P9-EDJ-599

Genesis and early man

VOLUME II: THE DOORWAY PAPERS

Genesis and early man

ARTHUR C. CUSTANCE

Drawings by the Author

**ZONDERVAN
PUBLISHING HOUSE** OF THE ZONDERVAN CORPORATION
GRAND RAPIDS, MICHIGAN 49506

GENESIS AND EARLY MAN

The Doorway Papers, Volume Two

Contents

Genesis 2:24	Genesis 28:1-2
4:1-2	29:1, 4-6, 9-28
4:19, 22, 23	38:2-30
9:20-25	Leviticus 18:17
11:25-31	2 Samuel 13:1
12:1, 5, 9-13	Matthew 1:25
20:1-12	Luke 15:11, 12, 31
15:2-4	Luke 15:20
16:1-3; 21:2, 8-14	Galatians 4:1, 4, 5
24:2ff.	

General Introduction

THE EXISTENCE of fossil remains of early man with grossly brutalized features and interpreted as proof of man's animal origin, poses a serious threat to Christian theology. Until these fossil remains became widely known, very few questioned the historicity of Adam and Eve. But today, whether Adam and Eve really existed in the historical sense that Genesis implies has become a matter of some debate even among Christian people.

Many still hold to a literal interpretation of these early records (as I most certainly do), whereas others feel that Adam and Eve are merely to be understood as symbolic representatives of the first truly human beings, who were in reality little more than made-over apes, evolved as to their bodies though with implanted "souls" to give them a unique constitution responsive to Divine influences and capable of fellowship with God. The idea of instant creation of man followed by a real temptation involving a real tree in a real garden is held to belong to the days of a naive faith no longer justified in the light of present knowledge. And no serious thought is given, as a rule, to the possibility that the first human pair could have been nearly as recent as the traditional biblical chronology invites us to believe, much less that the first woman was actually taken out of the first man by a Divine surgical operation of a sort.

But I am persuaded that when we abandon the concept of a truly historical Adam and Eve, experiencing a real temptation and Fall and expulsion from the Garden, we undermine the logical basis of the plan of salvation because that plan involves an undoing by a Second Adam of what the First Adam did, and it involves the reconstitution of a new family of human beings in the Lord Jesus Christ, capable of fulfilling the role for which Adam was originally created, and destined one day to do so. When we abandon the Genesis account of man's origin, we undermine the rationale of the biblical view of man's destiny.

What, then, are we to do with the current body of evidence which anthropological research has accumulated and which is almost universally interpreted in such a way as to challenge the biblical record of man's early history at almost every point?

I suggest we accept wholeheartedly whatever factual knowledge there is but apply to it an alternative interpretation. We cannot merely reject it, for that is to commit intellectual suicide. But it can indeed be interpreted otherwise than from the current evolutionary viewpoint; and the alternative interpretation proves, to my mind, to be thoroughly satisfying and reasonable. And by adopting this alternative interpretation of the data we are really only fulfilling an accepted scientific dictum which holds that we should explain the past as far as possible in terms only of known events or processes happening at the present. We need only qualify this to include what has happened within the recent past, within clearly historical times, for which we have adequate documentation.

Of the seven papers in this volume, the first *(Fossil Remains of Early Man and the Record of Genesis)* is just such a bold reinterpretation of the meaning of the fossil remains of early man, taking cognizance of certain facts relative to their distribution around the world. It is logical and does not ignore the evidence, but it rather views it from a new perspective. The question of the time element is not considered in this reconstruction, since I believe that the whole question of chronology is still in a state of flux and the techniques of establishing the time frame are by no means yet entirely dependable. The new framework is undoubtedly an oversimplification, but it does point the way to a viable alternative that ought to be explored.

The second paper *(Primitive Cultures: a Second Look at the Problem of Their Historical Origin)* revives an older view of primitive cultures in the light of far more information than its former proponents had at their disposal. This is an examination of the evidence, amply supported by comparatively recent historical events, that primitivism and barbarism are not necessarily the earliest stages of man's condition but are more probably the result of degeneration. Indeed, the evidence indicates that the higher a civilization the greater the degeneration is likely to be when it breaks down. It is no longer safe, then, to assume that primitive society provides us with a picture of the earliest condition of man, or to put it in a slightly different form, that our primitive contemporaries are our contemporary ancestors.

The third paper *(Establishing a Paleolithic I.Q.)* takes a second look at the achievements of early man as evidence of his intelligence. More recent experiments by modern man to accomplish the same tasks by his techniques force us to conclude that our early forebears were quite as intelligent, if not more so, than we are today.

The fourth paper *(The Supposed Evolution of the Human Skull)* shows how substantially environmental factors can modify the human skull and give it an ape-like cast that has no bearing whatever on phyletic relationships. The argument from comparative anatomy is seriously weakened in this respect in the light of present knowledge.

The fifth paper *(The Fallacy of Anthropological Reconstructions)* is almost entirely negative in its approach, yet it serves to show how very little validity there really is to so many boldly conceived reconstructions that purport to demonstrate evolution in current textbooks.

The sixth paper *(Who Taught Adam to Speak?)* deals with a particularly troublesome problem, the origin of language, a problem no nearer to solution than it was in Darwin's day. Indeed, it has proved so baffling from an evolutionary point of view that it has become almost indecent even to raise the issue for discussion in scientific circles.

Finally, one further paper *(Light From Other Forms of Cultural Behavior on Some Incidents in Scripture)* shows that the study of the subject matter of *cultural* anthropology can be thoroughly worthwhile for the Christian and sheds light on many situations in the Old Testament and the New which have hitherto largely escaped attention in biblical commentaries.

The Doorway Papers are a collection of writings earlier published by the author. This volume consists of several papers relating to a general theme; as a collection of papers, it is not to be regarded as a unified treatment of the subject, and there may be some duplication of material from one paper to the next.

The entire collection of the Doorway Papers is being published in nine volumes and an index volume by Zondervan Publishing House.

Part 1

Fossil Remains of Early Man and the Record of Genesis

Chapter 1
The Evolutionary Faith

"Man is a primate and within the order of primates is most closely related to the living African anthropoid apes."

SO WROTE F. Clark Howell recently,[1] providing us with a good example of the kind of confident announcement with which evolutionary literature abounds. As it stands, it is purely presumptive. Just because members of a family are apt to look alike, it is not at all safe to assume that all "look-alikes" are related. Howell's first statement "Man is a primate" is true enough; but his second statement, which is presented as though it were equally factual, is simple supposition without any positive proof whatever. Within the order Primates, man may most closely resemble living African anthropoid apes from an anatomical point of view, but it is quite another thing to state categorically that he is most closely related to them. Resemblance and relationship are by no means the same thing. Howell does admit in the next sentence that he is not sure how far removed the relationship is, but the basic assumption still remains that the blood relationship exists. Very few readers except those expert in the subject would discern the presumption in Howell's statement. All that the facts indicate is similarity. Relationship is totally unprovable by an appeal to morphology. If he had said, "Man is anatomically most like the African anthropoid apes," his statement would have been quite correct. As it stands, his statement is completely hypothetical. Howell is confusing hypothesis with fact.

The extent to which anthropologists today exercise faith, holding to be true and firmly established what in fact is only hopefully believed, is borne out by several of the following quotations, all of

---

[1] Howell F. Clark, "The Hominization Process" in *Human Evolution: Readings in Physical Anthropology,* ed. by Korn and Thompson, Holt, Rinehart and Winston, N.Y., 1967, p. 85.

which are from topflight experts in the field. Raymond Pearl, for instance, said — and this is a beautiful example of hopeful possibilities stated by circumlocution as high probabilities:[2]

> While everyone agrees that man's closest living relatives are to be found in the four man-like apes, gorilla, chimpanzee, orangutan, and gibbon, there is no such agreement about the precise structure of his ancestral pedigree. The evidence that he had a perfectly natural and normal one ... is overwhelming in magnitude and cogency. But exactly what the individual steps were, or how they came about, is still to be learned. There are nearly as many theories on the point as there are serious students of the problem. All of them at present, however, lack that kind of clear and simple proof which brings the sort of universal acceptance that is accorded to the law of gravitation, for example.
>
> Only on one point, and that one a little vague, can there be said to be general agreement. It is that, on the weight of evidence, it is probable that at some remote period in the past for which no clear paleontological record has yet been uncovered, man and the other primates branched off from what had theretofore been a common ancestral stem.

In this quotation the phrase "a perfectly natural and normal pedigree" means, of course, an evolutionary one. Pearl assures us that the evidence for this is overwhelming in magnitude and cogency, but in the next breath he speaks only of possibilities and adds that even for these there is no clear paleontological evidence. Many anthropologists today, twenty years after the above was written, would argue that the paleontological evidence is now at hand in the form of a wide range of catarrhine anthropoidea loosely catalogued together as pithecines. These creatures include such types as Dryopithecus, Ramapithecus, Kenyapithecus, and of course the more popularly known Australopithecines. But a study of the literature in which these fossils are described indicates first of all that there is considerable disagreement as to their precise status and relationship with one another, and secondly, that there is considerable debate whether they really stand in the line leading to Homo sapiens, though people like Robinson hopefully try to slide them across in the family tree so that they at least fall under the heading of hominoidea from which man is supposed to have evolved. At the present moment it appears to me that there has not been enough time yet to achieve a clear picture, and even if evolution *were* true it still seems unlikely that Homo sapiens arrived via a pithecine route.

The trouble is that the Australopithecines had very small brains, a mean cranial capacity of 575 cc.[3] compared with the normal

---

[2] Pearl, Raymond, *Man the Animal,* Principia Press, Bloomington, Indiana, 1946, p. 3.

[3] Clark, Wilfred LeGros, "Bones of Contention," Huxley Memorial Lecture, *Jour. Roy. Anthrop. Instit.*, 88, 2 (1958): 136-138.

for modern man of 1450 cc. and yet appear to have been tool users. Since by definition man is a cultured animal and tools are an essential part of his cultural activity, these primitive apes have been by some credited with culture and for this reason elevated to manhood, though at a very low level, of course. But there are many who hold that a creature cannot be said to be a "cultured" animal merely because it *uses* tools. Birds use tools for example, but this can hardly be considered as cultural activity.[4] There is no unequivocal evidence, that I am aware of, that the Australopithecines deliberately manufactured tools. There *is* evidence of what looks like manufactured tools, but it is highly debatable whether they were actually the work of the Australopithecines themselves. It has been argued that Australopithecines were hunted by early man and that these tools were left by the hunters. W. L. Strauss Jr.,[5] in a note appearing in *Science* entitled "Australopithecines Contemporaneous with Man?," said of these:

> Some of these artifacts are unquestionably worked, and all but one are composed of material foreign to the site and the immediate vicinity — an indication that they represent a true lithic culture. The stratigraphy seems to make it clear that the artifacts are of the same age as the red-brown breccia, and not intrusions. The industry is not of the most primitive character. . . .
>
> J. T. Robinson concludes that the advanced character of this stone industry makes its attribution to the Australopithecines dubious. . . . He believes that the most reasonable hypothesis at the present time is to attribute the industry to a "true man" that invaded the area before the time that this particular red-brown breccia was formed.

In the second place, it used to be held that cranial capacity and intelligence were closely related. This is seriously questioned today, although there is general agreement that a human being cannot be normal with a cranial capacity below about 800 cc., the so-called "cerebral Rubicon."[6] If there is no real relationship between these

---

[4] Tool Using: see Kenneth P. Oakley, "Skill as a Human Possession" in *A History of Technology,* ed. Charles Singer et al, Oxford, 1954, Vol. 1, pp. 1-37 for a discussion of animal tool-users. Also Mickey Chiang, "Use of Tools by Wild Macaque Monkeys in Singapore," *Nature,* 214 (1967): 1258, 9. Also K. R. L. Hall, "Tool-Using Performances as Indicators of Behavioural Adaptability," in *Human Evolution* (ref. 1), pp. 173-210; especially p. 195 for a remark by R. Cihak: "The author states that not tool-using but tool-making signalizes the critical stage in the transition from ape to human; but it ought to be pointed out that tool-making, as 'shaping an object for an imaginary future eventuality,' is the real boundary between ape and man."

[5] Strauss. W. L. Jr., "Australopithecines Contemporaneous with Man?" *Science,* 126 (1957): 1238.

[6] Weidenreich, Franz, "The Human Brain in the Light of Its Phylogenetic Development," *Sci. Monthly,* 67 (1948): 103-109, and P. V. Tobias, "The Olduvian Bed I Hominine with Specific Reference to Its Cranial Capacity," *Nature,* Apr. 4, 1964, p. 3.

two indices, then the very small Australopithecine brain might still qualify as "human." But there is certainly no general agreement on the matter. In any case, modern man with his far larger brain is represented by fossils which were contemporary with the latest in the Australopithecine line, so it still seems unlikely that Homo sapiens arrived via this route.

Leakey, writing in 1966 with reference to Homo habilis, a supposed *maker* of tools, for a number of reasons rejects any such lineal series as Australopithecus africanus — Homo habilis — Homo erectus (the latter being essentially man as we now know him).[7] "It seems to me," he said, "more likely that Homo habilis and Homo erectus as well as some of the Australopithecines, were all evolving along their own distinct lines by Lower Pleistocene times."[8] And again, "I submit that morphologically it is almost impossible to regard H. habilis as representing a stage between Australopithecus africanus and Homo erectus." He added:

> I have never been able to accept the view that Australopithecus represented a direct ancestral stage leading to H. erectus, and I disagree even more strongly with the present suggestion of placing H. habilis between them. . . . It is possible that H. habilis may prove to be the direct ancestor of H. sapiens but this can be no more than a theory at present. . . .
> All that can be said at present is that there was a time at Olduvai when H. habilis, Australopithecus (Zinjanthropus) boisei and what seems to be a primitive ancestor of H. erectus were *broadly contemporary and developing along distinct and separate lines* (my emphasis).

The debate continues, and though "no one" questions man's evolutionary origin, the conclusive links are still missing.

The problem is that although there *are* a substantial number of fossil candidates which can be manipulated into the proper kind of sequence, the chain seems to lead rather to modern apes — or to extinction — than to man. For certain periods of geological history there are promising successions of fossil forms which look as though they ought to lead to man, but they don't. Recently, Elwyn L. Simons observed:[9]

---

[7] Homo sapiens and Homo erectus are at least contemporary and may quite probably have been one species according to the latest studies made of the Talgai Skull by Anatomy Professor N. W. G. MacIntosh of Sydney University, Australia (*Science News:* Vol. 93, Apr. 20, 1968, p. 381).

[8] Leakey, L. S. B., "Homo habilis, Homo erectus, and AUSTRALOPITHECINES," *Nature,* 209 (1966): 1280, 1281.

[9] Simons, Elwyn L., "The Early Relatives of Man," *Sci. American,* July, 1964, p. 50. Simons' recent discovery in the Fayum of Aegyptopithecus reported in his article, "The Earliest Apes" (*Sci. American,* Dec., 1967, pp. 28-35) and which he describes as "the skull of a monkey equipped with the teeth of an ape," does not shed light on the nature of the missing link between ape and man — only between monkey and ape.

Within the past fifteen years a number of significant new finds have been made. . . . The early primates are now represented by many complete or nearly complete skulls, some nearly complete skeletons, a number of limb bones, and even the bones of hands and feet. In age these specimens extend across almost the entire Cenozoic era, from its beginning in Paleocene epoch some sixty-three million years ago up to the Pliocene which ended roughly two million years ago. . . . But they do not lie in the exact line of man's ancestry.

When the significance of the data itself is a subject of so much debate, it is clear that a great deal depends upon imaginative thinking, each authority being persuaded that he is merely reading the evidence. But the disagreement which exists between authorities demonstrates clearly that the evidence can be "merely read" in several different ways. For this reason, Melville Herskovits[10] observed that "no branch of anthropology requires more of inference for the weighing of imponderables, in short, of the exercise of scientific imagination, than prehistory."

Many years ago, Wilson D. Wallis[11] pointed out that there is a kind of law in the matter of anthropological thinking about fossil remains which goes something like this: the less information we have by reason of the scarcity and antiquity of the remains, the more sweeping our generalizations can be about them. If you find the bones of a man who has died recently, you have to be rather careful what you say about him because somebody might be able to check up on your conclusions. The further back you go, the more confidently you can discuss such reconstructions because there is less possibility of anyone being able to challenge you. Consequently, when only a few fossil remains of early man were known, very broad generalizations could be made about them and all kinds of genealogical trees were drafted with aplomb. A few wiser anthropologists today decry the temptation to draft genealogical trees which, as I. Manton said, are more like "bundles of twigs" rather than trees, in any case.[12] And when it comes to the reconstruction of a fossil find into a "flesh-and-blood" head and face, the degree of divergence can be even more extraordinary as is shown, for example, in those concocted to represent Zinjanthropus for the *Sunday Times* (London), the *Illustrated London News*, and for Dr. Kenneth Oakley by Maurice Wilson, respectively.[13] The reconstruction of man's evolutionary history is still

10 Herskovits, Melville, *Man and His Works*, Knopf, N.Y., 1950, p. 97.

11 Wallis, Wilson D., "Pre-Suppositions in Anthropological Interpretations," *Amer. Anthropologist*, July-Sept., 50 (1948): 560.

12 Manton, I., "problems of Cytology and Evolution in the Pteridophyta," Cambridge, 1950, quoted by Irving W. Knoblock, *Jour. Amer. Sci. Affil.*, 5 (3), Sept., 1953, p. 14.

13 *Sunday Times* of April 5, 1964; and *Illustrated London News and*

much more of an art than a science. I have redrawn these three reconstructions from the originals in Fig. 1 and 2.

The principle that the less the data the more freedom there is in interpreting it is widely recognized. In 1967 Takeuchi, Uyeda and Kanamori, in speaking about the Theory of Continental Drift, point out that "it often happens in science that while data are scarce, interpretation seems easy, but as the number of data grows, consistent argument grows more and more difficult."[14] Hallam L. Movius wrote very similarly in 1953 with reference to Paleolithic cultures and the presently existing data with which to reconstruct them. We now have so much more information than previously that "we can hardly compose them into anything even remotely approaching the ordered general scheme conceived by the earlier workers."[15] I predict that when we have *enough* evidence we shall find that the Biblical view of man's early history will not merely prove to be precisely correct but will seem self-evidently so to those who have that accumulated knowledge. In fact, they will wonder why the truth was not more obvious to those who preceded them. It is surprising how often a few additional facts act as a catalyst that seems to jog everything suddenly into place until one wonders how the truth could have been overlooked for so long.

Moreover, as has been recognized for many years and emphasized very recently by J. T. Robinson,[16] habits of life, climate, and diet can tremendously influence the anatomical features of the skull, indeed to such an extent that two series of fossil forms which may in fact be a single species are by some authorities put into different genera. I have in mind Australopithecus and Paranthropus. How can one take seriously family trees in which the lines of connection are drawn solely on the basis of similarity or dissimilarity in appearance when these similarities or dissimilarities could be nothing more than evidence of a difference in diet? Such cultural or environmental factors cannot only cause two members of a single species to diverge sufficiently to be put into two different genera, but two different genera can for the same reason *converge* until they have the appear-

Sketch, Jan. 1, 1960: see also "The Fallacy of Anthropological Reconstructions," by the author, Part V in this volume.

[14] Takeuchi, H., et al., *Debate about the Earth,* Freeman, Cooper & Co., San Francisco, 1967, p. 180.

[15] Movius. Hallam, "Old World Prehistory: Paleolithic," in *Anthropology Today,* ed. by A. L. Kroeber, Univ. Chicago Press, 1953, p. 163.

[16] Robinson, J. T., "The Origins and Adaptive Radiation of the Australopithecines," in *Human Evolution* (ref. 1), pp. 277, 279, and 294.

ance of belonging to the same species. There are some extraordinary examples of convergence.[17]

There is another factor which may very well have confused the issue, because it is possible that, for reasons worth considering briefly, early man may have tended towards the attainment of a certain "apishness" in his appearance because of the great age to which he survived. The Bible states categorically that men lived for centuries before the Flood, and even after it. We have specific records in Scripture of only a few people living for centuries after the Flood (Gen. 11:11-22), but it can scarcely be questioned that these individuals were merely singled out because they were important for other reasons. That many men besides them survived for centuries is hardly to be questioned, though the life span of man declined rather rapidly as generations succeeded one another after the Flood.

Now one of the "findings" of evolutionists is that certain animals may for obscure reasons experience the persistence of a youthful form into adult life. This is referred to technically as neoteny. The process leads to an adult who, although strictly adult chronologically, is nevertheless "immature" in form. Such individuals are said to be paedomorphic. As an illustration, man is said to be paedomorphic, for the following reasons and in the following respect: Assuming that he is derived from some ape-like ancestor who was covered with hair, it would be expected that he himself would likewise be covered with hair. But the hairiness of the adult ape is considerably greater than that of the newborn ape. If the comparative hairlessness of the newborn ape were to have persisted for some reason into the adult stage so that the full grown creature was as comparatively free of hair as its young is apt to be, then the adult would be termed paedomorphic, i.e., patterned (in this respect) like a child of its species. Since man is comparatively hairless over the general body surface he is believed to be paedomorphic, i.e., a hairy creature who didn't quite produce the hairiness that was expected of him on the basis of his ancestry. He has remained child-like, in this respect.

Sir Gavin de Beer is perhaps the most suitable authority to whom to refer the reader on this subject.[18] Neoteny refers to a condition

---

[17] Convergence: Leo S. Berg, *Nomogenesis: Or Evolution Determined by Law,* Eng. trans., Constable, Edinburgh, 1926; David Lack, *Evolutionary Theory and Christian Belief,* Methuen, Lond., 1957, p. 65; Evan Shute, *Flaws in the Theory of Evolution,* Temside Press, London (Can.), 1961, pp. 138ff.; and also Sir Alister Hardy, *The Living Stream,* Collins, London, 1965, pp. 199-202.

[18] de Beer, Sir Gavin, *Embryos and Ancestors,* Oxford, 1951, pp. 52f. and pp. 90f.

which is described as being due to "a relative retardation in the rate of the development of the *body* as compared with the reproductive glands," so that the body does not run through so many stages in the descendant as the ancestor did. Strictly speaking, paedomorphosis refers to a situation where "the larva becomes precociously sexually mature, whereas neoteny refers to a situation where the adult animal retains larval characters." "The production of phylogenetic change by the introduction into the *adult* descendant of characters which were youthful in the ancestor" by means of neoteny is termed paedomorphosis. Thus the comparative hairlessness of man as an adult is considered to be a case of a hairy ancestral type being replaced by a hairless descendant who is held to have retained to maturity the comparative hairlessness of the ancestral infant.

The assumption is made, further, that if man lived for a long enough time he would finally in fact achieve a fully adult form. The trouble is he dies too soon. In whatever way we may explain the fact that man's hairiness increases with age, it is a fact. If therefore man were to live for centuries it is conceivable that the developmental processes which he shares to some extent with other living creatures of a similar kind to himself might lead to a measure of convergence, not because of any relationship but simply through great age. If man lived to be hundreds of years old, and if the conditions of his life led to his being forced to surrender some of the mollifying influences of community life, so that he lived and died as a hermit or an isolated family, it may very well be that his remains, by their very unusualness, would confuse their finder into supposing that he was not man in the undoing but ape-becoming-man. Such great longevity might account for the comparatively large numbers of weapons and artifacts which make up the substance of prehistory but which are accompanied by so few skeletal remains. A very small population of individuals could leave the remnants of their settlements over tremendous territories if these individuals survived for centuries. And it seems highly probable that greatly extended experience through long years of trial and error would tend to accelerate somewhat the processes of improvement so that the progress from paleolithic, to mesolithic, to neolithic could easily occur in one generation, and neolithic weapons might have been used to kill Paleolithic Man as Dawson reported.[19]

It is evident, therefore, that morphology in itself is not really any guide at all to lineal relationships. Indeed, even the chance finding of the skeletons of a mother and a child together, although

---

[19] Dawson, Sir William, *Fossil Men and Their Modern Representatives,* Hodder and Stoughton, London, 1883, p. 123.

it may be presumptive evidence of a mother-child relationship, could never be taken as absolute *proof*. Almost all fossil remains are "proved" to be related in this way only in the sense that if you agree to the theory of evolution to start with, the relationship might be reasonably assumed. But in itself, similarity of form does not prove relationship. Those who see in their own finds, or who wish to see in them, more of man than of ape tend to classify them by tacking the suffix -*anthropus* on their name. Those who reemphasize rather the antiquity of their finds tend to classify them as -*pithecus*. Thus there are two alternative temptations, one being to stress the antiquity of man's supposed ancestors, and the other the humanness of them. Another factor clearly enters into these naming games and that is the prestige of having made a find which initiates a new genus, sub-family, or other category of some kind. Thus von Koenigswald calls his Javanese find Meg*anthropus,* whereas others see it as merely repre-sentative of one branch of Australo*pithecines.* Similarly, Leakey labels his Olduvai finds as Zinj*anthropus* whereas others would rob his specimens of their unique status by reducing them also to a mere Australo*pithecine.*[20] The unfortunate thing is that the very naming of these finds can give to them a weight of importance which can be quite unjustified. The name creates the significance, not the find itself.

Sir Solly Zuckerman,[21] in a paper with the intriguing title, *"An Ape or The* Ape," pointed out that far too much importance tends to be attached to small differences between specimens which but for these differences would certainly be classed as a single species. His argument was that the study of modern apes, and other creatures, demonstrates clearly and emphatically that within a single family of apes or monkeys there may be individuals whose divergence from one another is far greater than the divergence which may be observed in two particular fossils that on that account classified as not only belonging to a different species but even different genera. To quote one of his opening passages:

> Some students claim, or rather assume implicitly, that the phyletic relations of a series of specimens can be clearly defined from an assess-ment of morphological similarities and dissimilarities, even when the fossil evidence is both slight and noncontinuous geologically. Others, who in the light of modern genetical knowledge are surely on firmer ground, point out that several genes or several gene patterns may have identical phenotypic effects, and that when we deal with limited or

---

[20] Koenigswald, G. H. R., re: Meganthropus: see *Human Evolution,* (ref. 1), p. 280; and re: Zinjanthropus: see "The Fossil Skull from Olduvai," editorial comment in *Brit. Med. Journal,* Sept. 19, 1959, p. 487.

[21] Zuckerman, Sir Solly, *"An Ape or the* Ape," *Jour. Roy. Anthrop. Instit.,* 81 (1951): 57.

relatively limited fossil materials, correspondence in similar morphological features or in groups of characters does not necessarily imply
genetic identity or phyletic relationship.

Zuckerman subsequently quoted A. H. Schultz, one of the foremost
students of the Primates, as having said:[22]

> Among several hundred monkeys of one species, collected in the
> uniform environment surrounding one camp in the forest of Nicaragua,
> were found specimens with pug noses and those with straight profiles,
> some with large ears and others with small ones. In short, they differed
> from one another as widely as would an equal number of human city
> dwellers and this in spite of the fact that these monkeys all had the
> same occupation, the same diet, and the same climatic conditions, and
> this during thousands of generations.

In 1943, Gaylord Simpson had similarly written:[23]

> Earlier paleontologists had no real idea of the extent of morpho-
> logical variation that can occur in a single species. . . . Workable criteria
> have only slowly been achieved, hand in hand with similar work by
> neo-zoologists and with experimental work. . . .
> It is conservative to guess that among previously proposed species
> of fossil vertebrates, aside from types of currently recognized genera,
> not more than a quarter represent natural and distinct groups. The
> fraction of valid species is probably much lower.

In spite of these warnings it appears that minute differences in
measurements between this point and that or along some axis or
other of a fossil fragment that has already been distorted by its long
burial in the earth are made the basis of pontifical pronouncements
about the relationships and ancestral lines of potential candidates
for protohumanship. When Zuckerman presented his paper, he stated
specifically that he had in mind the current debates about the Australopithecines and other African fossil primate specimens. He argues
such statements are of highly doubtful validity, and these doubts
extend with equal force to the estimates made of cranial capacity.
And with respect to dentition, he argues that the impressive tables
designed to illustrate relationships, or otherwise, are fundamentally
exercises "in dental anatomy, not in primate phylogeny."

One thing is certain: no one is ever tempted to make any pro-
nouncement regarding their particular finds which puts the slightest
question mark against their evolutionary origin. Evolution is unchallengeable. Nor does Zuckerman challenge it.

LeGros Clark has pointed out that "practically none of the
genera and species of fossil hominoids [and this includes all the
Australopithecines according to Robinson] which have from time to

---

[22] Schultz, A. H., quoted by Zuckerman, ref. 21, p. 58.
[23] Simpson, G. G., quoted by Zuckerman, ref. 21, p. 59.

time been created have any validity at all in zoological nomenclature."[24] And again,[25]

> Probably the one single factor which above all others has unduly, and quite unnecessarily, complicated the whole picture of human phylogeny is the tendency for the taxonomic individualization of each fossil skull or fragment of a skull by assuming it to be a new type which is specifically, or even generically, distinct from all others.

In the popular mind, the Australopithecines are constantly being presented as though they were little by little filling the gap between man and his animal ancestors, and the temptation has been for "fossil-finders" to contribute to this confusion by attaching names to their finds which are intended to reinforce this impression.[26] In point of fact, not only are these names unjustified in many cases but the line itself now appears to have continued its imagined evolutionary development right up into Pleistocene times when modern man was already in existence. This has the unfortunate consequence of making man as old as his supposed ancestors, which seems nonsense to me, but in the evolutionist's credo, this is his faith — "the substance of things hoped for, evidence of things not seen...."

---

[24] Clark, LeGros, "Bones of Contention," in *Human Evolution* (ref. 1), p. 302.

[25] Ibid., p. 299.

[26] Thus Sir Solly Zuckerman, "Correlation of Change in the Evolution of Higher Primates," in *Evolution as a Process*, ed. Huxley et. al. Allen, Unwin, London, 1954, p. 301. "The fundamental difficulty has been that in the great majority of cases the descriptions of the specimens that have been provided by their discoverers have been so turned as to indicate that the fossils in question have some special place or significance in the line of direct human ascent as opposed to that of the family of apes."

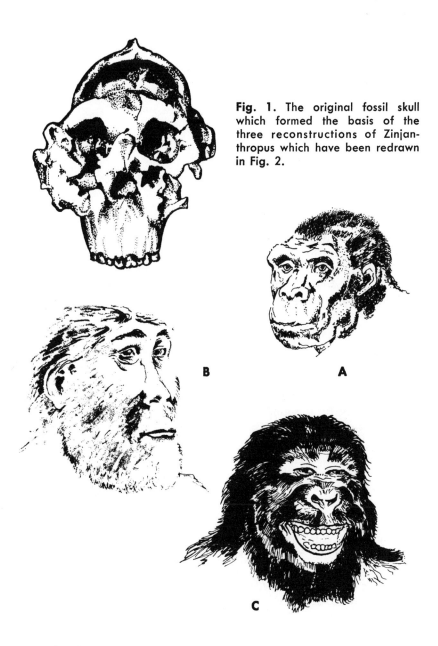

Fig. 1. The original fossil skull which formed the basis of the three reconstructions of Zinjanthropus which have been redrawn in Fig. 2.

B

A

C

Fig. 2. Zinjanthropus, as drawn (A) for the "Sunday Times" of London, 5 April 1964; (B) by Neave Parker for Dr. L. S. B. Leakey and published in the "Illustrated London News and Sketch," 1 January 1960; (C) by Maurice Wilson for Dr. Kenneth P. Oakley. All these are redrawn by the author.

Chapter 2
Faith Without Sufficient Reason

THERE IS no question that the theory of evolution is useful as a teaching aid to assist in the orderly arrangement of the data that is available. And there is no doubt also that when the theory is presented for popular consumption, i.e., omitting any mention of problems which yet remain to be solved before it can unequivocally be considered factually established, it has a certain compulsiveness about it, for it appears to explain everything. This, as a matter of fact, is one reason why there are a few authorities of stature within the camp who nevertheless feel somewhat uneasy about it all in its current theoretical formulation. For a theory which can be made to explain everything by manipulating the threads of the argument to suit the occasion is really unsound, for the basic reason that it could never be disproved. As Medawar observed,[27] if a theory is so flexible that the same explanation can be used to account for two entirely contrary tendencies, then the theory is meaningless. Once it was held that man's enlarging brain caused his emergence as Homo sapiens, the great tool-user, so that smaller brained creatures were lower in the scale. Now that small-brained creatures have turned up as tool-users, it is being argued that the very use of tools is what enlarged the brain to man size. Evolutionary theory is highly "adjustable." "When we speak," Medawar said, "as Spencer was the first to do, of the survival of the fittest, we are being wise after the event: what is fit or not fit is so described on the basis of retrospective judgment. It is silly to profess to be thunderstruck by the evolution of organism A if we should have been just as thunderstruck by a turn of events which would have led to the evolution of B or C instead."

A few years ago, T. H. Leith[28] underscored the fact, which I

---

[27] Medawar, Sir Peter B., *The Art of the Soluble,* Methuen, London, 1965, p. 55.
[28] Leith, T. H., "Some Logical Problems with the Thesis of Apparent Age," *Jour. Amer. Sci. Affil.,* 17 (1965): 119.

believe is of fundamental importance, that in order to be useful a theory must be so structured that some critical experiment is conceivable which, if it is actually false, could prove it to be so. As Medawar has pointed out,[29] since absolute proof is beyond our power (for there may always turn up one more piece of evidence which is irreconcilable), the best we can do in any area of research is to constantly seek for error in the hypothesis. The result of each experiment which does not demonstrate a flaw serves either to confirm the present hypothesis or to purify it by forcing its modification. But the theory of evolution is so flexible that it is simply not possible to conceive of a critical experiment which *could* disprove it. All research seems to be ultimately devoted to proving the theory, not to challenging it. How could one challenge it?

In the meantime, it may be useful enough, heuristically, or even as a philosophy which ministers to our materialism, but it is nevertheless held as an act of faith — indeed Huxley would even define it as a religion.[30] As such, there is a large element of emotion involved in its defence. In his recent book *This View of Life,* Simpson reveals this quite remarkably. There are some sections in which he reiterates ad nauseam the basic tenet of his faith: "Evolution is a fact."[31]

---

[29] Medawar, Sir P. B., *The Uniqueness of the Individual,* Basic Books, N.Y., 1957, p. 76. Similarly, Rudolf Flesch remarked, "The most important thing about science is this: that it isn't a search for truth but a search for error..." ("The Art of Clear Thinking," *Sci. Monthly,* 74 [1952]: 240). See also the editorial comment under "The Discipline of the Scientific Method," *Nature,* Aug. 1, 1959, p. 295: "Since, according to the code of science, no positive assertions are final and all propositions approximations, and indeed provisional, science is seen to advance more by denying what is wrong than by asserting what is right — by reducing, and eventually eradicating, errors rather than by heading straight towards some preconceived final truth."

[30] Huxley, Julian, "New Bottles for New Wine: Ideology and Scientific Knowledge," *Jour. Roy. Anthr. Instit.,* 80 (1950): 7-23, especially p. 15b; and the introduction to Teilhard de Chardin, *The Phenomenon of Man,* Collins, 1959, where Huxley hails him as the new prophet of the new faith!

[31] Simpson, Gaylord G., *This View of Life,* Harcourt, Brace and World, N.Y., 1964:
p. vii "one of the basic facts...."
p. 10 "Fact — not theory...."
p. 12 "no one doubts...."
p. 40 "all the facts support it...."
p. 51 "only dishonest biologists disagree...."
p. 62 "unassailable now...."
p. 63 "all problems being solved 'triumphantly'...."
p. 151 "Evolution is a fact ... creation a dogma...."
p. 193 "Evolution a fact ... the truth of evolution ... proofs ... all agree ... proofs of evolution."
In his article, "The Biological Nature of Man," (*Science,* 152 [1966]: 475), he wrote, "We are no longer concerned with *whether* man evolved, because we know that he did"! (emphasis his).

Circular reasoning plays a large part in current evolutionary anthropology, perhaps as large a part as it does in modern geology although it is not as readily admitted. The circularity of the reasoning goes something like this: we know that human evolution is true and therefore there must be a succession of forms from some protohuman being up to man spread over an appropriate time scale of millions of years. Since by disregarding geographical location and taking some liberties with an expansive time scale, one can line up a set of candidates in fossil form which make what is euphemistically termed a "nice sequence," this proves that human evolution is a fact. The possibility that there might be another explanation for similarity of form is not even considered. The point is that the mere arbitrary lining up of man-like fossils, even when the temporal ordering is correct, does not prove descent. The assumption is made that descent is the explanation, and the line-up is then used to prove the assumption.[32] This is as characteristically circular as much geological reasoning is.

This kind of evolutionary sequence was once very popular in *cultural* anthropology: artifacts developed progressively from simple to complex by known stages; religion evolved continuously from animism to monotheism; art passed from a very low stage of crude representation to its modern sophisticated (?) level of abstraction; in short, everything evolved. Little by little most of these classically familiar evolutionary schemes have been discarded as being either purely arbitrary mental creations or positively contrary to fact. Christian readers sometimes see references to the abandonment of these cultural evolutionary constructs and unfortunately gather the impression that all evolutionary ideas are being abandoned — which is not so at all. Unfailingly, human and prehuman fossil remains are still being set forth in such a way as to create the impression that linear relationships actually have been demonstrated between them. As Howell put it, "Man . . . is most closely related to the living African anthropoid apes"!

It is too soon for us to be able to see the true significance of the many new fossils from Africa and elsewhere, each of which tends, by its discoverer, to be hailed as *the* missing link, until it is challenged

---

[32] R. H. Rastall of Cambridge wrote "It cannot be denied that from a strictly philosophical standpoint geologists are here arguing in a circle. The succession of organisms has been determined by a study of their remains buried in the rocks, and the relative ages of the rocks are determined by the remains of organisms that they contain." (Encyc. Brit., 1956, Article on Geology, Vol. 10, p. 168). W. R. Thompson says of Simpson, "Simpson states that homology is *determined* by ancestry and concludes that homology is *evidence* of ancestry"! "Evolution and Taxonomy," *Studia Entomologica*, 5 (1962): 567.

as to its significance by the man who is lucky enough to find one even more primitive (or human-like!). A great deal tends to be made, by each discoverer, of those features of his own particular find which distinguish it markedly — so it is claimed — from other like finds and on that account justify its claim as a new link in the chain rather than part of an existing link. We have already referred to the fact that within any species there may be considerable variability, variability which is quite sufficient to justify the counterargument that many supposed links are not links at all but variant specimens of a single species. It is instructive to note a paper by Stanley M. Garn who, in discussing "the problem of fossil differences," makes the following series of observations which are extracted in the correct order from his paper but with much supplementary information omitted in the interests of brevity. He wrote:[33]

> In describing the pithecanthropus-sinanthropus fossils from Java and China and the various "Neanderthals," much is commonly made of differences between them and us. According to textbook descriptions (usually copied from previous textbook descriptions), these old-world fossils were unique in various ways. "Fossils" are supposedly characterized by unusually thick skulls, exceptionally large teeth, extramassive mandibular symphyses, and pattern of tooth size and tooth eruption not found in living man. Such characterizations heightened student acceptance of the notion that a "taxonomic chasm" separates the classical old-world fossil from contemporary man. . . .
>
> Now many of the fossils selected for description *were* thick skulled, if published measurements can be trusted. But they were not so unique in skull thickness as we were wont to believe. And it is not necessary to search museums for isolated cranial extremes simply to demonstrate this important point, nor is it necessary to center upon the thick-vaulted Florida and California coastal Indians. A contemporary series of living Americans extends well into the fossil range of skull thickness. With due precautions to exclude possible cases of Paget's disease, it is quite possible to show that contemporary Americans and paleanthropic fossils do not form separate distributions: the fossils are quite overlapped by living men and women.
>
> Many fossils have been described as big-toothed, and surely the megadonts of Asia and Africa were as big-toothed as their name properly suggests. But from Pithecanthropus on, the exceptional nature of fossil-tooth size (at least for premolars and molars) is again open to question. With perhaps one classical exception (Pithecanthropus 4) modern and fossil tooth sizes quite overlap. The Neanderthals, as variously described, fit comfortably within contemporary ranges, and this observation is remarkably true for the Lower-K teeth from Choukoutien. . . . It is clear that the distribution of tooth sizes in contemporary American whites encompasses the "fossil" range to the extent that, as with skull thickness, there is no suggestion of a true taxonomic chasm. . . .
>
> For some years, too, the notion has been current that fossil man

[33] Garn, Stanley M., "Culture and the Direction of Human Evolution," in *Human Evolution* (ref. 1), pp. 102, 103, 105, and 107.

and modern man were differentiated by the order of tooth eruption. Franz Weidenreich championed such a belief arguing a real toxonomic "chasm" in this respect. Broom and Robinson, and Dart, in turn, have gone further by suggesting different sequences of tooth eruption for individual australopithecines, sequences which they claim to be "unknown" in modern man. But the idea of one tooth-eruption sequence for fossils and another for modern man falls when subjected to careful review.... Actually, and as we have shown, the "fossil" order is the usual order of alveolar eruption in modern children....

Paleoanthropic fossils, according to the textbooks, are said to have massive mandibular symphyses, and high mandibular symphyses as well, as befits forms with supposedly massive dentition. Yet, by comparison to a rather small series of contemporary American adults (258 in all) it would seem that *we* hold equal claim to the extremes of symphyseal size and massivity. All except one or two fossil specimens fall within the contemporary combined-sex bivariate distribution. All other euhominid, erectus or sapiens (taken from the listing of Weidenreich), fall well into the contemporary American white distribution.... Once again it would appear that the fossils are not qualitatively different from us....

It would appear appropriate to observe that the facial skeletons of fossils and modern man are by no means so greatly different.

Since a great deal is made of the face of fossil man, the majority of reconstructions putting the major emphasis here *pro bono publico,* it is a useful corrective to have this admittedly rather long extract in front of one. Because it shows that if one is determined to provide man with ancestors from which he evolved, it is also necessary to show them as being significantly different in form in various ways, otherwise one cannot point to any evidence of "evolution." Evolution means change; and if there is no demonstrable change one cannot argue for evolution. So because of a consuming faith in an otherwise undemonstrable theory of human origins, it is necessary to find substance for it by overemphasizing the evidence to the extent of distorting it out of all proportion to its true significance. The facts do not justify this distortion as Garn's paper shows unequivocally. It is generally accepted as true that a view held without adequate evidence is held as an act of faith, no matter how reasonable it may otherwise seem to be.

What I am trying to underscore here is that the whole subject of man's supposed pedigree is loaded with dubious arguments based on an interpretation of the data which is often entirely arbitrary, its sole justification being that it lends support to a view of human origins which is held simply as an act of faith.

Even concerning the Cradle of Man the same dubious arguments are made to carry weight in the public mind because perfectly valid alternatives are ignored. Since most of the newer fossils have been turning up in Africa, it is popular to hail Africa rather than the

Middle East as the Cradle of Man, in spite of the fact that the Australopithecine line leads to modern apes and not to man at all, according to the many experts. . . . But there are ways in which the Middle East can still be shown to be the most reasonable Cradle of Man and that the group of fossils widely scattered over the world (in Asia, Africa, and Europe) which by general consensus of opinion *do* represent early man, such as the Homo erectus series, can be accounted for without making them man's *ancestors*. After all, there is no need to assume automatically that everything that looks like an ancestor *is* an ancestor — it could be a *descendant*. If one believes in evolution, the former is a reasonable enough assumption because these fossil skulls are so very primitive in appearance. If one believes that man was created, the logic of the argument is not nearly so compelling; for degeneration is as likely as improvement, for as we hope to show, there is a way in which all those fossil remains which are generally agreed to belong within the family of man, Homo sapiens, can be accounted for without appealing to evolutionary processes of any kind. And this way is not only reasonable in itself, but has substantial support from what we know of man's early history on the basis of archaeology, the records of antiquity, and modern research into the effects of food, climate, and habit of life on human physique.

Chapter 3
An Alternative Faith

WHETHER WE believe that the Flood in Noah's day was geographically local or universal, many who read this paper will
most certainly agree that from the point of view of the world's human
population the Flood was an overwhelming catastrophe, which left
this earth with eight sole human survivors. The same basic agreement
would, I believe, be found with respect to the period of time which
has elapsed since these eight souls began to repeople the world, a
period which cannot be much more than four or five thousand years
at the most.

It seems unlikely, even making all conceivable allowances for gaps
in genealogies which some are persuaded must exist,[34] that one could
push back the date of the Flood beyond a few thousand years B.C.
In this, we are forced to conclude that, except for those who lived
between Adam and Noah and were overwhelmed by the Flood and
whose remains I believe are not very likely to be found, all fossil
men, all prehistoric cultures, all primitive communities of the past
or the present, and all civilizations since, must be encompassed within
this span of a few thousand years. On the face of it the proposal
seems utterly absurd.

However, I think there are lines of evidence of considerable
substance in support of it. In setting this forth all kinds of "buts"
will arise in the reader's mind if he has any broad knowledge of
current physical anthropology. An attempt is made to deal specifically
with a number of these "buts" in other Doorway Papers by the
author,[35] but some problems remain unsolved, particularly the ques-

---

[34] On the question of gaps in the Biblical genealogies, see "The Genealogies of the Bible," in Volume VII.

[35] Custance, A. C., "The Supposed Evolution of the Human Skull," "Primitive Cultures: A Second Look at the Problem of Their Historical Origins,"
and "The Fallacy of Anthropological Reconstructions," all in this volume.

tion of the time element. However, one does not have to solve every problem before presenting a hypothetical reconstruction. After all, the prevailing view is shot full of them and yet it is still held to be a respectable one!

But it may be worthwhile to note how consistently the time factor in so many prehistoric sequences has tended always to be reduced rather than extended. There is only one possible exception. The exception relates to the duration of Pleistocene times which have been extended to almost double the original period. The shorter period proved in certain ways a source of embarrassment because more events had to be crowded into it than was considered feasible. But apart from this one exception, the rule of reduction is almost otherwise unbroken. Some reductions are so drastic as to put a big question mark against the validity of datings which remain unchallenged at present.

In 1953, during a symposium on anthropology which was published subsequently by Chicago University Press and which provided up to that time a kind of "last word" on the position of modern anthropologists, there are frequent notices of drastic reductions.

After careful criticisms of Zeuner's dating system as set forth in his classic study entitled "Dating the Past," we are presented with a series of incidences in which dates have been severely cut.[36] For example, a date of 10,000 years ago is reduced to 3,000, a date of 18,000 to 10,000, a date of 25,000 to 11,000, and a date of 1,000,000 to 50,000! And in a companion volume, the Magdelanian Culture once dated from 50,000 to 18,000 years ago is now dated from 15,000 to 8,000 years ago.[37]

In another Doorway Paper it is my intention to give a substantial number of examples of reductions of this kind which have been espoused, not by antievolutionists, but by those who hold firmly to a belief in man's evolution and who justify the reductions they propose on the basis of evidence which is now available and which is far more substantial and solidly based than was the evidence upon which the original expansive claims were made. Yet for all this, the public is still invited to think of man's origins as being rooted in a past so distant that the biblical chronology is made to appear utterly absurd. But only the use of astronomical figures allows the evolutionist room to float his theories. And this "antiquity" is presented as unchallengeable still.

---

[36] *Anthropology Today*, ed. A. L. Kroeber, Univ. Chicago Press, 1953, pp. 13, 9, and 47.

[37] *Appraisal of Anthropology Today*, ed. by Sol Tax *et al.*, Univ. Chicago Press, 1953, p. 7.

Many of the dates which are proposed are claimed to have been based upon physical and chemical processes which serve as time markers with strict objectivity. Unfortunately (or fortunately) some of these processes are perhaps being misread. A classical example was the estimate made by Lyell for the time which had been occupied since the Niagara River began to erode the lip of the Falls. He allowed a certain number of inches per year ending up with 30,000 to 100,000 years. This was what we were taught in university as the time at which the North American ice sheet retreated far enough to allow the water to drain over the escarpment at Queenston Heights. Many surveys have been made[38] since that time and more accurate data have established the fact that Lyell may have been by as much as 90,000 years wrong. Similarly, Antevs,[39] studying certain vanished lakes in the southern Californian desert, believed that they should have been dated about 25,000 years ago, but he now dates them at less than 10,000 years ago.

Many dates from proto- or early historic times have also been drastically reduced, as for example, Pendelbury concludes that the Neolithic Minoan culture must be brought down from 8,000 B.C. to 4,000 B.C.[40] This reduction resulted from the finding that whereas the accumulation of debris in Cnossos which was about 8 meters thick and that had been estimated to take 5100 years to form, is now believed to have been formed in between six and eight hundred years.

There are some other truly fantastic "potential" reductions. For example, Ernst Berl in 1940 developed a process for converting carbohydrate-containing material to coal and oil in one hour.[41] By contrast geologists currently hold that the coal beds took millions of years to form. John Klotz refers to a similar process of oil formation which was once believed to have taken several million years to complete but is now known to be possible in a few thousand years.[42] Boucher de Perthes, who estimated the age of certain Neanderthal remains in France, based his figures on the supposition that it took up to 20,000 years to deposit certain peat beds 26 feet deep. However, an American investigator found birch trunks three feet high in these

[38] For a series of maps see "Note on Niagara Falls," *Trans. Vict. Instit.,* 19 (1885): 90-92. And for a bibliography covering reports of surveys, see "Literature on Niagara Falls," *Trans. Vict. Instit.,* 40 (1908): 76.

[39] Antevs, Ernst, quoted by Kenneth Macgowan, *Early Man in the New World,* Macmillan, N.Y., 1950, p. 121.

[40] Pendelbury, J. D. S., *Archaeology in Crete,* Methuen, N.Y., 1939, p. 43.

[41] Berl, Ernst, referred to by John DeVries, *Beyond the Atom,* Eerdmans, Grand Rapids, 1950, p. 80.

[42] Klotz, John, *Genes, Genesis, and Evolution,* Concordia Publ., St. Louis, Mo., 1955, p. 115.

beds, rooted in place and extending up through from 3,000 to 2,000 years of deposits, according to de Perthes' estimated age. Roman remains were found in the peat indicating that it was not over 3,000 years old at the most.[43]

Much has been written in more recent times of the fact that anthropologists of an older generation tended to assume that "ages" were consecutive. Thus, having estimated the period supposedly occupied by Paleolithic Man, Mesolithic Man, and Neolithic Man, the sum of adding all these together was supposed to give a picture of the time involved. It is now realized that various ages may have been contemporaneous, just as the Indians of North America were still in a Stone Age when the Industrial Revolution began in Europe and some Australian aborigines were still in a Stone Age when the first atom bomb was dropped on Hiroshima. Hallam Movius,[44] in a paper entitled "Old World Prehistory: Paleolithic," in speaking of cultural contemporaneity, remarked, "In this connection it is of significance to note that *all* (his emphasis) the fundamental processes used by Paleolithic Man in Europe to produce tools are being used today, or have been employed during recent times by the Australian aborigine."

One of the first to call attention to such parallelisms was Sir Edward Tylor who, speaking before the Archaeological Institute in England in 1905, made the following statement:[45]

> I am not able to select and exhibit to the institute from among the flint implements and flakes from the cave of Le Moustier, in Dordogne, specimens corresponding in make with such curious exactness to those of the Tasmanian natives, that were it not for the different stone they are chipped from, it would be hardly possible to distinguish them.

Of course, the kind of time frame which is in view here is still nowhere near the traditional time frame of the Bible, even interpreted in the most expansive way that a genuine respect for its data will permit.

Concerning C—14 dating techniques there are, however, serious doubts being raised by men who nevertheless wholeheartedly accept the view that Man has evolved through a long slow process. As a

---

[43] Boucher de Perthes: quoted by Harold W. Clark, *The New Diluvialism,* Science Pub., Angwin, California, 1946, p. 187.
[44] Movius, Hallam L., "Old World Prehistory: Paleolithic," in *Anthropology Today* (ref. 36), p. 163.
[45] Tylor, Sir Edward: see in V. F. Calverton, *The Making of Man,* Modern Library, Random House, N.Y., 1931, p. 89.

single illustration, Charles A. Reed, in an article on animal domestication in the prehistoric Near East, wrote as follows:[46]

> A last difficulty, and at the moment one of the most frustrating,
> is the failure of the radiocarbon (C-14) technique to yield dates of
> certain dependability. Although it was hailed as the answer to the
> prehistorian's prayer when it was first announced, there has been in-
> creasing disillusion with the method because of the chronological un-
> certainties (in some cases, absurdities) that would follow a strict
> adherence to published C-14 dates.
>
> This is not to question the validity of the physical laws underlying
> the principle used or the accuracy of the counters now in operation
> around the world; the unsolved problem, instead, seems to lie in the
> difficulty of securing samples completely free from either younger or
> older adherent carbon.
>
> At least to the present, no kind or degree of chemical cleaning
> can guarantee one-age carbon, typical only of the time of the site from
> which it was excavated.
>
> What bids to become a classical example of "C-14 irresponsibility"
> is the 6000-year spread of 11 determinations for Jarmo, a prehistoric
> village in northern Iraq, which, on the basis of all archaeological
> evidence, was not occupied for more than 500 consecutive years.

Some use has been made of stalagmite and stalactite growth rates
to determine "ages since." The principle is that if a certain stalagmite
has built up to a certain height over some particular fossil remain
or artifact, and if one knows approximately the rate at which it
grows, then one can estimate a minimum time for the fossil remains.
However, John Curry, writing in *Nature*,[47] was able to show that a
stalagmite approximately 15 years old from a lead mine exactly
paralleled in form and height a stalagmite which in association with
human remains had been estimated by the experts as being 220,800
years old. I am not suggesting that similar mistakes are being made
today, but the fact remains that depth of burial is still considered a
very important index of probable age —by a rather similar process of
reasoning which could be equally faulty. Some time ago during the
excavation of a site in Australia a miner's pick was found at a depth
of 20 feet, which as it turned out afterwards, proved to have been
lost by the owner only 60 years previously.[48] As the report says, "How
it worked its way down to this depth is a total mystery." It could be
true of other such finds.

It is even being held by some authorities that the association of
human bones with the bones of supposedly long extinct animals may
not be proof of the antiquity of man but rather that these animals

---

[46] Reed, Charles A., "Animal Domestication in Prehistoric Near East,"
Science, 130 (1959): 1630.

[47] Curry, John, *Nature,* Dec. 18, 1873, p. 122.

[48] Miner's pick: noted by Dr. S. Thornton, "Problems of Aboriginal Art
in Australia," *Trans. Vict. Instit.,* London, 30 (1896): 229.

survived into much more recent times than was formerly believed.[49]

I am convinced that we do not yet need to surrender the position that Scripture seems to me to take rather clearly, namely, that the human race began with Adam's creation only a few thousand years ago.

Now it is our contention that Noah and his family were real people, sole survivors of a major catastrophe, the chief effect of which was to obliterate the previous civilization which had developed from Adam to that time. When the Ark grounded, there were eight people alive in the world, and no more.

Landing somewhere in the highlands north of Mesopotamia, they began to spread as they multiplied, though retaining for some time a homogeneous cultural tradition. The initial family pattern, set by the existence in the party of three sons and their wives, gave rise in the course of time to three distinct families of man who, according to their patriarchal lineage, may appropriately be termed Japhethites, Hamites, and Shemites, but in modern terminology would be represented by the Indo-Europeans (Caucasoids), the Mongoloid and Negroid peoples, and the Semites (Hebrews, Arabs, and some more ancient branches of the family such as the Assyrians, etc.).

At first they kept together, but within a century or so they began to break up. Subsequently some of the family of Shem, some of the family of Ham, and perhaps a few of the family of Japheth arrived from the East in the southern section of the Mesopotamian Plain.[50] Here it would appear from the evidence discussed elsewhere by the author[51] the family of Ham became politically dominant, initiated a movement to prevent any further dispersal by the erection of a monument high enough to be a visible rallying point on the flat plain, and brought upon themselves a judgment which led to their being forcibly and rapidly scattered to the four corners of the earth. Part of this we know only from the Bible; but part of it we know also from archaeological evidence.

The fact is that in every area of the world where Japhethites have subsequently settled, they have always been preceded by Hamites.

---

[49] Man and Prehistoric Animals: see, for example, William Howells, *Mankind So Far*, Doubleday, Doran, N.Y., 1945, p. 267. Also Ashley Montagu, *An Introduction to Physical Anthropology*, Thomas, Springfield, Mo., 1945, p. 110.

[50] The existence of the three "families" at this time is noted by Vere G. Childe in his *New Light on the Most Ancient East*, Kegan Paul, London, 1935, p. 18; and *What Happened in History*, Penguin Books, 1946, p. 81.

[51] Custance, A. C., "The Part Played by Shem, Ham and Japheth in Subsequent World History," "The Technology of Hamitic People," both in Volume I; and "The Confusion of Tongues," in Volume VI.

This pattern applies in every continent. In prehistoric times the circumstance seems always to be true, the earliest fossil remains of man being Mongoloid or Negroid in character and in head shape, whereas those that came last belong to the family of Japheth, i.e., Caucasoid. Indeed, in pre- and early historic times the pattern of events is repeated again and again, whatever cultural advances the pioneering Hamites had achieved tended to be swallowed up by the succeeding Japhethites. The record of Japheth's more leisurely spread (i.e., "enlargement," Gen. 9:27) over the earth has been marred consistently by his destruction of the cultures which were already in existence wherever he arrived in sufficient force to achieve dominion. It happened in the Indus Valley, it happened in Central America, it happened to the Indian tribes of North America, it happened in Australia, and only numerical superiority of the native population has hitherto preserved parts of Africa from the same fate.

Now, in spite of the claims made for and the implications based upon the South African discoveries of recent years, it still remains true that whether we are speaking of fossil man, ancient civilizations, contemporary or extinct native peoples, or the present nations of the world, all lines of migration which are in any way traceable or deducible seem to radiate like the spokes of a wheel from the Middle East.

Before presenting some of the evidence itself, it will be well to summarize briefly what the nature of this evidence is. Along any migratory route there will be settlements each of which differs slightly from the one which preceded it and the one which stems from it. As a general rule, the direction of movement tends to be reflected in the gradual loss of cultural artifacts which continue in use back along the line, but either disappear entirely forwards along the line or are less effectively copied or merely represented in pictures or in folklore. When several lines radiate from a single center, the picture presented is more or less a series of ever increasing circles of settlements, each sharing fewer and fewer of the original cultural artifacts which continue at the center, and each witnesses the appearance of completely new items developed to satisfy new needs which were not found at the center. The further from the center one moves along any such routes of migration, the more new and uniquely specific items one is likely to find which are not shared by the other lines, but there will yet be preserved a few particularly useful or important links with the original home base. Entering such a settlement without previous knowledge of the direction from which the settlers came, one cannot be certain which way relationships are to be traced without some knowledge of the culture content of settlements up and down the line in each direction. There is usually, however, some quite specific type of evidence which allows one to separate the artifacts which have been brought *with* newcomers, from those which have been developed on the site. This is particularly the case whenever complex items turn up. The materials for making them often would not be available locally. Sometimes the evidence is secondhand, existing in the form of an article which is clearly a copy and has something about its construction which proves it to be so. For example, certain Minoan pottery vessels are clearly copies of metal prototypes, both in the shape they take and in their ornamentation. Where the pottery handles of these vessels join the vessel itself, little knobs of clay are found which serve no functional purpose but which are clearly an attempt to copy the rivets which once secured the metal handle to the metal bodies of the prototype.[52] These prototypes are found in Asia Minor, and it is therefore clear which way the line of migration is to be traced, for it is inconceivable that the pottery vessel with its little knobs of clay provided the metalworker with the clues as to where he should place the rivets.

In the earliest migrations which, if we are guided by the chronology of Scripture, must have been quite rapid, it was inevitable that the tendency would be markedly towards a loss of cultural items common to the center as one moves out, rather than a gain of new items.[53] Thus the general level of culture would decline at first, although oral traditions and things like rituals and religious beliefs tend to be surrendered or changed much more slowly. In due time, when a large enough body of people survived in any one place that was hospitable enough to favor permanent settlement, a new culture center would arise with many of the old traditions preserved but some new ones established of sufficient importance that waves of influence would move out both forwards and backwards along the lines from which the settlers had come.

Accompanying such cultural losses in the initial spread of the Hamitic peoples would often be a certain coarsening of physique. Not only would people tend in many cases to be unsuited for the rigors of such a pioneering life and be culturally degraded as a consequence, but food itself would often prove grossly insufficient or unsuitable to their unaccustomed tastes, and not infrequently it would at first be inadequate for the maintenance of full bodily vigor and

---

[52] On this, see J. D. S. Pendelbury, *The Archaeology of Crete*, Methuen, N.Y., 1939, p. 68; and V. G. Childe, *The Dawn of European Civilization*, Kegan Paul, 5th ed., 1950, p. 19.

[53] Perry, W. J., *The Growth of Civilization*, Penguin Books, 1937, p. 123.

the development of entirely normal growth of the young, for dietary disturbances have their effects upon growth patterns. Indeed, as Dawson long ago observed,[54] the more highly cultured an immigrant is when he arrives at a frontier, the more severely is he handicapped and likely to suffer when robbed of the familiar accouterments of his previous life. This has been noted by those who have studied the effects of food deficiencies upon the form of the human skull, for example, a subject dealt with in some detail by the author elsewhere.[35] The effect upon the technological achievement of the newcomers is obvious enough, for a highly educated lady who had never made bread or mended her own clothes or cultivated a garden would be far worse off on the frontier when she first arrived than would a London charwoman. Thus the most likely cause of a particularly degraded society would, at the beginning, not be a low cultural background but a high one. And this is certainly the situation that Genesis presents us with immediately after the Flood.

Meanwhile, the occasional establishment along the various routes of migration of what might be called "provincial" cultural centers whose influences spread in all directions, would greatly complicate the patterns of cultural relationship in the earliest times. By and large, the evidence which does exist strongly supports a Cradle of Mankind in the Middle East, from which there went out just such successive waves of pioneers. And these were almost certainly not Indo-Europeans (i.e., Japhethites). They were Hamitic pioneers, either Mongoloid or Negroid in type for the most part but with some admixture, who blazed trails and opened up territories in every habitable part of the earth often at great cost to their own cultural heritage and to the detriment of the refined physique still to be found in their relatives who continued to reside at their point of origin. In each locality they ultimately either established a way of life which made maximum use of the resources available, or circumstances overwhelmed them and they died out leaving a few scattered remnants behind whose lot must have been appallingly difficult in their isolation, and whose physical remains bear witness to the effect. The Japhethites followed them in due course, often taking advantage of the established technology, as the Puritans were to do in North America thousands of years later, sometimes displacing them entirely, sometimes absorbing them so that the two stocks were fused into one, and sometimes educating them in new ways and then retiring. India has seen all three patterns. The Indus Valley people were over-

---

[54] Dawson, Sir Wm., *The Story of the Earth and Man*, Hodder and Stoughton, London, 1903, p. 390.

whelmed and entirely displaced or absorbed, and this admixture thousands of years later was once more educated in new ways by a further influx of Japhetic settlers, who have since surrendered their dominant status.

As we have already noted, there is a further factor that bears upon the degenerative form which so many of the earliest fossils of man seem to show. Although the life span of man is said to have declined quite rapidly after the Flood, for several hundred years many people did survive to what would today be considered an incredible old age. If we add to the isolation and deprivation of some of these more scattered early pioneers the possibility of their living well past a hundred years or perhaps even longer, the ultimate effect upon their physique would be tremendously accentuated. It has been noted, in fact, that the skull sutures are almost obliterated in some specimens, a circumstance which might reasonably be interpreted as evidence of very extreme old age. Extreme old age would often tend to modify the skull towards the conventional "man-ape" form.[55]

So much, then, for the broad picture. We shall now turn to a more detailed examination of the evidence (1) that the dispersal of man took place from a center somewhere in the Middle East and that this dispersal accounts for fossil man, and (2) that those who formed the vanguard were of Hamitic stock, using the term "Hamitic" to mean all the descendants of Noah who were not in the line of Japheth or Shem.

---

[55] Obliteration of Skull Sutures: Noted by Sir Wm. Dawson, *Meeting Place of Geology and History*, Revell, N.Y., 1904, p. 63.

Chapter 4
Where Did Man First Appear?

BEFORE MAN'S evolutionary origin was proposed, it was generally agreed that the Cradle of Mankind was in Asia Minor or at least in the Middle East area. Any evidence of primitive types elsewhere in the world, whether living or fossil, were considered proof that man had degenerated as he departed from the site of Paradise. When evolution captured the imagination of anthropologists, then primitive fossil remains were at once hailed as proof that the first men were constitutionally not much removed from apes. One problem presented itself almost from the beginning, however, and this was that these supposed ancestors of modern man always seemed to turn up in the wrong places. The basic assumption was still being made that the Middle East was the home of Man and therefore these primitive fossil types, which were turning up anywhere but in this area, seemed entirely misplaced. Osborn, in his *Men of the Old Stone Age,* accounted for this anomaly by arguing that they were migrants. He asserted his conviction that both the human and animal inhabitants of Europe, for example, had migrated there in great waves from Asia and from Africa. In the latter case, he wrote that it was probable that the source of the migratory waves was also Asia, North Africa being merely the route of passage. This was his position in 1915, and when a third edition of his famous book appeared in 1936, he had modified his original views only slightly. Thus he has a map of the Old World with this subscription, "Throughout this long epoch Western Europe is to be viewed as a peninsula, surrounded on all sides by the sea and stretching westwards from the great land mass of Eastern Europe and Asia — which was the chief theater of evolution, both of animal and human life."[56] However, in 1930 and contrary to expectations, H. J. Fleure had to admit:[57]

---

[56] Osborn, H. F., *Men of the Old Stone Age,* Scribners, N.Y., 1936, p. 19f.
[57] Fleure, H. J., *The Races of Mankind,* Benn, London, 1930, p. 45.

No clear traces of the men and cultures of the later part of the Old Stone Age (known in Europe as the Aurignacian, Solutrean, and Magdalenian phases) have been discovered in the central highland of Asia.

The situation remained essentially the same when, twenty years later, Wilhelm Koppers observed:[58]

It is a remarkable fact that so far all the fossil men have been found in Europe, the Far East, and Africa, that is, in the marginal regions of Asia that are most unlikely to have formed the cradle of the human race. No remains are known to us from central Asia where most scholars who have occupied themselves with the origin of man would place the earliest races.

It is true that some fossil men have now been found in the Middle East, but far from telling against this area as being central to subsequent migration, they seem to me to argue indirectly — and therefore with more force — in favor of it. We shall return to this subsequently.

Griffith Taylor of the University of Toronto, in speaking of migratory movements in general whether in prehistoric or historic times, wrote:[59]

A series of zones is shown to exist in the East Indies and in Australasia which is so arranged that the most primitive are found farthest from Asia, and the most advanced nearest to Asia. This distribution about Asia is shown to be true in other "peninsulas" [i.e., Africa and Europe], and is of fundamental importance in discussing the evolution and ethnological status of the peoples concerned....

Which ever region we consider, Africa, Europe, Australia, or America, we find that the major migrations have always been from Asia.

After dealing with some of the indices which he employs for establishing possible relationships between groups in different geographical areas, he remarked:[60]

How can one explain the close resemblance between such far-distant types as are here set forth? Only the spreading of racial zones *from a common cradleland* (his emphasis) can possibly explain these biological affinities.

Then, subsequently, in dealing with African ethnology, he observed:[61]

The first point of interest in studying the distribution of the African peoples is that the same rule holds good which we have observed in the Australasian peoples. The most primitive groups are found in the regions most distant from Asia, or what comes to the same thing, in the most inaccessible of regions....

Given these conditions it seems logical to assume that the racial

---

[58] Koppers, W., *Primitive Man and His World Picture,* Sheed and Ward, N.Y., 1952, p. 239.
[59] Taylor, Griffith, *Environment, Race and Migration,* U. of Toronto, 1945, p. 9.
[60] Taylor, G., ref. 59, p. 67.
[61] Taylor, G., ref. 59, p. 120, 121.

zones can only have resulted from similar peoples spreading out like waves from a common origin. This cradle-land should be approximately between the two "peninsulas," and all indications (including the racial distribution of India) point to a region of maximum evolution not far from Turkestan. It is not unlikely that the time factor was similar in the spread of all these peoples.

In a similar vein, Dorothy Garrod wrote:[62]

> It is becoming more and more clear that it is not in Europe that we must seek the origins of the various paleolithic peoples who successfully overran the west.... The classification of de Mortillet therefore only records *the order of arrival* (my emphasis) in the West of a series of cultures, each of which has originated and probably passed through the greater part of its existence elsewhere.

So also wrote V. G. Childe:[63]

> Our knowledge of the archaeology of Europe and of the Ancient East has enormously strengthened the Orientalist's position. Indeed we can now survey continuously interconnected provinces throughout which cultures are seen to be zoned in regularly descending grades round the centers of urban civilization in the Ancient East. Such zoning is the best possible proof of the Orientalist's postulate of diffusion.

Henry Field, in writing about the possible cradle of Homo sapiens, gave a very cursory review of the chief finds of fossil man (to that date, 1932), including finds from Java, Kenya, Rhodesia, and Heidelberg, and then gave a map locating them; and he remarked:[64]

> It does not seem probable to me that any of these localities could have been the original point from which the earliest man migrated. The distances, combined with many geographical barriers, would tend to make a theory of this nature untenable. I suggest that an area more or less equidistant from the outer edges of Europe, Asia, and Africa, may indeed be the center in which development took place.

It is true that these statements were written before the recent discoveries in South Africa, or in the Far East at Choukoutien, or in the New World. Of the South African finds we have already spoken — and they do not concern us here since there is no general agreement that they are truly fossils of man or even, in the opinions of some, ancestral to him. The finds at Choukoutien, as we shall attempt to show, support the present thesis in an interesting way. As for the

---

[62] Garrod, Dorothy, "Nova et Vetera: a Plea for a New Method in Paleolithic Archaeology," *Proceedings of the Prehistoric Soc. of East Anglia,* Vol. 5, p. 261.

[63] Childe, V. G., *Dawn of European Civilization,* Kegan Paul, London, 3rd ed., 1939. In the 1957 edition Childe in his introduction invites his readers to observe that he has modified his "dogmatic" orientation a little, but he still concludes at the end of the volume (p. 342): "the primacy of the Orient remains unchallenged."

[64] Field, Henry, "The Cradle of Homo sapiens," *Amer. Jour. Archeol.,* Oct.-Dec., 1932, p. 427.

New World, no one has ever yet proposed that it was the Cradle of Mankind. Nor do fossils in it antedate the supposedly earliest fossil men in the Old World. Thus the Middle East could still retain priority as the home of Man, although in the matter of dating it must be admitted that no authority with a reputation for orthodox scholarship at stake would ever propose it was a homeland *so recently* — by our reckoning only 4,500 to 5,000 years ago. The problem of time therefore remains. And at the moment we have no answer to it, but we can continue to explore further lines of evidence which in most other respects assuredly do support the thesis set forth in this paper.

Part of this evidence, curiously enough, is the fact of diversity of physical type found within what appear to have been single families (since the fossils are found all together and seem to be contemporary). This has been a source of some surprise, though readily enough accounted for on the basis of central dispersion. Some years ago, W. D. Matthew made the following observation:[65]

> Whatever agencies may be assigned as the cause of evolution in a race, it should be at first most progressive at its point of original dispersal....

Some comment is in order on this observation because there are important implications in it. Lebzelter pointed out that "where man lives in large conglomerations, physical form tends to be stable while culture becomes specialized: where he lives in small isolated groups, culture is stable but specialized races evolve."[66] According to Lebzelter, this is why racial differentiation was more marked in the earlier stages of man's history. The explanation of this fact is clear enough. In a very small, closely inbreeding population, genes for odd characters have a much better chance of being homozygously expressed so that such characters appear in the population with greater frequency, and tend to be perpetuated. On the other hand, such a small population may have so precarious an existence that the margin of survival is too narrow to encourage or permit cultural diversities to find expression. Thus physical type is variant but is accompanied by cultural conformity. Whereas in a large and well established community, a physical norm begins to appear as characteristic of that population, while the security resulting from numbers allows for a greater range of cultural divergence.

---

[65] Matthew W. D., "Climate and Evolution," *Annals of the New York Academy of Science,* 24 (1914): 180.

[66] Lebzelter, quoted by W. Koppers in his *Primitive Man* (ref. 58), p. 220. His view was sustained by LeGros Clark, *Jour. Roy. Anthrop. Instit.,* 88 (1958): 133.

At the very beginning, we might therefore expect to find in the central area a measure of physical diversity and cultural uniformity; and at each secondary or provincial center in its initial stages, the same situation would reappear. The physical diversity to be expected on the foregoing grounds would, it is now known, be exaggerated even further by the fact (only comparatively recently recognized) that when any established species enters a new environmnt it at once gives expression to a new and greater power of diversification in physical form. As LeGros Clark put it:[67]

> High variability (in type) may be correlated with the fact that (at that time) the rate of hominid evolution was proceeding rather rapidly with the deployment of relatively small and often contiguous populations into widely dispersed areas with contrasting and changing environments.

The fact of initial variability has been widely recognized. Ralph B. Goldschmidt spoke of it as a nearly universal phenomenon:[68]

> The facts of greatest general importance are the following. When a new phylum, class, or order appears, there follows a quick explosive (in terms of geological time) diversification so that practically all orders or families known appear suddenly and without apparent transitions.

Thus we have in reality three factors, all of which are found to be still in operation in living populations, which must have contributed to the marked variability of early fossil human remains, particularly where several specimens are found in a single site as at Choukoutien, for example, or at Obercassel, or Mount Carmel.

These factors may then be summarized as follows: (1) A new species is more variable when it first appears. (2) A small population is more variable than a large one. (3) When a species (or a few members of it) shifts into a new environment, wide variation again appears that only becomes stable with time. To these should be added a fourth, namely, that small populations are likely to be highly conservative in their culture, thus maintaining many links with the parent body though widely extended geographically.

Vere Gordon Childe observed:[69]

> Firmly entrenched instances, passionately held superstitions, are notoriously inimical to social change and the scientific advances that make it necessary. And the force of such reaction in a community seems to be inversely proportional to the community's economic security, a group always on the brink of starvation dare not risk a change.

---

[67] Clark, Sir W. LeGros, "Bones of Contention," ref. 1, p. 301.

[68] Goldschmidt, Ralph B., "Evolution As Viewed by One Geneticist," *Amer. Scientist,* 40 (Jan., 1952): 97; and see for additional material on this point, "The Supposed Evolution of the Human Skull," in this volume.

[69] Childe, Vere Gordon, *Man Makes Himself,* Thinker's Library, Watts, London, 1948, p. 99.

Fossil remains constantly bear witness to the reality of these factors, but the witness has meaning and the facts are best accounted for only if we assume that a small population began at the center and, as it became firmly established there, sent out successive waves of migrants usually numbering very few persons in any one group who thereafter established a further succession of centers, the process being repeated again and again until early man had spread into every habitable part of the world. Each new center at the first showed great diversity of physical type but as the population multiplied locally a greater physical uniformity was achieved in the course of time. Where such a subsidiary center was wiped out before this uniformity had been achieved and where chance preserved their remains, the diversity was captured and frozen for our examination. At the same time in marginal areas where individuals or families were pushed out even further by those who followed them, circumstances often combined to degrade them so grossly that fossil man naturally tends towards a bestial form — but for quite secondary reasons. This is supported by a statement of Le Gros Clark, for example. In discussing Heidelberg Man, he asks whether he represents a separate species of man or may not be "merely a deviant peripheral isolate."[70] Clark virtually admits the same possibility for Neanderthal Man. After referring to him as "an aberrant side line ... a sort of evolutionary retrogression," he goes on to say, "If the remains of Neanderthal Man are placed in their chronological sequence, it appears that some of the *earlier* fossils, dating from the earlier part of the Mousterian period are less 'Neanderthaloid' in their skeletal characters (and thus approach more closely to Homo sapiens) than the extreme Neanderthal type of *later* date (my emphasis) ."[71]

On the other hand, in the earliest stages of the migrations cul-

---

[70] Clark, LeGros, "Bones of Contention," in *Human Evolution* (ref. 1), p. 239.

[71] Clark, W. LeGros, *History of the Primates,* Phoenix Books, Univer. of Chicago, 1957, pp. 163, 164. The 1966 edition of the Encyclopedia Britannica, Vol. 14 (p. 738) has this observation: "In the early days of paleoanthropological discovery, Homo Neanderthalensis was commonly assumed to represent the ancestral type from which Homo sapiens derived. ...

But the accumulation of further discoveries made it clear that these apparently primitive features are secondary — the result of a retrogressive evolution from still earlier types which do not appear to be specifically distinguishable from Homo sapiens."

Wilfred E. LeGros Clark notes that Neanderthal Man "disappeared from Europe quite abruptly, to be replaced by a population of the modern Homo sapiens type. Presumably, the latter spread into Europe from a neighboring area, perhaps the Middle East, and by replacement led to the extinction of Homo Neanderthalensis." See his "The Crucial Evidence for Human Evolution," *Amer. Scientist,* 47 (1959): 303.

tural uniformity would not only be the rule in each group but necessarily also be found between the groups themselves. And this, too, has been found to be so. Indeed, following the rule enunciated above, the most primitive fragments which had been pushed furthest to the rim might logically be expected to have the greatest proportion of shared culture elements, so that links would not be surprising if found between such peripheral areas as the New World, Europe, Australia, South Africa, and so forth — which is exactly what has been observed.

Such lines of evidence force upon us the conclusion that we should not look to these marginal areas for a picture of the initial stages of man's cultural development nor for a picture of his original appearance. It is exactly in these marginal areas that we shall *not* find these things. The logic of this was both evident to and flatly rejected by E. A. Hooten who remarked:[72]

> The adoption of such a principle would necessitate the conclusion that the places where one finds existing primitive forms of any order of animal are exactly the places where these animals could not have originated. . . .
> But this is the principle of "lucus a non lucendo," i.e., finding light just where one ought not to do so, which pushed to its logical extreme would lead us to seek for the birthplace of man in that area where there are no traces of ancient man and *none of any of his primate precursors* (my emphasis) .

Nevertheless, the principle may be true — even if it does contradict evolutionary reconstructions.

William Howells has written at some length on the fact that, as he puts it, "all the visible footsteps lead away from Asia."[73] He then examined the picture with respect to the lines of migration taken by the "Whites" (Caucasoids) and observed that at the beginning they were entrenched in southwest Asia "apparently with the Neanderthals to the north and west of them." He then proposed that while most of them made their way into both Europe and North Africa, some of them may have traveled east through central Asia into China, which would explain, possibly, the Ainus and the Polynesians. He thought that the situation with respect to the Mongoloids was pretty straightforward, their origin having been somewhere in the same area as the Whites, from which they peopled the East. The dark skinned peoples are, as he put it, "a far more formidable puzzle." He thought that the Australian aborigines can be traced back as far as India with

[72] Hooten, A. E., "Where Did Man Originate?" *Antiquity,* June, 1927, p. 149.
[73] Howells, William, *Mankind So Far,* Doubleday, Doran, N.Y., 1945, pp. 295ff.

some evidence of them perhaps in southern Arabia. Presumably, the African Negroes are to be traced also from the Middle East, possibly reaching Africa by the Horn and therefore also via Arabia.

However, there are a number of black skinned peoples who seem scattered here and there in a way which he terms "the crowding enigma" — a major feature of which is the peculiar relationship between the Negroes and the Negritos. Of these latter, he had this to say:[74]

> They are [found] among the Negroes in the Congo Forest, and they turn up on the eastern fringe of Asia (the Andaman Islands, the Malay Peninsula, probably India, and possibly formerly in southern China), in the Philippines, and in New Guinea, and perhaps Australia, with probable traces in Borneo, Celebes, and various Melanesian Islands.
>
> All of these are "refuge" areas, the undesirable backwoods which the Pygmies have obviously occupied as later more powerful people arrived in the same regions....
>
> Several things stand out from these facts. The Negritos must have had a migration from a common point.... And it is hopeless to assume that their point of origin was at either end of their range.... It is much more likely that they came from some point midway which is Asia.

There is, then, a very wide measure of agreement that the lines of migration radiate not from a point somewhere in Africa or Europe or the Far East but from a geographical area which is to be closely associated with that part of the world in which not only does Scripture seem to say that man began physically populating the world after the Flood, but also culturally. Looking at the spread of civilization as we have looked at the spread of people, it is clear that the lines follow the same course. The essential difference, if we are taking note of current chronological sequences, is that whereas the spread of people is held to have occurred hundreds of thousands of years ago, the spread of civilization is an event which has taken place very recently. I think that man was making his long trek to the uttermost corners of the world while at the very same time civilization was blossoming at the center.

It used to be argued that although civilized man is a single species, these far-flung fossil remains of man formed separate species in their own right and were therefore not related to modern man in any simple way. Some have tentatively proposed, for example, a concept like this by looking upon Neanderthal Man as an earlier species or subspecies who was eliminated with the appearance of so-called

---

[74] Ibid., pp. 298, 299.

"modern man."[75] The association of Neanderthals with moderns in the Mount Carmel finds seems to stand against this.[76] And indeed, there is a very widespread agreement today that, with the exception of course of the most recent South African finds, all men — fossil, prehistoric, historic, and modern — are one species, Homo sapiens.[77]

Ralph Linton viewed the varieties of men revealed by fossil finds as being due to factors which we have already outlined. As he put it:[78]

> If we are correct in our belief that all existing men belong to a single species, early man must have been a generalized form with potentialities for evolving into all the varieties which we know at present. It further seems probable that this generalized form spread widely and rapidly and that within a few thousand years of its appearance small bands of individuals were scattered over most of the Old World.
>
> These bands would find themselves in many different environments, and the physical peculiarities which were advantageous in one of these might be of no importance or actually deleterious in another. Moreover, due to the relative isolation of these bands and their habit of inbreeding, any mutation which was favorable or at least not injurious under the particular circumstances would have the best possible chance of spreading to all members of the group.
>
> It seems quite possible to account for all the known variations in our species on this basis, without invoking the theory of a small number of distinct varieties.

Viewed in this light, degraded fossil specimens found in marginal regions should neither be treated as "unsuccessful" evolutionary experiments towards the making of true Homo sapiens types, nor as "successful but only partially complete" phases or links between apes and men. Indeed, as Griffith Taylor was willing to admit, "the location of such 'missing' links as Pithecanthropus in Java, etc., seems to have little bearing on the question of the human cradleland."[79] And he might in fact also have said, "on the question of human origins." He concludes, "They are almost certainly examples of a ... type which has been pushed out to the margins."

At a recent conference of anthropologists one speaker was reported as having said:[80]

> Many of the so-called "primitive" peoples of the world today, most of the participants agreed, may not be so primitive after all. They

[75] Weidenreich, Franz, *Palaeontologia Sinica*, Whole Series No. 127, 1943, p. 276.
[76] Romer, Alfred, *Man and the Vertebrates*, Univer. Chicago Press, 1948, pp. 219, 221.
[77] Fossils of man as a whole: see F. Gaynor Evans in a note on "The Names of Fossil Men," *Science* 101 (1945): 16, 17.
[78] Linton, Ralph, *The Study of Man*, Appleton Century, N.Y., 1936, p. 26.
[79] Taylor, Griffith, ref. 59, p. 282.
[80] Reported in *Science Yearbook*, 1966, p. 256.

suggested that certain hunting tribes in Africa, Central India, South America, and the Western Pacific are not relics of the Stone Age, as had been previously thought, but instead are the "wreckage" of more highly developed societies forced through various circumstances to lead a much simpler, less-developed life.

Thus the way in which one studies or views these fossil remains is very largely colored by whether one's thinking is in terms of biological or historical processes. And A. Portmann of Vienna has remarked:[81]

> One and the same piece of evidence will assume totally different aspects according to the angle— paleontological or historical — from which we look at it. We shall see it either as a link in one of the many evolutionary series that the paleontologist seeks to establish, or as something connected with remote historical actions and developments that we can hardly hope to reconstruct. Let me state clearly that for my part I have not the slightest doubt that the remains of early man known to us should all be judged historically.

This general approach towards the interpretation of the meaning of fossil man has been explored in some detail by Wilhelm Koppers who thought that "primitiveness in the sense of man being closer to the beast" can upon occasion be the "result of a secondary development."[82] He believed that it would be far more logical to "evolve" Neanderthal Man out of modern man than modern man out of Neanderthal Man. He held, in fact, that they were a specialized and more primitive type — but *later* than modern man, at least in so far as they occur in Europe.

Surprisingly enough, such a great authority as Franz von Weidenreich was prepared to admit unequivocably, "No fossil type of man has been discovered so far whose characteristic features may not easily be traced *back* to modern man" (emphasis mine).[83] Griffith Taylor has agreed with this opinion. He observed, "evidence is indeed accumulating that the paleolithic folk of Europe were much more closely akin to races now living on the periphery of the Euro-African regions than was formerly admitted."[84] Many years ago, in fact, Sir William Dawson pursued this theme and explored it at some length in his beautifully written but almost completely ignored work entitled *Fossil Man and Their Modern Representatives*.[85] At the Cold Springs Harbor Symposia on Quantitative Biology held in 1950, T. D. Stew-

---

[81] Portmann, A., *Das Ursprungsproblem*, Eranos-Yahrbuck, 1947, p. 11.

[82] Koppers, Wilhelm, ref. 58, p. 220 and 224.

[83] Weidenreich, Franz, *Apes, Giants and Man*, Chicago University Press, 1948, p. 2.

[84] Taylor, Griffith, ref. 58, pp. 46, 47.

[85] Dawson, Sir William, *Fossil Men and Their Modern Representatives*, Hodder and Stoughton, London, 1883, viii and 354 pp., ill.

art in a paper entitled "Earliest Representatives of Homo Sapiens" stated his conclusions in the following words, "Like Dobzhansky, therefore, I can see no reason at present to suppose that more than a single hominid species has existed on any time level in the Pleistocene."[86]

Korn and Thompson are prepared to admit the possibility that Heidelberg Man could be merely "a deviant peripheral isolate," which would suggest that he should no longer be viewed as a potentially early candidate ancestor on account of his "brutish" appearance.[87]

The Pithecanthropocines are all more or less peripheral to the traditional Cradle of Man. These include Vertesszolles Man in Hungary, Ternifine Man in Algeria, Olduvai Man in Tanzania, Swartkranz Man in South Africa, and Lantian and Pekin Man in Java and China. Neanderthal Man, on the other hand, occupies a position intermediate for cranial, facial, and dental characteristics between Pithecanthropus and Homo sapiens.[88]

The most primitive types being at the margins and only essentially modern types so far found where civilization had its source, it is to be expected that combinations and intermediate forms would be found in the geographic areas in between. Alfred Romer observed in commenting on the collection of fossil finds from Palestine (Mughâret-et-Tabun, and Maghâret-es-Skuhl), "while certain of the skulls are clearly Neanderthal, others show to a variable degree numerous neanthropic (i.e., 'modern man') features."[89] Subsequently he identified such neanthropic skulls as being of the general Cromagnon type in Europe — a type of man who appears to have been a magnificent physical specimen. He proposed later that the Mount Carmel people "may be considered as due to interbreeding of the dominant race (Cromagnon Man) with its lowly predecessors (Neanderthal Man)." The assumption is still being made that the lower Neanderthal form *preceded* the higher Cromagnon Man. William Howells said of the Skuhl fossil group, "It is an extraordinary variation. There seems to have been a single tribe ranging in type from

---

[86] Stewart, T. D., "Origin and Evolution of Man," *Cold Springs Harbor Symposia on Quantitative Biology,* 15 (1950): 105.

[87] Korn, N. and F. Thompson, *Human Evolution: Readings in Physical Anthropology,* Holt, Rinehart & Winston, N.Y., 1967, p. 239.

[88] McCowan, T. D., "The Genus Palaeoanthropus and the Problem of Superspecific Differentiation Among the Hominidae," *Cold Springs Harbor Symposia on Quantitative Biology,* 15 (1950): 92.

[89] Romer, Alfred, ref. 76, pp. 219, 221.

almost *Neanderthal* to almost *sapiens*."[90] LeGros Clark was even prepared to omit the "almost."[91]

As an extraordinary example of the tremendous variability which an early, small isolated population at the periphery can show, one cannot do better than refer to the finds at Choukoutien in China, from the same locality in which the famous Pekin Man was found. These fossil remains came from what is known as the Upper Cave, and consist of a group of seven people who appear to be members of one family: an old man judged to be over 60, a younger man, two relatively young women, an adolescent, a child of five, and a newborn baby. With them were found implements, ornaments, and thousands of fragments of animals.

A study of these remains has produced some remarkably interesting facts, the most important of which in the present context is that, judged by cranial form, we have in this one family a representative Neanderthal Man, a "Melanesian" woman who reminds us of the Ainu, a Mongolian type, and another who is rather similar to the modern Eskimo woman. In commenting on these finds, Weidenreich expressed his amazement at the range of variation. Thus he wrote:[92]

> The surprising fact is not the occurrence of paleolithic types of modern man which resemble racial types of today, but their assemblage in one place and even in a single family considering that these types are found today settled in far remote regions.
> Forms similar to that of the "Old Man," as he has been named, have been found in Upper Paleolithic, western Europe and northern Africa: those closely resembling the Melanesian type, in the neolithic of Indo-China, among the ancient skulls from the Cave of Lagoa Santa in Brazil, and in the Melanesian populations of today; those closely resembling the Eskimo type occur among the pre-Columbian Amerindians of Mexico and other places in North America and among the Eskimos of western Greenland of today.

He then proceeded to point out that the upper Paleolithic melting-pot of Choukoutien "does not stand alone."[93] In Obercassel in the Rhine Valley were found two skeletons, an old male and a younger female, in a tomb of about the same period as the burial in Choukoutien. Weidenreich said, "The skulls are so different in appearance that one would not hesitate to assign them to two races if they came from separate localities." So confused is the picture that he observed:[34]

---

[90] Howells, William, ref. 73, p. 202.
[91] Clark, Sir W. LeGros, in *Human Evolution* (ref. 1), p. 302.
[92] Weidenreich, Franz, "Homo sapiens at Choukoutien," News and Notes, in *Antiquity*, June, 1939, p. 87.
[93] Ibid., p. 88.
[94] Ibid.

Physical anthropologists have gotten into a blind alley so far as the definition and the range of individual human races and their history is concerned. . . .

But one cannot push aside a whole problem because the methods applied and accepted as historically sacred have gone awry.

This extraordinary variability nevertheless still permits the establishment of lines of relationship which appear to crisscross in every direction as a dense network of evidence that these fossil remains for the most part belong to a single family, the descendants of Ham.

Griffith Taylor linked together Melanesians, Negroes, and American Indians.[95] The same authority proposed a relationship between Java Man and Rhodesian Man.[96] He related certain Swiss tribes which seem to be a pocket of an older racial stock with the people of northern China, the Sudanese, the Bushmen of South Africa, and the Aeta of the Philippines.[97] He would also link the Predmost Skull to Aurignacian folk and to the Australoids.[98] Macgowan[99] and Montagu[100] were convinced that the aboriginal populations of central and southern America contain an element of Negroid as well as Australoid people. Grimaldi Man is almost universally admitted to have been Negroid even though his remains lie in Europe.[101] But indeed, so widespread is the Negroid type that even Pithecanthropus erectus was identified as Negroid by Buyssens.[102]

Huxley maintained that the Neanderthal race must be closely linked with the Australian aborigines particularly from the Province of Victoria;[103] and other authorities held that the same Australian people are to be related to the famous Canstadt Race.[104] Alfred Romer related Solo Man from Java with Rhodesian Man from Africa.[105] Hrdlicka likewise related the Oldoway Skull with LaQuina Woman;

---

[95] Taylor, Griffith, ref. 59, p. 11.

[96] Ibid., p. 60. His argument here is based on head form, which he considers conclusive.

[97] Ibid., p. 67. He feels only a "common cradleland" can possibly explain the situation.

[98] Ibid., p. 134.

[99] Macgowan, Kenneth, *Early Man in the New World*, Macmillan, N.Y., 1950, p. 26.

[100] Montagu, Ashley, *Introduction to Physical Anthropology*, Thomas, Springfield, Illinois, 1947, p. 113.

[101] Weidenreich, Franz, ref. 92, p. 88.

[102] Buyssens, Paul, *Les Trois Races de l'Europe et du Monde*, Brussels, 1936. See G. Grant MacCurdy, *Amer. Jour. Archeol.*, Jan.-Mar., 1937, p. 154.

[103] Huxley, Thomas, quoted by D. Garth Whitney, "Primeval Man in Belgium," *Trans. Vict. Instit.*, London, 40 (1908): 38.

[104] According to D. Garth Whitney, ref. 103.

[105] Romer, Alfred, ref. 76, p. 223.

Lachapelle and others to the basic African stock;[106] and held that they must also be related to Indian, Eskimo, and Australian races. Even the Mauer Jaw is held to be Eskimo in type.[107]

We cannot do better than sum up this general picture in the words of Sir William Dawson who, far in advance of his time, wrote of fossil man in Europe, in 1874:[108]

> What precise relationship do these primitive Europeans bear to one another? We can only say that all seem to indicate one basic stock, and this is allied to the Hamitic stock of northern Asia which has its outlying branches to this day both in America and in Europe.

Although it is perfectly true that the thesis we are presenting has against it in the matter of chronology the whole weight of scientific opinion, it is nevertheless equally true that the interpretation of the data in this fashion makes wonderful sense and, indeed, would have allowed one to predict both the existence of widespread physical relationships as well as an exceptional variableness within the members of any one family. In addition to these anatomical "linkages" there are, of course, a very great many cultural linkages. One such linkage is the painting of the bones of the deceased with red ochre — a custom which not so very long ago was still being practiced by the American Indians and which has been observed in prehistoric burials in almost every part of the world.

The circumstances are worth a moment's consideration because it is hard to explain the phenomenon as simply evidence "that men's minds work pretty much the same everywhere." It might be true of the use of flint for weapons, the making of wooden spears, or the use of leather for clothing, because all these things serve needs which men everywhere are apt to experience. But painting bones with red ochre serves no strictly "useful" purpose, nor can it be said that in most known cases the practice contributed to beautification. It is difficult to know precisely what purpose it did serve. But it certainly was very widespread.

One of the first notices of this practice was the finding in 1823 by William Buckland of a female skeleton in a cave near Paviland which was painted with red ochre.[109] His find came to be known as "The Red Lady of Paviland." In the New World the same practice

---

[106] Hrdlicka, Ales, "Skeletal Remains of Early Man," Smithsonian Inst., *Misc. Collections*, 83 (1930): 342ff.

[107] Ibid., p. 98. And see William S. Laughlin, "Eskimos and Aleuts: Their Origins and Evolution," *Science*, 142 (1963): 639, 642.

[108] Dawson, Sir William, "Primitive Man," *Trans. Vict. Instit.*, London, 8, (1874): 60, 61.

[109] Buckland, quoted by Kenneth Macgowan, ref. 99, p. 52.

recurs, though much later in time. Thus between A.D. 700 and A.D. 1100, in the cultural sequences which have been established in the Illinois area in the United States, there is what has been termed the "Red Ochre Culture," so-called because in almost every case bodies were sprinkled with haematite. Sir William Dawson[110] had noted this circumstance in other parts of the New World and remarked upon one burial from the St. Lawrence Valley dated (at that time) as about 300 years old, in which warriors were buried with iron oxide treatment of the face precisely similar to those discovered by Dr. Riviera in a cave at Mentone on the border between France and Italy. He suggested that in the case of the Indian burials it was an attempt to provide the dead with the means to appear in the presence of their ancestors with the appropriate war paint. Perhaps Dawson was not too far from the truth when he argued that prehistoric man quite probably enjoyed a culture very similar to that of many Indian tribes when first discovered by the White Man. He proposed that the very epithet "Red Indian" derives from this use of red ochre. The Crow Indians painted the newborn baby with grease and red paint,[111] which seems to suggest that the substance was held to be of great potency in guaranteeing vitality — both to the newborn, the warrior, and to those who had gone to join the spirits of their ancestors.

So powerful is this coloring material, and so widespread is its use, that the Australian aborigines in the central areas of Australia coat with it everything except their spears and spear throwers.[112] Coon observes, "It is hard to say how much this served them as a protection and lubricant." Even some of their spear throwers are treated with red ochre (I have one), though it is hard to know whether this is a concession to tourists.

At the other end of the world, it appears that the Saxons also buried their dead, at least upon occasion, in the company of red ochre, if not originally actually painted with it.[113]

Surely such a custom could hardly arise everywhere indigenously

---

[110] Dawson, Sir William, ref. 19, pp. 19, 142, 143.

[111] Murdock, G. P., *Our Primitive Contemporaries,* Macmillan, N.Y., 1951, p. 275.

[112] Coon, Carleton S., *A Reader in General Anthropology,* Holt, N.Y., 1948, p. 226.

[113] Childe, V. G., ref. 63, p. 168; and elsewhere in Europe, see pp. 209, 254, 259. See also C. S. Coon, *Reader in General Anthropology,* Holt, N.Y., 1948, p. 226; George P. Murdock, *Our Primitive Contemporaries,* Macmillan, N.Y., 1934, p. 275; Kenneth Macgowan, *Early Man in the New World,* Macmillan, N.Y., 1950, p. 52; Sir William Dawson, *Fossil Men and Their Modern Representatives,* Hodder & Stoughton, London, 1883, p. 19, 143; and in the Time-Life Publications, *Early Man (Life* Nature Library), 1965, p. 156, and *The Epic of Man,* 1961, pp. 40, 41.

simply as an expression of the tendency of men's minds to find similar answers to similar needs, for where was the need? It seems much more reasonable to assume it was spread by people who carried it with them as they radiated from some central Cradle of Mankind.

And this brings us once more to the question of the geographical position of this Cradle. Evidence accumulates daily that, culturally speaking, the place of man's origin was somewhere in the Middle East. No other region in the world is as likely to have been the Home of Man if by man we mean something more than merely an intelligent ape. Vavilov[114] and others[115] have repeatedly pointed out that the great majority of the cultivated plants of the world, especially the cereals, trace their origin there. Field remarked:[116]

> Iran may prove to have been one of the nurseries of Homo sapiens. During the middle or upper Paleolithic periods the climate, flora, and fauna of the Iranian Plateau provided an environment suitable for human occupation. Indeed, Ellsworth Huntington has postulated that during late Pleistocene times southern Iran was the *only* (his emphasis) region in which temperature and humidity were ideal, not only for human conception and fertility but also for chances of survival.

Many speculations exist as to the routes taken by Caucasoids, Negroids and Mongoloids, as the world was peopled by the successive ebb and flow of migrations, and while not one of these really establishes with certainty *how* man originated as *man*, almost all of them make the basic assumption that western Asia is his home as a creator of culture.

From this center one can trace the movements of an early migration of Negroid people, followed by Caucasoid people, in Europe. From this same area undoubtedly there passed out into the East and the New World successive waves of Mongoloid people, and the time taken need not have been so great. Kenneth Macgowan said it has been estimated that men might have covered the 4,000 miles from Harbin, Manchuria, to Vancouver Island in as little as twenty years,[117] while Alfred Kidder said,[118] "A hunting pattern based primarily on big game could have carried man to southern South America without the necessity at that time of great localized adaptation. It could have been effected with relative rapidity, so long as camel, horse, sloth,

114 Vavilov, N. I., "Asia, the Source of Species," *Asia,* Feb., 1937, p. 113.
115 Cf. Harlan, J. R., "New World Crop Plants in Asia Minor," *Sci. Monthly,* Feb., 1951, p. 87.
116 Field, Henry, "The Iranian Plateau Race," *Asia,* Apr., 1940, p. 217.
117 Macgowan, K., ref. 99, p. 3 and map on p. 4.
118 Kidder, Alfred, "Problems of the Historical Approach: Results," in *Appraisal of Anthropology Today,* ref. 37, p. 46.

and elephant were available. All the indications point to the fact that they were." According to de Quatrefages,[119] 600,000 people made a trip from a point in Mongolia to China during winter and under constant attack in just five months, covering a distance of 700 leagues or 2100 miles; and though this seems to be a staggering trip in so short a time, it actually works out to an average of 14 miles per day.

In Africa, Wendell Phillips,[120] after studying the relationships of various African tribes, concluded that evidence already existing makes it possible to derive many of the tribes from a single racial stock (particularly the Pygmies of the Ituri Forest and the Bushmen of the Kalahari Desert), which at a certain time must have populated a larger part of the African continent only to retreat to less hospitable regions as later Negroid tribes arrived in the country. H. J. Fleure[121] held that evidence of a similar nature towards the north and northeast of Asia, and on into the New World, was to be discerned by a study in the change of head forms in fossil remains, and it has even been suggested that the finds at Choukoutien mean we have encountered some of these first pioneers on their way to the Americas. Moreover, wherever tradition sheds light on the subject, it invariably points in the same direction and tells the same story. Many primitive people having recollections of a former higher cultural standing, a circumstance explored elsewhere by the writer at considerable length.

And thus we conclude that from the family of Noah have sprung *all* the peoples of the world, prehistoric and historic. The events described in connection with Genesis 6 to 10 and particularly the prophetic statements of Noah himself in Genesis 9:25-28 with respect to the future of his three sons, Shem, Ham, and Japheth, together combine to provide us with the most reasonable account of the early history of mankind, a history which, rightly understood, does not at all require us to believe that modern man began with the stature of an ape and only reached a civilized state after a long, long evolutionary history, but made a fresh start as a single family who carried with them into an unpeopled earth the accumulated heritage of the pre-Flood world.

In summary, then, what we have endeavored to show in this paper may be set forth briefly as follows:

(1) The geographical distribution of fossil remains is such that they are most logically explained by treating them as marginal repre-

---

[119] de Quatrefages, A., *L'Espece Humaine,* Balliere et Cie., Paris, 14th ed., 1905, pp. 135, 136.

[120] Phillips, Wendell, "Further African Studies," *Sci. Monthly,* Mar., 1950, p. 175.

[121] Fleure, H. J., ref. 57, pp. 43 and 44.

sentatives of a widespread and, in part, forced dispersion of people from a single multiplying population, established at a point more or less central to them all, which sent forth successive waves of migrants, each wave driving the previous one further towards the periphery.

(2) The most degraded specimens are representatives of this general movement who were driven into the least hospitable areas where they suffered physical degeneration as a consequence of the circumstances in which they were forced to live.

(3) The extraordinary physical variability of their remains stems from the fact that they were members of small, isolated, strongly inbred bands; whereas the cultural similarities which link together even the most widely dispersed of them indicate a common origin for them all.

(4) What is true of fossil man is equally true of vanished and of living primitive societies.

(5) All these initially dispersed populations are of one basic stock — the Hamitic family of Genesis 10.

(6) They were subsequently displaced or overwhelmed by the Indo-Europeans (i.e., Japhethites) who nevertheless inherited, or adopted and extensively built upon, their technology and so gained the upper hand in each geographical area where they spread.

(7) Throughout this movement, both in prehistoric and historic times, there were never any human beings who did not belong within the family of Noah and his descendants.

(8) Finally, this thesis is strengthened by the evidence of history, which shows that migration has always tended to follow this pattern, has frequently been accompanied by instances of degeneration both of individuals or whole tribes, and usually results in the establishment of a general pattern of cultural relationships, which are parallel to those that archaeology has since revealed from antiquity.

Part II

Primitive Cultures: A Second Look at the Problem of Their Historical Origin

Introduction

A FRIEND OF mine once sat down to dinner with a famous old gentleman of foreign extraction. During the course of the conversation my friend remarked upon the beauty of the view from the dining room window and pointed out to his guest that when the sun rose over the Hudson River below it created an ever-changing kaleidoscope of colorful reflections as the ships of many nations moved up and down stream. "But," complained the great man, "Dat iss der vest, nod der east!" His host hastened to assure him that he must have got turned around and was making a mistake. The argument, however, reached such a point that it seemed nothing short of a compass on the table would convince the old gentleman of his error. So a compass was produced which bore out the observation made by the host who had sat in that window many, many times. "Then," said the old man, after considerable pause, "der kompass is wronk!" Since he had spoken with such complete conviction, further discussion of the subject was pointless and the matter was dropped.

This story sounds so absurd as to be almost unbelievable, nevertheless it really happened. It is a beautiful illustration of the extent to which a preconceived idea can prevent the admission of a truth when that truth is contrary to expectation. In the minds of most anthropologists a preconception about the nature of man when he first appeared on the scene as a creature little removed from the apes has likewise led to their complete repudiation of the early chapters of Genesis as a compass to the past. For Genesis pictures the first man as anything but an animal, and his first efforts to build a civilization as anything but primitive. But this is quite the opposite of what is believed today of the first human beings. With the elderly gentleman of our story, they simply say, with finality, "Der kompass iss wronk." Yet rightly understood, the record of Genesis accounts for many of the anomalies of prehistory.

It seems to me a matter of very grave concern that not a few Christian anthropologists, when publishing their views, no longer feel it necessary to make any real attempt to square what they say as anthropologists with their theology as Christian believers. In the desire to be up-to-date, no Christian can afford to embrace the latest orthodoxies merely because they are accepted by the authorities. There is no guarantee that what is latest is necessarily truer than what preceded, and in fact it will be shown subsequently that quite the reverse may be the case, and older beliefs may reappear in a new light and be accorded greater respect. For my part, I believe it is both wiser and safer to make Scripture the touchstone of truth, even in the matter of anthropology — and wait.

During the last hundred years the pendulum of opinion has tended to be carried from one extreme to the other. First of all, everyone was convinced that man's Fall was so complete that no progress whatever was possible and everything must be in a state of decay. When this gloomy picture was rejected, it was replaced by a philosophy of progress which gave birth, towards the end of the last century, to an age of great optimism in which the key was progressive evolution. Degeneration became a naughty word. But two devastating world wars tempered such visionary philosophies and forced us all to take a fresh look at the course of human history. Was it, after all, a record of progress from primitive to civilized, from simple to complex, from superstition to pure worship, from savage to refined? A few who suggested that perhaps we should reexamine primitive cultures with a view to understanding how they came to be what they are, found it unwise to propose forthrightly that they might be degenerate, because the climate of opinion was against any concept which reflected in any way the idea of a Fall of man. As Liberal theology lent its weight to the disposal of this particular aspect of Christian faith, fewer scholarly voices were heard defending the traditional view. At the same time, it became less dangerous for a non-Christian writer to admit the possibility of degeneration, and this they have consequently often tended to do.

When Lyell formulated his principle that in explaining geological phenomena, appeal to forces not known to be operating in the present ought to be avoided, he was attempting to discourage the Catastrophists who frequently introduced forces that were so unusual as to be practically supernatural. The general belief is that the science of geology profited very greatly by following Lyell's advice.

In dealing with the early human prehistorical period, the time scale and background is geological, and anthropologists were easily persuaded that this same general principle should be applied to their discipline also. However, while they accepted Lyell's rejection of all appeals to supernatural forces, they did *not* follow his rule of explaining the past only in terms of the known "present." If they had done so, they could never have assumed cultural evolution to have taken place in the way they say it did.

Furthermore, Lyell's Principle obviously could not apply to the matter of origins — for example, to the origin of the Universe. Nor can it apply to the origin of civilization. At this point we have no such guide to the interpretation of the past. In a sense, herefore, it was not reason but bias which led to the rejection of the biblical record. But the time is perhaps ripe now for a reexamination of the whole issue.

The references found at the foot of each page of this Doorway Paper may seem inordinately numerous. My purpose is to extend the scope of the text somewhat by providing an additional list of bibliographical references where further interesting information will be found.

Such information is sometimes only indirectly related to the subject, but it is worthwhile in any case, and contributes in other ways to some of the wider implications of the paper.

Chapter 1
The Changing Climate of Opinion

DURING THE nineteenth century, partly as a result of the development of more rapid means of travel, partly as a result of the establishment of the British Empire, making it possible for people to journey safely in many parts of the world hitherto considered inaccessible, and partly as a result of an extraordinary increase in missionary activity, the ways of primitive people became a subject of popular interest to an unprecedented extent. The Journal of the Royal Anthropological Institute recently carried an article entitled "Anthropology and the Missionary," which paid tribute to the great service done by these earlier missionaries in the understanding of primitive cultures.[1] Such men as Livingstone in Africa, for example, receive prominent mention. But the list is surprisingly large. Acknowledgment is made of the scholarliness of the writings of these pioneers. The rise of large publishing houses which greatly accelerated the dissemination of this kind of literature also helped to bring before the civilized world in Europe and America the unexpected diversity of patterns of living, and the cultural backwardness (viewed materialistically) of a very large part of the world's population.

It was during the latter half of the nineteenth century that genuinely Christian scholars formed themselves into societies to present papers before the public, which were an attempt to show how the rapid extensions of knowledge in this and other areas were related to Scripture, and particularly to the Old Testament. Always the assumption was that the Bible is true and that when the findings of these young sciences were not in harmony with it, the fault lay not with Scripture but with the sciences. This approach is revealed clearly in the earlier papers of the Transactions of the Victoria Institute in London,[2] the Exeter Hall Papers presented before the newly formed

---

[1] Rosenstiel, Annette, "Anthropology and the Missionary, *Jour. Roy. Anthrop. Instit.*, 89 Pt. 1, Jan.-June (1959): 107-115.

[2] For example, the very first volume of the Transactions of the Victoria

YMCA,[3] and the Present Day Tracts contributed by some of the greatest authorities of the times.[4] These papers dealt with geology, astronomy, archaeology, and so forth — and not a few with the question of the origin of civilization and how primitive cultures had come into existence.

It is important to an understanding of the events which followed to realize that initially it was not at all thought that such primitive cultures were representative stages through which Western civilization had passed. The biblical record of the childhood of mankind starting with the creation of a completely human and highly intelligent being, Adam, followed by the rapid rise of city life, the almost immediate appearance of trades and skills evidencing a division of labor supportable only by a higher civilization — all these were seen by most people as normal to the beginnings of human history. No primitive stages were visualized for man as a whole during this process. When, for the first time, stone arrowheads and associated fossil remains were brought to the attention of the public, they were not taken to be manifestations of man in the making, but as the relics of man under condemnation.[5] The existence of primitive people was unanimously interpreted as proof of the Fall of man. Very few people

Institute published in 1866 contained papers on the existing relations between Scripture and science, on the difference in scope between Scripture and science, on the various theories of man's past and present condition, on the origin of speech, on miracles, on the lessons taught us by geology in relation to God, on the mutual helpfulness of theology and natural science, and on the past and present relations of geological science in relation to the Sacred Scriptures. In the succeeding years papers were presented with such titles as, "Some Uses of Sacred Primeval History," "The Common Origin of the American Races with Those of the Old World," "On True Anthropology," and on "Man's Place in Creation." These papers were written, in many cases, by men who were prominent figures in England and on the Continent.

[3] The Exeter Hall Papers, published in London by Nisbet, were even earlier, running from 1845 to 1865; and being addressed to a more popular audience were not quite as scholarly but dealt with the same basic problems. It is some reflection on the seriousness of the membership of the YMCA in those days that these papers treated such serious subjects as "Patriarchal Civilization," "Biblical Statements in Harmony with Scientific Discoveries," "The Natural History of Creation," "Geological Evidence of the Existence of the Deity," "The Common Origin of the Human Race," "God in Science," and so forth.

[4] The Present Day Tracts were a series of learned papers in 13 volumes published by the Religious Tract Society from 1883 on. They, too, dealt with problems such as "The Age and Origin of Man Geologically Considered," "The Mosaic Authorship and Credibility of the Pentateuch," "The Philosophy of Mr. Herbert Spencer," "Points of Contact Between Revelation and Natural Science," "The Ethics of Evolution Examined," and so forth.

[5] Wendt, Herbert, *I Looked For Adam*, Weidenfeld and Nicolson, London, 1955, p. 15 ff.

considered them as evidence of man's evolution. So firm was the belief in the idea that Adam was a vastly superior being and early civilization reflected some of this superiority, and that the Christian civilizations of the day had somehow preserved this superiority, that all other forms of culture were looked upon as decadent, and primitive people as the most degenerate of all. The idea of any kind of progress apart from Christian influence was simply not countenanced.

But another and entirely different view of history was beginning to find favor in England and elsewhere as a result of the Industrial Revolution and the great advances being made in technology, advances which seemed to be completely independent of any Christian indebtedness. This took the form of a philosophy that was Darwinian in spirit but actually owed nothing to him. Some of the most generative concepts of this particular view of history, such as the survival of the fittest for example, were borrowed from Spencer and others who shared his views. Tennyson's famous poem, *In Memoriam,* which pictures Nature as red in tooth and claw was actually published ten years before *The Origin of Species.* What is even more important in the context of this Doorway Paper is that during the latter half of the nineteenth century the social anthropologists who wrote about primitive people in general had also been strongly influenced by the Spencerian philosophy of progress. And they, *entirely independent of Darwinism,* were busily engaged in ordering and arranging these primitive cultures in tidy little evolutionary sequences. Thus as Melville Herskovits pointed out:[6]

> It is essential for an understanding of cultural evolutionism that it be regarded as more than just a reflex of the biological theory of evolution, where it is customarily held to have been derived. Teggart, the student of intellectual history, has pointed out how Darwin's work *The Origin of Species* that appeared in 1859 was "just too late to have an effect upon the remarkable development of ethnological study in the second half of the nineteenth century." The works which initiated this development, such as the contributions of the Germans, Waitz, Bastian, and Bachhofen, or the English scholars, Maine, McLennan, and Tylor, appeared between 1859 and 1865. This means that they were being planned and written about the same time Darwin was carrying out his researches and organizing and writing down his conclusions. Teggart, moreover, shows that cultural and biological evolutionism differed in certain important theoretical respects. He points out that "Tylor, in 1873, and McLennan, in 1876," were "disclaiming dependence upon Darwin, and maintaining their allegiance to an earlier tradition of development or evolution. The concept of 'evolution' in ethnology is, in fact, distinct from the type of evolutionary study represented in Darwin's writings."

When Maine and McLennan began to publish their views, they

[6] Herskovits, Melville J., *Man and His Works,* Knopf, N.Y., 1950, p. 464.

had not the slightest doubt as to the propriety of arranging the cultural materials to demonstrate evolutionary progress. Things had always improved in the past, and they would therefore continue to do so in the future. Science was merely accelerating a natural process, performing more and more miracles as the Church unhappily seemed able to perform fewer and fewer. A very concrete heaven could be built right here on earth, and the appeal to a spiritual heaven to come in another world increasingly lost its force. Morality based on man-to-God relationships was being steadily replaced by ethics based on man-to-man relationships. A person could be good and completely non-Christian. Of this new spirit Melvin Rader wrote:[7]

> At the dawn of modern science, men were immensely confident that its uses would be beneficent. The great medieval seer, Roger Bacon (one of the first "moderns") was fired by the deep enthusiasm for the new world that science could create. It would reveal the past, present and future; and secure the vast improvement and the indefinite prolongation of life! Similarly such Renaissance thinkers as Giordano Bruno, Leonardo da Vinci, and Tomasso Companella, harbingers of the modern scientific and technological revolution, were intoxicated with its infinite promise. Such optimism found ample expression in the work of Francis Bacon who believed that science would enlarge "the bounds of human empire to the effecting of all things possible" and in writing the *New Atlantis,* jubilantly imagined the Utopia he believed scientific progress would achieve.

In its initial stages of development such an intellectual climate was completely suited to the launching of a work like *The Origin of Species.* It was almost inevitable, for as Calverton rightly pointed out:[8]

> The very simultaneity with which Darwin and Wallace struck upon the theory of natural selection and the survival of the fittest was magnificent proof of the intense activity of the idea at the time. Every force in the environment, economic, and social, conspired to the success of the doctrine.

As we have already noted, anthropology in its initial stages developed entirely independently of Darwinism. But it was not long before its findings were recognized as providing additional confirmation of Darwin's views as applied to human origins. The literature of this new discipline quickly gained popular acclaim, because it so completely suited the "zeitgeist" of the time. Yet this popularity was in the end to prove a hindrance. For anthropology began to achieve the status of a science chiefly because of its evolutionary bias in much the same way that geology and zoology were considered sciences be-

---

[7] Rader, Melvin, "Technology and Community," *Sci. Monthly,* June, 1949, p. 502.

[8] Calverton, V. F., "Modern Anthropology and the Theory of Cultural Compulsives," in *The Making of Man,* Modern Library, N.Y., 1931, p. 2, and italicized statements on p. 27.

cause they subscribed to the view that everything must be explained in completely naturalistic terms without any appeal to the supernatural. The hindrance lay in the fact that evolutionary principles were soon uncritically applied where they never should have been, and when the mistake became apparent to anthropologists themselves, they did not dare to speak out against the tendency for fear of being termed unscientific.

Lack of courage on the part of those who could see what was happening, led younger students to get an entirely biased view of the evidence. Thus, to use the words of Abram Kardiner:[9]

> The study of "primitive man" held out high hopes that it would supply valuable information about man's cultural evolution. In a measure — a small one — this hope was satisfied. But when a new area of investigation is the by-product of a parent hypothesis, it is natural that its first efforts will be directed by sustaining its progenitor.
> The study of primitive man was therefore biased at its inception. The great names of Edward B. Tylor, James Frazer, Lucien Levy-Bruhl, and Emile Durkheim were associated with these early efforts. They were determined to show cultural evolution by demonstrating that archaic, simple forms of thought and social organization changed into more complex and integrated forms.
> The fallacy of this early approach was not only that it colored the conclusions from observed data, but also that it dictated what data should be considered relevant. This is where the theory of cultural evolution did its greatest damage. For these evolutionists were not studying the adaptation of primitive man to his environment. They hopped, skipped, and jumped from one culture to another, picked what they wanted from each, and fitted it into their master plan.

Meanwhile this humanistic philosophy was reinforced in its popular appeal by the prodigious labors of the Higher Critics who steadily succeeded in providing thoughtful people with more and more excuses for dismissing the authority of Scripture by pronouncing it essentially mythological. There was no doubt that everything tended to evolve, and the Bible was wrong in its emphasis on the natural tendency of man to degenerate. In the opposing camp, a quite formidable array of Christian scholars were insisting with equal assurance that the evidence from archaeology and ethnology were completely against any such universal progress. There was no doubt that everything tended to degenerate, and the Bible pointed to the final and utter corruption of all things pertaining to the cultures of the world. Perhaps both views have been in error by exaggerating one side of the picture only. Not everything degenerates — nor does everything evolve into something higher.

---

[9] Kardiner, Abram, in a review of "Posthumous Essays by Bronislaw Malinowski," in *Sci. American*, June, 1948, p. 58. An excellent illustration of how this bias operated will be found, with reference to Eoliths, in H. V. Vallois and M. Boule, *Fossil Men*, Dryden, N.Y., 1957, p. 101.

As we shall see, there has been a change of opinion even among non-Christian anthropologists, and the initial artificial evolutionary sequences created by Maine and Tylor, et. al., have been largely repudiated in their original form, though they are still often used for teaching purposes. However, it should be noted that when modern authorities state their disbelief in "Evolution," they do not mean by this that they doubt man's animal ancestry, but only that they are rejecting the kind of cultural evolution which, to use Wallis' words, "dominated the findings" of the earlier social anthropologists. The point is an important one, because Christian writers who are not aware of this background sometimes quote modern authorities as having repudiated the theory of the evolution of man as a whole. This is a mistake. These writers are referring only to cultural evolution and not to biological evolution. But this is a recent change of mind. Such a change has resulted partly from the fact that the vastly increased body of evidence from prehistoric times could no longer be fitted into the older scheme and partly because of more refined methods of dating. Wilson Wallis a few years ago said in an address before the American Association in 1947, certain basic assumptions are currently made by anthropologists when dealing with prehistoric man.[10] To use his words, "The further we proceed into the gloom of the prehistoric, the clearer our vision. Hence things which could not possibly be inferred if the data were contemporary man, can, thanks to this illumination in the gathering dusk of remote ages, be inferred with confidence." Of course, the secret is that when there is no possibility of being proved wrong, one can afford to state with complete assurance that one is right. In fact, this tendency to take advantage of the scarcity of the data has been sharply rebuked by such men as Harry L. Shapiro of the American Museum of Natural History, who remarked:[11]

> No doubt the competitive struggle for attention for one's ideas may motivate the form in which they are presented, and unquestionably many of us in our zeal may speak with honest if unwarranted conviction: but this does not excuse anthropology or anthropologists from the consequences of what we permit to stand as anthropological gospel. . . . [What is needed is] the development of a rigorously critical attitude towards the speculations and developments embodied in anthropological writings. This is all the more essential since anthropology, as well as the other social sciences, lacks the experimental procedures that exert a profound salutary control on the growth of the experimental sciences. Among them, a claim can be immediately checked

[10] Wallis, Wilson, "Pre-Suppositions in Anthropological Interpretations," *Amer. Anthropol.*, 50 (1948): 560.

[11] Shapiro, Harry L., "The Responsibility of the Anthropologist," *Science*, 109 (1949): 323, 326.

under similar control in hundreds of laboratories.... On the contrary our investigations do not lend themselves readily to this kind of testing.... It is for this reason that I regard it as essential for the continued health of anthropology that we be severely critical in appraising the theories and investigations that are issued as representative of anthropology.

But one also notes an amazing failure to examine the fundamental assumptions and premises of new lines of investigation which, like a new fashion in women's wear, appear to exercise a kind of tyranny that no one dares to question.

I do suggest that such critiques are desirable, and I do know a number of anthropologists who do not hesitate privately or in their classrooms to offer critical comment — yet they are strangely silent in print.

Perhaps he had in mind Wallis, who in the same connection and on another occasion had also written:[12]

Since the day of Darwin, the evolutionary idea has largely dominated the ambitions and determined the findings of physical anthropology, sometimes to the detriment of the truth.

These self-criticisms are comparatively recent. But even when anthropology was a young science divorced from any reference to biblical statements, there were notable exceptions to the general rule that the most prominent authorities were dedicated to the evolutionary idea. In fact, E. B. Tylor himself, who has been quite properly called the Father of anthropology, and who firmly held the progressive view of culture which evolution seemed to demand, nevertheless was not unaware of the fact that cultural degeneration was very real. Thus in his classic work he wrote with keen insight:[13]

It does not follow from such arguments as these that civilization is always on the move or that the movement is always progress. On the contrary history teaches that it remains stationary for long periods and often falls back.

To understand such decline of culture it must be born in mind that the highest arts and the most elaborate arrangements of society do not always prevail, in fact they may be too perfect to hold their ground for people must have what fits their circumstances.

There is an instructive lesson to be learnt, from an Englishman at Singapore, who noticed with surprise two curious trades flourishing there. One was to buy old English ships, cut them down and rig them as junks. And the other was to buy English percussion muskets and turn them into old fashioned flint locks! At first sight this looks like mere stupidity, but on consideration it is seen to be reasonable enough. It was so difficult to get Eastern sailors to work ships of European rig that it answered better to provide them with the clumsier craft they were used to; and as to the guns, the hunters far away in the hot damp forests were better off with gun-flints than if they had to carry and keep a dry stock of caps. In both cases what they wanted was not

12 Wallis, Wilson, "The Structure of Prehistoric Man," in *The Making of Man*, Modern Library, N.Y., 1931, p. 75.
13 Tylor, E. B., *Anthropology*, Hill and Co., N.Y., 1904, pp. 14, 15.

the highest product of civilization, but something suited to the situation and easier to be had.

Now the same rule applies both to taking in new civilizations, and keeping up old. When the life of the people is altered by a migration into a new country, or by war and distress at home, or mixture with a lower race, the culture of their forefathers may be no longer needed or possible and so dwindles away.

Such degeneration is to be seen among the descendants of Portuguese in the East Indies, who have intermarried with the natives and fallen out of the march of civilization, so that newly-arrived Europeans go to look at them lounging about their mean hovels in the midst of luxuriant tropical fruits and flowers as if they had been set there to teach by example how man falls in cultures where the need of effort is wanting.

Another frequent cause of loss of civilization is when people once more prosperous are ruined or driven from their homes like those Shoshonee Indians who took refuge from their enemies the Blackfeet, in the wilds of the Rocky Mountains where they now roam. They are called "Digger Indians" from the wild roots which they dig for as part of their miserable subsistence. Not only the degraded state of such outcasts, but the loss of particular arts by other peoples, may often be explained by loss of culture under unfavorable conditions. For instance, the South Sea Islanders though not a very rude people when visited by Captain Cook, used only stone hatchets, and knives, being indeed so ignorant of metal that they planted the first iron nails they got from the English sailors in the hope of raising a new crop. Possibly their ancestors were an Asiatic people to whom metal was quite well known, but who through emigration to ocean islands, and separated from their kinsfolk, lost the use of it and fell back into the Stone Age.

Here is a great authority writing at a time when the concept of progress dominated everyone's thinking and required the interpretation of all history to lend its support, nevertheless drawing attention to the fact that there are circumstances in which devolution and not evolution is almost inevitable. As a matter of fact, one of the great Christian protagonists of that day, Sir William Dawson, enunciated the principle that if mankind enjoyed a high civilization at the very beginning we might often *expect* to find a very low civilization at the end by reason of its initial brilliance, because the more refined a culture the more sensitive it is to imbalance and decay. When such a culture broke down, it would probably sink as much lower as it had once been higher, the more advanced its earlier stages, the more degraded its later. A gentlewoman becoming a pioneer wife might be found in greater straits for her gentility than her laundrywoman, but the subsequent findings of her rude handicrafts would be no indication whatever of whether she were a primitive or a cultured person. Accustomed to silk, she could not weave for herself the coarsest sackcloth, accustomed to silverware she would be able to devise only the crudest of wooden spoons, having no palette or paints she would scarcely exhibit her highly trained artistic talents except in the crudest way. Should we subsequently come upon these evidences of her presence, must we therefore conclude that she was a member of a tribe scarcely civilized at all? As Dawson put it:[14]

> As well might it be affirmed that a delicately nurtured lady is an "utter barbarian" because she cannot now build her house or make her own shoes. No doubt in such work she would be far more helpless than the wife of the rudest savage, yet she is not on that account to be held as an inferior being.

To us now this conclusion seems almost self-evident although at the time Dawson wrote, scarcely anyone paid any attention to his arguments. But inevitably the artificiality of these reconstructions of culture history became apparent even to those who had not the slightest doubt that man began his career as little more than an ape. Today the tide of opinion has begun to turn and modern authorities often take pains to show the weaknesses of some of these earlier views. I think one reason for this is that we no longer have any recognized and authoritative Christian school of thought upholding the biblical view of man's early superiority and subsequent degeneracy. Therefore social anthropologists today are no longer afraid of being accused of a Christian bias when they look with more favor upon the possibility of cultural devolution. Such frank admissions are no longer felt to give any comfort to the enemy.

Let me illustrate this point by a few extracts from recent literature. To quote Herskovits again:[15]

> Every exponent of cultural evolution provided an hypothetical blueprint of the progression he conceived as having marked the development of mankind, so that many examples of unilinear sequences have been recorded. Some of these progressions were restricted to a single aspect of culture, as has been indicated. Not all students, moreover, were equally insistent on the inevitability of the developmental stages they sketched. As we move away from the heyday of the evolutionary hypothesis, we encounter a greater degree of tentativeness and flexibility. Yet some sequence is always described in these latter works, whatever exceptions to them may be noted.
> Of the evolutionary sequences that were formulated in the classical works of this school, none is more specific than that given in Morgan's *Ancient Society*. Three principal periods in human sociocultural development were distinguished by Morgan — savagery, barbarism, and civilization. The first two of these were each held to have been divided into older, middle, and later periods, marked by conditions of society to which were applied the designations lower, middle, and upper status of savagery or barbarism.

Herskovits then goes on to illustrate how Morgan rearranged history

[14] Dawson, Sir J. William, *The Story of the Earth and Man*, Hodder and Stoughton, London, 1903, p. 390.
[15] Herskovits, Melville, ref. 6, p. 467.

to validate his interpretation. Starting with the very primitive Australians with descent through the female, he then drew a line leading to the American Indians with a change in descent from the females to the males. The sequence then moved to Grecian tribes in the protohistoric period, with descent firmly established in the male line, but no strict monogamy. The last entry in this ascending scale was, of course, represented by modern civilization with descent in the male line and strict adherence to monogamy. This was only one of Morgan's sequences and was constructed to show how what he considered was a very loose family organization had evolved into a close one. On this sequence Herskovits commented as follows:[16]

> But this series, from the point of view of a historical approach, is quite fictitious, since only the last two items in it are historically related. In terms of actual time, the series should be arranged in this way:

Grecian Tribes.
|
Modern Civilization. American Indians. Australian Aborigines.

> Placed in this fashion, it is at once seen to be no series at all, but rather a comparison of data existing on a given plane, arranged according to a predetermined scheme of development.

This is an illustration of a principle which was applied right across the board to the development of art, religion, toolmaking, etc. Thus European prehistory was neatly divided into a series of ages, Paleolithic, Mesolithic, and Neolithic. The fact that the American Indians were still living in the Old Stone Age (Paleolithic) when Europe was passing through an Industrial Revolution did not at the time appear to challenge this neat little scheme of things. Sir William Dawson wrote his *Fossil Men and Their Modern Representatives* as a protest against such blindness, but in spite of the fact that he wrote with authority and eloquence, and without rancor, it seems that no one paid much attention to his work.[17] However, as we have said, the tide is turning.

A recent symposium in Chicago at which experts from several countries presented papers covering the whole field of anthropology, included a paper by Hallam L. Movius entitled "Old World Prehistory: Paleolithic." He opened with these words:[18]

[16] Ibid., p. 476.
[17] Dawson, Sir J. William, *Fossil Men and Their Modern Representatives,* Hodder and Stoughton, London, 1883, viii and 354 pp., index and illustrations.
[18] Movius, Hallam L. Jr., "Old World Prehistory: Paleolithic," in *Anthropology Today,* Chicago, 1953, p. 163.

During the last twenty-five years, our knowledge of the Paleolithic period has been greatly extended beyond the confines of Western Europe. This has not resulted in the establishment of as coherent a picture of man's early attempts to develop a material culture as was originally expected. For, when we examine the bewildering array of primitive Stone Age assemblages that are constantly being augmented by fresh discoveries, we can hardly compose them into anything even remotely approaching the ordered general scheme conceived by the early workers.

It all seems so very obvious now. Ruth Benedict stressed this when she pointed out:[19]

> Early anthropologists tried to arrange all traits of different cultures in an evolutionary sequence from the earliest forms to their final development in Western civilization. But there is no reason to suppose that by discussing Australian religion rather than our own we are uncovering primordial religion, or that by discussing Iroquoian social organization we are returning to the mating habits of man's early ancestors.
>
> Since we are forced to believe that the race of man is one species, it follows that man everywhere has an equally long history behind him. Some primitive tribes may have held relatively closer to primordial forms of behavior than civilized man, but this can only be relative and our guesses are as likely to be wrong as right. There is no justification for identifying some one contemporary primitive custom with the original type of human behavior.

But Ruth Benedict herself almost fell into the trap of stating that early man must have been somewhat like modern primitives. Or, to put it slightly differently, that our primitive contemporaries are in effect our contemporary ancestors. However, there must have been a fundamental difference between early man and modern primitives because, in the Middle East at least, culture though beginning in a comparatively simple way, very rapidly advanced into complexity, whereas backward people today no longer seem to have the power to elevate themselves.

Contact with higher civilizations sometimes brings a great advance, but almost as frequently it brings their extinction. In examining the question of how civilization arose in the first place, Lord Raglan had this to say:[20]

> The term "backward races," which is almost universally applied to savages ... implies that they are now in the stage that we were in

[19] Benedict, Ruth, *Patterns of Culture,* Mentor Books, N.Y., 1951, pp. 16 and 17. See also on this subject Herskovits, ref. 6, p. 618; Goldenweiser, Alexander, *Anthropology,* Crofts, N.Y., 1945, p. 507; Shapiro, H. L., *Race Mixture,* UNESCO, Paris, 1953, pp. 31, 32; also Lowie, R. H., *Social Organization,* Rinehart, N.Y., 1948, pp. 122 ff.; Evans-Pritchard, *Social Anthropology,* Cohen West, Lon., 1951, 24.
[20] Raglan, Lord, *How Come Civilization?* Methuen, London, 1939, pp. 28, 29.

a few thousand years ago, and, if left alone, would in time rise to something similar to the stage in which we are now.

Not a single fact can be adducted to support this theory. All the available evidence suggests that no savage society, if left to itself, has ever made the slightest progress. The only change that takes place in isolated societies is change for the worse.

This lack of evolutionary sequence applies in the realm of man's religious history also. Thus E. O. James in a paper read before the Royal Anthropological Institute said:[21]

> It is impossible to maintain a unilateral evolutionary development in religious thought and practice in the manner suggested by the rationalistic classifications of Tylor and Frazer, following along the lines of the "Law of the Three Stages," enunciated by Auguste Comte. Neither the Euhemeran speculation that the idea of God arose in ancestor-worship, revived by Herbert Spencer, nor the Frazerian evolution of monotheism from polytheism and animism as a result of a process of the unification of ideas, can be reconciled with the shadowy figure of a tribal Supreme Being now known to have been a recurrent feature of the primitive conception of Deity.
>
> Largely as a result of the persistent researches of Pater Wilhelm Schmidt, following the lead of Andrew Lang who in 1895 first called attention to the High Gods of Low Races in his *Making of Religion,* it is now fairly established that, independent of influences from missionaries, or any other contacts with higher cultures, the recognition of an All-Father is an integral element in the religion of such simple people as the Pygmies, the Fuegians, the Australian aborigines, the Californians, and the Andamanese. This cannot be described as monotheism in the strict sense of the term, since there is no suggestion of a single omnipotent Deity being the ground and source of all existence; or even as monolatry, inasmuch as the All-Father is not the sole god of his people like Jehovah in pre-exilic Israel. Nevertheless, the belief in Supreme Beings precludes a clear-cut evolutionary interpretation of the idea of God as distinctly stratified as the geological sequence in the rocks.

Similarly, Goldenweiser pointed out how misleading the theory of evolution became when applied to other human institutions and activities. He warned that "having been impregnated almost fatally with the seed of evolutionary thinking, we like to conceive of everything in the history of culture as a series of transformations."[22] He then went on to show how misleading such thinking can be. For example, he said:[23]

> Nor is it true, as some social scientists have once supposed, that the primitives were addicted to communal or group ownership rather than the ownership of things by individuals. The patent facts do not at all support this *a priori* conception which must be regarded as one of the *ad hoc* concoctions of the evolutionists who were looking for

[21] James, E. O., "Reality and Religion," *Jour. Roy. Anthrop. Instit.,* 80 (1950): 28.
[22] Goldenweiser, A., *Anthropology,* Crofts, N.Y., 1945, p. 134.
[23] Ibid., p. 47.

something less specific than individual property from which it could be derived, and who found this "something" in communal ownership.

Even with regard to early art history, evolution proved wanting as a key. It was assumed at first that pictorial representations would naturally precede the use of symbols, since the latter are of a higher conceptual order. But this, too, proved to be unsupported by the evidence from prehistory.[24] As we have shown in another Doorway Paper,[25] evolutionary theory applied to the origin of language proved to be a block to any further understanding of the problem and has since been discarded. At the moment no "satisfactory" alternative has been found. Darwin himself remarked upon the stimulating effect of mistaken theories as compared with the sterilizing effect of mistaken observations.[26] But a false theory can be very useful in spite of its falsity, provided only that it is not erected into a dogma and presented as *fact*. Theories are essential to the progress of understanding in science because they structure experiment and inspire the asking of pertinent questions. When facts do not support the theory, it may be modified and continue to serve as inspiration for further investigation. But when a theory which is tentative is presented as fact, it no longer serves to inspire questions but rather to predetermine answers. To my mind, this is the present position of evolutionary theory. It has become "fact" and to challenge it is to run the risk of excommunication. In Medieval times, too, excommunication was one of the penalties for challenging the accepted view of things. At that time the test of whether any new theory was true or false was, as John Randall points out, whether it fitted harmoniously into the orthodox systems of belief and not whether it could be verified by experiment.[27] This is exactly the position today; ecclesiastical dogma has been replaced by biological dogma[28] which, as "dogma," has been detrimental to the truth.

---

[24] Ibid., p. 166.

[25] Custance, A. C., "Who Taught Adam to Speak?" in this volume.

[26] White, Andrew D., *A History of the Warfare of Science With Theology,* Braziller, N.Y., 1955, p. 43.

[27] Randall, John H. Jr., *The Making of the Modern Mind,* Houghton Mifflin, N.Y., 1940, p. 98. Carl C. Lindegren pointed out that "the chronological sequence in which scientific discoveries are made has a direct bearing upon the way in which they are interpreted." As a consequence of this he says, "Dates that confirm a well established theory are generally accepted without critical evaluation" (*Science,* July 6, 1956, p. 27). See also on this P. G. Fothergill, *Historical Aspects of Organic Evolution,* Hollis and Carter, London, 1952, p. 116.

[28] During the International Symposium on Anthropology held in New York under the chairmanship of A. L. Kroeber in 1952, there was remarkable freedom of discussion and criticism of the tendency of some authorities to become emotionally dogmatic when orthodox views were challenged in any

One of the unexpected results of archaeological research was the quite frequent validation of classical historians like Herodotus[29] and others, and upon occasion quite remarkable confirmations of specific traditions which had formerly been considered entirely fictitious. A good illustration of this was the rediscovery of Troy. But archaeology in general in the Middle East area tended to strengthen greatly our confidence in much that had been viewed as an illustration of the rather natural desire of any people to glorify their own past history. Melvin Kyle summed up the situation this way:[30]

> Archaeology, in both the Biblical and the classical fields, has started without assumptions and has proceeded uniformly towards trustworthiness of ancient documents. The whole underlying Homeric stories, the account of the ruined palace and splendor of King Minos and the story of Menes, the first king in Egypt, all formerly regarded as legendary or mythical, have now taken their place in sober history. Herodotus, and Strabo and Josephus, so often charged with inaccuracies, have again and again been found to be correct. In the Biblical field not a single statement of fact has been finally discredited.

Quite remarkable have been some of these findings. No one took the story of the Golden Fleece seriously until it was found that the traditional home of this fabled pelt had in earlier times been the scene of much gold mining activity. The natives apparently panned gold from the local streams and were in the habit of using sheep skins with the wool still intact as sieves. Such skins became heavily gilded, the gold being recovered subsequently by burning them.[31] It seems highly likely that one of these was seized by a traveler who did not understand its purpose or origin and the trophy, finally came to Colchis where it easily became the basis of the classical story. From this same heroic age came the stories of Nestor and Telemachus. Nestor has come to life, and with his resurrection much that was mythical has turned out to be history. Even the bath tub in which Telemachus was refreshed by Nestor's youngest daughter, perhaps

---

way. For example, see the remarks made by M. Bates with reference to the domineering attitude of Dobzhansky, as reported in *An Appraisal of Anthropology Today*, edited by Sol Tax *et al*, University Chicago, 1953, pp. 271, 272.

[29] *The Illustrated London News* (Dec. 10, 1927, p. 1058) contained an article by Margaret Taylor on the unique rock painting in Southern Rhodesia, which shows a whole orchestra about to begin a performance! The circumstances surrounding this painting are believed to confirm a statement made by Herodotus whch was completely discredited because it stated that about 600 B.C. Pharaoh Necho sailed round Africa. This was held to be extremely unlikely. But it appears that it may very well have occurred, this orchestra having belonged to the Egyptian king.

[30] Kyle, Melvin G., "The Antiquity of Man According to the Genesis Account," *Trans. Vict. Instit.*, London, 57 (1925): 127.

[31] Simpich, Frederick, "Men and Gold," *Nat. Geog. Mag.*, Apr., 1933, p. 482.

the first "Order of the Bath," may have been rediscovered.[32] When Layard recovered for us much of Assyria's past, its fabled kings and conquerors likewise became historic characters.

When early Christian societies, to which reference has already been made, were being formed, a great number of papers appeared dealing with the traditions of ancient people and their relationship to the biblical record. A number of very learned works of a more extended nature appeared dealing with the same subject including those of Lord Arundell of Wardour,[33] Francois Lenormant,[34] and, of course, Alexander Hyslop with his famous "The Two Babylons."[35] This general interest in Middle East traditions was extended in due time to an interest in the traditions of people from other parts of the world, such as is reflected in the work of Charles F. Keary[36] and, of course, more extensively in the writings of Sir James Frazer[37] whose massive scholarship and extraordinary literary eloquence earned him worldwide recognition. It may be noted in passing that Frazer had no desire to uphold the veracity of Scripture nor do his writings reflect any great spirit of reverence. The revival of interest in tradition which called forth his monumental work was evidently very widespread and extended far beyond the circle of Christian readers.

Writing at the time of this surge of fresh interest, the great Orientals scholar, George Rawlinson pointed out the significance of this increasing verification of traditions in so far as they relate to the origin of civilization and the condition of early man. He said:[38]

> It will scarcely be denied that the mythical traditions of almost all nations place at the beginning of human history a time of happiness and perfection, a "golden age" which has no features of savagery or barbarism, but many of civilization and refinement. In the Zendavesta, Yima-khshaeta (Jemshid), the first Aryan king, after reigning for a time in the original Aryanem vaejo, removed with his subjects to a secluded spot, where he and they enjoy uninterrupted happiness. In

---

[32] Blegen, Carl W., "King Nestor's Palace," *Sci. American,* May, 1958, p. 111 and photo of the bathtub, p. 113!

[33] Arundell, Lord, of Wardour, *Tradition: Principally with Reference to Mythology and the Law of Nations,* Burns, Oates and Co., London, 1872, xxix and 431 pp., index.

[34] Lenormant, Francois, *The Beginnings of History According to the Bible and the Traditions of Oriental People,* Scribners, N.Y., 1891, xxx and 588 pp., with appendices.

[35] Hyslop, Alexander, *The Two Babylons,* Partridge, London, 1903, 3rd edition, xxiv and 320 pp., index and illustrations.

[36] Keary, Charles F., *Outlines of Primitive Belief Among the Indo-European Races,* Scribners, N.Y., 1882, xxi and 534 pp., index.

[37] Frazer, Sir James G., *The Golden Bough: The Magic Art and the Evolution of Kings,* 2 Vol. ed., Macmillan, N.Y., 1935.

[38] Rawlinson, George, *The Origin of Nations,* Scribner, N.Y., 1878, pp. 10 and 11.

this place was "neither overbearing, nor mean-spiritedness, neither stupidity nor violence, neither poverty nor deceit, neither puniness nor deformity, neither huge teeth nor bodies beyond proper measure." The inhabitants suffered no defilement from the evil spirit. Their cattle were the largest, best, and most beautiful breed; their food ambrosial, and never failed them. The Chinese speak of a "first heaven" and an age of innocence, when the "whole creation enjoyed everything that was good, all beings were perfect in their kind." Mexican traditions tell of the "golden age of Tezeuco," and Peruvian history commences with the "Two Children of the Sun" who established a civilized community on the borders of Lake Titicaca. And of course the Greeks pointed in the same way to a beautiful past. Such is the voice which reaches us on all sides from the dim and twilight land, where the mythical and the historical seem to meet and blend together inseparably.

Of course, Rawlingson is speaking for the most part of people known to us only as civilized. However, primitive people also have many traditions concerning their own origin and past history and almost invariably they look back upon a past very different from their present situation. As we shall see later, some of them have traditions of techniques such as the making of pottery, canoes, woven fabrics, and even the making of fire which they no longer were able to do. In one instance there was a recollection of terms appropriate only for a culture which supported a king and his court, but these terms no longer applied to anything extant in their culture.[39] The conflict of cultures in the Indus Valley when a high initial civilization was virtually wiped out by invading hordes of barbaric Aryans, led to an epic literature, the RigVeda, written by the latter to commemorate their victory. The care taken subsequently to preserve this record with exactitude illustrates how much importance was attached to traditions related to the earliest steps towards nationhood taken by any people. In this connection Stuart Piggott wrote:[40]

> I think we are justified in accepting the Rigveda, on archaeological grounds. as a genuine document of the period, preserved intact by the constant fear of the consequences if the magic word were altered by a hairsbreadth.

It is a curious thing that tradition, preserved by word of mouth where literature is not in existence, may be even more perfectly preserved, perhaps because the absence of writing makes it more necessary to exercise memory. For example many of the traditions of the Iroquois Indians in North America were recorded by early mission-

---

[39] The Polynesians in their eastward drift into the Pacific lost textiles, pottery, metalworking, and gave up the use of the bow. See Roland Dixon, *Building of Cultures*, Scribner, N.Y., 1928, p. 280. For reference to loss of words regarding court life, see Rich Taylor, *New Zealand and Its Inhabitants*, undated, p. 6 as quoted by Lord Arundell, ref. 33, p. 122.

[40] Piggott, Stuart, *Prehistoric India*, Penguin Books, Eng., 1950, p. 256.

aries in the "Jesuit Relations" during the first half of the 17th century. Franz Boas investigating the same subject about 300 years later found that the descendants of these same Indians had preserved the same traditions word for word in spite of all the cultural changes that had taken place during the interval. The fact is that people in reduced circumstances tend to cling all the more tenaciously to any recollections they may have of a once happier past. As W. J. Perry put it:[41]

> In dealing with native tradition it must always be remembered that the accounts of the beginnings of their culture are usually among the most cherished possessions of any community. Often, where youths are initiated into the tribe when they are about to become men, they are taught the traditions, and are enjoined to preserve them as close secrets, to keep them from the knowledge of women, children, and the uninitiated. Among many peoples a knowledge of his family-tree is an essential part of the training of a member of the ruling group. So greatly do peoples the world over value their traditions.

In his *History of Science* George Sarton remarked upon the fact that some of the Greek philosophers were highly suspicious about the desirability of teaching anyone to write: He said:[42]

> This was because mnemonic traditions were so satisfying that many people, including highly educated ones, did not feel the need of writing. For example, such traditions must have been very strong in the Golden Age of Hellenism; otherwise Socrates' diatribe against the art of writing in Phaidros would hardly be intelligible.

The aid to memory resulting from written records was felt to be detrimental to the powers of memory. We ourselves are so accustomed to keeping records that we never fail to marvel at the feats of memorization found among unlettered people. Where the Bible is scarce it is not unusual to find native Christians who have memorized prodigious sections of it and are word perfect in recitation. It is a curious thing that the Higher Critics argued against the reliability of the early chapters of the Bible on the grounds that since they were not supposed to have been put into writing till the time of Ezra, and since writing had not even been known before Moses, the very detailed nature of these early records told strongly against the possibility of their transmission over so many centuries without error. They were therefore fabrications. Paradoxically, anthropologists and others were at the same time pointing out that the preservation of oral tradition was the more exact as the culture had less means for keeping written records.

---

[41] Perry, W. J., *The Growth of Civilization*, Penguin Books, Eng., 1937, p. 137.
[42] Sarton, George, *A History of Science*, Harvard, 1952, pp. 111 and 116.

The so-called myths of Genesis which had been thus dismissed as of no historic importance, are increasingly turning out to be recorded fact. It is true that such validation has not yet applied much beyond Abraham, and the periods prior are still very largely unsupported from archaeology, but the confirmations already available are so remarkable that one's confidence in the earlier portions of Scripture is greatly strengthened.

While one cannot suppose that Adam had at first the technical skills which would enable him to proceed at once to the creation of a high civilization, there are statements in the Genesis record, that we shall subsequently consider, which clearly imply an exceedingly rapid development of culture from simple to complex. The Flood introduced a very serious break into this development. But Noah and his family reestablished the process so that once more within a very few centuries a high civilization flourished in a number of centers including Asia Minor, Egypt, Palestine, the Indus Valley, and in Mesopotamia.

Scripture records an event, however, which disrupted this ancient civilization and led to the forced dispersal of man, at the time of the building of the Tower of Babel, in such circumstances that many of those who migrated surrendered one element after another of the basic culture, descending lower and lower in the scale (except in a few notable instances) as they receded further and further from their original home. In the next chapter we shall examine from archaeology some of the evidence which supports the general conclusion that the trend of culture is not normally towards improvement but towards degeneration. This does not mean that no culture evolves in the commonly accepted sense of the term, but rather that there is no law of evolution which would guarantee that each succeeding generation will inevitably improve upon the techniques of their forebears in such a way that, for example, a crude toolmaking industry automatically becomes a superior one, that superstition becomes an elevated religious faith, that grunts become speech, that scribbles become fine art, that a promiscuous herd becomes a monogamous family. Then in the chapter following we shall give some examples of the breakdown of whole cultures under conditions which probably paralleled quite closely those prevailing in these earliest times. And finally we shall consider some of the factors which may have accounted for the extraordinarily rapid rise of civilization at the very beginning of human history.

Chapter 2
Climax at the Beginning

THE PURPOSE of this chapter is to establish two points. First, in that area of the world from which all existing civilizations have derived their inspiration and which might, therefore, properly be called the Cultural Cradle of Mankind, the time lapse from the establishment of the earliest human settlements to the building of the first cities was remarkably short. Secondly, when new techniques and arts and skills make their first appearance they are frequently at the peak of their achievement and the course of their subsequent development is one of decline, not evolution.

Let me elaborate these two points somewhat. First, the rapidity with which civilization developed after the Flood, for which there is archaeological evidence, must have been paralleled by a similar rapidity of development from Adam to Noah. During this earlier period, although archaeological evidence is still lacking, there were special circumstances which account for the acceleration and these will be discussed in the final chapter. My own impression is that when the Flood came, mankind had not spread very far from the traditional "home" of the race. With the destruction of all that preceded except for those elements of that culture which were carried over the Flood by Noah and his sons, a new start was made. But if an analogy may be used, the new beginning did not represent the first faltering paces of a child but rather the steps of an adult who has recently emerged from an operation intended to remove a sickness which could only have rendered further progress in civilization disastrous. It is this circumstance which I believe accounts for the remarkably rapid transition from Sialk and other Iranian Highland Plateau settlements to the advanced cultures of Elam, the Indus Valley, Mesopotamia, Palestine, and Egypt.

Secondly, with respect to the evidence for cultural degeneration, it must first of all be admitted that cultural progress does undoubtedly take place. Within the past 75 years, so many advances have been made in the means of communication and travel, in medicine and in our control of the enviroment in general, that it would be foolish to deny it. Such advances have not all been gain, but fundamentally man's heart, and not his head, has been the cause of this. But we have been so bombarded with the concept of evolutionary progress that the reverse process has been almost overlooked. Hence in the chapters which follow the emphasis is upon degeneration, not because we wish to deny a general trend in the opposite direction, but rather because such emphasis is necessary to produce a balanced view of history. The almost complete occupation by earlier Christian scholars with the evidence for degeneration led to a reaction which prepared the way for an evolutionary philosophy, which was accepted not merely with openness but with relief and unbounded optimism. Perhaps it is time to take a fresh look at the situation.

Although to many people diagrams are a hindrance rather than a help, for the few who find them illuminating the two graphs (shown on pp. 84, 85) have been drawn to summarize the substance of the previous paragraphs.

Graph I is intended to represent the currently accepted view of things. The first man started at an animal level (A) but with something which enabled him gradually to elevate himself until he reached (B) after an interval of perhaps 500,000 years. This point marks what has been called by some archaeologists and prehistorians the Neolithic Revolution.[43] It is essentially the time at which man is believed to have established the first permanent settlements by achieving the domestication of some animals and cereals, thus becoming a food producer for the first time. Previously man had been a nomadic hunter. From this point on a steady cultural evolution took place, occupying perhaps 10,000 years up to the present time.

In Graph II we have an entirely different kind of picture, although the end result is much the same. At (G) we have the creation of Adam already removed far above the animal level. He began with certain instructions from his Creator, certainly in language which lies at the root of culture, and perhaps in the making of clothes and in the matter of worship. These legacies and probably others were his from the very first and (G) starts, therefore, clearly above the animal line. From there to (H) which marks the time of the Flood was a very rapid rise. The time interval is a matter of a very few thousand years, contrasting sharply with the length of the line AB in Graph I.

---

[43] I think the originator of this term was V. Gordon Childe. He uses it, for example, in his *Man Makes Himself*, Watts, London, 1948, Chap. 5, pp. 66 ff.

At H, much of the cumulative technology of the pre-Flood world was lost: but much remained for a fresh start. This is shown by beginning the next curve a little distance down from H, at K.

From K to J there is a steady rise but it is not a smooth curve. It is made up rather of a series of sharp rises followed by a collapse, each new rise starting at some point on the falling line of the previous arc. This is the picture which history gives us: it is the pattern of events which was first seen clearly by Vico[44] and has subsequently intrigued most philosophers of history including Toynbee,[45] Spengler[46] and others.[47] Each civilization seems to have had a birth followed by a rapid development to a Golden Age and then a slow decline. Somewhere in the declining period, another culture takes over and raises the cumulative thread of cultural development to a slightly higher level than before, only to pass into a subsequent descendancy like all its predecessors. In a sense there is evolution, but it carries with it the inevitable consequence of leaving behind strewn about the world the decadent remnants of each civilization — some of which continued their decline until rediscovered centuries later by the White Man as he set forth to dominate what he had previously thought were the uninhabited regions of the world. Such backward peoples as he found everywhere in marginal areas were not representatives of prehistoric man striving to elevate themselves to a higher cultural level, but the sad reminders of the fact that no civilization however accomplished it may be, has the power within itself to maintain itself against ultimate decay. In some instances the process of decay carried man culturally so low that he approached nearer than ever before to the animal line. It is a frightening thought, but one that must be faced, that isolated individuals found now and then as feral children may even have crossed this line also.[48] History, far from being characterized

---

[44] Giovanni, Battista Vico (1668-1744) was an Italian philosopher whose chief work was published in France by Michelet in 1827 under the title *Principes de la Philosophie d'Histoire.*
[45] Toynbee, Arnold, *A Study of History,* Oxford Univer. Press, 1946-1957, in which the rise and fall of 19 civilizations is presented in such a way as to suggest that history repeats itself according to what is almost a spiritual law. Karl Marx believed the determining factor was an economic one, Ellsworth Huntingdon that it was a climatic one.
[46] Spengler, Oswald, *Decline of the West,* Allen and Unwin, London, 1926.
[47] For a discussion of Vico's views, see R. G. Collingwood, "Oswald Spengler and the Theory of Historical Cycles," *Antiquity,* Sept., 1927, pp. 311-325; and also "The Theory of Historical Cycles," Dec., 1927, pp. 435-446. A. L. Kroeber has several worthwhile contributions on the subject of Cultural Determinism and Historical Cycles. These deterministic trends in culture he refers to as the "superorganic," *Amer. Anthrop.,* 19 (1917): 162-213. This concept was elaborated in many of his subsequent works.
[48] There are possibly four or five fairly well authenticated cases in com-

Two Contrasting Interpretations of Man's Cultural Development

Graph I

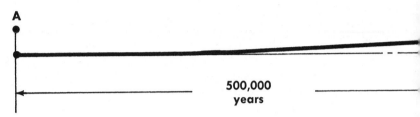

Fig. 3. A to B represents Palaeolithic time, possibly 500,000 years. B to C = Neolithic time to the present, possibly 8,000 to 10,000 years. G to H = from Adam to the Flood, possibly 2,000 to 4,000 years. K to J = from the Flood to the present, possibly 4,000 years. K = the point at which civilization took a fresh but slightly regressed "beginning." H to K represents the cultural loss resulting from the Flood.

Curve BC is smooth with a few divergencies, but essentially a steady evolution of culture. BL typifies the course taken by primitive people as a whole who have shared little in the evolution of culture.

KJ is less a curve than a series of arcs. It intends to show that culture has not enjoyed the steady evolution shown by BC, but has been marked by a series of rises and falls as one historical culture succeeded another — one habitually starting out of the preceding one and springing from some level near the top. This is a cyclic view of history.

Point A represents the departure of Homo sapiens from the animal level, rising slowly to B. Point G = the creation of Adam, well above the animal level. Though all his descendants have tended to remain above the animal level, on occasion members of the race (feral children) have fallen below it, at F.

As each arc in KJ reaches its point of decline, a series of cultures of increasingly lower level has resulted. This may account for many features to be found in primitive people, living and extinct. Thus the "Law of Cultural Development" seems to involve a decline from which some fragments tend to sink lower and lower, unable to retain or recover the initial level, without a reintegration with the main stream; such reintegrations have been few and far between, the attempt usually leading to complete extinction of the lower society.

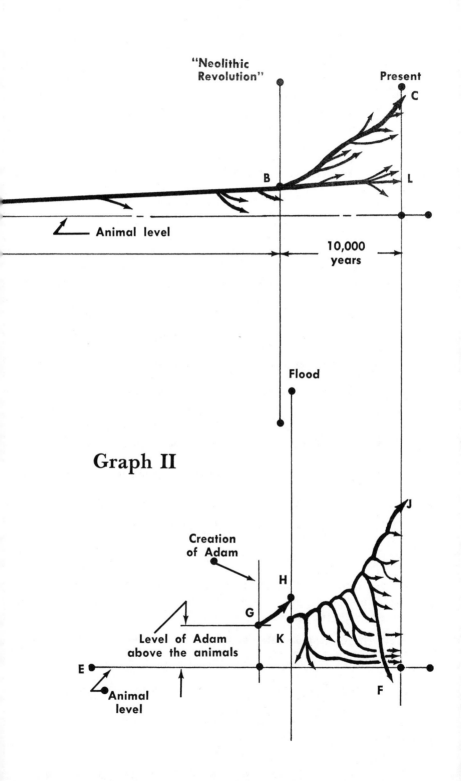

"Neolithic Revolution"

Present

C

B

L

Animal level

10,000 years

Flood

Graph II

J

Creation of Adam

H

G

Level of Adam above the animals

K

E

Animal level

F

by progress from savage to barbarian to civilized, is in fact more frequently characterized by regression from civilized to barbaric (albeit, refined at times) to savage.

In these two graphs, therefore, we have two contrasting views of man's history, the one presenting a long, slow, unbroken climb from animal almost to superman: the other showing the effect of three great facts, namely, that man was created with a vast superiority over the animals; secondly, that his ingenuity quickly proved too dangerous and had to be curbed by the Flood; and thirdly, that what ingenuity he still retains is constantly subject to the decaying effects of sin so that his great achievements are never lasting although their cumulative effect gives the impression of continuous upward progress.

The picture of the growth of civilization based upon prehistoric research in Europe is one of a vastly extended and very gradual progress from crude stone implements, the absence of cereals or domesticated animals, no pottery and no established settlements — to more refined stone and metal tools and weapons, pottery, cereals, domestic animals, and more or less permanent settlements. This process is said to have taken 500,000 years.

By contrast, as already noted, archaeology has revealed in the Middle East — but not elsewhere— a tendency for people to begin almost immediately to congregate in larger and larger numbers, at first in camps (at M'lefaat), soon after in villages (Jarmo, Sialk, Tell Halaf, etc.), then towns (Susa, Jericho, etc.), and then cities (Al Ubeid, and in the Indus Valley, and Egypt), all of this taking place in a matter of centuries.

The difference in pattern between Europe and the Middle East is significant, for as it has been noted by several authorities,[49] the "city-idea" is not an Indo-European one but originated with the non-Indo-European peoples. In fact, neither Indo-Europeans nor Semites had a word specifically for "city," in both cases using a borrowed term.[50]

The English word "borough" and its older form "burg" are both derived from a more ancient root appearing in classical antiquity in the form "perg-" (as in Pergamos, for example) which is also reflected in the Greek word for "tower," namely, *purgos*. In fact, our

paratively recent times. Reference is made to these by Susanne Langer, *Philosophy in a New Key*, Mentor Books, N.Y., 1952, p. 87. Also in the works of Ernst Cassirer: see "Who Taught Adam to Speak?" in this volume.

[49] See on this Stuart Piggott, *Prehistoric India*, Penguin Books, Eng., 1950, p. 263; H. J. Fleure, *The Races of Mankind*, Benn, London, 1930, p. 68; A. H. Sayce, "The Aryan Problem," *Antiquity*, June, 1927, p. 214.

[50] See Robert Eisler, "Loan Words in Semitic Languages Meaning 'Town'," *Antiquity*, Dec., 1939, pp. 449ff.

words "town" and "tower," being derived from the same root, indicate the association between the two ideas. This association is a very ancient one and is found in the case of Babel, in Genesis 11:4. The root form "perg" has been carefully traced by Eisler to the more ancient word *"uruk,"* the name of a very famous early city. This name in turn is found in Cuneiform in an alternative form *"unuk."* It is a curious thing that while the names of all cities in Cuneiform are identified as cities by the use of a small determinative sign preceding the name, *unuk* is a sole exception. There must be a very good reason for this, and I suggest the reason is to be found in Genesis 4:17. Cain, representing only the second generation of Homo sapiens, is said to have built the first city and to have named it after his son Enoch. Being the first city, its name became virtually synonymous with the concept "city" and when after the Flood a new Unuk was built it never seemed necessary to identify it with a special determinative sign. It was not altogether unlike the way in which local people in the country will speak of going "to town" without feeling it necessary to be more specific. Everyone knows which town they mean.

The purpose of introducing this point here is that it indicates, I think, that when Noah and his family began to repeople the Middle East it was only to be expected that they would proceed within a very short time to the reestablishment of villages or towns, since city life had been normal to man from the time of Cain. People who have always lived in the country and never known urban life do not automatically proceed to assemble themselves into large aggregations. It is not, therefore, a "natural" thing that cities should have appeared so quickly, but they resulted from the circumstances in which the fresh start was being made, and this is evidence, indeed, in favor of the record of events in the early chapters of Genesis. It is a remarkable testimony of the truth of what might otherwise be considered a very innocent remark in Genesis 4:17, which being thus shown to be fact reveals how short the time interval really was between the appearance of the first man and the building of the first city. This is very different, surely, from the picture presented to us in most textbooks of prehistory which, of course, are based upon an examination of the evidence in Europe. Perhaps what took place in Europe must be accounted for in some entirely different way. This is the subject, in part, of Chapter 3. In the meantime we may say with a measure of certainty that the rapidity with which civilization developed in the Middle East as revealed by archaeology accords remarkably well with what is stated in Genesis but is in almost complete contradiction with that one ought to expect if human evolution were a fact.

But we may go even further and say that not only did civilization appear suddenly, but in many ways its earliest stages of development tended to be its finest. One of the surprises of early archaeology in the Middle East was the discovery that in the very area in which man was supposed to have begun what Crawford has termed "the conquest of culture,"[51] there was no truly primitive stage even in such sites as Sialk and Jarmo, and in the very lowest levels at Jericho and Tell Halaf there is evidence of the rudiments of civilized life though naturally at a simple level. But the domestication of animals, the growing of wheat, and skill in the manufacture of weapons and tools is there at the outset. Long antecedent periods of development from an entirely nomadic food-gathering kind of life to the community life of these early settlements is, of course, assumed but is still unsupported by evidence. A. H. Sayce in 1899, in spite of the fact that he knew nothing of the subsequent finds in the Iranian Plateau to the north of Assyria, was still essentially correct when he said,[52]

> The history of the ancient East contains no record of the development of culture out of savagery. It tells us indeed of degeneracy and decay in time, but it knows of no period when civilization began. As far as archaeology can teach us the builders of the Babylonian cities, the inventors of the cuneiform characters had behind them no barbarous past.

When these words were penned, it was still confidently asserted by others that further excavation would change the picture, and that in the end it would become apparent that this great cultural surge which marked the beginning of the truly historical period had a perfectly "normal" (by which was meant evolutionary) development from a primitive stage such as marginal groups possess. For this development it was necessary to postulate thousands of years, for in other areas where Stone Ages were known, progress from the lowest levels to a high state of civilization was felt to have taken literally hundreds of thousands of years. On the other hand, while such sites as Jarmo and others do reveal an initially simple stage, the time taken to reach a zenith of cultural achievement can be measured in centuries, not millenia, much less hundreds of thousands of years. Evidently something different was taking place at the center.

Let us deal with areas, one at a time, and see what the authorities have to say. Since Egypt is so familiar to us all (but not because of any priority in time), let us begin with a review of the evidence

---

[51] Crawford, M. D. C., *The Conquest of Culture*, Fairchild, N.Y., 1948, xii and 449 pp., index. A very useful summary of technical achievements, but without documentation.

[52] Sayce, A. H., *Early Israel and the Surrounding Nations*, London, 1899, p. 270.

from the valley of the Nile. P. J. Wiseman said in this connection,[53]

> No more surprising fact has been discovered by recent excavation than the suddenness with which civilization appeared in the world. Instead of the infinitely slow development anticipated, it has become obvious that art, and we may say science, suddenly burst upon the world. For instance, H. G. Wells acknowledged that the oldest stone building known to the world is the Sakkara Pyramid. Yet as Dr. Breasted pointed out, "From the earliest piece of stone masonry to the construction of the Great Pyramid less than a century and a half elapsed."
>
> Writing of this Pyramid, Sir Flinders Petrie stated that "the accuracy of construction is evidence of high purpose and great capability and training. In the earliest pyramid the precision of the whole mass is such that the error would be exceeded by that of a metal measure on a mild or a cold day: the error of leveling is less than can be seen with the naked eye. The conclusion seems inevitable that 3000 B.C. was the heydey of Egyptian art."
>
> Dr. Hall in referring to this sudden development says, "It is easy to say that this remarkable outburst of architectural capacity must argue a long previous apprenticeship and period of development: but in this case we have not got this long period."
>
> In the face of these facts the slow progress of early man is a doubtful assumption, and the idea that an infinitely prolonged period elapsed before civilization appeared cannot be maintained.

G. A. Reisner says that the quality of "the art of the Old Kingdom of Egypt . . . has rarely been reached by the art of any other period or region: but authentic specimens are not common, and popular judgment is usually formed by *inferior* examples of *later* ages."[54]

Vere Gordon Childe in speaking of early Egyptian pottery remarked:[55]

> The pottery vessels especially those designed for funerary use, exhibit a perfection of technique never excelled in the Nile Valley. The finer ware is extremely thin, and is decorated all over by burnishing before firing, perhaps with a blunt-toothed comb, to produce an exquisite rippled effect that must be seen to be appreciated.

Walter Emery, speaking of the tombs of the first Pharaohs, remarked:[56]

> One great tomb after another was cleared (from 1935 to the end of World War II) each showing that civilization during the period of the First Dynasty was far more advanced than we had supposed . . . showing that a highly developed culture existed in Egypt by 3000 B.C. . . .

---

[53] Wiseman, P. J., *New Discoveries in Babylon About Genesis,* Marshall, Morgan and Scott, London, 2nd ed., rev., undated, pp. 28, 31, 33.
[54] Reisner, G. A., *The History of the Giza Necropolis,* reviewed in *Antiquity,* Mar., 1938, p. 104.
[55] Childe, Vere Gordon, *New Light on the Most Ancient East,* Kegan Paul, London, 1935, p. 67.
[56] Emery, Walter B., "The Tombs of the First Pharaohs," *Sci. American,* July, 1957, pp. 107, 112, 116.

The scattered contents of their tombs show that they had a well developed written language, a knowledge of the preparation of papyrus, and a great talent for the manufacture of stone vessels, to which they brought a beauty of design that is not excelled today. They also made an almost unlimited range of stone and copper tools, from saws to the finest needles. Their decorative objects of wood, ivory, and gold are masterly, and their manufacture of leather, textiles, and rope was of a high standard. Above all they had great artistic ability.

This advanced civilization appears suddenly in the early years of the third millennium B.C.; it seems to have little or no background in the Nile Valley....

The monumental architecture of the First Dynasty has been compared to that of the Jamdet Nasr period in Mesopotamia, and I think the similarity is beyond dispute.

This Jamdet Nasr period is dated around 3500 B.C. by Meek,[57] being the last of four pre-Dynastic periods in Mesopotamia of which the first was the Al Ubeid period to which reference is made subsequently.

R. E. Bewberry pointed out that "the essentials of the Egyptian system of writing were fully developed at the beginning of the *first* dynasty. It must have been the growth of many antecedent ages, yet not a trace of the early stages of its evolution have been found on Egyptian soil."[58] Vere Gordon Childe put it this way:[59]

On the Nile and in Mesopotamia the clear light of written history illumines our path for fully fifty centuries, and looking down that vista we already descry at its farther end ordered government, urban life, writing, and conscious art. The greatest moments — that revolution when man ceased to be a parasite ... have passed before the curtain rises.

W. J. Perry, quoting de Morgan,[60] said, "What appears at a very early date in Egypt is perfection of technique. The Egyptian appears, from the time of the earliest Pharaohs, as a patient, careful workman, his mind like his hand possesses an incomparable precision ... a mastery that has never been surpassed in any country."

Of course, archaeologists have turned up some ancient remains which seem to be more simple and more like the Palaeolithic remains of Europe, yet even in these sites pottery is found, and of this pottery W. E. Taylor of the University of Toronto assured us that "crude as it may appear it was in actual workmanship *never excelled*. The flint tools chipped and ground so very carefully are the finest that have ever been found anywhere!"[61] It may be strange to refer to their

[57] Meek, T. J., "Magic Spades in Mesopotamia," *Univ. of Toronto Quarterly*, 7, No. 2 (Jan., 1938): 235-237.
[58] Bewberry, R. E., quoted by C. Urquhart, *The Bible Triumphant*, Pickering, London, 1935, p. 36.
[59] Childe, V. G., ref. 55, p. 2.
[60] Perry, W. J., ref. 41, p. 54.
[61] W. E. Taylor in a lecture given before the Orientals Dept. of the Univ. of Toronto, Spring of 1936.

pottery as crude and yet as never excelled ... but the fact is that Egypt did not possess a source of clay for good pottery, and thus their best efforts were not comparable to the pottery of other ancient civilizations. Nevertheless, the best they ever made was made at the very beginning.

Moving northward from Egypt, towards the Cradleland, we come to Palestine and then to Syria. It is fairly certain that those who entered Egypt came either around the Fertile Crescent from Mesopotamia following the natural route which was followed by Abraham, settling first in the Nile Delta towards the sea and then subsequently settling the Upper Nile and Ethiopia, or across Southern Arabia to the Horn of Africa and flooding out across the African continent.

Although it is not usual to look for the origins of culture in Palestine, it will be valuable in passing to note a remark by M. G. Kyle with respect to the pre-Israelite times, when the country was possessed by the Canaanites and the Philistines and other tribes mentioned in the early chapters of Genesis. He said:[62]

> Wherever it has been possible to institute a comparison between Palestine and Egypt, the Canaanite civilization in handicraft, art, engineering, architecture, and education has been found to suffer only by that which climate, materials, and locality impose. In genius and in practical execution it is equal to that of Egypt and only eclipsed, before Graeco-Roman times, by the brief glory of the period of Solomon.

To the north lay Syria. The recent excavations at Ras Shamra and more especially at Tell Halaf have revealed much of the wealth and culture of the very earliest periods. This is particularly and, for our purposes, significantly true of the very earliest period at Tell Halaf. T. J. Meek in discussing the achievements reached by the people who occupied the site at the very beginning remarked:[63]

> Tell Halaf has revealed the most wonderful hand-made pottery ever found. Although the lowest strata here are probably representatives of the oldest culture so far definitely attested, yet it is already clearly chalcolithic. From various indications we know that metal was used, although not very extensively. In this period great skill was shown in the working of obsidian into knives and scrapers. ... The pottery of Tell Halaf was made by hand, unbelievably thin, indeed not thicker than two playing cards, and shows an extraordinary grasp of shape and decorative effect in color and design. The pottery was fired at great heat in closed kilns that permitted indirect firing with controlled temperatures. The result of the intense heat was the fusion and vitrification of the silicates in the paint so that it became a

---

[62] Kyle, M. G., "Recent Testimony of Archaeology to the Scriptures," in *The Fundamentals*, Biola Press, Los Angeles, 1917, p. 329.

[63] Meek, T. J., "Mesopotamian Studies," in *The Haverford Symposium on Archaeology and the Bible*, 1938, p. 161.

genuine glaze that gives the surface a porcelain finish quite different from the gloss of burnished ware so common later.

Technically and artistically the Tell Halaf pottery is the finest handmade pottery of antiquity and bears witness to the high culture of its makers.

Mallowan said of the use of metal at this early period, "It should be noted that in one of the oldest strata in which Tell Halaf pottery occurs, a copper necklace-bead has been found."[64]

The people who came to Tell Halaf and thus began the civilization of Syria and Palestine, evidently arrived from two directions. Some seem to have come from the north, from Anatolia, and possibly some from Mesopotamia due east, i.e., from northern Babylonia. We must look further to the east, therefore, for the roots we are seeking.

Turning to the Mesopotamian plains, the story is exactly similar to the story of Egypt. The Greatness of Egypt is monument-al. The greatness of Sumerian civilization is of a different nature. Despite the fact that they had no stone with which to erect memorials of their culture as Egypt erected theirs, yet once the search had begun it became increasingly apparent that not only was Sumerian civilization equal in every respect to that of Egypt, it was prior. The earliest culture of the long series which culminated in the great cities like Nineveh and Babylon is termed the Al Ubeid Culture. Of these people Vere Gordon Childe wrote:[65]

> The authors of the Al Ubeid culture cannot have sprung from the marsh bottom, yet the culture itself shows no sign of having developed locally from any more primitive mesolithic forerunner.

C. J. Gadd remarked:[66]

> The Sumerians possessed the land since as far back in time as anything at all is seen or even obscurely divided, and it has already been remarked that their own legends which profess to go back to the creation of the world and of men, have their setting in no other land than their historical home.... But the shapes of the earliest flints are not those of a pure stone age, nor has any certain evidence been found in Iraq of a population so primitive as to have no knowledge of metal.

And again, subsequently, he said:[67]

> Works of art which astonish by their beauty have been found (not least at Ur itself) to be the relics of the first, not the last ages. Nothing but the good fortune that they were discovered by regular

---

[64] Mallowan, M. E. L., *The Excavations at Tell Chagar Bazar and an Archaeological Survey of the Habur Region, 1934-35*, Oxford, 1936, reviewed in *Antiquity*, Dec., 1937, p. 502.

[65] Childe, V. G., ref. 55, p. 145.

[66] Gadd, C. J., *The History and Monuments of Ur*, Chatto and Windus, London, 1929, p. 24 and p. 17.

[67] Ibid., p. 27.

excavation could have avoided the ludicrous misconception of their date.... Gold is the material of their possessions and the symbol of their superfluity. In the flourishing days and at their lavish court, the arts of manufacture rose to a perfection and beauty in their products which was never seen again. The articles made were, indeed, of much the same kind as those of later ages, but they were at this very early period marked by a richness and splendor rather of Egyptian sumptuosity than the supposed sobriety of the River-lands. These deposits amaze by their riot of gold: silver also is there in great profusion evidently nothing accounted of.

Sir Leonard Woolley[68] came to the conclusion that "so far as we know, the fourth millennium before Christ saw Sumerian art at its zenith." And Childe likewise remarked upon the same phenomenon,[69] "These (recent discoveries) suffice to show that, even more than in Egypt, civilization has reached a very high level by the end of the fourth millennium B.C., that was not surpassed during the whole of the pre-Sargonid epoch." And Wiseman pointed out:[70]

This discovery is the very opposite to that anticipated. It was expected that the more ancient the period, the more primitive would excavators find it to be, until traces of civilization ceased altogether and aboriginal man appeared. Neither in Babylonia, nor Egypt, the lands of the oldest known habitations of man, has this been the case. In this connection Dr. Hall writes in his *History of the Near East,* "When civilization appears it is already full grown." And subsequently, "Sumerian culture springs into being ready made." And Dr. L. W. King in his book *Sumer and Akkad* remarks, "Although the earliest Sumerian settlements in southern Babylonia are to be set back in a comparatively remote past, the race by which they were founded appears at that time to have already attained to a high level of culture."

Yet it is not possible to push back the habitation of man in the Mesopotamian plain vast millennia into the past, for the very simple and conclusive reason that the more southern Mesopotamian land must have been formed within the last 10,000 years or so. We know that owing to the peculiar nature of the rivers in bringing down silt, and depositing it at the entrance to the Persian Gulf, the land has been formed gradually during the past few thousand years, and the land is still being added to by this means. Ur of the Chaldees was once on the edge of the Persian Gulf, and is now over one hundred miles from it.

J. L. Myers pointed out that the shore line has been advancing rapidly within historic times: Eridu, for example, which was a chief port of early Babylonia, lies now 125 miles from the sea.[71] If the present rate of advance, about a mile in thirty years, may be taken

[68] Woolley, Sir Leonard, *The Sumerians,* Clarendon Press, Oxford, 1928, p. 44.
[69] Childe, V. G., ref. 55, p. 19.
[70] Wiseman, P. J., ref. 53, pp. 28 and 29.
[71] Myers, J. L., *Dawn of History,* Williams and Norgate, London, undated, p. 85.

as an average, Eridu may have begun to be mud-bound about 1800 B.C.

T. J. Meek in a lecture given at the University of Toronto stated that "the Sumerian culture springs into view ready made, and there is yet no knowledge of the Sumerians as savages: when we find them in the fourth millennium B.C. they are already civilized highly. They are already using metals and living in great and prosperous cities."[72]

Citizens stamped their correspondence with cylinder seals that were rolled over the soft clay. Such seals were beautifully carved in the very ancient times with animal figures that portray motion. The later seals, even those of only a few centuries later, are vastly inferior from an artistic point of view. Inspiration belonged to the earliest ages, not to the later.[73] When compared with their present descendants, if brain size means anything, according to Sir Arthur Keith even in this they were superior.[74]

Now the record of Genesis tells us that those who first settled in Mesopotamia entered the land *"as they journeyed from the East."* This implies that they did not originate there; and since this piece of historical information is presented to us some time after the Ark had landed, and after men had begun to spread abroad somewhat, it seems fairly certain that these people had come down on the eastern side of the Zagros Mountains towards the site of Susa. Here they effected a settlement before going on towards the west and there "finding" a plain, the plain of Mesopotamia. Susa thus stands in a parental or at least a prior relationship to the Al Ubaid culture exactly as the excavations show. We ought in theory to be one step nearer the beginning when we have arrived back at Susa.

Yet even here, the story is repeated. H. G. Spearing wrote of Susa:[75]

> The earliest colonists at Susa were well civilized before they left the country of their parenthood and arrived there. For in their burial ground outside the city walls are found the bronze hatchets of the men and the mirrors and needles and the ointment vases of the women; there are also relics of delicate fabrics finely woven on a loom. . . .
> The pottery is wonderfully thin and hard, not much thicker than a couple of post cards, and it rings like porcelain, though it is not so

[72] Meek, T. J., in a lecture before the Orientals Dept., University of Toronto, Fall of 1936.

[73] Frankfort, Henri, in an article on Khafaje in the *Illustrated London News,* Nov. 13, 1937, pp. 840, 841, gives some photos of such seals.

[74] Keith, Sir Arthur, "Physical Anthropology," *Sci. Progress,* Oct., 1936, p. 333.

[75] Spearing, H. G., "Susa, The Eternal City of the East," in *Wonders of the Past,* Vol. III, Putnam, N.Y., 1924, p. 583.

transparent. The forms are simple and graceful; they were produced on a rudimentary pottery wheel used with a skill that looks like the inherited experience of many generations of craftsmen.

Nearly all the bowls and vases were elaborately decorated either inside or outside with strange designs, most of which have no similarity with other designs found in other parts of the world, so that we have no clue to the country where these potters learned their art, though we can be fairly sure that they brought it from some center of civilization where it had been undergoing a long period of development.

How inevitable this conclusion always seems to be!

Where shall we look now for the origins of the people who created this pottery? It seems we cannot look further to the east, though in this direction lies the Indus Valley Civilization. But this culture owes its origin to a people who themselves manifestly came from the *west*, and who shared much with the creators of the Sumerian culture. Nevertheless, the earliest levels at two sites, Changu Daru and Harappa in the Indus Valley, are remarkably reminiscent of the earliest levels at Tell Halaf in Syria, and in keeping with the fact that the Tell Halaf settlers arrived there from the north and east towards Ararat, it is clear that the Indus Valley people came from somewhere in the same direction. Thus Ernest Mackay[76] said, "There seems no doubt that... we must look to the Iranian Highlands for the region whench civilization was brought to India."

In his report to the *Illustrated London News*, Mackay remarks upon the finds at the earliest levels in Changu Daru,[77] and describes the extraordinary way in which the city was laid out in blocks with draining systems and underground sewers. Some of the drain pipes are illustrated in his article and he remarks of them that they "are quite modern in design... some having pigots which fit into each other, and some conical shaped so that the smaller end fits into the larger end of the next one."

He tells of a hoard of beads found.[78]

> Some of the beads made of steatite were astonishingly small; a quantity had been kept for safety in a small jar, and when placed end to end they ran to 34 to an inch. Their holes were so tiny that they could only have been threaded on a hair, and how these beads were made and bored it is hard to comprehend....
> As at Mohenjo Daro (another Indus Valley site) practically every house had its bathroom and latrine from which the water ran into the street drains and was thus carried well outside the city. Indeed, the draining system was remarkably well planned, every street being supplied with two or more drains, built, like the houses, of burnt brick. A number of pottery drain pipes, some of which were found in situ,

---

[76] Mackay, Ernest, "Great New Discoveries of Indian Culture in Prehistoric Sind," *Illus. London News,* Nov. 14, 1936, Plate I.

[77] Ibid., p. 860, Fig. II.

[78] Ibid., pp. 860 and 894.

testify that these ancient people were expert sanitary engineers; moreover, falls were arranged so that there should be as little splashing as possible, and when a corner had to be turned the bricks were carefully rounded off to reduce friction. The drain pipes are quite modern in design; except for being made of porous pottery, they would well serve the same purpose today.

As a matter of fact, anyone who has had experience with a septic tank disposal system will know that in reality this porosity was a great advantage, for much of the content of the system is bled through the pipe walls into the surrounding soil, thus relieving the lead at the disposal end.

Some remarkable seal amulets were also found at the lowest levels, with illustrations of elephants, oxen, and single-horned Urus ox. These seals are beautifully carved, with almost perfectly formed reproductions of the animals they portray, showing absolutely correct proportion and musculature. Copper and bronze instruments and weapons abound everywhere.

How well such sanitation and such household furnishings contrast with the modern eastern villages whose inhabitants have the unpleasant habit of casting all refuse into the street for the rain to wash away. But where did these people come from? Dr. Mackay says we must look towards the Iranian highland plateau. Wherever they came from, it seems they entered the Indus Valley already cultured. It is amazing to find at two of the earliest sites, Harappa and Changu Daru, evidence of such artistic taste and skill, coupled with a remarkable engineering knowledge.

At Mohenjo Daru, another site in the same complex, was found a male dancing figure and the torso of a nude female figure which, according to Childe,[79] are "modelled with a liveliness of attitude, and the musculature and contours of the bodies delineated with an attention to detail and verisimilitude, found nowhere else before classical Greek times. Indeed so modern is the treatment that the sculptures have been attributed to the Greco-Bactrian age." Their artistic taste was no less highly developed than their technology.

But if these settlers came from the highland zone surely we ought to find their remains there? It seems that the site of Sialk is such a village. Excavation of this site was undertaken by a French expedition from the Louvre Museum, beginning in 1933 and working continuously till 1938, and with further work in the area since World War II. In charge of the expedition was R. Ghirshman who has reported

---

[79] Childe, Vere Gordon, "India and the West Before Darius," *Antiquity*, Mar., 1939, p .10.

his work in numerous journals and recently given a very comprehensive account in a volume entitled "Iran."[80]

In this, and in earlier papers, he set forth some of his findings which may be summarized somewhat as follows. The site is quite near the famous city of Kashan known for its rugs, and not far south of Teheran the capital of Iran. It was first occupied in the fifth millennium B.C., at which time the evidence shows that the climate of the region was just changing from a very wet one to an arid one. The central part of the Iranian highland plateau had apparently escaped the glaciation which had engulfed the rest of Europe but had been experiencing a very, very heavy rainfall, and this had led to the formation of "an immense lake or inland sea" into which many rivers ran from the high mountains. As this large, but shallow, inland sea dried up it left in its place many swamps which became grassland and savannah. Game was abundant and man "moved in first to hunt and then to settle permanently." He had, by this time, already domesticated certain species such as the ox and the goat.

Ghirshman also found that the occupants were highly artistic. To use his own words:[81]

> Never before in the systematic explorations which have brought to light the remains of extinct civilizations have such objects carved out of bone or of stone been found in this region. The Sialk excavations have now revealed the existence of a marvellous art of carving on bone, which had already made noteworthy progress at the period we are now considering. Among the remains of the dwellings, we found recently a whole series of flint holders, with handles finished off with an animal head or a carved human figure....
>
> The figurine which decorates the handle of one of these tools may be regarded as the oldest carved human image ever found in Western Asia. The statuette, which perhaps represents a chief or a priest, has a little cap on its head; round the hips is a loin-cloth, the upper part of which is rolled under to form a sort of belt. The arms of the figure are crossed, and the torso is slightly bent forward.
>
> It is not possible to believe that an art capable of creating such an object as this statuette was in its initial phase. The artist reveals awareness both of proportions and of technical approach. The way in which the attitude of the man is treated, his muscles, his clothing, show close observation, and also much practice and skill....

The inhabitants soon domesticated also pigs, dogs and the horse, this being the first evidence of the existence of the latter in Iran at such a remote period. Vere Gordon Childe remarked on the surprising fact that at the earliest levels the inhabitants were also spinning and weaving to make fabrics, though the fibers they used have not yet

---

[80] Ghirshman, R., *Iran*, Penguin Books, Eng., 1954, 368 pp., Index, ills.
[81] Ghirshman, R., "At Sialk: Prehistoric Iran," *Asia*, Nov., 1938, p. 646.

been identified for certain.[82] Ghirshman also referred to the earliest known records in the form of simple tablets which were clearly to be related with the earliest tablets found by a French expedition in the lowest levels of Susa — thus establishing what he considers a direct ancestral link from the north to the south.

It seems therefore that Sialk represents a settlement made by the people who, travelling further towards the south, established themselves at Susa some little time later. But Ghirshman would go one step further, for he views the people of Sialk as being related also to the Indo-European civilization, and to that of the Phrygians of Asia Minor, a people of the Indo-European race closely related to the Illyrians who immigrated there from Thrace, which "entitles us to regard the inhabitants of Sialk as belonging also to the same Indo-European family."[83] It is only to be expected that there should be evidence at this early time of the close association of all three of the sons of Noah. It would almost seem as though they were still together at this time, though doubtlessly their families had greatly enlarged. But shortly afterwards they began to divide. The children of Japheth went towards the north and settled up into Asia Minor and into Europe. The children of Ham went south and coming into the Indus Valley established themselves there. But they also went via Susa round into Mesopotamia arriving at the southern end soon afterwards to establish the Al Ubeid culture. Perhaps the children of Shem went towards the west and then down into northern Syria, settled at Tell Halaf and later turned towards the east again and to northern Mesopotamia where in the time of Nimrod they fell under the domination of the Sumerians from the south.

In speaking of Sialk, Childe is careful to note how quickly the people who occupied it moved forward in their civilization. He wrote:[84]

> The earliest culture found at Sialk can be matched at other sites upon the plateau and northward up to Anau in the Merv oasis in Russian Turkestan [the route followed by the children of Japheth?]. At Sialk a second phase can be seen in the villages built on the ruins of those described. The houses are no longer built just of packed clay, but of molded bricks dried in the sun. Food-gathering is less prominent in the communal economy: horses have been added to the domestic flock. Shells are brought across the mountains from the Persian Gulf. Copper is commoner, but it is still treated as a superior sort of stone,

---

[82] Childe, Vere Gordon, *What Happened In History*, Penguin Books, Eng., 1946, p. 64.

[83] V. G. Childe also refers to the evidence for the existence of a Japhetic people dwelling in early times in the highlands from the Zagros Mountains westward (ref. 55, p. 18).

[84] Childe, V. G., ref. 82, p. 64.

worked by cold hammering. Equipment is made from local bone, stone, and chert, supplemented by a little imported obsidian. But special kilns are built for firing pots.

Then with Sialk III the village was removed to a new site close by the old one and watered by the same spring. Equipment is still mainly home-made from local materials. But copper is worked intelligently by casting to make axes and other implements that must still be luxuries. Gold and silver are imported, and lapis lazuli from northern Afghanistan. Potters appear who make vessels quickly on a fast spinning wheel, instead of building them up by hand. And men use seals to mark their property. Finally Sialk IV is a colony of literate Elamites. ...

In other words, life at the very beginning in these places was necessarily simple, but it seems that it was not only technically proficient, it was also artistic and therefore cultured. And it developed extremely rapidly.

From Sialk it is now customary to go back to the lower levels at Jarmo and to other sites in Iraqi Kurdistan which appear to represent an earlier stage, a stage without pottery (roughly contemporary with and similar to the lowest levels of Jericho even though it was already a fortified town by this time).[85] But can we really be sure that such sites are prior merely because there is no evidence of pottery? Is this not a biased interpretation? There is really no absolute reason for placing these cultures "earlier" other than the argument that they ought to be earlier merely because they appear to be simpler. The supposed law of evolutionary development may demand this interpretation, but in itself the evidence is quite neutral, until something turns up which positively established priority.

When Noah and his family stepped out of the Ark somewhere in this general region, they certainly must have had a knowledge of metals, for by this time metal-working was already centuries old (Gen. 4:22).

Now, it is argued that sites without pottery in this area must be earlier. The criterion is the absence of pottery. However, it is known from other sites, especially in Greece,[86] that the use of metals can *precede* the use of pottery, pottery vessels being subsequently based upon metal prototypes. In such sites, although the metal originals have disappeared, they must have existed in order to give rise to what are manifestly substitutes. It follows from this that in those periods

---

[85] For a useful summary of these associations and time correlations, see Seton Lloyd, *Early Anatolia*, Penguin Books, Eng., 1956, pp. 53, 54.

[86] Excellent illustrations of such pottery will be found in E. J. Forsdyke, "Marvels of the Potter's Art," in *Wonders of the Past*, Vol. 2, Putnam, N.Y., 1924, Plate at p. 426. Such forms occur widely in early Helladic sites as at Asea, Gournia, Korakou, Vasiliki, etc. Even the rivets are sometimes reproduced in pottery!

when vessels were commonly made from metal, there may have been an absence of pottery, and this absence would be evidence, not of a lower level of technology, but rather of a higher one. Thus the reason why Jarmo and the lower levels of Jericho are considered to be more primitive, i.e., the absence of pottery, may be quite unsound. In fact, when pottery does finally appear in these sites, it takes a form which could easily be the result of inspiration derived from the use of metal wares. The fact that no metal wares were found at these lower levels is not too significant for the simple reason that such vessels would not be easily broken and would not be thrown away. The point of this discussion is simply that those sites which by reason of their lower culture are considered to be antecedent, may actually be later: they may be, in fact, settlements established by the first off-shoots from the main body on the highland plateau.

Thus although Jarmo and early Jericho are assumed to be older than Sialk, I do not think the point is established. Possibly they were, but the assumption rests, as stated above, on the lower level of cultural development as gaged by what was left behind by the inhabitants. The dating for Jarmo established by Braidwood is in any case not so very ancient. He gives the figure 6000 B.C., but adds that this date is likely to be reduced, when the evidence is more fully assessed.[87] Jericho is dated by Kenyon at 8000 B.C.,[88] but Zeuner who was chiefly responsible for the investigations on which the figures were based states "most emphatically" that caution is needed in accepting these C-14 dates.[89]

Such then is the picture. Somewhere in the Iranian highland there settled a small group of people who needed little time to develop sufficiently to create the later culture-complex which characterized the upper levels at Sialk. From here, or from some similar sites in about the same stages of development, emigrants set out towards the West to settle at Tell Halaf, for example. Others went south, dividing into two bands, one passing around the lower end of the Zagros Mountains where they came up into the plains of Mesopotamia from

[87] Braidwood, Robert J., "From Cave to Village," *Sci. American*, Oct., 1952, pp. 62ff. This is an excellent summary with useful illustrations and graphic presentations of the evidence as he sees it. To the uninitiated, the matter is clearly settled. But Miss Kenyon disagrees.

[88] Kenyon, Kathleen M., "Ancient Jericho," *Sci. American*, Apr., 1954, pp. 76 ff. In her article, "Some Observations on the Beginnings of Settlement in the Near East," *Jour. Roy. Anthrop. Instit.*, Jan.-June, 1959, pp. 35ff., she explains why she believes Jericho is older than Jarmo and criticizes Braidwood's interpretation of the Archaeological evidence from Jarmo — which shows how difficult it is to be certain about sequences at this early date.

[89] Kenyon, Kathleen, *Jour. Roy. Anthrop. Instit.*, Jan.-June, 1959, p. 41.

the south, and the other turning to the east, finally establishing themselves in the Indus Valley.

From Mesopotamia and Northern Syria it seems, more adventurous spirits travelled on until they reached Lower and Upper Egypt; and all this took place within a remarkably short time.[90]

This is manifestly a gross oversimplification, for some of the settlers, in lower Mesopotamia, subsequently travelled around the southern boundary of Arabia and entered Africa via the Horn. And the Japhetic branch of the family of Noah quite possibly spread at a much more leisurely pace toward the north (into the Caucasus) and towards the west (into Asia Minor and on into Greece and Europe), only much later returning towards the south and east into Persia and into the Indus Valley. Yet even though this reconstruction is artificial in its simplicity, the time factor is not likely to be changed very much. The tendency has been, rather consistently, to reduce rather than to extend the over-all chronology.[91]

All the initial movements seem to have taken place within a period of about 1,000 to 1,500 years, showing how quickly the transition was made to the cultural level at Al Ubeid, for example. And while Al Ubeid stands at the beginning of Sumerian civilization, within a few hundred years the Sumerians had achieved a level of technical proficiency greater than that to be found in many parts of Europe just prior to the Industrial Revolution.

---

[90] A very stimulating and concise evaluation of the evidence for these early migrations was given by M. E. L. Mallowan in "Mesopotamian Trilogy," *Antiquity,* June, 1939, pp. 159-170.

[91] In discussing one of the papers presented at the Anthropological Symposium (ref. 29), Grahame Clark made the remark regarding new techniques of dating, "They seem to suggest that the Magdalenian cave artists, far from ending at 18,000 B.C., probably ended at more like 8,000 B.C.; and far from beginning anywhere near so early as 50,000 B.C., began about 15,000 B.C., or perhaps even later.

"I conclude by asking a question which I hope Hallam Movius (see ref. 18) will take up. If the only date in the Zeuner-Milankovitch system (on which ref. 92 is based) we are in a position to check by means of C−14 is found to be as badly wrong and as grossly overinflated as this, how much reliance should we place on the long-range dating for the early phases of the ice age? I only ask this question. I don't know the answer" (*Appraisal of Anthropology Today,* Chicago, 1953, p. 78). On this see also, Oakley, *Man,* Oct., 1951, p. 142.

The same authority said subsequently (p. 37), "C−14 dating seems to suggest that the Upper Paleolithic developments came rather later than we thought, and this only heightens the impression of a very great speed-up in cultural development and differentiation."

A. L. Kroeber (p. 39) strongly reinforced Clark's words, underlining the change in view regarding both Old and New World chronology. In the *Illust. London News,* Sept. 14, 1935, Henry Frankfort suggests that "the

One is inevitably faced with the question of what had been happening in the rest of the world that progress had been so fantastically slow, *if* it really had occupied a time of some quarter to half a million years to reach the lowest levels at Sialk. Such a long period with so little progress is almost impossible to conceive of, especially when one realizes that the art of the European caves attributed to Cromagnon Man was according to Zeuner in the process of development some 72,000 years ago.[92] In fact he admitted his own amazement at the slowness of development in some cases. Thus in speaking of cultures during the Last Interglacial he wrote:[93]

> The interesting feature of this evolution of the hand-axe industries is the small amount of change observed, notwithstanding the huge time span covered. Judged by the standards of, say the upper Palaeolithic, the evolutionary rates of the Crag "industries" and of the Abbevillian, covering about 60 thousand years each, are small; but smaller yet is that of the Acheulian which lasted through 300 thousand years of which something like 200 thousand years appear to have been occupied by the "middle stage." This conservatism of the Acheulian is one of the most striking phenomena in the chronology of the Palaeolithic.

It is strange indeed. Observe the sequence: for perhaps a quarter of a million years intelligent men, to all intents and purposes apparently much like ourselves in many respects, advanced their culture scarcely at all. Then appeared a settlement in the Iranian highlands near the traditional site of the landing of the Ark, which within a period of perhaps 1,500 years developed into a culture in the Mesopotamian plains, which in turn, within a thousand years, gave rise to a series of high cultures scarcely paralleled until comparatively modern times.[94] And finally, after this sudden burst of activity lasting possibly a further 1,500 years or so, which witnessed some of the finest cultural achievements in Babylonia, Egypt, and the Indus Valley which the Middle East has ever seen, the process was once more slowed up until many prosperous centers decayed and disappeared, and much of India, Africa, and Europe remained in a state of semibarbarism till

---

earliest periods of civilization in Mesopotamia are more closely related and extend over a shorter period of time than is generally assumed."

[92] Zeuner, F. E., *Dating the Past,* Methuen, 1958, p. 299, fig. 81.

[93] Ibid., pp. 285 and 288.

[94] We now have a new "twist" in the interpretation of the evidence. The fact that there is no paleolithic phase in the Middle East cannot, of course, be taken to mean that man was civilized almost as soon as he appeared. This is not "evolutionary thinking." So it must be assumed that the absence of the earlier phase is due to the fact that it *never* was the Cradle of Mankind — never was a "centre of hominid dispersion." The fact that all lines of migration lead back here is simply discounted, and the evidence is completely reinterpreted to support current assumptions. See F. Clark Howell, "The Villafranchian and Human Origins," *Science,* 130 (1959): 833, col. c.

well on toward Roman times, and in some instances till much later.

The sequence takes the form, then, of an unbelievably long time with almost no growth; a sudden spurt leading within a very few centuries to a remarkably high culture; a gradual slowing up, and decay, followed only much later by recovery of lost arts and by development of new ones leading ultimately to the creation of our modern world. What was the agency which operated for that short period of time to so greatly accelerate the process of cultural development and produce such remarkable results? And is the long prior period of slow "progress" merely a figment of imaginative thinking resulting from a mistaken interpretation of the facts? Is it possible to account for palaeolithic man in some other way? Could he have been descended from rather than ancestral to the people who so quickly created the cultures of the traditional Cradle of Civilization?

I think this is so. The sudden rise of high culture in the Middle East is most readily accounted for by reference to certain explicit statements in the early chapters of Genesis, and to some reasonable implications based upon them. And further, I am convinced that one can only account for the extraordinary slowness of early cultural development in Europe and elsewhere by reviewing those cultures in the light of what we actually know from the history of primitive societies since the White Man first made contact with them and began to record his observations about them.

Chapter 3
Cultural Degeneration

SOMEWHERE AROUND 3000 B.C. the cultural position of mankind seems to have been somewhat as follows: A remarkably high civilization represented in several areas in the Middle East, more particularly in Mesopotamia, Egypt and the Indus Valley, was circled by a number of subsidiary settlements established as colonies reflecting some but not all of the core civilization which was ancestral to them. As we move away from the center, the light grows dimmer. Here and there circumstances, the nature of which is not altogether clear, permitted the light to flare up more brilliantly, quite early in China[95] and considerably later in Central America. On the whole,

95 A number of authorities have suggested that Chinese civilization was rather directly descended from early Sumerian. Its script may have been related (S. L. Caiger, *Bible and Spade*, Oxford, 1936, p. 2). There are apparently some close resemblances between Sumerian and very early Chinese music (M. E. L. Mallowan quoting F. W. Galpin, *The Music of the Sumerians*), Cambridge, 1937, in *Antiquity*, June, 1939, p. 169). W. J. Perry in his *Growth of Civilization* (Pelican Books, Eng., 1937, p. 125) refers to some very striking architectural parallels. Lord Raglan (*Jour. Roy. Anthrop. Instit.*, July-Dec., 1957, p. 144) argues that Chinese civilization progressed only so long as contact with the outside world was maintained. Carl Whiting Bishop in his paper, "The Beginnings of Civilization in Eastern Asia" (*Smithsonian Instit. Annual Report*, 1940, pp. 431-446), discusses in an interesting way the question of whether cultural centers such as Sumeria and China could have arisen in entire independence. He argues that the large number of common elements in these earliest civilizations, what he described as "homogeneity in fundamentals" (p. 433) cannot be attributed simply to the fact that men's minds work pretty much the same everywhere. There seems to be little question as to the relatedness of them all. Joseph Needham underscores the fact that while Sinanthropus seems to antedate the beginnings of Chinese civilization by an immense period of time, there is a complete hiatus from this to the first clear evidence of widescale settlement in 2,500 B.C. Note this time — it is not very far from the traditional date of the Flood. Thereafter he says, "Then suddenly, about 2,500 B.C., the apparently empty land begins to support a large and busy population. There is evidence of hundreds, even thousands, of villages, inhabited by people of agricultural as well as pastoral economy, acquainted with carpentry, textiles,

104

however, it appears to have been a general rule that the cultural level was lower as it moved further from the original source of inspiration. Any people who migrated either at will or under pressure so far that they passed beyond the stream of influence of the central core and no longer enjoyed the stimulation of continuous culture-contacts, descended lower and lower in the scale, losing one element after another, until they reached that position with respect to culture that the body may reach with respect to disease where its energies are reduced so low as to render it unable to restore itself without outside aid. Unfortunately, just as the wrong restoratives may destroy the sickly patient, so the contact of the White Man and his vastly more complex civilization has tended to destroy the more primitive cultures, even when he honestly sought to improve their condition. Not a few peoples have shown themselves to have reached such a low ebb that the penalty of meeting a higher civilization has been total extinction; they sang their swan song and disappeared. If such primitive people really did in any way represent early man, one wonders whether cultural evolution ever could have occurred seeing that there does not appear to be any power of self-improvement.

Those societies which suffered most from culture-contacts with the White Man have tended to be the most "degraded," and their degeneration resulted invariably from the extreme harshness of their environment. This very harshness has, however, discouraged higher civilizations from any desire to dispossess the aboriginal inhabitants until quite recent times, a fact which saved them from being brought to extinction. It is difficult in the first place to understand why any people should choose to settle in some parts of the world where the environment is so hostile. The Eskimo in the Arctic, the Ona and Yaghans in Tierra del Fuego, the Semang of the Malay Peninsula, the Bushmen of the Kalahari Desert, or the Ituri Pygmies in the hot humid forests of the Congo — these would surely not choose such a habitat unless some circumstance had forced their ancestors into doing so, their descendants thereafter becoming accustomed to it and accepting it as normal for themselves. In many of these cases the margin of survival is so small that once a safe pattern of living has been established such societies cannot permit the slightest deviation.[96]

and ceramics" (*Science and Civilization in China,* Cambridge, 1954, Vol. 1, p. 80). Incidentally, the same "sudden" appearance of civilization applies to Japan also (Ingram Bryan, *The History of Japan,* Benn, London, 1928, p. 9). The Central American Cultures are, of course, far later.
[96] Radcliffe-Brown, A. R., *Andaman Islanders,* Cambridge, 1922, illustrates this point very forcibly for this particular people whose culture is very low indeed, showing that they will not allow the introduction of even the most

The culture becomes "of a piece," and any changes tend to be disastrous unless they are from within. Goldenweiser refers to this as cultural involution,[97] which occurs without conflict, as opposed to evolution which depends *upon* conflict. It is for this reason that contacts with other cultures are feared and are avoided as far as possible. It seems likely that this characteristic of all primitive people has always existed. Such conservatism stands firmly against any kind of progressive evolution as an automatic process resulting from the Struggle to Survive, because this kind of change almost always had a detrimental effect on the culture. Involution can take place quietly. Indeed, it is only ever permitted when this is possible. Thus, the evolutionary concept of Struggle for Survival, per se, does not benefit a primitive society. Their resources are far too small.

On the other hand, cultural devolution can be shown to have occurred many times in history. To summarize this situation, we may see that progress has only taken place in the mainstream, in those cultures which derived their inspiration and renewed it from time to time from the initial explosive development which was the subject of the first part of this paper. The moment any culture broke contact, its history thereafter tended to be characterized by the loss of old elements rather than the gain of new ones. Gains were made in some cases, but almost always by involution. Moreover, once the break had occurred and lack of contact continued for some time, renewal of contact tended to be harmful rather than beneficial. We do not have any case on record of any culture once so isolated having thereafter enjoyed a continually progressive development to a higher level. If we allow the biblical view of a high civilization at the very beginning, resulting from the circumstances of man's original creation and special endowment, followed by the disaster of the Flood and the scattering of man shortly after while he still enjoyed a high civilization, the subsequent cultural history of mankind makes good sense. The evolutionary picture of man beginning as an animal and slowly educating himself for better and higher things until after half a million years he reached a Neolithic stage, from which he quickly improved his own lot and soon became highly civilized, may appear to be reasonable, but is not really supported by the evidence.

Now these two alternative views have always existed, although today no anthropologist of reputation in the world would be willing

---

useful items (such as traps, p. 37) because of their fear of changing the slightest part of their culture. He repeatedly emphasizes this conservatism (cf. p. 302).

[97] Goldenweiser, A., *Anthropology*, Crofts, N.Y., 1945, p. 414, fn. 4.

to admit holding the first. But E. B. Tylor, while believing strongly in the second alternative, nevertheless admitted that the biblical view was at least possible. Notice, however, the curious form in which this admission appears. To use his own words:[98]

> The thesis which I venture to sustain, within limits, is simply this, that the savage state in some measure represents an early condition of mankind, out of which the higher culture has gradually been developed or evolved, by processes still in regular operation as of old, the result showing that on the whole, progress has far prevailed over relapse.
>
> On this proposition, the main tendency of human society during its long term of existence has been to pass from a savage to a civilized stage.

Yet he continued:

> This progression-theory of civilization may be contrasted with its rival, the degeneration-theory. . . .
>
> This theory has received the sanction of great learning and ability. It has practically resolved itself into two assumptions, first, that the history of culture began with the appearance on earth of a semi-civilized race of men, and second, that from this stage culture has proceeded in two ways, backward to produce savages, and forward to produce civilized men. The idea of the original condition of man being one of more or less high culture, must have a certain prominence given to it on account of its considerable hold on public opinion. As to definite evidence, however, it does not seem to have any ethnological basis whatever.

In spite of the tenor of his final conclusion here, he nevertheless proceeds to state that modern primitives, though they are representatives of Paleolithic Man in his view, are actually a very poor witness for the progressive theory since they never seem to show any evidence of progress themselves. He observes that Niebuhr, in attacking the progressionists of the 18th century, had been one of the first to make the point "that no single example can be brought forward of an actually savage people having independently become civilized."

Whately[99] appropriated this remark, which indeed forms the kernel of his well-known lecture "On the Origin of Civilization." "Facts are stubborn things," he said, "and that no authenticated instance can be produced of any savages that ever did emerge unaided from that state, is no theory but a statement hitherto never disproved of as matter of fact." With this view Tylor had little patience;[100] yet

---

[98] Tylor, Edward B., *Primitive Culture*, Vol. I, Murray, London, 2nd ed., 1891, pp. 32 and 35.

[99] Whately, Archbishop of Dublin, "On the Origin of Civilization," *Exeter Hall Papers, 1854-55*, Nisbet, London, p. 23. This whole essay is still well worth reading in spite of its date.

[100] Tylor, E. B., *Anthropology*, New Science Library, Hill, N.Y., 1904, pp. 14ff.

he was honest enough to admit that there were known cases of degeneration within the historical period. As a matter of fact, in another work he devoted considerable space to further instances, and to some of the factors which bring such degeneration about. For his more evolutionary minded successors such admissions gave far too much comfort to the enemy and consequently were seldom if ever alluded to in "official" literature until, as we have previously pointed out, there came a gradual revolt among anthropologists against this dogmatic insistence that everything in man's cultural past must have an evolutionary history. There is another fact that better acquaintance with existing primitive people has brought clearly to light which also challenges the view that early man started with little more intelligence than an animal and only after hundreds of thousands of years evolved into a superior and more cultured being. This is the discovery that in spite of all appearances to the contrary, existing primitive people are every bit as intelligent as we are and in many cases a whole lot wiser. It is customary to suppose that early man was so slow in improving his lot because he was at first little more intelligent than the other primates, whose world he shared, Not till an immense period of time had passed did he have sufficient intelligence to settle in one spot and make a serious attempt to control his environment by domestication of plants and animals, replacing a nomadic life by a settled one. But we know now that the lowest of all primitive people of recent times are every bit as educable as ourselves, the difference being one of environment, training, and opportunity.

Loren Eiseley in an article reviewing Darwin's ideas about the development of man's brain pointed out that Wallace himself long ago admitted men with simple cultures possess the same basic intellectual powers which the Darwinians maintained could only be developed by competitive struggle. This struggle was conceived of as having been a very greatly extended one, but as Eiseley remarked:[101]

> Natural Selection could only have endowed the savage with a brain little superior to that of an ape, whereas he actually possesses one but little inferior to that of the average of our learned societies. . . .
> Wallace insisted that artistic, mathematical, and musical abilities could not be explained on the basis of Natural Selection and the struggle for existence.

In a similar vein Franz Boas cautioned:[102]

---

[101] Eiseley, Loren C., "Was Darwin Wrong About the Human Brain?" *Harpers*, Nov., 1955, p. 67.

[102] Boas, Franz, *The Mind of Primitive Man*, Macmillan, N.Y., 2nd ed., 1939, pp. 16, 17.

By analogy we associate lower mental traits with brute-like features. In our naive, everyday parlance, brutish features and brutality are closely connected. We must distinguish here, however, between anatomical, muscular development of the face, trunk and limbs due to habits of life....We are also inclined to draw inferences in regard to mentality from a receding forehead, a heavy jaw, large and heavy teeth, perhaps even from inordinate length of arms or an unusual development of hairiness.

It appears neither cultural achievement nor outer appearance is a safe basis on which to judge the mental aptitude of races.

In one of the Oxford pamphlets on World Affairs, Sir Alfred Zimmern makes the interesting point that the reverse is also true, namely, that in our own culture "every baby that is born...is a Stone Age baby."[103] The significance of this is that human potentialities have never really changed either for good or for ill. In spite of all appearances to the contrary, you and I are not one bit more gifted by nature than a baby born in a contemporary primitive society. Zimmern was attempting to underscore the fact that a modern European (he had in mind the Nazis) can be by nature as savage as any "savage." A higher "culture" does not mean superior intelligence. Nor, by the same token, does a lower culture signify a lower intelligence. Many recent writers have stressed this point. Thus Nicholson recently reviewing a work by Oscar Lewis, *Five Families: Mexican Case Studies in the Culture of Poverty*, concluded from the evidence:[104]

> The progress from poverty to riches is a progress from deep to shallow religious perception, from more to less serious reading, from earthy to diseased sexual problems, and from a kind of rough contentment based on a full day's work to an almost constant cantankerousness resulting from artificial pleasures and twisted values.
> This trend should give food for thought to those who still believe that the trend from an underdeveloped to a developed economy is necessarily and in itself desirable.

Moreover, part of the awakened interest in this subject has been due to the fact that World War II revealed how utterly inhuman so-called "civilized" man could be, the more inhuman as he is the better educated. E. J. Holmyard in an editorial on this point remarked:[105]

> That the average man of 1946 is very much better informed than his predecessors of even a century ago must surely be ascribed to better methods for the dissemination of knowledge rather than to an increased power of assimilating it. And it can hardly be disputed that one of the chief reasons for our present troubles is this wide extension

---

[103] Zimmern, Sir Alfred, *The Prospects of Civilization*, Oxford Pamphlets on World Affairs, No. 1, Oxford, 1940, p. 23.
[104] Nicholson, I., Book reviews, *Discovery*, London, Dec., 1959, p. 540.
[105] Holmyard, E. J., "The Future of Man," *Endeavour*, Imp. Chem. Indust. Ltd., London, Jan., 1946, p. 2.

of knowledge to people whose minds are not sufficiently cultured to make proper use of it.

We have to be careful how we judge lower cultures when we have information only about the simplicity of their weapons and commodities. There is plenty of evidence that their children make first class, and sometimes superior, scholars when given opportunity.[106] The same must apply to Early Man. As Kenneth Oakley has recently pointed out:[107]

> We have no reason to infer that all Early Paleolithic men had brains qualitatively inferior to those of the average man today. The simplicity of their culture can be accounted for by the extreme sparseness of the population and their lack of accumulated knowledge. A supposed hallmark of the mind of Homo sapiens is the artistic impulse, but archaeological evidence suggests that this trait manifested itself almost at the dawn of tool making.

As a matter of fact, it is instructive to turn the tables upon ourselves and learn what primitive people have sometimes thought of the White Man — when he could be persuaded to express his opinion in spite of the restraint of his own natural politeness. Consider, for example, the reply delivered to the Virginia Commission in 1744 when that worthy Body offered to educate six Indian youths in William and Mary College.[108]

> Several of our young people were formally brought up in colleges of the Northern Provinces: they were instructed in all your sciences; but when they came back to us, they were bad runners, ignorant of every means of living in the woods, unable to bear either cold or hunger, knew neither how to build a cabin, take a deer, or kill an enemy, spoke our language imperfectly, were therefore neither fit for hunters, warriors, or councillors; they were totally good for nothing.
> We are, however, not the less obliged by your kind offer, though we decline accepting it; and to show our grateful sense of it, if the gentlemen of Virginia will send us a dozen of their sons, we will take great care of their education, instruct them in all we know, and make men of them.

It is not stated in the source from which I obtained this interesting quotation whether any young men of Virginia took advantage of the offer of being properly educated. It shows, however, that we may be so frightfully culture-bound that we fail to see in a primitive society any of the real values which exist there and how lacking they may

---

[106] A whole series of such "experiments" will be found cited by J. Mildred Creed in *Nineteenth Century*, 7 (1905) : 89 ff. See also *Nature* (England), 40 (1889) : 634. The interest at the time was much greater than it is now, since the fact was so unexpected.

[107] Oakley, Kenneth, "The Evolution of Human Skill," in *A History of Technology*, Vol. I, ed. by Singer, Holmyard and Hall, Oxford, 1957, p. 27.

[108] Quoted from Wallbank and Taylor, *Civilization — Past and Present*, Vol. 1, Scott Firesman, Chicago, 1942, pp. 499 and 500.

actually be in our own. We look upon such people as grown-up children playing rather foolish games, easily angered and generally immature in their behavior. It may, therefore, come as a surprise to read the following assessment of the White Man made to Rasmussen by an Eskimo.[109]

> It is generally believed that White Men have quite the same mind as small children. Therefore one should always give way to them. They are easily angered, and when they cannot have their will they are moody, and like children have the strangest ideas and fancies.

In her book *Ishi, a Biography of the Last Wild Indian in North America,* Mrs. Theodora Kroeber writes a very sensitive appraisal of a truly "primitive" man, who survived only by accident into the modern world. She and her husband (A. L. Kroeber) established complete rapport with this remarkable and gentle man, and as a result, were able to discern his genuine impressions of the White Man who came as a total stranger to him as he did to them. He considered the White Man to be "fortunate, inventive, and very, very clever: but child-like and lacking in a desirable reserve and in a true understanding of Nature." Just before he died (in 1916) he reaffirmed his view of us as sophisticated indeed but "still only children— smart but not wise."[110] And this man was a representative of a people we took for granted were untaught, superstitious savages, a condition supposedly once characteristic of our own prehistoric forebears.

And just to keep the record straight early Britons, when they were first contacted by the Romans, were looked upon much as we have looked upon our primitive contemporaries. Cicero wrote back to Rome:[111]

> Do not obtain your slaves from Britain because they are so stupid and so utterly incapable of being taught that they are not fit to form part of the Household of Athens.

This might be another way of looking at the old battle cry, "Britons never, never, never shall be slaves." Much more recently the African native has begun to find courage enough, and words, to express his candid view about the White Man. He has never failed to admire our technology but his feelings about our cultural behavior are something else. Since the original statement which I have

---

[109] Spoken by an Eskimo named Kuvdluitsoq and quoted in "The Seal Eskimos," by Knud Rasmussen, in *A Reader in General Anthropology,* ed. C. S. Coon, Holt, N.Y., 1948, p. 119.
[110] Kroeber, Theodora, *Ishi: A Biography of the Last Wild Indian in North America,* Univ. California Press, Los Angeles, 1971, pp. 229 and 237.
[111] Cicero, quoted by Kenneth Walker in *Meaning and Purpose,* Penguin Books, England, 1950, p. 147.

in mind here is rather long, the following summary may suffice. The writer was an African native visiting Europe and America.[112] He was genuinely shocked at the manner in which children are not only allowed but almost encouraged to be disrespectful to their elders. "The white women," he says, "appear to be chattering like birds all the time. Their remarks ... are not to be taken seriously." He observed that the White Man gets all excited and speaks exaggeratedly of things he himself would consider of no particular significance. They are so ill at ease with one another, he felt, that they must be talking all the time, afraid of silence. We think of native people as quite lacking in individualism, but this African gentleman was surprised to find how great was our fear of being thought "different." He further observed, "Men appear even more mysterious. It may seem to us that they even play the role of children in the house. They are looked after very carefully and told what they are supposed to like, to eat, to wear, and to do." He was amazed at the fear of age, which to him was a prerequisite of mature judgment. For all this he was also a wise man for he said, "We know such an interpretation is not accurate, and so we should not attach too much importance to our first general impressions." In this observation he had in mind also to warn the European visitor against premature judgments of native ways based on insufficient understanding.

Such things should serve to correct some rather common preconceptions about people of "lower" cultures in general. If they are as wise and as intelligent as we are and if they do represent prehistoric man in any way, then prehistoric man was no less fully human and wise and intelligent than ourselves. Why, if this is so, did he take so long to develop a civilization? Or, to put the question in a slightly different form, why have his modern counterparts never been known to elevate themselves, except by contact with a higher civilization? The cause for this latter phenomenon has been tentatively identified: namely, that existing or recently extinct primitive societies have reached their conditions by degeneration, and when this condition results, no power of self-recovery remains. Would it not therefore be logical to suppose that Paleolithic cultures were also degenerate fragments resulting from the initial break-up of the high civilization in the Middle East? These prehistoric cultures never did show any progressive development except that which resulted by the subsequent infiltration of later fragments from the core civilization. Of course, such a picture appears to fly in the face of all the chrono-

---

[112] African view: reported under the title, "Different People — Different Ways," in *South African Pioneer*, SAGM, Apr.-June, 1955, p. 15.

logical evidence. To many, this difficulty may appear to be insuperable. We shall leave this aspect of the problem for the present, and only point out that such a reconstruction of prehistory in Europe, Africa and Asia — as well as in the New World — makes remarkably good sense of the available cultural evidence. Moreover, if the initial fragmentation and scattering of mankind resulted in successive waves of migration, some groups of people would inevitably be pressed into the most marginal areas where it is almost certain that individuals or single families might wander even further and die in their isolation reduced to circumstances which would leave them little if anything above the beasts who shared their environment. One might suppose that such oppression would break not only the spirit of man, but physically degrade the human form also, and that for this reason the most primitive fossil remains would be found — as indeed they invariably are — not near the center where man originated, but at the edges where in his final degradation he breathed his last.[113] This might account for the otherwise anomalous fact that the most primitive fossil types, such as Sinanthropus, could still produce flint weapons "sometimes of fine workmanship."[114] Even as he died, thousands of miles away his not too distant relatives were pressing forward toward the creation of some of the most remarkable civilizations that the ancient world ever knew.

How far down the scale can man go when circumstances cause him to be uprooted from the stabilizing influences of the mainstream of culture? And how long is this process likely to take? Exotic arts might be lost readily enough, but is it likely that any people who once had a fair range of *useful* arts would ever abandon them or forget the techniques of their manufacture?

In some ways the New World presents a clearer picture of what can actually happen than the Old, because compared with the total time periods involved in Europe as currently interpreted, the span here is so very much shorter, even if we allow the maximum figures given for human remains and artifacts (i.e., up to 25,000 years or so). The whole interval is certainly less than one tenth of that involved in Europe by such a reckoning, and could even be no more than one twentieth, if Paleolithic times in the Old World lasted for 500,000 years. Actually it is far less than 25,000 years, for the decay of the New World Culture is almost (though not quite) an event of the last 2,000 to 2,500 years at the most.

---

[113] This point is explored further in "The Supposed Evolution of the Human Skull," in this volume.

[114] Sinanthropus' tools: on this point see Marcellin Boule and Henri V. Vallois, *Fossil Men*, Dryden, N.Y., 1957, p. 145, fn. 45.

Moreover, the settlement of the New World by the White Man was accompanied by the gradual eclipse of degradation of a number of aboriginal peoples and such events were chronicled by eyewitnesses at the time. This is strictly a matter of historical record in many cases. We do not have to surmise what would happen if this kind of dislocation took place on a wide scale — we actually know. Sometimes it was the displacement of people still to all intents and purposes at a Stone Age level by others who were much further advanced — a phenomenon which may also have happened though perhaps less dramatically to prehistoric man in Europe if we knew enough. The now generally recognized "contemporaneity of cultures," which were formerly always looked upon as successive, may bear on this. Dawson[115] reports on a case where Paleolithic men were found with Neolithic arrowheads in their bones.

In other instances it was a case of the catastrophic destruction of high civilizations, as in Central America for example, chiefly by duplicity but also by superior weapons. This, too, has happened more than once in history and may account for the disappearance of some African civilizations, such as that which lay behind the ruins of Zimbabwe.[116] In the Island of Yezo,[117] now inhabited only by the primitive Ainu, there are numerous vestiges of large cities, roads, canals, and mines skillfully worked, and other traces of towns and castles embedded in the forests, evidences of a high civilization which may have been desolated as the Indus Valley Cultures were "destroyed" by the "barbaric" Aryans.[118]

Continuing to this day one may still see the gradual extinction of primitive people in the New World such as those of Tierra del Fuego in the extreme south, again chiefly because of the White Man's presence and the introduction of diseases against which the natives had no natural defense. Who knows but what Neanderthal Man disappeared in Europe (if indeed he did) for a similar reason? The reduction in the population of a tribe so situated can be fantastic, even without any actual warfare. Lincoln Barnett says that the Alacalufes, canoe people of the Western Channels, numbered 10,000

---

115 Dawson, J. W., *Fossil Men and Their Modern Representatives*, Hodder and Stoughton, London, 1883, pp. 109, 123.

116 Pollock, David, "Zimbabwe: Mystery of Mashonaland," in *Wonders of the Past*, Vol. III, Putnam, N.Y., pp. 601-605; a very interesting report.

117 Allen, F. A., "On the Evolution of Savages by Degradation," *Trans. Vict. Instit.*, London, 19 (1885-86) : 133.

118 Childe, V. G., "India and the West Before Darius," *Antiquity*, 1939, p. 15: "The Aryans ... are disclosed as the destroyers rather than the creators of the Indian civilization."

in 1831 at the time of Darwin's visit; now there are hardly 100.[119] The Onas, an inland tribe of the Archipelago, were massacred by sheep farmers in quest of grazing land; today only 7 of an original 4,000 are still alive. Such massacres, it seems, occurred in prehistoric times. The prehistoric inhabitants of the Upper Cave at Choukoutien in China, whose fossil remains were found in 1929, seem to have come to such an end.[120]

The Eskimos to the north are in many ways unique because, although they have been looked upon as modern representatives of men of the Old Stone Age, they have proved themselves highly adaptable to new cultural influences. They have always been remarkably inventive and mechanically minded, and in fact the White Man's teacher when it came to his first introduction to an Arctic environment.[121] They are possibly representatives of the people who first entered the New World, probably across the Bering Straits from Siberia to Alaska. These first-comers were presumably the makers of the Folsom, Yuma, and other well-known spear or arrow heads. One has only to examine such weapons to be struck with the skill that went into their manufacture. The work of these craftsmen bears the hallmark of genius: simplicity of design, beauty of form, perfection of workmanship. It is quite clear that the men who made them were not experimenting nor were they simply interested in making "some kind of a point." These are not weapons only, they are works of art — like some of the older rifles — finished with an attention to detail, which speaks volumes for the kind of people who made them. Kenneth Macgowan says of one particular style, "the Yuma point is easily the finest job of flint knapping in the New World and it is equalled only by the later (sic!) Neolithic daggers of Egypt and Scandinavia."[122]

Settlement thereafter throughout the whole of the New World may have been quite rapid, for this particular tool-making industry is found from Alaska to the Southern States. In fact Macgowan suggests that far less time may have been required for some parts of this migratory movement than is usually supposed, even pointing out

[119] Barnett, Lincoln, "Darwin's World of Nature: Part IV. Uttermost Region of the Earth," *Life,* June 1, 1959, p. 68.
[120] All seven people in the Upper Cave at Choukoutien, China, had evidently met violent deaths (*Antiquity,* Notes and News, June, 1939, p. 243).
[121] Ackerknecht, E. H., "The Eskimo's Fight Against Hunger and Cold," *Ciba Symposia,* 10, 1 (July-Aug., 1948): 894, points out that the White Man only survived in the Arctic at first because he accepted the Eskimo's advice on almost every feature of the design of his original equipment and clothing.
[122] Macgowan, Kenneth, *Early Man in the New World,* Macmillan, N.Y., 1950, p. 116.

that it could have taken as little as 20 years to make the trip from Harbin, Manchuria, to Vancouver Island.[123]

At this point of initial entry into the New World, well-organized but small settlements were very early established, and from here man moved down into and across the continent. In the Mississippi Valley and in the Southwest, larger settlements soon appeared and wherever they persisted, colonies sharing a large number of culture-traits mushroomed as explosively as the original Middle East cultures had done. We do not know how it came about that the Mayas, Aztecs, Incas, and others ultimately rose to such a high level, but Raglan suggested a combination of favorable environment, readily available natural resources, and constant contacts with other native cultures.[124] There may, of course, have also been influences from across the Pacific; but the question is far from settled yet.

What we do know, however, is that gradually the tide of development turned, and the levels of culture began to regress everywhere except perhaps in the very center. Possibly the continued retreat of the great ice sheet to the north changed the climate and rendered the land less fertile and more arid. The decay was, of course, greatly accelerated by the coming of the White Man, but, and this is an important point, American Indian tribes of lower culture seem already to have begun to degenerate in pre-Columbian times. Among the numerous monuments of these less well-known aboriginal societies are the huge earth works of the Mound-Builders, one of which is actually the largest pyramid in the world.[125] One enclosure has been found occupying an area of 4 square miles. Tylor mentions their cultivated fields, their pottery and their stone implements, and by comparison he says, "If any of the wild roving hunting tribes now found living near these huge earth works of the Mound Builders are the descendants of this somewhat advanced race, then a very considerable degradation has taken place."[126]

For one reason or another, not one of the original American

<hr>

[123] Ibid., p. 3. On their way, it seems such people created remarkable cultures in Siberia, which were afterwards deserted. The ruins of such settlements were noted long ago by Allen in his paper (referred to in ref. 117 above) p. 132, and more recent reference to one of these "cities" with a central heated palace covering 1,500 sq. yds. appeared in the newspapers (*Hamilton Spectator*, Canada, Jan. 28, 1947). The Russians have now issued an official report entitled, "Ancient Population of Siberia and Its Culture," reviewed in *Science*, 30 (1959): 1467.
[124] Raglan, Lord, "Some Aspects of Diffusion," *Jour. Roy. Anthrop. Instit.*, July-Dec., 1957, p. 147.
[125] Known now as Monk's or Cahokia Mound, near St. Louis, Missouri.
[126] Tylor, E. B., *Primitive Culture*, Vol. I, p. 56.

cultures was able to maintain itself at a high level. Changes of climate, migration induced by an increase in population,[127] or because of disease introduced by newcomers, and by what seems to be a "natural" tendency for more arts to be lost than are newly invented — all these, and other factors, brought a gradual drop in cultural levels all over the continent. Such a generalized pattern of events is summed up by W. J. Perry who wrote:[128]

> We find in the region of northern Mexico and Arizona which is rich in ruins of the settlements of people who had installed great irrigation systems along the sides of canons, that the present-day Indian tribes are in no way the equals of their predecessors, culturally speaking. Throughout this area, as well as in Mexico and Central America, there are numerous tribes who live amidst the ample traces of ruins of a vanished past of which they have but little knowledge. . . .
>
> It is found as an invariable rule that, as time goes on, the cultural level in all parts of North America consistently drops. One element of culture after another is lost.

It is true that this was originally written in 1926, and it is true also that Perry was a "diffusionist," with rather exaggerated views about the importance to the world of Egyptian Civilization, nevertheless, since he wrote, archaeological research in the New World has only tended to confirm his impressions of a steady decline.

Roland B. Dixon stresses the fact that this decline had already begun prior to the White Man's coming, i.e., in pre-Columbian times. Some ferment was at work uprooting the older cultures and causing widespread movements of whole tribes. He pointed out:[129]

> The semiagricultural and sedentary Woodland tribes of Algonkian and Siouian stock, abandoning their former habitat, moved westward out into the Plains, lost agriculture, pottery making, and their semi-sedentary mode of life, and became buffalo-hunting nomads.

And he adds that widespread dislocations in the center had repercussions even in the very tip of South America. As he says,[130] "The Yaghans appear to have been crowded into this inclement and harsh environment and there to have retrograded somewhat and lost some of their cultural traits such as the bow which they once possessed."

---

[127] Cunningham Geikie refers to a statement of an Admiral Osborn who observed that a tribe wandering along the extreme northern edge of the Siberian coast had recently driven another tribe across the Frozen Sea to an island lying so far north that only its mountain tops could be seen from the Siberian headlands. This was entirely the result of a chain-effect, due to a population increase on the mainland (*Hours With The Bible,* Vol. I, Alden, N.Y., 1886, p. 134).

[128] Perry, W. J., ref. 41, p. 136 and p. 123.

[129] Dixon, Roland B., *The Building of Cultures,* Scribners, N.Y., 1928, p. 280.

[130] Ibid.

Considering that Tierra del Fuego abounds with trees, one wonders how on earth a people could lose the art of making bows, but the loss of pottery seems equally surprising. Pottery is found everywhere in Iroquois and other sites in Ontario, New York State, etc., yet it, too, became a lost art here just as it had among the Plains Indians of whom Dixon speaks. This would have seemed a most unlikely occurrence since pottery vessels are of all things the most common possessions of "rich" and poor alike, but evidently such has been the case on a number of occasions, and this only goes to show how easily lost even the most useful of arts may be, when a society is dislocated and forced to move into a new environment. Humphrey Johnson has put it:[131]

> The anthropologists of the latter half of the last century, so obsessed with the idea of the evolution of culture, were too prone to denounce as reactionaries those who believed that cultural degeneration had occurred alongside of it. This attitude was still dominant when the present century began, and as late as 1911 Sir E. B. Tylor was able to write, "Had the Australians or New Zealanders, for example, ever possessed the potter's art they could hardly have forgotten it." Yet, only the very next year Dr. W. H. Rivers, one of the leading ethnologists of his day, addressing the British Association voiced a view diametrically opposed to it. "In many parts of Oceania," he said, "there is evidence that objects so useful as the canoe, pottery, and the bow and arrow, have once been present where they are now unknown or exist only in degenerate form. . . . Some of the widely accepted theories of anthropology depend on the assumption, which rests on the application of our utilitarian standards of conduct to cultures widely different from our own, has been shown to be without justification."

In another part of the world, the Bushmen of the Cape region, like the North American Indians and the Polynesians, lost the art of making pottery when they were driven south by the Bantu.[132] Originally the Bushmen were *exceedingly* fine artists.[133] Today their artistic production is virtually nil.

Of the Polynesians, Dixon wrote:[134]

> There is no evidence anywhere in Polynesia that pottery was ever made, yet the ancestors of the Polynesian people in their earlier Indonesian home probably were in possession of the art, and one can see no adequate reason why the manufacture of this useful product should have been given up. But lost the art certainly was, and so thoroughly that not even a tradition of it now remains.

---

[131] Johnson, Humphrey J. T., *The Bible and the Early History of Mankind*, rev. ed., London, 1947, pp. 70f. An R. C. publication.

[132] Wendt, Herbert, *I Looked For Adam*, Weidenfeld and Nicolson, London, 1955, p. 393; Rivers, W. H., *The Disappearance of Useful Arts*, Brit. Assoc. Report, 1912, pp. 598, 599; Raglan, Lord, *Home Came Civilization*, Methuen, London, 1939, p. 35.

[134] Dixon, R. B., ref. 129, p. 147.

[133] Adam, Leonard, *Primitive Art*, Penguin Books, England, 1949, p. 97.

Whatever was the cause for its abandonment by the Bushmen, it is likely that in the case of Polynesia the volcanic islands had no suitable material for pottery making, as Prince John Loewenstein recently pointed out.[135] The Plains Indians perhaps became altogether too nomadic to be able to take the time to build the necessary furnaces, etc.

Here, then, we see the loss of two cultural elements which would appear to be of great value and importance — the bow (which vastly increased man's effective range of attack on his enemies or for the taking of game), and pottery which is both inexpensive in terms of raw materials, highly useful for storage of water and other products, and for cooking, etc., as well as providing plenty of scope for man to express his artistic impulses. In each case the loss was due to dislocation of the culture, resulting in the disappearance of the original skills or the absence of suitable material in the new environment.

Sometimes isolation is sufficient in itself to bring about the decay and final disappearance entirely of almost every art by which man is to be distinguished from the animals. The Tasmanians enjoyed one of the finest temperate climates in the world and animal life abounded. Their island is well watered, fertile, and amply supplied with wood. Yet they were unquestionably the lowest of any people known to modern man. Why? George Murdock[136] said, "Not climate or topography, but isolation is responsible for this condition." Fish abounded, yet they had entirely lost the art of fishing, nets and fishhooks being unknown to them. Sollas said:[137]

> The primitive ancestors of the race may have been widely distributed over the Old World: displaced almost everywhere by superior races, they at length became confined to Australia and Tasmania, and from Australia they were finally driven and partly perhaps absorbed or exterminated by the existing aborigines of that continent who were prevented from following them into Tasmania because by that time Bass Strait was wide enough to offer an insuperable barrier to their advance.

So complete was the break that both the bow and arrow, and the boomerang, were entirely lost.

Contrary to some popular accounts, the Tasmanians still had fire. But there is at least one tribe, the Pygmies of the Epilu River of Central Africa, who although they *use* fire still do not make it for

[135] Lowenstein, Prince John, "Who First Settled Polynesia," *The Listener,* BBC, London, Apr. 23, 1959, p. 712.
[136] Murdock, George P., *Our Primitive Contemporaries,* Macmillan, N.Y., 1951, p. 1.
[137] Sollas, W. J., "The Tasmanians," in *The Making of Man,* ed. by Calverton, Modern Library, Random House, N.Y., 1931, p. 87.

themselves. They "purchase" it from neighbors.[138] If they should ever become as isolated as the Tasmanians, it seems likely they would lose it entirely, for they seem quite unwilling or uninterested in learning to make it for themselves. Whatever the reason for this, the dependence on others is there even in such a basic element of civilization as the making of fire, and separation from the source of supply would rob them of it altogether. To revert to my original analogy of a very sick man, it is as though the patient had not merely lost the ability to recover but even the will to do so, for it appears from Montagu that they do not even *want* to learn how to make fire.

In many cases the loss is not sudden but gradual. The art decays until the product is no longer useful and in time it is discarded. Any "natural tendency" for techniques to improve with time simply is not there. It *looks* as though things always improve, as though the new is better than the old, but this is apt to be true only of those cultures which have maintained a vital connection with the original main stream. The examples of trait degeneration which could be given are simply legion. In Britain, after pottery first appeared it thereafter steadily declined.[139] Early Neolithic pottery in Europe, both in richness of form and technique, contrasts sharply with the lesser achievements of later Neolithic times.[140] In Thessaly, the earlier pottery is far superior to that of subsequent generations.[141]

Other arts tend to follow the same pattern. Early Navaho weavers were far more skillful than their descendants, and their techniques were much more complex and varied.[142] The art of making gold jewelry was lost by the Indian tribes of Central America.[143] Schliemann found the bronze age at Hissarlik (Troy) was at a level below the Stone Age, thus reversing the "normal" order of cultural evolution,[144] just as the very high Minoan Civilization degraded to a neolithic level after the breakdown of the culture for some still un-

---

[138] Montagu, Ashley, *Man: His First Million Years*, Mentor Books, N.Y., 1958, p. 159.
[139] Scott, Sir Lindsay, "Pottery," in *A History of Technology*, Vol. I, ed. by Singer et al, Oxford, 1954, p. 377.
[140] MacCurdy, George G., reviewing *Le Neolithique Lacustre Ancien*, in *Amer. Jour. of Archaeol.*, July-Sept., 1935, p. 413.
[141] Hanson, Hazel D., *Early Civilization in Thessaly*, Johns Hopkins Press, Baltimore, 1933, pp. 44 and 72.
[142] Stirling, Matthew, "Indian Tribes of Pueblo Land," *Nat. Geog. Mag.*, Nov., 1940, p. 571.
[143] Dawson, Sir J. W., ref. 115, p. 147.
[144] Schliemann, Heinrich, reported by Frank S. de Hass in *Buried Cities Recovered*, Bradley Garretson, Phila., 1884, pp. 509, 510. Schliemann's interpretation of the levels may have been misguided, but the reversal of the expected order was never in doubt.

ascertained reason.[145] One of the first stone axes in the world, a truly beautiful object, came from one of the lowest levels of Troy.[146] The culture of the Swiss Lake Dwellers during the Stone Age degenerated as time went on.[147] The earliest remains of Eskimo culture in Alaska were often superior to their present achievements, except where contacts with the White Man have inspired or provoked new techniques.[148] As already noted, the finest points in the New World were made at the first, not at the last, just as in Egypt some of the earliest flint weapons were unexcelled and never subsequently approached for technical perfection. Degradation of civilization is amply born out by the gigantic ruins in Java and Cambodia.[149] In Abyssinia and the Anglo-Egyptian Sudan there is everywhere evidence of a once high civilization with immense stone structures about which the present inhabitants know nothing.[150] In northeast Kenya, wells and cairns abound which are never made by the present natives.[151] Well-fortified villages are found in West Central Angola, quite beyond the abilities of the present natives there.[152] The Transvaal tells the same story, and so does the coastal region of West Africa, especially near Gambia.[153] In Nigeria in the Bauchi country,[154] there are numerous stone bridges and walled cities but the present inhabitants no longer build with stone at all. In Uganda, Tanganyika, and elsewhere, are ruins of systems of terraced cultivation abandoned probably at least 800 years ago and quite beyond the capabilities of the present inhabitants of these areas.[155] Within the terraced area in Kenya are what appear to be lines of carefully graded ancient roads,

---

[145] See on this the review by S. Casson of J. S. Pendlebury, "The Archaeology of Crete," in *Antiquity*, Dec., 1939, pp. 482ff., and in the same issue, "The Volcanic Destruction of Minoan Crete," by Sp. Marinatos, pp. 425-439. Also, Pendlebury, *Palace of Minos: Knossos*, Parrish, London, 1954, p. 36.

[146] Pictured in a beautiful photograph, illustrating a note, "Battle Axes From Troy," *Antiquity*, Sept., 1933, p. 337.

[147] Reported in *Science*, 90 (1939) : 10. Their earlier pottery was "a magnificent product," their later potter — and general economy — was far inferior.

[148] Hrdlicka, Ales, "Where Asia and America Meet," in *Asia*, June, 1939, pp. 354 ff.; Rainey, Froelich G., "Discovery of Alaska's Oldest Arctic Town," *Nat. Geog. Mag.*, Sept., 1942, pp. 319 ff.

[149] Smith, Sir G. Elliot, *In the Beginning*, Watts, London, 1946, p. 21.

[150] Evans-Pritchard, E., "Megalithic Grave-Monuments in the Anglo-Egyptian Sudan and Other Parts of East Africa," *Antiquity*, June, 1935, pp. 151 to 160.

[151] Watson, C. B. G., in *Man*, Roy. Anthrop. Instit., 1927, p. 30.

[152] Hambly, W. D., *Source Book For African Ethnology*, Publication Nos. 394 and 396, Field Museum, Anthropology Series, Chicago, Vol. XXVI, Part 1, p. 154.

[153] Lowe, C. van Riet, *Jour. Roy. Anthrop. Instit.*, 1927, p. 227.

[154] Justice, J. N., in *Man*, Roy. Anthrop. Instit., 1922, p. 3.

[155] Wilson, G. E. H., in *Man*, Roy. Anthrop. Instit., 1932, p. 45.

but Africans today never make roads except under the influence of and using the White Man's machines.[156]

In religious beliefs and practices, the same sad story prevails. According to Rivers,[157] one of the most primitive tribes in India, the Toda, probably arrived in that country with well-defined religious beliefs which have since become completely meaningless to them. Among the Digger Indians of California,[158] ancient fragments of a higher religious faith were preserved until recently without any knowledge of their original meaning, including the putting of shoes at the feet of the dead, a practice which they could no longer explain. Thomas Bridges noted that the Yaghan had a word for "death" which meant "to go up or fly," but by 1870 they had no conscious conception of a hereafter.[159] In South Africa some tribes were reported in 1873 which appeared to have no religious beliefs whatever, yet some of the older men used the word "Morimo," which had apparently been employed by their forefathers to describe the Great Spirit.[160] But these same old men attached no definite idea to it at all. Here we have four primitive cultures, the Toda of India, the Digger Indians of California, the Yaghans of the tip of South America, and certain unnamed primitive people of South Africa (quite possibly Bushmen), all of whom had degenerated in their religious beliefs almost to the point of being without religion at all.

Now Perry thought that the settlement of the New World was merely one aspect of a very general migration from the original Cultural Center of mankind, which led in due time to the initial peopling of every corner of the globe as the Middle East populations expanded:[161]

> This movement took 3,000 years, more or less, to accomplish its journey, but it can be traced with fair accuracy for thousands of miles. . . . The distribution of culture can obviously have been the outcome of a great process of growth from the center, the effect of the stimulus growing fainter as the original focus became more remote. . . .
> The demonstrable fact that degradation of culture, and not advance, is the rule in so many of the outlying parts of the world makes it more probable than ever that civilization began in one place. . . .
> Transplantation involves dislocation, the proper workmen are not there, they have not the requisite skill or knowledge and the

---

[156] Huntingford, G. W. B., in *Man,* Roy. Anthrop. Instit., 1932, p. 45.

[157] Rivers, W. H. R., quoted by G. P. Murdock, *Our Primitive Contemporaries,* Macmillan, N.Y., 1951, p. 133.

[158] Coon, C. S., *A Reader in General Anthropology,* Holt, N.Y., 1948, p. 77.

[159] Ibid., p. 98.

[160] Stated by a Mr. C. Graham, in the discussion of James Reddie "On Civilization: Moral and Material," *Trans. Vict. Instit.,* London, 6 (1872-73) : 35.

[161] Perry, W. J., ref. 41, p. 123.

product is inferior. Even in the country of origin the product is not always maintained at the original level. The Egyptians only made their wonderful stone vessels in their full perfection for a few centuries; the craft was destined to languish. Painted pottery in Susa soon degenerated and finally disappeared. Innumerable instances could be quoted of this process.

Thus he echoes more forcibly the reluctant admission of Tylor quoted above (p. 69), and underscores again the fact that such degeneration tends always to accompany migration, especially when it is under pressure from behind and even more particularly when the new environment is harsher than the old. History is full of instances of it. George Rawlinson, for instance, remarked:[162]

> While progress is the more ordinary process or at any rate the one which most catches the eye when it roves at large, there are not wanting indications that the process is reversed occasionally. Herodotus tells us of the Geloni, a Greek people, who having been expelled from the cities on the northern coast of the Euxine, had retired into the interior and there lived in wooden huts and spoke a language half Greek and half Scythian. By the time of Mela this people had become completely barbarous and used the skins of those slain by them in battle as covering for themselves and their horses. A gradual degradation of the Greco-Bactrian people is evident in the series of their coins which is extant and which has been carefully edited by the late H. H. Wilson and by Major Cunningham. The modern Copts are very degraded descendants of the ancient Egyptians, and the Roumans of Wallachia have fallen away very considerably from the level of the Dacian colonists of Trajan.

Similarly, Dr. W. Cooke, writing some years ago of how separation from the centers of civilization may bring people very rapidly into a state of barbarism, illustrated his point by the following reference:[163]

> The Greenlanders, it is believed, at an early period used metals, but after ceasing to have intercourse with Europeans for about 300 years, sank down to the use of implements of bone and wood and stone. Sir John Lubbock speaking of the Australians, says that in a cave on the West Coast of that country, there are tolerably correct figures of sharks, porpoises, turtles, lizards, canoes, etc., and yet the present natives of the country are incapable not only of producing similar imitations, but even of realizing the most vivid artistic representations as the work of man, and they ascribe the drawings in the cave to diabolic agency.

In 1787 *The Bounty* under Captain Blight set sail for the Island Tahiti in the South Seas, to transplant food-bearing trees to uninhabited islands in the same group in order to make them more habitable, and so to add to the King's dominions. After a voyage of

---

[162] Rawlinson, George, *The Origin of Nations*, Scribners, N.Y., 1878, p. 4.
[163] Cooke, W., *The Alleged Antiquity of Man*, Hamilton Adams, 1872, p. 99.

ten months, the ship arrived at her destination and a further six months were spent collecting bread-fruit palm saplings. The sailors, meanwhile, had formed strong attachments with the native girls and, upon receiving the order to embark, they mutinied, sent the captain and a few men adrift in an open boat, and returned to the island. Captain Blight, however, survived his ordeal and eventually arrived home in England from whence a punitive expedition was sent out which captured fourteen of the mutineers. But nine had transferred to another island where they formed a new colony. Here, in the language of the Encyclopedia Britannica, they degenerated so rapidly and became so fierce as to make the life of the colony a hell on earth. Quarrels, orgies, and murders were a common feature of their life. Finally all the native men and all the white men except one were killed or had died off. Alexander Smith alone was left with a crowd of native women and half-breed children. So quickly can the cultural influences of a society be lost.

In the 17th Century, the Dutch held Formosa for 38 years until driven out by the pirate Coxinga, who in turn had to cede it to the Chinese.[164] It is said that during their stay the Dutch "civilized" the aboriginal tribes, but when they left the latter returned to a worse savagery than ever, even to cannibalism, resembling thenceforth the Dyaks of Borneo and the Malay Polynesians. This is a remarkable commentary on 2 Peter 2:22. Some of these people were even taught to read and write, but they entirely lost the art within about a hundred years. What deeds and contracts remained came to be treasured very greatly, though completely unintelligible to the owners.[165]

Evidently piracy contributed not a little to the degenerative process by disrupting long established cultures. According to Tylor, the very primitive Orang Samba,[166] who have no agriculture and no boats (though they live near the sea), give a remarkable account of themselves that they are descendants of shipwrecked Malays from the Bugis country, but were so harassed by pirates that they gave up civilization and cultivation, and vowed not to eat fowls because they betrayed their presence by crowing. So they plant nothing, but eat wild fruit and vegetables, and all animals but the fowl. "This," observed Tylor, "if at all founded on fact, is an interesting case of degeneration."

The same authority records another striking instance of comparatively recent degeneration:[167]

---

[164] "Formosa and Its Pirate Chief," in *Times,* London, Feb. 9, 1885.
[165] Allen, F. A., ref. 117, p. 140.
[166] Tylor, E. B., ref. 98, Vol. 1, p. 52.
[167] Ibid., p. 47.

The degradation of the Cheyenne Indians is a matter of history. Persecuted by their enemies the Sioux, and dislodged at last even from their fortified village, the heart of the tribe was broken. Their numbers were thinned, they no longer dared to establish themselves in a permanent abode, they gave up the cultivation of the soil, and became a tribe of wandering hunters, with horses for their only valuable possession, which every year they bartered for a supply of corn, beans, pumpkins, and European merchandise, and then returned into the heart of the prairies. When in the Rocky Mountains, Lord Milton and Dr. Cheadle came upon an outlying fragment of the Shushwap race without horses or dogs, sheltering themselves under rude temporary slants of bark or matting, falling year by year into lower misery, and rapidly dying out; this is another example of the degeneration which no doubt has lowered or destroyed many a savage people.

How far can man degenerate? How much further could some of these tribes conceivably go? How long is the process likely to take? In some of the more recent historically attested cases it was a matter of one or two generations only. Is it likely that useful arts will be lost? It seems so: indeed, in a few instances almost the only thing left to distinguish man from the lower animals has been the retention of the powers of speech, since no tribe has ever been known to lack a full and sufficient means of verbal communication.

If one further question should be asked, In what circumstances is this degenerative process most likely to occur? — the answer seems clear enough: *emigration, under pressure, into an unfamiliar environment, of a people who once have known a high civilization.* Each of these factors is a specific component in the total picture. Each of these factors was almost inevitably in operation if the early history of mankind was as recorded in Scripture.

Surely in the face of the evidence, it is difficult to see how civilization could ever have evolved at all if early man was to all intents and purposes like our primitive contemporaries; situated in an environment that was no less hostile and may have been much colder. If man had not been originally provided with special endowments of a high order by his Creator, could he ever have survived?

Chapter 4
Some Considerations, Some
Causes, and Some Conclusions

STUDENTS OF prehistoric times who occupy themselves with imaginative reconstructions of man's origin and original estate at a time when he was very little removed from the animals, never fail to stress the idea that his position must have been precarious in the extreme. Compared with the other creatures who competed with him for possession of the earth, he is pictured as a pretty poor animal. Without either a natural covering or dependable instincts, with a long period of almost complete helplessness in childhood, and a population growth rate far below that of most other species, he was, as Kipling said of Mowgli, "indeed a naked frog."

Even granting that his superior intelligence made up somewhat for other physical deficiencies in this unequal engagement, his energies must have been so completely occupied with the problems of mere survival that he could have had no more free energy for the creation of culture than his supposed modern counterparts among lower primitive peoples have had. Grahame Clark expressed this limitation very forcibly:[168]

> The basic characteristic of savagery is dependence on wild sources of food supply with all the disadvantages that this implies. The idea that savages enjoy some advantage over civilized man through consuming only "natural" foods is very far removed from the truth, when in fact we find among them an "extremely wide prevalence of malnutrition, deficiency diseases, and a general lack of resistance to infection" (A. I. Richards, "Land, Labour, and Diet in Northern Rhodesia," London, 1939, p. 1), not to mention a low average output of energy. The ever-present fear of starvation causes the bulk of economic effort to be turned directly to the quest for food, the chief occupation of every active member of the community. This preoccupation with the basis of subsistence combined with a low average of vitality, is of itself sufficient to set narrow limits to the possibilities of cultural achievement under a state of savagery....

[168] Clark, Grahame, *From Savagery to Civilization,* Cobbett Press, London, 1946, p. 28.

> The low cultural status of savage societies can best be illustrated by considering the amount of energy at their disposal.... Taking one man-power as the equivalent of one-tenth horsepower, and making due allowance for infants, the aged, and the sick, we arrive at one horsepower as a fair measure for the maximum energy of the largest social groups normally encountered under conditions of savagery....
>
> It has to be remembered also that not even this meager supply was adequately applied among men subject to a greater or lesser degree of malnutrition and incapable of long sustaining labor.

Hypothetical as such figures are, I think they are at least of the right order. In experimental work, my own findings are that one-sixteenth horsepower of work sustained for an hour or so requires a man to be in good shape. The figure of one-tenth horsepower given by Clark is, if anything, on the high side. Yet consider the average home as we know it. There may be at least one small electric motor of one-eighth horsepower and probably of one-quarter horsepower in a mixer or floor-polisher, and we employ this "to save ourselves the work involved," even though we have all the food and rest one could ask for. In other words, with every advantage of modern living from the mechanical point of view, we still find mixing a cake or whipping cream a burden sufficient to justify the use of a power-source, and in the New World at least, a floor-polisher has now become almost a "necessity." For all this, we may still find ourselves with hardly sufficient energy to sew on a button. Yet somehow we imagine that people who must be hunting for food perhaps 75% of their time would have all kinds of free energy to build a civilization by the continual improvement of their own circumstances, and this without the stimulation (or provocation) of the example of the "Jones" next door!

Lyell formulated the principle that in seeking to explain geological phenomena we ought not to make any appeal to the action of forces which cannot be shown to be operating at the present time. If this rule were to be applied to prehistory, we would be hard put to find anything within the historic period to support current reconstructions of the origins of civilization. One must conclude that such reconstructions are therefore figments of the imagination; philosophical concepts, not scientific ones. Yet virtually no one apparently feels there is really any difficulty in squaring current theories with knows facts. Sir Francis Galton, in his justly famous work *Hereditary Genius,* had no hesitation whatever in asserting:[169]

> My view is corroborated by the conclusion reached at the end of each of many independent lines of ethnological research — that the

---

[169] Galton, Sir Francis, *Hereditary Genius,* Watts, London, 1950 reprint, p. 337.

human race were utter savages in the beginning; and that, after
myriads of years of barbarism, man has but very recently found his
way into the paths of morality and civilization.

And very few would quarrel with him today. The emphasis is laid
on the superiority of man's brain, though how this came about is not
quite clear. But it is held that in this, and in this alone, lies the
secret of the appearance of culture, that phenomenon of human ac
tivity which is uniquely his and entirely lacking among the animals
C. E. M. Joad argued that this intellectual superiority was more than
merely a greater cleverness.[170] It included also man's moral and his
artistic sense; the former being important because man's long child
hood, so greatly to his advantage in extending his period of teachable
ness and flexibility, was a great gain only because man was also
capable of willingly making the necessary sacrifices for his children
to advance themselves even beyond his own capabilities during this
learning period. Animals permit their young to learn up to their
level of learning, but not beyond this point if they can prevent it. As
soon as an animal offspring shows any signs of having achieved
superiority over the parents, the latter will if possible see to it that
the process stops right there. For various reasons, man has the capacity
of sacrificing his own interests and by this making progress of this
kind possible. His artistic sense led to the development ultimately of
symbolic forms of communication and opened the way for the intro
duction of writing, that great extender of knowledge and spur to
cultural advance.

But, true though all this may be, it does not *really* solve any
thing, because virtually all authorities are also agreed that the human
brain evolved by very small stages and therefore in the beginning
when the test was most severe, the superiority would also be exceed
ingly slight. Everything might work out very reasonably once the
first critical period was over, but how did man survive this period.
Somewhere there had to be a first man and a first woman who were
of the species Homo sapiens. If they were evolved, these two, what
were they like when they first arrived on the scene as newborn infants?

It is possible, of course, that some kind of half-man and half-ape
creature might have wandered away from his immediate family and
"parental" influences, and thereafter have continued his evolution
alone thus establishing a new species, Homo sapiens. But this is
surely a very hypothetical and unlikely event. Quite apart from the
fact that speciation involves a chromosomal change and that such a

---

[170] Joad, C. E. M., *For Civilization,* Macmillan War Pamphlets, No. 7
1940, p. 3 especially and pp. 4-7.

change must have taken place at the same time in at least two such creatures, there are equally serious difficulties to be faced in another direction. Suppose we assume that a baby was born to some primate family whose *brain* was like that of a man but whose *body* was also essentially human (because it is increasingly apparent today that a human brain in an animal body would be a monster and not a man) : what chances of survival would such a strange creature have in such a setting? Are we to imagine that the ape-family is going to make a supreme effort to keep this new man-child alive despite the fact that he must be warmed, fed and guarded for so much longer a period of time than his own generation of "brothers and sisters" who remained apes? And having survived this unusual circumstance and been raised by the extraordinary "forbearance" of all the rest of the band, did he then chance to find that another primate group somewhere nearby had produced, conveniently for him, an equally unusual female child with whom he could mate and thus propagate a new species, the race of man? Probably such a reconstruction would strike most evolutionists as completely absurd. Yet the break had to be made somewhere and no one, as far as I know, has actually attempted seriously to visualize what the first steps would be. The effect of mutations is sudden and if man's qualitatively different brain was suddenly changed, a new situation such as we have postulated seems inescapable at some point along the line.[171] The child who suddenly thought to arm himself with weapons would presumably also think to use them against his own family when food was scarce. Such a child would surely invite disaster and would need to have not only an inventive mind capable of devising a new way of increasing his own fighting strength but also a superior cunning to survive the immediate reaction of a host of contemporaries. It is a mistake to assume that if man had just the right kind of brain at the beginning he could have overcome his other physical deficiencies. So he might, after a period of learning. But the question is whether he could survive while he learned. His brain made him teachable in a unique way, but we cannot look for this first teacher among the animals.

Granted that a body of knowledge and fund of wisdom and experience is at hand, man is beautifully equipped to make the best use of it. But at the beginning this fund did not exist. How did it arise? As we have already noted, primitive people do not tell us much, for they are not progressive. Such people may not be like our

---

[171] It is generally agreed that the possession of language, that "Vehicle of Culture" which is man's peculiar creation, was the result of a "lucky mutation." See on this, A. L. Kroeber, *Anthropology*, Harcourt Brace, N.Y., 1948, p. 71; and Ernst Cassirer, *Essay on Man*, Yale, New Haven, 1948, p. 30.

supposed Paleolithic ancestors, but the reason they are denied this privilege is not because they are "primitive" (which our distant ancestors are also assumed to have been), but because they are found to be as intelligent and as fully human as the rest of us which our earliest ancestors are assumed *not* to have been. But if they were less intelligent than our primitive contemporaries and if the latter do not today show any progressive tendencies, what likelihood is there that they would have or could have created culture in the first place? A superior child has only an advantage in the presence of a superior teacher. Without any teacher whatever such a child is at a disadvantage, as we know from the few authenticated instances of infants deserted by their parents who nevertheless by some strange circumstance survived the experience and were later "captured" as feral children. They have proved conclusively that being human does not mean automatically creating a culture appropriate to human status. All cultured behavior is learned, and in the absence of this learning — in the absence of a teacher — a human being turns out to be something almost less than an animal. Ruth Benedict pointed this out:[172]

> Not one item of man's tribal social organization, of his language, of his local religion, is carried in his germ cell. In Europe, in other centuries, when children were occasionally found who had been abandoned and had maintained themselves in forests apart from human beings, they were all so much alike that Linnaeus classified them as a distinct species Homo ferus, and supposed that they were a kind of gnome that man seldom ran across.
>
> He could not conceive that these half-witted brutes were born human, these creatures with no interest in what went on about them, with organs of speech and hearing that could hardly be trained to do service, who withstood freezing weather in rags and plucked potatoes out of boiling water without discomfort. There is no doubt, of course, that they were children abandoned in infancy, and what they had all of them lacked was association with their kind through whom alone man's faculties are sharpened and given form.

But this is exactly what must have been the position of the first child to be born a human being of animal parents.

Rightly understood, this one fact disqualifies from serious consideration any other view of human origins than the biblical one. How is it that anyone can imagine some evolutionary process accidentally casting up a creature so unlike its parents that it would almost certainly be ejected from the band the very moment its "differentness" was recognized by the rest of the family, promptly going out and finding a mate with whom to create a new order of society on a human level ... when such feral children as have been authenticated could hardly be deserving to be called human at all and were

---

[172] Benedict, Ruth, *Patterns of Culture*, Mentor Books, N.Y., 1951, p. 11.

in many respects far less fitted to survive just because they *were* human beings and not animals.

Some years ago James Reddie stated the case rather eloquently:[173]

> What I argue is that all nature has a beauty and perfection and fitness of its own exhibited in every element and in every plant and every animal, save man; we are bound from analogy to argue that as the ant, the bee, the spider, the beaver, the elephant, the dog, have each their peculiar and marvellous instincts and intelligence adapted to their nature and place in creation, so man — when originally created — would surely in like manner come perfect from the hand of his Creator with an intelligence and an enlightened reason adapted to his superior place in creation. If not, we should have a solecism in nature: in other words, it is unnatural and irrational to come to such a strange conclusion.

Reddie continues by pointing out that man *is* now a solecism and only because the very quality which constitutes his superiority in creation is, in his present state, the cause of most of his anxieties. In other words, man realizes his superiority only if he is willing to listen to a superior Teacher. By nature he no longer has any claim to this higher status, it being a potential rather than a real one. At the very beginning it was entirely real, but because of his fallen condition, he has continually tended to lose it by degeneration. At the first the Creator gave him sufficient instruction to provide the initial impetus for him almost immediately to take steps towards achieving his appointed dominion over the earth. That his brain could easily have been capable of receiving such instruction in spite of the simplicity which must have characterized his culture at first is admitted by some of the best authorities. The earliest prehistoric men were not essentially any different in this respect from ourselves. Robert Braiffault put it:[174]

> It may be doubted whether the modern civilized individual differs greatly as regards inherited capacities from his ancestors of the Stone Age; the difference between savagedom and civilization is not organic (i.e., it is circumstantial). The increase in our knowledge of ancient types of man has, in some respects, accentuated rather than attenuated the abruptness of the transition from animal to human: the oldest human remains and the tools associated with them indicate a brain capacity which is not markedly, if at all, inferior to that of existing races.

In a similar vein Goldenweiser remarked, "Broadly speaking, there is no such thing as a primitive mind: primitive man is potentially like modern man or any other kind of man."[175]

---

[173] Reddie, James, "On Civilization: Moral and Material," *Trans. Vict. Instit.*, London, 6 (1872-73) : 23 and 24.

[174] Briffault, Robert, "The Evolution of the Human Species," in *The Making of Man,* ed. by Calverton, Modern Library, N.Y., 1931, p. 763.

[175] Goldenweiser, A., *Anthropology*, Crofts, N.Y., 1945, p. 407.

It may be exclaimed, "But you don't really mean that prehistoric man is to be accounted for in this way? What about the time factor? You postulate a few thousand years for all this, whereas we 'know' that man is at least half a million years old!" But do we? It is not yet time to say with absolute certainty that the basic assumptions of C—14 dating methods are completely sound. Are we quite sure that the same atmospheric conditions existed prior to the Flood? It could make all the difference if the answer were no.

Suppose for the sake of argument that there was very little conversion of nitrogen to C—14 in the upper atmosphere prior to the Flood, due either to some change in the earth's magnetic field or to a greatly increased percentage of carbon dioxide in the earth's atmosphere, reducing the relative proportion of radioactive carbon dioxide. At present the proportion of carbon dioxide in the atmosphere is about 0.04%, but this might easily have been considerably greater before the Flood. Or suppose the atmosphere had in some way been blanketed against neutron bombardment, then once more the percentage of radioactive carbon dioxide would be greatly reduced. The end result is the same in either case: and we would have the following situation. An organism dying one year before the Flood might have an extremely small amount of radioactive carbon dioxide. By C—14 decay-counting methods, the sample would be estimated to be very, very old, let us say, 30,000 years. On the other hand, an organism dying two years later, that is to say, one year after the atmosphere had been modified somewhat as a side-effect of the Flood, might be found by radiocarbon dating to be only 4,500 years old. Thus the two objects separated in actual fact by only two years, would by C—14 dating methods be separated by 25,000 years.

Of course, radiocarbon dating is not the only method used to establish the chronology of prehistory: but tree-ring counting is limited to 2,000 to 3,000 years as a rule, and varve counting, though sometimes considered useful up to 10,000 years, is challenged by some very excellent authorities who would limit its usefulness to little more than half this period. These three are virtually the only "absolute" means of dating the past, and they may well be limited in their validity or feasibility to post-Flood times.

Besides these three methods, we have only relative means based on associated flora and fauna, etc., which are tied in with climatic changes related to the glacial and interglacial periods. Datings based on the recession of the Niagara Falls, the erosion of river beds, or the silting up of deltas have proved rather indeterminate. Lyell has allowed 30,000 years for the recession of Niagara Falls, which is believed to have begun when the ice retreated north of the Niagara Escarpment. This figure had served to establish approximately the time since the last great advance of the ice sheet over North America. But more recent studies have consistently reduced this to 10,000 years or even to 8,000 years. Such revisions of dates downwards are very frequent, as we show in another Doorway Paper.[176] And some of these revisions are quite extraordinary.[177]

It may be objected that such a suggestion runs so completely counter to everything we have been taught for the last fifty years that there is not the slightest possibility of its obtaining a sympathetic hearing. The theory of evolution is so widely accepted and has proved so useful in the ordering and systematizing of modern knowledge, especially in the life sciences, that a few fragments of contrary evidence will not undermine it, no matter how serious these contradictions are. But in spite of all this, the historical evidence stands clearly against its basic postulate of continuous progressive development, and in the end it will be found necessary to abandon it just as social anthropologists have abandoned it as a key to the history of art, language, religion, and many human institutions. The alternative, the Scriptural view, is far more consonant with the findings of archaeology as well as what we know from more recent historical events.

Now, as we have seen, two things stand out in even a cursory reading of the first few chapters of Genesis. The first is the exceedingly rapid development of civilization. The other is the exceedingly rapid development of wickedness. Two individuals are singled out who happen to have been contemporaries since both were the seventh generation from Adam: one of these was Lamech and the other was Enoch. In the brief reports which have been preserved for us of these two men, we have on the one hand a picture of a vicious and revengeful man threatening to murder any one who dares to oppose him, and on the other hand an individual whose saintliness was so outstanding that God took him home without permitting him to see death. The one has left a record of vengefulness which apparently became a proverb among men, and the other a record of godliness

---

[176] "Fossil Remains of Early Man and the Record of Genesis," in this volume.

[177] For example, Kenneth Macgowan (*Early Man in the New World*, p. 187) gives a series of such cases, involving a reduction from 4,000 B.C. to an A.D. figure! He mentions one authority who has now argued that man came into the New World not as a primitive paleolithic 25,000 years ago, but as fairly civilized at the beginning of the Christian era! A. L. Kroeber believes that chronologists have been far too free with years (*Anthropology*, 1948, p. 654). He says, "One can believe the (Milankovitch-Zeuner dating system) : but one does not have to" (p. 655, fn. 9) .

which was recalled with wonder 3,000 years later in the New Testament. In either case we have the feeling that developments, for good or for ill, were greatly accelerated.

When, a thousand years after Enoch, the earth had become so full of violence and corruption that the wickedness of man knew no restraints, only one patriarch was left whose heart was still right before the Lord and whose family seemed worthy to be saved. The catastrophe of the Flood, destroying the whole race probably still concentrated in a comparatively limited area, reduced the family of man to eight people only; and we have a unique circumstance in history. Here was now a small society of cultured and technically trained individuals, inheritors of a great proportion of all that had been achieved in the past two or three thousand years, making a new start under conditions which may well have been in many respects ideal. For one thing, all the immediate dangers from wild beasts and from unfriendly neighbors had been completely removed.[178] Well supplied with stock and probably with food, such a small group with the experience of the past to guide them, could make progress very rapidly, especially with the structure of the Ark at hand to supply them with many building materials already prepared. But the population of this first settlement would in time increase to the point where, for various reasons, the ties of close association began to be broken. Possibly Noah and his wife remained as a kind of focal center but each of the three sons, Shem, Ham, and Japheth, presumably began to spread apart in different directions.[179] What happened thereafter has been by implication the subject of this paper. The phenomena which resulted in the course of time from this initial circumstance are of a very specific nature and can be summarized as follows:

(1) In the Middle East progress from the first evidence of settlement to the appearance of cities was exceedingly rapid.

(2) A circle of slightly lower but obviously derived cultures surrounded the central core within a few centuries as population pressures increased.

(3) There was a gradual loss of shared cultural elements as the circle widened, until contact was lost almost entirely in the more marginal areas where much lower cultures arose. At the extreme margins all culture contacts ceased.

(4) The most primitive of all fossil remains are those found

---

[178] This may seem a small matter, but actually it may not have been so. It was such a danger that lay behind the statement in Deut. 7:22 apparently.

[179] The early existence of these three groups as distinct communities has recently been substantiated for the Middle East Area (cf. V. G. Childe, *What Happened in History*, Penguin Books, Eng., 1946, p. 81).

at the extreme edges of this radial pattern with less primitive remains a little nearer to the center and transitional-to-modern forms within the Middle East area itself (as in Skuhl and Shanidar finds).

(5) Modern types of man (Fontechevade and Swanscombe) in some cases antedated more primitive types in Europe where migrants who had more recently left the central area reached distant points quite by chance but failed to establish themselves, and died out leaving the territory to earlier settlers who were already there.

(6) Primitive cultures which lost vital contact with the mainstream steadily degenerated but never to the extent of losing the power of speech and a well-developed language.

(7) Where complete isolation of adult individuals occurred, it is probable that extreme physical degeneration was experienced, accounting for some exceptionally primitive fossil remains (Pithecanthropus, Sinanthropus, etc.). In more recent times where complete isolation in childhood (ferals) has occurred, all cultural elements are lost including language.

(8) Occasionally old cultures reestablished vital contact with the mainstream in a beneficial way and achieved a notable revival to a much higher level (China, for example). Upon rare occasion, a culture was established in a highly favorable environment surrounded by many smaller societies developing independently, and because of its central position a high civilization arose (as in Central America, for example).

(9) High cultures are susceptible to complete breakdown, as in the case of the Minoan, thus demonstrating that civilization is a plant of delicate growth rather easily withered.

(10) The contact of high cultures with low ones is apt to be detrimental to the latter. One particular circumstance, to be considered later, may prevent such ill-effects.

It is very difficult to account for these things by any other than the biblical view of man's origin and early history. There is one aspect of pre-Flood times which has often been commented upon and considered to be quite exceptional — the extraordinary rapidity with which civilization developed in the first three or four generations, considering the fact that no precedence existed and every cultural element had to be engineered from scratch. Several factors may account for this, provided that we allow the biblical record to speak for itself. These are —

(1) The great age to which man lived.

(2) The temperateness of the climate.
(3) The uniformity of language.
(4) The concentration of population.
(5) The nature of the original endowment of man by his Creator.

Let us examine these very briefly. There is a tendency by many to question whether men really did live to such extraordinary ages. The evidence that the record here has not been tampered with but is sober history is the subject of another Doorway Paper.[180] This evidence, to my mind, is very satisfying. Consider what it would mean for most of us if we could extend the period of research and learning in a normal life time by ten or fifteen times. Even as it is, most of us are impressed with our older colleagues who have an advantage over us of as little as ten years. What if they had the advantage over us of 900 years! Moreover, communication takes time and for many of us the weeks are not long enough to allow us to keep up with what is being done elsewhere even in our little fields of enquiry. Just suppose for one moment that we had the time to discuss with Leonardo da Vinci or with Isaac Newton or with any of the "greats" of a few hundred years ago, not merely what they were doing for a few fleeting years but what they have been doing ever since. The situation is one which is so outside our experience that it is even hard to conceive its implications. But surely there is no question that if everyone was surviving for centuries, the cumulative effect of man's inventiveness and curiosity would be fantastic — both for good and for ill. Longevity must have contributed enormously to the process of speeding up the development of civilization even in those first few generations. The fact that Scripture not only records that men lived to be very old but also that within two generations of Adam city life and art and technology were already highly developed, is evidence of its reliability, for the one finds its most logical explanation in terms of the other. And if either were true, the other is most likely to have been also.

The second factor is perhaps less certain, namely, climatic uniformity. We do not know that such uniformity really existed. But I think that the most logical way to interpret the events associated with the Flood and, more particularly what may perhaps have been the first appearance of a rainbow, as meaning that rain as we understand it had not fallen previously since the creation of Adam. It has been suggested that the atmosphere was in some way different and that man may have lived, protected from certain types of cosmic radiation

---

[180] Custance, A. C., "Longevity in Antiquity and Its Bearing on Chronology," in Volume V.

in a kind of hothouse that was not oppressive but did contribute to his longevity.

The third factor is the uniformity of language which may be assumed since the break-up of languages did not occur until after the Flood. The very circumstance of the judgment which took place at Babel is sufficient indication of how uniformity of language could contribute to the acceleration of man's cooperative efforts, for it was this very factor which evidently made such an enterprise feasible, and by its reversal the enterprise was abandoned. One of the bugbears of our own highly technical civilization is the curse of specialization which has led to the development of technical jargons constituting so many different languages that a man trained in one discipline can scarcely understand or be intelligible to a man trained in another discipline. As a matter of fact, William Temple suggested that God had had a hand in this and brought it about in order that He might once more prevent men from achieving sufficient unity of purpose to attempt the erection of a second "Tower of Babel."[181] It is interesting to find that Dante interpreted the events at the building of the Tower of Babel as being just this[182] — the rapid rise of technical jargons which made communication between tradesmen difficult.

The fourth factor is the concentration of population, which allows for the maximum exchange of ideas with the least possible delay. This, again, is one of the critical factors in our own generation since, in spite of our means of rapid communication, distances are still great enough to prevent the immediacy of verbal exchange which comes with personal contact. This is one of the enormous gains of scientific conferences where almost as much is achieved in conversation vis-à-vis over a cup of coffee as is achieved by the formal presentation of papers. As we have already seen, isolation almost inevitably leads to stagnation. Sir Flinders Petrie stressed the importance of contacts between cultures when developing his cyclic view of history, attributing every renaissance to fresh culture contacts.[183] Ernst Kretchmer arrived at the conclusion, with regard to the share which the Nordic race had in Western culture, that their most marked

---

[181] Temple, Archbishop William, "Babel and Pentecost," in *The Church Looks Forward,* Macmillan, London, 1944, pp. 174 ff.
[182] On Dante, see Alexander Gode, "The Case for Interlingua," *Sci. Monthly,* Aug., 1953, p. 83.
[183] Petrie, Sir Flinders, *Revolutions of Civilization,* Harper, London, 1911, p. 114. He commits himself to the statement that "in every case" it was the result of an infiltration of a new people. J. C. Curry held that this stimulus was more often than not due to an Aryan infiltration ("Climate and Migrations," *Antiquity,* Sept., 1928, p. 301), and this opinion was not due to any sense of racial superiority on his part.

contributions were developed only in those regions where it had been exposed to an intense mixture with other races.[184] Fenton Turck credited the initial vitality of American civilization to the fact that the population formed an amalgam of people from so many different cultural traditions.[185] Such an amalgamation means the sharing of new ideas which would otherwise have remained the property only of their originators. When ideas are wedded there is a tendency not merely for a kind of "hybrid" to result but for entirely *new* ideas to appear which were not latent in either of the originals when considered alone. The process tends to be multiplicative rather than additive. Where the original population was still compact we may assume, especially in view of longevity, that the total wealth of ideas resulting from a vastly extended range of experience would be compounded in ways which are not known today.

And finally, there is the matter of man's original endowment. This is a subject which really requires (and receives in other Doorway Papers) [186] much fuller treatment than can be afforded at this point. It is my conviction that man has three kinds of capacity: inventive, philosophical, and spiritual, and that at the time of the Flood God distributed these three capacities in a special measure between the three sons of Noah respectively. Shem was made responsible for the spiritual welfare of mankind, Ham for the physical welfare of mankind, and Japheth for the intellectual welfare of mankind. When race mixture or culture contacts have brought together these three contributions in a balanced way, there has always resulted a great advancement of civilization. But when any one of these three contributions has been either neglected or overemphasized, the civilization which resulted from the amalgam has begun the process of decay.

I believe that in Adam and his descendants, until the Flood brought an end to the old world, these three capacities were by and large combined within each person individually though, of course, not always in exactly the same measure, just as not everyone now has the same level of intelligence. But each man carried within himself a threefold potential which after the Flood was very greatly reduced and more often than not was limited to a capacity chiefly in

[184] Kretschmer, Ernst, quoted by Franz von Weidenreich, *Apes, Giants and Man,* Chicago, 1948, p. 90.

[185] Turck, Fenton B., "The American Explosion," *Sci. Monthly,* Sept., 1952, p. 191.

[186] Custance, A. C., "The Framework of History from the Biblical Point of View," "The Part Played by Shem, Ham, and Japheth in Subsequent World History," in Volume I, cover part of this general thesis.

one direction. In another work, the thesis has been examined rather carefully that *science* results only where philosophy (the contribution of Japheth) is wedded to technology (the contribution of Ham), just as *theology* only arises where philosophy is wedded to spiritual insight based upon revelation (which was the specific contribution of Shem). On the whole, those who are highly inventive and mechanically minded are rarely of a philosophical turn of mind, and philosophers tend to be rather impractical. Whenever these two capacities do happen to appear in one man, we have the scientific individual. Unfortunately, scientifically minded people tend to be somewhat indifferent about spiritual things that are matters of faith. And since man is primarily a spiritual creature, science has often tended to be one-sided and inadequate, sometimes rather futile, and frequently dangerous because it encourages a sceptical attitude. But consider what would happen if every man had within himself a large capacity for invention and could extend the application of his own inventiveness as greatly as scientists have recently extended the basic technology of the previous 6,000 years of civilization. The progress of the past 100 years might have been crowded into the first few centuries of human history, and Adam's grandson might have seen the development of city life, the erection of very large buildings, the appearance of the arts including all kinds of music, the extended use of metals, and the establishment of cattlemen and farmers on a large scale — as evidently Cain's children did (Gen. 4:17-22).

But, as always seems to have been the case, man's spiritual capacity tended to suffer from disuse, or even abuse, and the evil in man was fortified very rapidly to an extraordinary degree by the exercise of his other capabilities, until the Lord looked down from Heaven and saw that it was too dangerous for the individual to be endowed so fully. After the Flood, what had been combined in Adam was thenceforth divided between Shem, Ham, and Japheth. During pre-Flood times, however, it seems that the capacity of the individual was so much greater that the processes of civilization were all enormously accelerated.

By themselves, representatives of any one of these three branches of the race have always suffered cultural stagnation or degeneration. Association is essential for progress, and it is this association which stamps the main stream for what it is. In isolation, man is still a special creature of God but his capacity is enormously reduced. Nevertheless, how ever far down he goes, he remains — unlike the animals — essentially a human being. Of the few cases of feral children who might almost be an exception to this, we know far too little to be certain. But we do know that the most isolated and exceedingly primitive of peoples are quite capable of responding to education. We know something more than this, namely, that unless this education has a very clear and spiritual component capable of leading to a full assurance of faith, the educative process is only partially effective, and may even be highly detrimental.

When the Dutch were forced out of Formosa and could not carry the education of the natives further, those natives returned to a more serious kind of barbarism than they had known before. One of the Tierra del Fuegians, named Jeremy Button, who was taken by Darwin and educated in England was later returned to his own people apparently without any evidence of conversion and subsequently became even more barbarous than they.[187] *But* when missionaries with a vital Scriptural faith — who during this Age of Grace stand in the world community for a season in the place of Shem (Gen. 9:27) undertake to contribute their vital part in the education of such people and succeed in communicating that faith to them — their condition is changed for the better in a striking and lasting manner, as Darwin himself was only too willing to admit of the Tierra del Fuegians.[188] It is true that with the missionary come also other less happy influences from Western Culture and not a few of its diseases so that in the end such cultures have not always benefitted as a whole. Education without this spiritual component has surprising limitations. On the other hand, Herman Merivale,[189] one-time Professor of History at Oxford, after a careful study of the effects of colonization and education of native peoples, came to the conclusion that history could point to no single successful attempt to introduce civilization to "savage tribes in colonies except through the agency of religious missionaries."

Thus it appears that only so long as the light of true spiritual faith, the basis of which is the Word of God, forms an essential

[187] Jeremy Button ended up many years later as the instigator of the subsequent massacre of a small congregation of natives who had been converted and were, with the white missionary, in the act of worshipping in a half-finished church building (Lincoln Barnett, *Life,* June 1, 1959, p. 87).

[188] Charles Darwin, according to the biography by his son Sir Francis Darwin, in later years wrote personally to Admiral Sir James Sullivan asking permission to be elected as an honorary member of the Mission to the del Fuegians, the South American Missionary Society, which he had "prophesied would be an utter failure" but had been a "most wonderful success." James Orr, in his *God's Image in Man,* Eerdmans, Grand Rapids, 1948, reprint, p. 164, gives an equally striking case of what true missionary effort may ultimately do to a whole primitive society.

[189] Merivale, Herman, *Colonization and the Colonies,* p. 294, quoted in *Trans. Vict. Instit.,* 19 (1885) : 128.

element of a culture can it lay any claims to being or becoming a part of the main stream; and only so can it hope, therefore, to preserve itself against or recover itself from, the invidious processes of degeneration. The main stream is only "main" so long as the Christian faith is contributing to its current in a vital way. This may not always engender its *advance,* indeed it probably never does specifically, but it does prevent its degeneration. In this sense the church of God in so far as it supports this true faith has the preservative qualities and function of "salt" (Matt. 5:13).

If we may revert once more to our opening thoughts, we see that there is neither automatic cultural evolution nor automatic cultural devolution. The deciding factor is whether vital contact has been retained with the main stream which is only so by reason of the fact that it represents a composite of spiritual, intellectual, and technological enlightenment sustained thus by Shem, Japheth, and Ham. This circumstance did not arise by chance evolution but by the direct creative activity of God at the beginning; and high civilizations which have passed away, and primitive people — living and extinct, and even feral children — all bear witness to the fact that in the absence of any one of these essential components of truly human, as opposed to animal, society, man must inevitably suffer degeneration. Civilization is a phenomenon which arose at the very beginning only because man was not evolved but was created by God with the necessary endowment, an endowment which even in his fallen state is still permitted to find expression according to the forbearance of God in very remarkable ways.

Part III

Establishing a Paleolithic I.Q.

Definition of *Intelligence:*
"Quickness of mental apprehension."
(Oxford English Dictionary)

Introduction

THIS ESSAY (bearing its present title) was originally presented in fulfillment of a requirement by the Department of Anthropology in the University of Toronto during one of my courses there. And although, as will be seen from the approach taken, my thesis was anything but favorable towards the evolutionary view adopted without question by the department, when the essay was returned to me it had written across it: "A very excellent and scholarly treatment of the subject." Underneath that, it was marked "A++."

This circumstance made it seem worthwhile expanding it a little bit though without changing its essential character and presenting it as a Doorway Paper.

Although there is nothing specifically "Christian" about it, it nevertheless presents evidence that the biblical picture of Early Man which shows him as not one bit less intelligent than ourselves from the beginning may, after all, be the true one.

Chapter 1
The Intelligence of Early Man

ARCHAEOLOGISTS WORKING in Mexico, Peru, and Yucatan realize that such achievements in the arts of living as were found in these three regions could only have arisen over thousands of years. So wrote Jurgen Thorwald.[1] Now, it is a principle in advertising that if a statement is repeated often enough, people will come to believe it whether it is true or not. And the view that early cultural development was always pitifully slow has similarly been repeated so often that it has come to be accepted as unquestionably true.

Early Man, it was held, may have had a fair measure of animal cunning, otherwise he probably would never have survived, but the kind of intelligence which we associate with inventiveness and the advancement of culture he can have had very little indeed, hence the tremendous time lapse between each significant advance. And this was held to be true for three reasons: first of all, he was so nearly animal himself, and animals are not culturally progressive; and secondly, there are certain primitive people who have not advanced culturally either, and this fact is popularly attributed to the same cause, namely, "low intelligence" — thus providing us with an actual picture of what fossil man was like when he roamed the earth. These people, we are told, are Paleolithic Men who happen to be still living! And thirdly, he had such brute features and such a small cranial capacity, both of which were taken to be clear evidence of his low level of mental development. He looked idiotic and therefore was idiotic.

These views accord so well with and, until recently, have formed such an integral part of evolutionary philosophy that they were never seriously questioned. There must have been a long time in the process of man's evolution from ape to protoman to Homo sapiens,

---

[1] Thorwald, Jurgen, *Science and Secrets of Early Medicine,* Harcourt, Brace and World, N.Y., 1963, p. 249.

and since everyone knows how forward-looking and progressive modern man is now, the earliest representatives of our race must have had a low I.Q. to remain so long at one cultural level. All the evidence seemed to dovetail, and the existence of primitive cultures which are marked by "backwardness" and whose members appear to lack "nobility of countenance" as we see it, seemed to provide the ultimate demonstration of the reasonableness of the current view of prehistoric man.

For many people, it is simply self-evident that the earliest human beings had a low I.Q. because an evolutionary view of things demands that this be so. But if we follow Lyell's dictum of interpreting the past only in the light of the known present, it can be shown that most of the available evidence stands squarely against the current view of early man's lack of intelligence. There is absolutely no historical record of any primitive culture whose children were so lacking in intelligence that they could not hold their own with the children of civilized parents, when provided with comparable opportunities. Thus, although it is felt by many people that our primitive contemporaries are backward enough to be our contemporary ancestors, it is also important to underscore at the same time the well recognized fact that our own newborn babies are not essentially different from those of any other culture, advanced or backward. Man seems always to start with about the same intellectual endowment regardless of whether he happens to be a member of some primitive tribe or a member of some well-to-do European family where it may be presumed opportunity for intellectual development is very high. It is opportunity that makes the difference. The apparent backwardness of some modern native cultures and the extreme simplicity of the tools and artifacts of Paleolithic Man are not, in either case, evidence of inferior intelligence but more probably due to a historical circumstance which it is well worth examining.

If this can be established, an important argument in favor of the supposed evolution of man from some animal form is weakened. And the object of this essay is simply to examine the evidence in the light of present knowledge. How intelligent *was* Paleolithic Man?

Chapter 2
Are Intelligent People Inventive?

I KNEW A MAN who had a small summer cottage with a kind of kitchenette occupying one corner of it. The sink was set in a counter. From the sink to the corner wall, there was about eighteen inches of counterspace, perhaps a little less. On the other side of the sink, there was a total of about five feet of counterspace. When the dishes had to be done, it invariably happened that in clearing the table everything was piled beside the sink on the five foot section. Consequently, when the dishes were washed, they were always put to drain on the tiny little eighteen-inch section. The suffering (?) male was therefore forced to stand between the lady of the house, who was washing the dishes, and the wall in a space which barely allowed enough room to turn around, let alone dry a large plate or a pitcher or some such thing. After enduring this for probably a couple of years, it was suggested quite casually that it might be better to pile the dirty dishes on the eighteen-inch section so that the drier could do his duty in the wide open spaces on the other side — where he always put the clean dishes in any case. It was quite amazing how much more pleasant it made the whole burdensome operation! One day, when he tried to explain this little program change to a friend, the friend expressed only incredulity that it could have taken two perfectly intelligent people so long to make such a simple "discovery." They were two intelligent people, but it still took two whole years. . . . Whereby hangs a moral.

The moral is that all too frequently the most obvious solutions to the simplest of problems stare us in the face, but we quite fail to observe them. *After* one has the solution, it tends to appear very obvious indeed. Before one has the solution, it is far from obvious. My own experience in a research laboratory has strongly confirmed in my mind the fact that most of us see things pretty much as they are and have little or no power to envision possibilities which are not foreshadowed in the immediate present. We all tend to be great critics of what is, and a few are able to act as improvers, but the man who can produce genuine innovations is rare.

The very simplicity of many important new developments, once a technology has reached a point which allows the making of them, tends to deceive us almost wholly into supposing that there is really nothing to them. As a child I used to be tremendously impressed with the engineering achievement which lay behind the construction of what we used to call a Pacific type locomotive. Later on, when I learned that Hero of Alexandria had proposed a steam engine of sorts (working on a steam jet principle) to hoist fuel into the tower of the Pharos Lighthouse at Alexandria in Egypt,[2] around 120 B.C., I was not at all impressed. But history shows that it was Hero's steam engine which, 17 centuries later, inspired Branca to devise similarly steam-driven toys. As Elliot Smith remarked,[3] "in the course of time Worcester, Savery, Papin, Newcomen, and Watt as the outcome of a century's intensive research devised a practical steam engine that was of economic value." I had seen an illustration of Hero's steam engine and it was unimpressive: it was far too simple. But in point of fact the Pacific locomotive was, strictly speaking, a "child" of Hero's steam engine.

It is very tempting to hold that the improver is more intelligent than the originator, especially if — as usually happens — the improvement introduces the element of complication. The complication as a rule has the effect of impressing us because it is beyond our immediate comprehension. The original simple invention we can understand at once and hence we unthinkingly suppose that the originator thought it up "at once," i.e., the moment the need presented itself. The improver so complicates, and thus conceals, the prime element of novelty by the addition of dials, knobs, and switches, which perform functions that we no longer perceive directly, that we imagine much greater intelligence is required by the latter. Much greater knowledge may be required — but not much greater intelligence. Here is where the confusion arises. It is obvious that as we grow older we accumulate knowledge but there is evidence that intelligence per se does not increase much after adolescence is reached. It appears to do so because judgment is improved (hopefully) as a result of experience, so that we expect a man to be wiser and more mature in his judgments than a youth is. But it has yet to be established that this involves any increase in intelligence.

---

[2] Hero: Clive Bell, *Civilization*, Pelican Series, 1947, p. 63.
[3] Smith, Sir G. Elliot, *In the Beginning*, Thinker's Library, 2nd ed., 1946, p. 2.

Intelligence is rather like a potential: wisdom and knowledge build upon intelligence but do not, probably, determine it. Thus while we stand on the shoulders, technically speaking, of our predecessors, we cannot seriously look upon ourselves as more intelligent than they. For we have to remember that the day will come when others who follow will stand upon our shoulders, and to them our technology may appear to be primitive indeed. And so it will be by comparison, undoubtedly. But we do not judge ourselves on that account to lack intelligence. We have therefore to be very careful to distinguish between the growth of knowledge and an increase in intelligence.

But we must go one step further than this and learn from history the fully documented but little recognized fact that the power of invention belongs to a very few. These very few are people with a peculiar mental bent. They are very often difficult to get on with and may even be positively antisocial. In some respects, they may have only an ordinary intelligence. They just seem to be able quickly to see solutions which are entirely new in conception. Their antisocial behavior often stems from the fact that their own society, far from being enthusiastic about their invenions, tends to be either hostile towards them or — which is worse — quite indifferent. Until very recent times we have not on the whole been enamoured with novelty as we often suppose, although the influence of a century of evolutionary philosophy has certainly broken down our resistance to change by allowing our thinking to become dominated by the idea that change in itself is progress, thus making a virtue out of novelty.[4] When we have thrust upon us an advertisement stating that something is "new, New, NEW," what is really meant is "changed, Changed, CHANGED," and what we almost inevitably interpret it to mean is "better, Better, BETTER." Again, it is necessary to underscore the fact that neither resistance to change nor enthusiasm for it are necessarily an index of the level of intelligence. The *zeitgeist* of the times can so envelope us without our knowing it that we may accept change as a good thing, whether it is or not. By contrast, as we shall show, primitive people may refuse change whether it is good or not.

And then there is the matter of "need." Necessity is in a sense the mother of invention, but history shows that millions of intelligent people can get along without something which later proves to be a necessity. Indeed, Lord Raglan defined the civilizing process as being "the progressive conversion of luxuries into necessities." This is a

---

[4] Shepard, W., "Our Indigenous Shangri-La," *Sci. Monthly*, Feb., 1946, p .163.

profoundly true observation. But necessity itself does not enable the majority of people to see how the need can be satisfied. This tends to be left to a comparatively small number of individuals, and as a rule their solutions or provisions are, at first, essentially simple in conception. And when they are observed by the rest of us they frequently seem self-evident. The inventor naturally must have intelligence to father his invention, or in rare cases, to recognize the invention he has hit upon accidentally. People often make discoveries but do not recognize their discoveries for what they are. And this, again, is no indication of their intelligence or lack of it: it is just that they lack a certain peculiar turn of mind.

We may safely conclude, therefore, that where there does not appear a need for improvement, improvement is not likely to come, and so long as an existing invention *or* development serves the purpose for which it was made, it may remain for centuries with little or no elaboration. Indeed, elaboration is not always improvement. Tylor reported that when native people in the tropics first received modern rifles, they found them quite unsuitable for that environment.[5] At that time, cartridges became so damp as to be useless, so the natives then rebuilt their equipment into a flint-lock firing system, carrying their powder in horns where they could keep it dry. Similarly, metal tools, especially copper ones, are better than flint tools in some circumstances but native people soon found that for shaving hair off, the cutting edge of a flint is far superior and more readily renewed.[6] A modern example is the use of a piece of broken glass in the very finest microtomes for cutting sections of muscle tissue 100 to 200 angstrom units in thickness for electron microscope examination.[7] The usual steel blade is not sharp enough. Recent experience has shown that flint weapons can be unexpectedly effective. Whole houses of simple design have been built with them and whole carcasses have been butchered with comparative ease and in a remarkably short time using nothing but flint tools, some of them believed to be thousands of years old.[8]

The Australian aborigines who had been accustomed to stone spearheads, did not take readily to metal ones since they are not as

[5] Tylor, E. B., *Anthropology*, Hill and Co., N.Y., 1904, pp. 14 ff.

[6] Razors: one such flint razor was found recently in a late Bronze Age interment in Wiltshire, England, which had been used to shave off the eyebrows of the mourners (See *Man*, Oct., 1950, p. 144).

[7] Huxley, H. E., "The Contraction of Muscle," *Sci. American*, Nov., 1958, p. 72.

[8] Custance, A. C., "Stone Tools and Woodworking," *Science*, 160 (1968): 100, 101. This brief article provides a very useful summary of the present evidence.

easily worked. Consequently, when the Australian government ran telephone lines across some of their territories, the natives took to knocking down the glass or porcelain insulators out of which, by a technique familiar to them, they were able to make very beautiful spearheads.[9] The government found this so distressing that they came to terms with the natives and agreed to leave at the foot of every pole a certain number of extra insulators on the understanding that the natives would not knock them down from the poles any more.

Thus, in these three cases, conservatism was not because of lack of intelligence but resulted from experience. The continued use of flint-lock guns, of stone razors, and of glass or glasslike weapon heads, was simply because the more advanced substitutes were not suitable. As a matter of fact, it could be said that, in the circumstances, the behavior of the users was perhaps more intelligent than ours would have been with our tremendous urge always to change to something different and more "modern."

This is not to imply that primitive people automatically refused innovations. The revival of Zuni pottery by Maria Marinez is a case where one individual began something new and persuaded her own people to support her.[10] There are a number of recent cases where individual native people have undertaken to introduce entirely new things into their own culture. We are apt to suppose that these natives would never have thought of departing from traditional ways and introducing new elements into their own culture if the inventive White Man had not provided the stimulus in the first place. But as we have demonstrated elsewhere[11] at some length and over a very wide range of items, it has not been the Indo-Europeans who were the originators of a large part of our technological heritage but the non-Indo-European peoples, the people of Africa, the American Indians, the natives of South America, the Mongols generally (especially the Chinese), and many others. Yet these same people are apt to be thought of, and indeed are on the whole, highly conservative and resistant to change. To this extent, they are like Early Man apparently, who may have been equally inventive therefore.

Thus it may fairly safely be said, and the point needs underscoring heavily because it is so easily forgotten, that intelligence is

[9] The Royal Ontario Museum (Toronto, Canada) has several beautiful specimens of recently worked glass weapons in the "Pacific Gallery."
[10] Zuni pottery: described by A. Goldenweiser, *Anthropology*, Crofts, N.Y., 1945, pp. 199 ff. There are other excellent examples from the Solomon Islands given by J. M. Mello, in a paper titled, "Primitive Man: Neolithic Man," *Trans. Vict. Instit.*, London, 30 (1896) : 292; also R. Linton, *Study of Man*, Appleton, N.Y., 1936, p. 313.
[11] "The Technology of the Hamitic People" in Volume I.

not necessarily to be equated with inventiveness, the majority of intelligent people never inventing anything. This is the first important fact to bear in mind. And there is a second equally important fact that needs underscoring: that the complexity of a device or technique is, per se, no measure of the intelligence required to develop it. As a matter of fact, it is quite generally agreed that the essence of genius is simplicity of design. This applies to much creative activity. It applies in music, in art, in architecture, in engineering, in literature, perhaps in most things. What could be simpler than the basic theme of Beethoven's "Moonlight Sonata," or some of the profound observations put into the mouths of Shakespeare's characters, or such a formula as $E = mc^2$?

And having said all this, it may be asked, What has it to do with the subject of this essay? My purpose has been to underscore the fact that when we look back into prehistoric times, we should not be deceived by the simplicity of their cultural possessions into supposing that they were any less intelligent than we are today. Where we do have their artifacts, we almost always find that they were designed not merely with utility in mind, but also with a marked sense of formal beauty and symmetry. Many of them are as much works of art as any of the highly engraved revolvers and rifles of more recent times. And, of course, their powers of observation, at least among those who were artists in the community, were equal to the best artists of today. Moreover, the Portuguese and other early traders, when they first met their counterparts among native Africans and elsewhere, were both surprised and, to be truthful, chagrined to discover that the natives were a match for them in business acumen.[12]

We conclude, therefore, that if we follow the strictly scientific principle of being guided in our estimates regarding events in the past which we cannot know directly, by observing the evidence of the present which we *can* observe directly, we must conclude that as soon as true man appeared on the scene he was probably no different from ourselves in intelligence and the potential for the development of culture. He was, in fact, intelligent enough to know that the simple necessities of life were best obtained by simple devices, the needless elaboration of which was not in the interests of survival until a sufficient mastery of the environment had been achieved and a large enough population was present to allow for specialization in the arts and, with specialization, leisure. Archaeology shows that as soon as this occurred, civilization developed with extraordinary rapidity, thus demonstrating that the capability was there once the total situation

---

[12] Davidson, Basil, *African Kingdoms,* Time Inc., N.Y., 1966, p. 102.

permitted it to find expression. Man had not become suddenly more intelligent with the appearance of the early high cultures of the Middle East: it was merely that his potential was being realized.

Chapter 3
The Intelligence of
Our Contemporary Ancestors

IT IS DIFFICULT to treat separately the underlying assumptions which are set forth at the beginning. They are so inter-related that to some extent one has to deal with them all at the same time. However, an attempt will be made to give a structure to this section by reviewing first what we know about the intelligence of primitive people viewed in the light of their backwardness or conservatism, and then by considering the relationship between intelligence and the willingness or the desire to be progressive in outlook.

There are reasons why people are backward, which have nothing to do with intelligence, and conversely, there are reasons why people may be highly progressive yet very lacking in wisdom. Those who have come to know primitive people intimately are the first to admit that some of their forms of social behavior appear to us to be very foolish, but side by side with this apparent capacity for "foolishness" there is almost always found to exist a remarkable amount of very sound wisdom. Curiously, the older members of such cultures may be exceedingly wise even when that culture is exceedingly primitive. And, as we shall see, these same older people are very likely to look upon the highly civilized man as both childish and ignorant. A. P. Elkin,[13] a medical man by training, spent some time with the Australian aborigines and was so impressed with the genuine wisdom of some of their witch doctors, a class of people who are usually thought of as complete charlatans, that he wrote a book about them with the odd title *Aboriginal Men of High Degree,* by which he meant that he was presenting a study of primitive men who had the equivalent of the highest degrees which our universities are able to offer. Of

---

13 Elkin, A. P., *Aboriginal Men of High Degree,* 1944 Queensland University John M. Macrossan Memorial Lectures, published by Australasian Publications, 1946.

course, technically speaking, these aboriginal M.D.'s and Ph.D.'s could have been no match for our own graduates, but in point of wisdom in dealing with sick people and in dealing with problems which were strictly sociological in nature, these most primitive people were very wise indeed. And it is interesting to read how completely frank these witch doctors were with Elkin, once he had gained their confidence, in admitting that very often the health or recovery of the patient depended as much upon the patient's faith in the power of the "doctor" to heal as it did in his knowledge of what was wrong with him. Indeed, Elkin says that one of the best proofs of the effectiveness of their treatment and of their honesty lay in the fact that they always sent their own children, when they became ill, to another witch doctor — and not, except as a last resort, to one of the government doctors.

If primitive people have appeared at times to be inhumanly savage and beastly, it has virtually without exception been the direct result of provocation due to the inhumanity and beastliness of the more powerful White Man in his treatment of them. It can be stated almost as a rule that the more primitive a people is, and therefore by modern estimates the more nearly they are like our Paleolithic ancestors, the more ideally humane they have proved to be. Speaking of one tribe of Australian aborigines,[14] Thomson says that the Bindibu when they first had contact with the White Man were "friendly, fearless, poised, and happy."

Some of the most tragic episodes in human history have accompanied the final stages of the contact between the "civilized" White Man and primitive people when, reduced to utter poverty and degradation, many of these once quite extended societies sang their swan song and disappeared forever. The ultimate extinction of the Tasmanians, as an example, is unbelievably sad and resulted from a final act of barbaric savagery on the part of white settlers in that unhappy island. It leads one to wonder whether even the Nazis were the most brutal of modern oppressors. It is described by Murdock[15] who observes that the colonists regarded the aborigines "not so much as human beings as wild beasts to be ruthlessly exterminated. Even more barbarous in their treatment of the natives were the bushrangers, convicts who had escaped into the bush where they lived a life of brigandage. These outlaws hunted the blacks for sport." One

[14] Bindibu: quoted by John Hillaby, reporting for Mr. Thomson in an article, "Journey into the Stone Age," in *The New Scientist,* Feb. 25, 1965, pp. 507-509.

[15] Murdock, G. P., *Our Primitive Contemporaries,* Macmillan, 1951, pp. 16 ff.

particular individual used to hunt the natives "in order to provide his dogs with meat." Within a few years the population was reduced from around 5,000 to 203. Twelve years later, in 1847, only 40 remained. In 1876, with the death of the woman, Lawla Rokkh, the Tasmanian race became extinct. As Murdock concludes, "This, in brief, is one chapter in the history of the triumph of 'civilization' over 'savagery.' "

All the studies made of these people show that although, physically speaking their civilization was simple in the extreme, being strictly at the early Paleolithic level, they attached great importance to family life and showed great fondness for their children. Morality by our standards was high; and although the women were entirely naked, delicacy marked the association of the sexes, and great modesty was shown in the matter of self-exposure. Fidelity in marriage was strictly insisted upon and adultery extremely rare before the coming of the White Man. They believed in a life to come, which was thought to resemble this life except that it was divested of its evils. They were fond of decorating themselves with bright colored flowers, and their songs, though pitched largely in a minor key, were soft, plaintive and melodious. They did not mutilate their bodies as some higher cultures have done, and the sick were treated with remedies that were evidently of considerable worth. And they had a keen sense of humor. Such, then, is the true picture which emerges of a people who lived at the very bottom of the cultural scale (viewed from the White Man's point of view), and are by many people believed to be representative of a stage in the development of man which was not merely Paleolithic but even early Paleolithic.

This picture is by no means a solitary one. Indeed, it may safely be said that the "lower" in the scale such societies are found to be, the freer they are apt to be from the kind of barbarism which has been attributed to them. Whenever they have become cruel and savage, it has been under provocation. By nature and undisturbed, they are not savage. There are some authorities who hold that the Australian aborigines, perhaps the next people in the scale of "primitiveness," are actually the world's most outstanding sociologists in dealing with interpersonal relationships within their own community.[16]

Increasingly one reads of the passing of such cultures. In 1953, the last of the Australian Dieri died.[17] According to one authority,

---

[16] Levi-Strauss, Claude, *Race and History,* The Race Question in Modern Science, UNESCO, Paris, 1952, p. 27.

[17] Dieri: Les Bingham, "Vanishing Stone Age Men of Australia," *The Montrealer,* Nov., 1953, p. 44.

the last of the pureblood Easter Islanders died in 1914.[18] Less than a decade ago, there remained only seven people of the Tierra del Fuegians who, when Darwin visited them, numbered perhaps 20,000 or 30,000 people.[19]

The pathos that really lies behind such happenings is sharpened now and then by some strange circumstance. A case in point is mentioned by Humboldt who, in 1806, said that in Maypures there was an old parrot still living whose stream of chatter was no longer understood, for he was the only living creature left to perpetuate for a few more years some fragments of the language of the Atures who, being dead, yet continued to rebuke the world which had brought about their extinction.[20] So defenseless have such people been against the weapons and diseases and so-called civilizing influences of the White Man with his strong materialistic bent and his impatience with a system of values that does not favor his own acquisitiveness, that they were often treated with brutal indifference to their common humanness and were looked upon as undesirable animals. It is no wonder that they turned against their oppressors with the ferocity of desperation. Foreman's eloquent account of what he called "the last trek of the Indians" as the white settlers displaced them in parts of North America,[21] is a record of how completely opposed the value systems of two cultures can be, and what are the inevitable consequences to the less well defended party in the conflict. Not unnaturally, ruthlessness on the part of the White Man led the natives to have recourse to similar forms of savagery — for which they were promptly condemned and judged as being less than human.

Thus it came about that to their seeming poverty of possessions was added a reputation for inhumanness, especially in the treatment of captives; and it is not altogether surprising that the more primitive of such people came to be viewed as backwater survivals of what Homo sapiens must at first have been before the humanizing influences of civilization turned him into "cultured man," whatever that means. And that such primitive peoples never apparently exploited the territories they occupied in the way that the White Man succeeded in doing once he had dispossessed them, seemed only to demonstrate conclusively that they were incapable of so exploiting the land be-

---

[18] Easter Islanders: Mrs. Scoresby Routledge, "The Mysterious Images of Easter Island," in *Wonders of the Past*, Vol. III, Putnam, London, 1924, p. 803.

[19] Moore, R., *Evolution*, Life Nature Library, Time Inc., N.Y., 1962.

[20] Atures parrot: quoted by Hugh Miller, *The Testimony of the Rocks*, Ninno, Edinburgh, 1873, p. 231.

[21] Foreman, G., *The Last Trek of the Indians*, Univ. Chicago Press, 1946.

cause they lacked the mental capacity. Thus was strengthened the common view that very early man whose artifacts showed so many parallels could have been similarly little raised above the animals, both savage in temperament and of low intelligence.

But today, almost too late, it has come to be recognized that such primitive people — where a few still remain — are not mentally incompetent at all. One of the best illustrations of this in modern times is to be found in the continued existence and growing prosperity of the Eskimo, who have, by many writers, been hailed as the nearest possible living representatives of Paleolithic Man that survived into the historic period. The parallelisms between the cultures of the latter and Early Man are not surprising, in a way, since Early Man seems in many places to have lived in a cold hostile environment rather similar to the Arctic environment of the Eskimo. And they therefore created a very similar culture.

These similarities have been widely explored. Boyd Dawkins,[22] towards the end of the last century wrote extensively, especially in his *Early Man in Britain,* setting forth the similarities between Paleolithic cavemen and modern Eskimos. It is even stated that Paleolithic Man wore gloves very similar in design to those worn by the Eskimo. Many other writers since have reinforced these observations, especially with respect to the design of hunting weapons, harpoons, and such things. There are those who do not agree, however, for example, Frederica de Laguna,[23] who has written at some length on a comparison of Eskimo and Paleolithic art, which she feels are not truly parallel. Nevertheless, more recently the older view has been strongly reinforced,[24] although there is a tendency to equate them with the cultures of the Middle Stone Age rather than the Old Stone Age. Such European Mesolithic traits as pottery lamps, steep-sided conical based cooking pots, and barbed bone, fish and bird spears, occur in prehistoric Eskimo sites. Moreover, geometric designs in European Paleolithic and Mesolithic levels are comparable to bone and ivory designs found in early Eskimo sites. Even more recently, one series of articles designed for the general public by a well-known publisher has set forth pictorially (with the use of some imagination) how well the Eskimo way of life reflects the culture of very Early Man. Here,

---

[22] Dawkins, W. Boyd, *Early Man In Britain, Tertiary Period,* Macmillan, 1880, pp. 238-239.

[23] de Laguna, Frederica, "A Comparison of Eskimo and Paleolithic Art," *Amer. Jour. Archaeol.,* Part I in Oct.-Dec., 1932, pp. 447-511, and Part II in Jan.-Mar., 1933, pp. 77-107.

[24] Krieger, A. D., "New World Culture History: Anglo-America," in *Anthropology Today,* ed. A. L. Kroeber, Univ. Chicago Press, 1953, p. 246.

herefore, is Paleolithic Man. What, then, do we know of the intel-
ctual capacity of the Eskimo, by which we might assess the I.Q. of
arly Man?

For many years people have written about the Eskimo because
hey occupy a part of the world which has always had a strange
ascination for people. Many who have done duty in the Arctic have
poken of its beauty and its appeal, in spite of the intense cold and
he dangers inherent in such an environment. In recent years more
nd more people of western cultural tradition have been stationed
here, many of them being men with a high degree of technical com-
etence. Such people have come increasingly to look upon the Eskimo
s being extraordinarily adaptable, quick-witted, mechanically adept,
nd highly intelligent.

Dr. Erwin Ackerknecht, one of the best of modern authorities in
is respect, has said:[25]

> The Eskimo is one of the great triumphs of our species. He has
> succeeded in adapting himself to an environment which offers to man
> but the poorest chances of survival. . . .
> His technical solutions of problems of the Arctic are so excellent
> that white settlers would have perished had they not adopted many
> elements of Eskimo technology.

Like most other human beings, the Eskimo had to concern him-
lf with three basic physical needs: the provision of clothing, the
uilding of a shelter, and the obtaining of food. Considering these
ery briefly, we may note, for example, that Frederick R. Wulsin, an
uthority on clothing problems in the cold, admitted candidly that
here is "no doubt that Eskimo clothing is the most efficient yet de-
ised for extremely cold weather."[26] And in addressing a scientific
ymposium in Ottawa in 1955, Dr. O. Solandt stated categorically:

> The White Man has not introduced a single item of environ-
> mental protection in the Arctic which was not already being used by
> the natives, and his substitute products are not yet as effective as the
> native ones. Only in his means of production has he the edge.

t seems that to the Eskimo must probably go the credit for develop-
ng what is, strictly speaking, the first "tailored clothing," and in
iew of this, perhaps not unnaturally, the first thimbles.[27] We cannot
e absolutely sure of this claim to priority because needles of re-

---

[25] Ackerknecht, Erwin, "The Eskimo's Fight Against Hunger and Cold,"
iba Symposia, 10 (July-Aug., 1948): 894.
[26] Wulsin, Frederick R., "Adaptations to Climate Among Non-European
eoples," in The Physiology of Heat Regulation and the Science of Clothing,
l. by L. H. Newburgh, Saunders, Phila., 1949, p. 26.
[27] Thimbles: C. W. Jeffreys, A Picture Gallery of Canadian History, Vol. I,
yerson, Toronto, 1924, p. 113.

markably modern appearance have been found in some very ancient Paleolithic sites in Europe, a fact which only underscores the parallelisms between the two cultures.

With respect to the provision of shelter, the Eskimo igloo is familiar to almost everyone, but what is not at all familiar to most people is (1) the difficulty of building one, (2) the remarkable size which some of them attain, and (3) their effectiveness in terms of heat insulation. It might be thought that once the idea was conceived, the construction of such a house would be comparatively simple. Actually, it is remarkably difficult to construct a dome without any means of supporting the arch while in the process of completing it. As the wall rises, it converges upon itself. Each new block overhangs more and more until near the top they rest almost in a horizonal plane. The problem is to hold each block in place until the next one ties it in, and then to hold that one until it, too, is tied in place. Given enough hands, the process is not so difficult, but the Eskimos have overcome the problem so effectively that one individual can, if he has to, erect his own igloo single-handed without too much difficulty. The solution is to carry the rising layers of blocks in a spiral instead of in a series of horizontal levels. The starting block is pie-shaped. Thus as each block is added it not only rests on the lower level, but against the last block. One block would simply tend to fall in, and by experience, so do two or even three, when a new layer is started if the tiers are horizontally laid. But the Eskimo method overcomes the problem entirely. The solution is, of course, amazingly simple — once it is known. Most solutions are, when someone has discovered them for us. The problem is to visualize the solution before it exists. We tend to assume we would discover the way quite quickly — but experience shows that this is not true.

The size of some of these igloos is remarkable, often being of the order of eighteen feet in diameter with corresponding headroom, of course. By hanging skins on pegs built into the wall and by correctly designing the floor level so that the cold falls into a "pool" which is avoided by the occupants, and by covering the used areas of floor surface with furs, the Eskimo ends up with a roomy enough dwelling that soon becomes so warm as to require the occupants to strip most of their clothing off.

In obtaining food, the ingenuity of the Eskimo seems almost unlimited. Consider how he deals with one particular problem. Dr. Edward Weyer, in an article properly titled "The Ingenious Eskimo," has this to say:[28]

---

[28] Weyer, Edward, "The Ingenious Eskimo," in *Natural History*, Nat. History Museum, N.Y., May, 1939, pp. 278-279.

Take the Eskimo's most annoying enemy, the wolf, which preys on the caribou and wild reindeer that he needs for food. Because of its sharp eyesight and keen intelligence, it is extremely difficult to approach in hunting. Yet the Eskimo kills it with nothing more formidable than a piece of flexible whalebone.

He sharpens the strip of whalebone at both ends and doubles it back on itself, tying it with sinew. Then he covers it with a lump of fat, allows it to freeze, and throws it out where the wolf will get it. Swallowed at a gulp, the frozen dainty melts in the wolf's stomach and the sharp whalebone springs open, piercing the wolf internally and killing it. . . .

Such ingenuity is deceiving in its very simplicity, yet this simplicity is characteristic of almost everything he does. He makes hunting devices of all kinds that are effective, inexpensive in time, easily repaired, and use only raw materials immediately available. His harpoon lines have floats of blown-up skins attached so that the speared animal is forced to come up to the surface if he dives. To prevent such acquatic animals from tearing off at high speed dragging the hunter and his kyack, he attaches baffles to the line which are like small parachutes that drag in the water. All he needs is a bone hoop, a skin diaphragm stretched over it, and some thongs. To locate the seal's movement under the ice, he has devised a stethoscope which owes nothing to its modern western counterpart but works on the same principle.[29]

Recently, a native "telephone" was discovered in use made entirely from locally available materials, linking two igloos that were several hundred feet apart with a system of intercommunication, the effectiveness of which was demonstrated on the spot to a Hudson's Bay agent, a Mr. D. B. Marsh. At the end of his report, Marsh makes this statement:[30]

> The most amazing thing of all was that although doubtless they may have heard of them from their friends who time to time visit Churchill, no one in that camp had ever seen a telephone.

Moreover, it is exceedingly unlikely that any of these friends who had seen the telephone would ever have seen the kind of arrangement this Eskimo had devised which, of course, used no batteries. As children, we used to make a similar kind of thing with string threaded through the bottom of a tin can, but they were never of much use; whereas in this case the Eskimo had used fur around the diaphragm to cushion it and the sound came through quite as well as it often does on country phones of modern design. The Eskimo has developed

---

[29] Stethoscope: an illustration of such an instrument is given by A. Goldenweiser, ref. 10, p. 85.

[30] Marsh, D. B., "Inventions Unlimited," *The Beaver*, The Hudson's Bay Co., Dec., 1943, p. 40.

another item for outdoor use which the White Man has likewise found indispensible in the Arctic, namely, snow goggles. I have in my possession a pair of these, of native manufacture, and it is doubtful if they are any less efficient in protecting the eyes against a very unpleasant ailment of snow blindness than the more sophisticated White Man's product which was patterned after them. They also have this advantage that they never fog up in the cold, which manufactured goggles are very apt to do.

The Eskimos, unlike many other primitive people who somehow suffered rather than gained by contact with the White Man, have proven themselves well able to adapt to the mechanics of our civilization. They are adept in handling machinery, and not only quickly learn how to use sewing machines but also how to repair them. Similarly the repair of watches seems to present no problem to them.

When we are assured that Paleolithic Man made and used the same kind of weapons, clothed himself with the same kind of raw materials in an environment which must have been very similar at times, and hunted the same kinds of animals for a livelihood, it is difficult to believe that he was less intelligent. The slouching, half-brute creatures which adorn (?) the pages of books for popular consumption dealing with our earliest ancestors, might very well rise up in indignation against us for our gross misrepresentation of their intellectual capacity.

When we find that all those primitive people of recent or modern times who have been taken as representatives of man in his earliest stages of evolution are people who, upon better acquaintance, prove themselves to be intelligent, musical, creative within the limits of their environment, peaceable, fond of their children, and with a highly developed sense of morality and social responsibility within their own group, it is clear either that the choice of them as models of Early Man is entirely wrong, or Early Man had all the capacities of which modern men can boast.

It should be admitted that the older view of such primitive societies as supplying us with a picture of what Early Man was like, has fallen into disfavor as those societies have come to be better understood. It has turned out that the word "primitive" is no longer strictly appropriate. In the recent well known *Life* publication, *The Epic of Man*,[31] a chapter is devoted to a dramatization of the daily life of one tribe of Australian aborigines and one family of Caribou Eskimo. The chapter is entitled, "Stone Age Cultures of Today,"

[31] By the Editors of *Life* Magazine, *The Epic of Man*, Time Inc., N.Y., 1961, pp. 243 f.

and in the introductory paragraphs, it is stated that "these are people of the twentieth century who still hunt, eat, and obey codes and taboos just as all men did in the Stone Ages." The section which deals with the Caribou Eskimo is accompanied by a number of photographs taken prior to the very recent contact of these people with the White Man's civilization which occurred as late as 1949, and these photographs are then said to "stand as a record of patterns of living little changed from those evolved by Middle Stone Age Man, some 10,000 years ago."

It is true that Middle Stone Age Man is, by many standards of assessment, recent. But some of the other primitive societies, such as the Tasmanians for example, have customarily been taken to reflect *Old* Stone Age man. The point of importance here is that no matter how primitive these living examples have been found to be in terms of the kind of artifacts which would survive the passage of time if buried in the ground and which would thus be taken by future archaeologists as a means of assessing their status as human beings, we know in point of fact that such people are essentially no different from ourselves. Their chief lack was, or is, a dearth of sources of power and tools to master their environment, and a sophisticated form of keeping written records. As we shall see, the absence of these things gives to their culture a primitive aspect which belies the true character of the people themselves.

Well established habits of thought die hard and the popular press, even when it pretends to being scientific, does little to dispel the view that the simplicity of their culture is due to their being, individually, very low in the evolutionary scale of Homo sapiens. Anthropologists themselves in their more serious moments repudiate this view entirely, yet when addressing the general public through the medium of the popular press they have a tendency to support the common view.

However, it may be worthwhile pointing out that although they do in fact repudiate the view that these people are truly representative of Paleolithic Man, they do so because they believe that such primitive societies no longer qualify as acceptable models. Upon closer acquaintance they have been found to be far too intelligent... which the earliest human beings, they say, cannot possibly have been. We thus find a curious twist in the development of anthropological theory which first of all seized upon them as undeniable proofs that early man was very primitive and lacking in intelligence, and then had to confess that the analogy was not sound because they turned out to have far too much intelligence. But the public has not been allowed yet to observe this little comedy of errors because, if a little muddled thinking is allowed, the analogy still has considerable heuristic value.

In such articles as that so beautifully illustrated in *The Epic of Man,* the reader is being invited to draw the conclusion for himself that these really are representatives of Stone Age types. What is seldom pointed out in this kind of article, as far as I have been able to determine, is that any one of the individuals thus portrayed is capable, if taken young enough and given the right opportunities and environment, of proving himself as educable and as intelligent and as forward-looking as ourselves. One is forced to conclude that if any one of their very ancient forbears in Europe and elsewhere of Paleolithic times, whose artifacts suggest they were living at the same kind of cultural level, had been set down in a modern industrial community and protected against the environment as we are protected and nurtured in childhood as we are nurtured and educated as we are educated, he would have been as intelligent and forward-looking as any of us moderns. We can say this with some measure of confidence because we now have a better understanding of the capabilities of native people who, in individual cases, have had these opportunities and have easily demonstrated their competence. Frithjof Schoon has recently said:[32]

> The mental distance between a living so-called "primitive" and a "civilized" person is regarded as equivalent to thousands of years, but experience proves that this distance, where it exists, is equivalent to no more than a few days, for man is everywhere and always man.

Theodosius Dobzhansky a little while ago observed:[33]

> The cranial capacity of the Neanderthal race of *Homo sapiens* was on the average equal to or even greater than that in modern man. Cranial capacity and brain size are, however, not reliable criteria of "intelligence" or intellectual abilities of any kind. The painters of the Altamira and Lascaux Caves may have been no less talented than Picasso.

As a matter of fact, for all we know, we may actually have in our possession some of their fossil remains — yet we reconstruct their cranial fragments to look appropriately primitive, if not brutal, and reward ourselves with congratulations upon our own cultural superiority. Yet most of us could scarcely draw a thing! Dobzhansky said, "It is indeed possible, though not proved, that even if we were

---

[32] Schoon, Frithjof, *Light on the Ancient Worlds,* Perennial Books, London, 1965, pp. 107-108.
[33] Dobzhansky, Theodosius, "Changing Man," *Science,* 155 (1967): 410, 411.

brought up to lead the life of our Paleolithic ancestors we would be less efficient in their environment than they were."[34]

A few years ago it was reported that an Australian aborigine named Harold Blair, then 24 years of age, was writing his Ph.D. thesis on 15th and 16th century composers. It was stated that he spoke German, Italian, and English fluently.[35] At a time when the successful education of the children of such primitive people was a matter of great surprise, there were many such reports. The Hon. J. M. Creed,[36] writing in the well-known English journal, *Nineteenth Century* (it is now called *Nineteenth Century and After*) in 1905, gave a number of striking illustrations. Repeatedly the writer states that these Australian aborigine children not only held their own against white children but very frequently indeed showed themselves to be superior in intelligence. Similar reports appeared in the English journal *Nature* towards the end of the last century.[37] This is admitted every so often by various anthropologists. Robert Braidwood, in his useful little book *Prehistoric Men* has an intriguing series of illustrations in which flint weapons and tools are imposed over their modern counterparts in order to show how closely the ancient designs anticipated modern ones, or in other words, how little we have really improved on their basic design, per se.[38]

We have to be careful how we judge lower cultures, especially when we have information only about the simplicity of their weapons and commodities. And since we do have plenty of evidence that their children can make first class scholars when given opportunity, we ought to bear this in mind when assessing the intelligence of early man. Kenneth Oakley recently pointed this out:[39]

> We have no reason to infer that all Early Paleolithic Men had brains qualitatively inferior to those of the average man today. The simplicity of their culture can be accounted for by the extreme sparseness of the population and their lack of accumulated knowledge. A supposed hall-mark of the mind of Homo sapiens is the artistic impulse — but archaeological evidence suggests that this trait manifested itself almost at the dawn of tool making.

A corollary of the argument that Paleolithic Man was not essentially

---

[34] Ibid., p. 411.
[35] Harold Blair: reported by Canada Press, in *Toronto Evening Telegram*, Mar. 17, 1949.
[36] Creed: quoted by E. L. Heermance, *The Unfolding Universe*, Pilgrim Press, N.Y., 1915, p. 170.
[37] See *Nature*, 40 (1889) : 634.
[38] Braidwood, Robert J., *Prehistoric Men*, Popular Series, Anthropology # 37, Chicago Nat. Hist. Museum, 1948.
[39] Oakley, Kenneth, "The Evolution of Human Skill," in *A History of Technology*, ed. Singer, Holmyard, and Hall, Vol. I, Oxford, 1957, p. 27.

different in mental capacity from ourselves is, of course, that *we* are not ourselves essentially different from Paleolithic Man in mental capacity. Jacobs and Stern observed, "Available knowledge supports the conclusion that during the Pleistocene epoch following the appearance of fire and of cutting tools of stone, the mental potentialities ... were equal, and have continued to be equal ever since."[40] This is quite generally agreed upon today, at least to the extent that it is freely admitted that our children are not in any way mentally superior when they begin their education. Robert Briffault observed:[41]

> It may be doubted whether the modern civilized individual differs greatly as regards inherited capacities from his ancestors of the Stone Age; the difference between savagedom and civilization is not organic but cultural. The increase in our knowledge of ancient types of man has, in some respects, accentuated rather than attenuated the abruptness of the transition from animality to humanity; the oldest human remains and the tools associated with them indicate a brain capacity which is not markedly, if at all, inferior to that of existing races.

Indeed, the anthropologist, William Howells,[42] considered that "there are no signs whatever to indicate that the Neanderthals were our inferiors in intelligence," and he adds that this could in fact be "a statement which is more flattering to us than to them."

Sir Alfred Zimmern, in one of the Oxford Pamphlets on World Affairs, after speaking briefly on how the barbarities of World War II were shattering our naive beliefs in automatic linear progress, said:[43]

> We know today that these hopes were unwarranted. Acquired characters are not inherited, at least not in any form or degree which are relevant for sociologists and political scientists. For all practical purposes, the material of human nature, the stock of instincts and impulses, of qualities and attitude, with which our statesmen have to contend is the same as that with which not merely Pharaoh and Nebuchadnezzar but the tribal leaders of the Stone Age had to deal.
> Every baby that is born ... is a Stone Age baby. ... It is the problem of primitive man in the modern world.

We are dealing here with early man, not with so-called ape-men or creatures who are hopefully presented as missing links between men and apes. We are comparing the intelligence of modern man with the intelligence of the earliest identifiable *men*. The point is important because we are not trying to prove anything more than that the earliest true men were quite as intelligent as ourselves, and

[40] Jacobs, Melville and B. J. Stern, *Outline of Anthropology,* Barnes and Noble, N.Y., 1947, p. 29.

[41] Briffault, Robert, "Evolution of Human Species," in *The Making of Man,* ed. V. F. Calverton, Modern Library, N.Y., 1931, p. 763.

[42] Howells, W., *Mankind So Far,* Doubleday Doran, N.Y., 1945, p. 166.

[43] Zimmern, Sir Alfred, *The Prospects of Civilization,* Oxford Pamphlets on World Affairs, 1939, p. 23.

that the simplicity of their culture was not because they were nearer to the apes than modern man is but because of other circumstances which are entirely historical (i.e., in no sense biological), which we shall examine subsequently. Goldenweiser was speaking the simple truth when he wrote:[44]

> Broadly speaking there is no such thing as a primitive mind; primitive man is potentially like modern man or any other kind of man.... Primitive mind is primitive because it is rooted in a primitive culture.

The truth of the matter is that the intelligence of a man expresses itself only so far as his cultural milieu will allow it to, and if for historical reasons this cultural environment is conservative rather than progressive, the individuals who are born into it will seldom have the opportunity to display their intellectual potential, and by the time they are mature, even the desire to think independently will have virtually disappeared. What are the factors, then, in a primitive society which render its spirit so intensely conservative, stifling initiative and leading first to stagnation and, then, all too frequently, to degeneration?

A small group of even the most intelligent people in a hostile environment and without any of the resources that we now take for granted may find itself, after having been pressured into this position from behind (a subject which is discussed at some length in another Doorway Paper),[45] placed in such a position that the margin of survival is so tenuous that only dependable and well-tried techniques of obtaining food, clothing, shelter, and warmth can afford to be countenanced. An experimental failure can mean the demise of the experimenter and his family, a real possibility in many situations, which discourages curiosity as it discourages the development of all arts which are not strictly practical in their aim. There is plenty of evidence that primitive people, in areas where the struggle to survive is intense, have tended to relinquish one by one certain less essential elements of their cultural heritage simply because the total life of the community had reached such a low ebb that there was neither the energy nor the will to sustain them. In a few extreme cases we have a situation in which the community is rather like a man inadequately protected against extreme cold. He stands shivering and restless at first until he finds a spot that offers some shelter, if not from the cold at least from the wind. Gradually he draws himself in, wraps himself about, as it were, with his own body in the desperate need to conserve

---

44 Goldenweiser, A., ref. 10, p. 407.
45 "Primitive Cultures: Their Historical Origins" in this volume.

heat. Movement of any kind becomes more and more of a threat to comfort and he therefore extends himself less and less. He finally reaches the ultimate position in which heat conservation in vital areas is maximum — and fearful of making the slightest move, he slowly freezes to death.

He may know, in the early stages of the ordeal, that he could do something else besides merely conserving heat. He may know quite well that if only he will break away and be active he can *generate* heat. But starting with little enough energy and soon having even less will, the idea of changing his position becomes less and less attractive and his refusal to act is soon justified on the ground that he would only be risking the present small comfort for an initial discomfort, the advantages of which cannot be guaranteed. So he moves as little as possible and seeks comfort and assurance by making no changes. That this comfort steadily diminishes is compensated for, in part, by the fact that as the life processes grow steadily feebler, so does the urge to do something about it becomes less. Ultimately, of course, he dies —as primitive cultures die in like manner once the margin of survival has become small enough.

Now, while all this is true of primitive cultures within the historic period, it may not have been true, of course, of Paleolithic Man. Paleolithic Man was perhaps not always being pressured from behind, but he did share this in common with modern primitive cultures, that he had very small resources in terms of power and cultural heritage and was in the truest possible sense of the term pioneering in virtually every step he took. Any solutions that he found to the pressing problems of providing food, clothing, shelter, and warmth which were at least for the time being sufficient for his immediate needs, tended to be preserved unchanged as long as the margin of survival was small. Only after there came to be a measure of superfluity was there time to sit back and think of other ways of doing things. We have tremendous power resources at our finger tips, a fact which provides us with leisure to rethink. We have learned how to dominate our environment to a large extent. Grahame Clark,[46] in his book *From Savagery to Civilization,* has made some interesting calculations on the total power resources in the whole of Europe in Paleolithic times and concludes that it was probably less than the power available to us now in one single well designed gasoline engine.

This consciousness of power gives us a very different feeling towards the forces of Nature. Early Man, like primitive man, had no

[46] Clark, Grahame, *From Savagery to Civilization,* Cobbett, London, 1946, p. 28.

such assurance, and this lack of assurance persisted well into the historical period of Egyptian and Babylonian times, and is reflected in earlier forms of religion. His view of reality led him to seek to enter into a contract with the powers of Nature whereby, if he fulfilled certain obligations and avoided certain "intrusions," he expected Nature to do the same with him. To man in such a precarious position, the feeling of community with Nature is very close. She must not be offended in any way, or, for example, the caribou will not come back to provide food and raiment next winter, and the rains will not come to fertilize the seed planted hopefully in the parched desert, and so forth.

The simplicity of a culture bears upon the ingenuity of its solutions to the problems of getting food. Nature is sensitively balanced as we know only too well, and primitive people are aware of this, though they treat the word "sensitively" in its psychological sense. A rabbit, a bird, a fish, or a bear must be killed respectfully and cooked in the proper way. One does not cook certain forms of life together, simply because these forms of life are antagonistic in Nature. The Indians of North America were horrified at the first plows of iron used by the White Man. One should use wood which grows out of the earth, if one wishes to plow Mother Nature. Nor should a steel knife be used to cut fish, but only bone, because the fish are accustomed to having bone in their flesh. When killing certain types of animals, such as bears, one apologized, especially if bears were scarce, so that the spirit of the bear would go away peaceably and return again in due time. The Naskapi Indians always had a threefold Blessing for food before eating it: "Thank you Creator, for sending the Caribou; thank you Caribou, for being obedient and coming; and thank you Cook, for preparing it so well."

This meant that one did not simply go out and kill animals. There was a wrong way and a right way, a dangerous way and a safe way. The safe and proper way must be taught to the rising generation. It usually involved a great deal of sound factual knowledge. The chains of cause and effect were more carefully noted than we are apt to suppose: but the interpretation was entirely different from ours. Yet it worked. When it was a matter of life and death, observation had to be precise and clear.

But another important consideration in this transfer of exact knowledge and skill is the fact that there were no written records of it. This inevitably made the older members of the community the only "knowing" or educated people. A young man could not short-circuit experience by reference to a handbook that at times might make him more knowing than his teacher. He had to learn the correct way to kill and prepare a bear or a bird from an older man. And when learning is the preserve of the older members of the community, it is far more conservative, for only youth wants to change things all the time.

Besides, animals and people are related. One had to be careful not to kill a relative. The Australian aborigines believe that at one time animals and men were kind of animal-men creatures. Then one day they were separated. Some men parted from a kind of ostrich-man, some from a rabbit-man, some from a walla-walla-man, and so forth. Thus each tribe has a totem or brother animal that is taboo as food, since it is a relative. Once a year however, a ceremonial communion feast is held in which the men dress up like their totem animal, and eat the flesh of that particular animal ceremonially. This unites the tribe with its animal brothers, and momentarily restores the ancient days before the division existed. These feasts are very solemn occasions. All kinds of ritual are prescribed. The slightest error in recitation or dance step or body movement or "table manners" can be fatal, for the ostrich or the rabbit will be offended and will then warn all the other animals which are not taboo as food, and the plants too, of the unworthiness of the tribe to be permitted to continue its existence. So there is much to learn, and it is learned only by rote, not by understanding. And the movements, dances, and costumes are learned from the older men in secret and cannot be learned any other way.

The Australian is no exception in this, though better known because many of his traditional beliefs have survived into the present. But what is true of the aborigine in Australia is true of the Eskimo, the American Indian, and the African native. We distinguish between the supernatural and the natural with a kind of precision that is totally beyond the native. To him, there is no such division. The contract between man and the world about him was always a contract between persons, though he himself was a very minor party in this agreement.

Such guarantees for the safety of the community were carried out only by the older men who knew how. There were no short-cuts for precocious children, any more than we would send an inexperienced youth on a very grave mission to some powerful monarch. Nature was not considered as It, but as Thou, and the relations between men and Nature were personal, not impersonal. The forces of Nature were more like Wills than forces, just as the characteristics of things were Characters. One did not ask, "What happened?" One asked, "Who did it?" The kind of question determined the kind of search. Cause and effect were interpreted accordingly. Thus in the presence of any situation that demanded attention, the attitude of the individual was one of involvement. In exactly the same way that we cannot normally treat people as things (doctors are therefore reluctant to operate on their relatives), in this same way these people could not stand in the presence of Nature as a "thing." The native lore of the American indians has a real beauty to it — it is the beauty of long experience with life and it is not communicated quickly. Education in such a society is education in wisdom, as well as in knowledge — indeed, more than in knowledge.

Moreover, in such a personal view, the concept of experimenting to "find out" is akin to sacrilege. It seems to the native rude and improper to tamper with things just to see what would happen. Events are not analyzed intellectually, they are experienced individually. Emotional involvement concentrates all attention on the detailed present, and freedom for the objective association of ideas in the past is virtually denied. Man becomes entangled in the immediacy of his perceptions. This attitude is viewed as the proper one. It is analogous to "paying attention" and "being respectful." Such a precept was taught as fundamental to survival to every youngster about to become a man. It formed the basis of his search for a vision to guide him in the choice of an emblem or guardian spirit. He had to find some special "power" in Nature with whom to establish specific relations as a kind of go-between or mediator.

The sense of weakness in the face of the Wills of Nature is very marked, and it even continued to a large extent in Europe until the Greeks challenged it. Among the Hebrews it was converted from "superstition" to reverence, and awe: but the idea of tampering with Nature was still quite abhorrent. The world continued to be confronted not with detachment, but as equally involved in the service and worship of God. Hence the strong element of animation in the Psalms. We may interpret this now as being one way of declaring the appropriateness of God's every created thing. But to the Hebrew it was probably something more than this. Even in Babylonia and in Egypt, man in society accompanied the principal changes in nature with appropriate rituals, which were viewed not as merely symbolic, but as "willed" counterparts, part and parcel of the cosmic events. Man *shared* in these events, just as the Hopi rainmaker shares in the making of rain. The same clearly is true of early China. The festivals are but later reflections of such ancient beliefs, though they have lost much of their meaning because of cultural changes induced by contacts with the West.

There is logic in much of what is done. The Hopi stamps his feet to wake up the earth so that it will be quite ready to receive the rain that heaven is about to give. Some things are more alive than others. Fire is particularly so. But then some animals are more alive than others, so it seems. When a man makes an image of an enemy and commits this to the flames, he is asking the fire to judge between him and his foe. If the fire burns the image furiously, the fire has given a clear decision in his own favor. It would not occur to a native to ask whether perhaps the wood of the image was particularly dry, and therefore burnt quickly on that account. The fire was asked to give a clear decision, and this decision was given. That settles the matter.

Frankfort summarized this view so manifest in Mesopotamia and Egypt, where, though culture was certainly not "primitive" in the accepted sense, the attitude towards nature persisted for a surprising length of time, thus showing how strong such feelings can be:[47]

> The Universe did not, like ours, show a fundamental bipartition into animate and inanimate, living and dead, matter. Nor had it different levels of reality: anything that could be felt, experienced, or thought had thereby established its existence, was part of the cosmos. In the Mesopotamian Universe everything, whether living being, thing, or abstract concept — every stone, every tree, every notion — had a will and a character of its own.
>
> World order, the regularity and system observable in the Universe, could accordingly be conceived of in only one fashion: an order of wills. The Universe as an organized whole was a Society, a State.

In this State man was very powerless. Even animals had more power at times; and of course earthquakes, thunder and lightning, mighty floods, and eclipses were overpowering in their willful destruction and terrifying aspects. Such forces are not to be played with.

Thus it was important to be able to discern Nature's mood of the moment. One must always be on the lookout for evidences of enmity or disapproval in Nature. The slightest irregularity in events boded ill for the observer. It is no wonder, therefore, that the exception — not the rule — was the object of chief interest. Signs and omens, not laws, were the center of attention. Education was intended to render this awareness more acute. Moreover, if one can cajole or persuade Nature to be friendly or merciful toward oneself, obviously one ought to be able to persuade Nature to be injurious to an enemy. So arises the use of both White and Black Magic, and the battle of

---

[47] Frankfort, H. et al., *The Intellectual Adventure of Ancient Man,* Univ. Chicago Press, 1946, p. 149.

"lobbyists" in this giant republic begins. Education becomes not merely a matter of learning to preserve the cultural values and skills as such, but also of learning to preserve oneself in a rather hostile environment where conspiracy is rampant and where true safety lies in knowing either the right people (spirits) or the right formulae (i.e., rituals). The exactness of one's response was all important. Errors could be fatal.

The more precarious the society, the more suspicious will it be of the exceptional or outstanding individual; and the less favorable will it be to innovations either in word or deed on the part of one of its members. Such innovations can only have a secret and dangerous meaning. There is no room for the brilliant child or for the individualist in the clan.

All these considerations have a profound bearing on the problems of the education of the next generation and therefore the future evolution of the culture itself. In the first place, the whole emphasis would be upon the survival of the community as a whole, and not upon the encouragement of the individual as such. Conformity would be the watchword, preservation of existing knowledge the goal. In a situation where the old men hold the keys of knowledge, tradition and conservatism rule the day. Youth has no power to effect changes. Furthermore, the older men would be jealous of the younger man who proved exceptionally gifted. Since the method of injuring one's enemies is by the use of magic in which the old men are skilled and the young are not, a young man dare not risk running foul of a superior. Discretion rules the day and serves very nicely to discourage ambition before it can feed upon itself and express itself overtly.

The main emphasis in all education of this sort is on memorization rather than on creative mental activity. The young are taught to *learn*, not to think. Since a creative mind must create or cease to be creative, any who might have had new insights and new ideas were soon rendered mentally docile and inactive for lack of encouragement.

But this leads naturally to a consideration of inventions. What happens when a man has a new idea — can he introduce it? The answer is, yes and no. He may introduce it if it does not conflict with an already existing pattern in the society. Too much is involved, too many ramifications, to permit much disturbance. It is analogous to the "disappearance" of the occasional invention of, say, a new carburetor that cuts down gas consumption by 75%. The oil companies cannot allow this, so it is said. However, the rejection of such an invention in our culture is a completely rationalized and objective one; in other cultures it may be an emotional one.

Let us say that an invention appears which does not conflict with existing patterns, and is accepted. Then what happens? Can it be improved upon? Again, the answer is Yes and No. Yes, by the originator; No, by anyone else. To attempt to improve the invention is an insult to its inventor. It is analogous to adding a mustache to a friend's photograph to improve his appearance. We just don't do that kind of thing, even if we are sure it will improve his appearance and sure that he will never see it again.

In the same way that every symbol is wedded to the "thing" for which it stands and which called it forth, so every invention is wedded to the circumstance which called it into being. It cannot be used by transfer in some other application. It is just conceivable that wheels, for example, were first used for toys in the New World, and that *for this reason* they were never subsequently applied to larger vehicles.[48] It is however, true also that they had no draft animals. Yet wheeled platforms could have been used for the moving of stones, etc., especially in view of their road systems. At any rate, to divorce the invention from its inventor or its original application was not wise. This is not so strange really, for anyone in our society with an inventive mind will experience the same kind of feeling of identity with his invention and will tend to resent its modification unless the modification is initiated by himself. It seems like robbery otherwise. Thus even though the originator was dead, his spirit could be dangerously offended if his invention were in any way changed. So development, the evolution of civilization, was restrained by such beliefs. On the other hand, a stranger could introduce a new idea, and it might be welcomed — if it did not conflict with other elements in the culture. If the stranger then withdrew his invention could be safely modified. His spirit was no longer around to make such activity dangerous. But again, if a native of the culture radically modified the invention, it could then come to be identified as *his* invention and thenceforth its modification was taboo.

It was also important, in this exchange of ideas, that the right kind of person sponsor the innovation at the beginning. A king who favored some device of no value whatever could "stick" his people with it for the rest of their cultural history. But an unpopular or despised member of a society who happened to be the first contact to introduce a new device would thereby cast a shadow over it so that it might never gain acceptance no matter how desirable it was intrinsically.

---

[48] For a photograph of a wheeled toy, see P. Herrman, *Conquest by Man,*

This is not only true of new devices — it is equally true of new *ideas*. As Robert Lowie said:[49]

> Training, accordingly, was not in the interests of expanding but of preserving knowledge: and if new observations ran palpably counter to the old they were not treasured but discarded. The conscious striving by trained workers to increase knowledge regardless of past convictions is unknown in primitive and early cultures.

In a primitive society the community largely takes precedence over the individual, and communities as such are not progressive. The individual provides the motive power for revision of the status quo. It was Lebzelter who formulated the principle that small communities are variant in physical type but homogeneous in culture, whereas large societies tend toward the opposite in each case — uniform in physical type but more variant in cultural patterns.[50] The variability of physical type is due to the existence of mutant genes which have a better chance of finding phenotypic expression homozygously in a small community. The cultural pattern is, however, uniform, because there is not sufficient room for a man with different tastes.

There is a parallel in modern society. The individual worker feels so powerless in the presence of a strong employer. Only by identifying himself with a union can he feel secure. A small culture with little total power in the face of Nature presents the same condition, and the individual within it has only one hope in the struggle, and that is to identify himself completely with the group which then acts as a "giant self." The odd man, the individualistic thinker, is suspect, just like the man who refuses to join the union. Clive Bell put it well. The native who stops to think in such a society runs the risk of stopping altogether.[51] By the same token the little man cannot afford to arouse the suspicions of his union.

Now, under such circumstances, as early societies developed, there would be an increasing measure of control of the environment until some degree of personal liberty would be permissible. Yet so long as the feeling of kinship with an all powerful Cosmos existed, such individualism would be restricted. The idea of an Egyptian "gentleman" was a man who never disturbed things. The same has been true in Chinese society. It was true in England until new forces came into play which upset the old accepted patterns.

Harper, N.Y., 1954, fig. 32; and for a short bibliography, see K. Macgowan, *Early Man in the New World*, Macmillan, 1950, p. 26, ref. 2.

[49] Lowie, Robert, *Introduction to Cultural Anthropology*, 2nd ed., Farrar, N.Y., 1940, p. 336.

[50] Lebzelter, Viktor, quoted by Wilhelm Koppers, *Primitive Man and His World Picture*, Sheed and Ward, London, 1952, p. 219, ref. 252.

[51] Bell, Clive, *Civilization*, Penguin Books, 1938, pp. 43, 44.

Even the expression of emotion is discouraged, for it reveals the inner feelings to who knows what hostile invisible (or visible) forces. If one must express feelings, then they are to be shown violently, as a warning. This is the way primitive man thinks about such things.

Goldenweiser has spoken of the occasional new insight and its fate.[52] He said:

> It is, of course, inevitable with man that deliberation and therefore awareness will here and there break into the course of the industrial process. But the spark of intellectual discernment flickers but for a moment, presently to go out again. What is passed on to the following generation is the objective result, not the intellectual insight. This is so because these pursuits, one and all, are direct and pragmatic. What is aimed at is achievement, not understanding.

He thus refered to such culture growth as being by involution rather than by evolution:[53]

> This feature has often been commented on by observers of primitive life. The all pervading ceremonialism of the Todas, the interminable exchanges of presents attending Trobriand marriages, the minute apportionment of a hunting booty among the Central Australians (just such and such a piece to such and such a relative), the elaborateness of Maori or Marquesan Art (arts that overreach themselves), the ravages of tabu in Polynesia (tabu run amok) — all of these and many similar cultural traits exhibit development by involution.

So each society permits development by slight changes in the existing pattern but always within itself. An extra little kick of the foot in a ceremonial dance, a new gesture added (at first with much trepidation) in a traditional pantomime, a very slight change of angle in a pattern used for vase decoration. And so on. By these, men preserved some small measure of individualism.

But extraordinary limitations were placed on ritual modifications, simply because in the ritual the whole universe, including the society performing it, was personally involved as a single unit. The "crowd" character here asserted itself enormously. The individual had ceased to exist. Yet not entirely, for the group was drawn into one person and personally represented by the king or priest.

In all this, preservation is the watchword. Tradition is the wisdom of the ages. The old men were its repositories, and they kept their knowledge in secret societies to which no youngster was admitted.

This pattern of distrust for innovation survived even in Europe and England until remarkably recent times. The reception accorded a series of inventions which we take for granted now was at first uniformly hostile. Samuel Martin made a special study of this some

---

[52] Goldenweiser, A., ref. 10, p. 411.
[53] Ibid., p. 414.

years ago.[54] Among the products to which great resistance was offered he listed coal, printing, the ribbon loom, the stocking loom, table forks, the sawmill, the steam engine, tea, the spinning-jenny, steamboats, railways, the use of gas, macadamized roads, and some other items that seem essential to us today, which were at first refused in almost every case on the grounds that they would upset the status quo of society.

We have a series of chains of cause and effect. No matter how intelligent early man may have been, when he faced Nature with very limited resources without the prophetic vision that such resources as we have would ever become available, he must have quickly learned (as primitive people show) to come to terms with Nature, not by dominating it but by identifying himself with it mystically. The sheer impotence of man thus situated when faced with the prodigious powers of Nature as well as the inbuilt wisdom of the animal world, must have been so driven home to him that he had no alternative but to adopt a very humble attitude, looking upon himself not as the lord of creation but as one of the feeblest and least wise of all creatures. As Childe put it:[55]

> Man is now, and was apparently even at his first appearance in the Pleistocene, inadequately adapted for survival in any particular environment. His bodily equipment for coping with any special set of conditions is inferior to that of most animals. He has not, and probably never had, a furry coat like the polar bear's for keeping the body's heat under cold conditions. His body is not particularly well adapted for escape, self-defence, or hunting. He is not, for instance, exceptionally fleet of foot, and would be left behind in a race with a hare or an ostrich. He has no protective coloring like the tiger or the snow leopard, nor bodily armor like the tortoise or the crab. He has no wings to offer escape and give him an advantage in spying out and pouncing upon prey. He lacks the beak and talons of the hawk and its keenness of vision. For catching his prey and defending himself, his muscular strength, teeth, and nails are incomparably inferior to those of the tiger.

If he had not possessed superior intelligence, it is very doubtful indeed whether man could ever have survived at all in such circumstances, especially in view of the very extended period of dependency that his children have upon him. Most animals can fend for themselves very quickly: but not so human beings. One might suppose that if he did have superior intelligence, he would quickly have revealed it by the invention of all kinds of devices compensating for his innate weaknesses, but, as we have seen, intelligence and the

---

[54] Martin, Samuel, "Opposition to Great Inventions and Discoveries," in the *Exeter Hall Papers,* London, 1854-55, pp. 461-500.

[55] Childe, V. G., *Man Makes Himself,* Watts, London, 1936, p. 23.

power to invent are unfortunately related only rather indirectly. Instead of new devices, early man like primitive people, developed, rather, a philosophy of life which in curious ways appears to have allowed survival in environments and circumstances which otherwise must have seemed to be entirely impossible. Whenever this philosophy, as exemplified in modern times in primitive cultures, was undermined by the White Man, the whole system of cultural survival — indeed, the very physical continuance of the people — was endangered. The result was usually fatal, a fact which in itself bears witness of a kind to the practical workability of such philosophies of life where they are preserved intact. The equilibrium between man and nature is very sensitively balanced. And it is well established that history bears testimony to the fact that when individual white men were bereft by circumstances of their own culture and thrown among such primitive people for a long enough period to enter into the spirit of their culture, they tended to adopt its set of values and its ways of survival. It is seldom if ever recorded that such adopted sons introduced any striking changes such as one might suppose their pretended intellectual superiority would inevitably lead them to do. It thus appears that intelligence is not to be equated with the power to innovate or advance a culture, and the tendency to assume that conservatism stems entirely from lack of intelligence while progressiveness is to be equated with it is entirely unwarranted.

At a certain cultural level conservatism is equated with survival, and so long as that level remains unchanged, conservatism is probably the most intelligent philosophy. The conservatism of Paleolithic Man may have been a result of the circumstances in which he found himself and a reflection of practical good sense.

Chapter 4
Intelligence as Judged
by Facial and Head Forms

T HERE IS NO doubt that some people who look intelligent, are intelligent: and there is no doubt that some people who look idiotic, are idiots. In both cases we are guided as a rule by the appearance of the face — not by the shape of the skull. The point is an important one. It is possible for an artist to impose upon the same skull whether it is large, normal, or small a face which suggests a philosopher or a moron, according to his fancy. It is not true that everyone who looks intelligent *is* intelligent, but there is truth in the observation that the man who looks like an idiot is likely to be one. Faces can be deceiving, but there is no question that we do make judgments on the basis of something we see there, whether it is apathy or animation, sparkle or vacuity, or whatever it may be: and in a large number of cases our judgment is apt to be correct.

Thus, if we had actual portraits of Paleolithic Men, we might be in some position to judge more precisely whether their faces were intelligent faces or as vacuous as the face of an ape. But since we do not have such portraits (there may be a possible exception),[56] since we have only skulls and often only a small part at that, there really is no way in which we can assess their intelligence on the basis of bone structure.

There are, of course, certain configurations of the cranium which appear to us to imply brutality or nobility, according to whether the form approaches the idealized White Man both with respect to proportion and to size (i.e., as to cranial capacity). But it is very impor-

---

[56] This exception is possibly to be found in the beautiful ivory head discovered by Dr. Karl Absolon at Vestonice which he suggests is the earliest known portrait of a human being. Several beautiful photographic reproductions appear in *Illustrated London News,* London, Oct. 2, 1937; and see also the Doorway Paper "The Fallacy of Anthropological Reconstructions," in this volume.

tant to keep in mind that the human skull under certain conditions is very plastic and can, due to influences which result from eating habits, and certain diseases, be deformed in a way which increasingly approximates the gorilla-type of skull configuration. And it is equally important to bear in mind that there does not appear to be any clearly established relationship between mental capacity and cranial capacity, some geniuses having surprisingly small heads and some idiots surprisingly large ones. Yet so strong is the pressure of evolutionary philosophy upon our thinking that whenever we are presented with a reconstructed head in which the features have been brutalized by the artist, and whenever we are informed in the accompanying text that the owner's cranial capacity was less than that of modern man by such and such an amount, we automatically and inevitably assume that the creature was something more nearly animal than human in mental capacity. Franz Boas has rightly observed:[57]

> By analogy, we associate lower mental traits with brute-like features. In our naive everyday parlance, brutish features and brutality are closely connected. We must distinguish here, however, between anatomical, muscular development of the face, trunk and limbs due to the habits of life.... We are also inclined to draw inferences in regard to mentality from a receding forehead, a heavy jaw, large and heavy teeth, perhaps even from inordinate length of arms or an unusual development of hairiness.
>
> It appears that neither cultural achievement nor outward appearance is a safe basis upon which to judge the mental aptitude of races.

We shall now consider very briefly these two factors, the brutalization of the facial form and the assessment of cranial capacity in fossil men. And, since this is a more straightforward matter, we will consider first the significance of cranial capacity.

Perhaps the most succinct and comprehensive review of the significance of cranial capacity as an index of intelligence was written by Weidenreich in 1948. His opening words in this article were as follows:[58]

> The discovery of the remains of Peking Man in the cave of Choukoutien, and evidences of a relatively advanced culture at the same site, confronted paleontologists with a new, unexpected and vital problem.
>
> The find of ash layers and burned stones and bones revealed that the man who lived there had knowledge of fire; and the find of stone implements, some of them skillfully chipped, proved that this man was already an able artisan.
>
> On the other hand, the anatomical record of the skulls shows that the cave dwellers represented a very primitive type, morphologically

---

[57] Boas, F., *Mind of Primitive Man*, Macmillan, 2nd ed., 1939, pp. 16 f.

[58] Weidenreich, Franz, "The Human Brain in the Light of Its Phylogenetic Development," *Sci. Monthly*, Aug., 1948, p. 103.

inferior to any fossil human type unearthed up to that time. The cranial capacity of the first skull to be found is not much over 900 cc.

Marcellin Boule, in discussing these finds, was so convinced that a creature with a cranial capacity so small could not possibly have produced this kind of culture that he therefore had to assume that some higher race, morphologically more modern, had overwhelmed the primitives with their small brains, whose bones were represented by Peking Man, and after so doing had left the artifacts and other cultural evidences which were therefore their own work and not that of Peking Man.[59] Weidenreich used this proposal by Boule as a springboard for a most conclusive essay which showed that the underlying concept which relates brain size to culture level is quite unsupportable from the evidence. And, in Weidenreich's view, the convolutions or surface complexities of the brain do not give any indication of level of intelligence either.

He deplored the confidence with which the statement is often made that "cranial capacity is a fairly accurate measure of the mental status from the most primitive primates to Homo sapiens."[60] And he said, "We do not know of any fact which proves that the mere increase of the size of the brain is tantamount to an advance in mental ability."[61] He pointed out that the famous phrenologist himself, Gall, Anatole France the French novelist, and Gambetta the French statesman, each had a cranial capacity of about 1100 cu. cm. At the other extreme, we have the English writer Dean Jonathan Swift, the English poet Lord Byron, and the Russian novelist Turgeniev, all with a cranial capacity of about 2000 cu. cm.[62] So Weidenreich properly posed the question, "Had Turgeniev really twice the mental ability of Anatole France?" And he pointed out that one of the first fossil specimens of Early Man which seemed to support the view that man was more brutish at the beginning, was Neanderthal Man whose cranial capacity was around 1650 cu. cm., which is considerably above the average modern European.

It is sometimes said that man has a larger brain relative to his body weight than any other creature. This, too, said Weidenreich, is quite wrong, for man is far surpassed in this respect by the dwarf monkeys of South America, the marmosets, which have one gram of brain per 27 grams of body substance as opposed to man's one gram of brain substance to 44 grams of body weight.[63] And he is even more

[59] Ibid.
[60] Ibid.
[61] Ibid., p. 104.
[62] Ibid., p. 105.
[63] Ibid., p. 104.

far surpassed by the Capuchin monkey with one gram of brain substance to every 17.5 grams of body substance, i.e., approximately two and a half times as great, relatively speaking.

Again, in the matter of complexity of surface, there is no evidence in man's favor. For, "in the pattern of the surface of the hemispheres, primates and man do not differ from other mammalian orders with regard to the presence and abundance of the wrinkle system."[64] For example, the Capuchin monkey, which many experimental psychologists regard as equal to any highly gifted chimpanzee, possesses an almost smooth brain surface: on the other hand, the whale has the greatest number of finest wrinkles all over the hemispheres of its brain and the most intricate arrangement of all animals. Thus Weidenreich concluded:[65]

> All recorded facts indicate that neither the size nor the form of the brain, the surface of the hemispheres or their wrinkled pattern in general or in detail furnishes a reliable clue to the amount and degree of general or specific mental qualities.

In keeping with this general conclusion, it is not too surprising to find Weidenreich express the opinion that in the face of all these facts, "It is hard to understand why people cannot get rid of the idea that mere size or configuration of a special convolution or fissure must give a clue to mental qualities."[66]

It has been argued that any otherwise normally built man, the cranial capacity of whose head is less than 900 cc., cannot but be an idiot. Nevertheless, under certain circumstances, a remarkable amount of brain tissue can be to all intents and purposes rendered inactive, and yet the patient may continue to act as an intelligent and effective member of society — indeed, more effective for the loss sustained. The former principle of measuring intelligence by the number of cubic centimeters of grey matter is now well recognized to be without foundation, and yet this popular view which seems to fit so nicely into an evolutionary philosophy is still kept alive, simply because it does agree so well with that philosophy. There is almost no factual basis for it.

Turning, then, to the brutalization of the face. Unlike other animals, man is a very slow-maturing creature both physiologically and psychologically. This allows for a great deal of bone modification to take place before the final "set" is given to the face. Some primitive cultures deliberately distort the bone structure to an extraordinary

---

[64] Ibid., p. 106.
[65] Ibid., p. 107.
[66] Ibid., p. 106.

degree by pressure applied with bandages during the first ten or fifteen years of growth.[67]

Thus, there is remarkable plasticity here, and certain factors of an environmental or a cultural nature can have tremendous effect in modifying features. In another Doorway Paper,[68] we have explored at some length and illustrated with a number of line drawings the effect of such "pressures" in order to show that the normal tendency is for the bone structure of the face and head to be brutalized wherever these pressures result from primitive conditions of living. The eating of uncooked or partially cooked foods has the effect, especially in childhood, of strengthening the jaw mechanism and causing it to become more massive in structure, and the increased musculature deforms the skull in certain unmistakable ways. The overall effect is to depress the forehead, rendering the brow ridges more prominent, and forcing outwards the zygomatic arch, thus accentuating the cheekbones. The tugging of flesh from bone in the absence of knives may also accentuate these modifications of the normal jaw structure. Squatting in the absence of chairs may have a tendency to arch the back and lead to the head being carried more forward with respect to the shoulders, so that the muscles that hold the head erect are not only increased in mass but cause also a corresponding enlarging of the bone where the anchorage occurs along the occipital torus. These effects may be particularly pronounced when the diet is lacking in bone hardening substances.

Thus the overall effect in a primitive society is very often to produce a facial form that is peculiarly brutalized, not for genetic reasons but for historic ones, i.e., reasons in the life history of the individual. That this kind of brutalization can take place even among a people who have once known a higher culture and have been forcibly thrust out into a harsh environment, is borne out by what happened to certain Irish families of whom Robert Chambers spoke so eloquently.[69] Thus Professor Wallis wrote:[70]

> It follows that a return to the conditions of diet and life which characterized prehistoric man would be followed by a return to his physical type. Yet if there were this transition to a type more simian

---

[67] For some photographs showing the extraordinary extent to which the human head can be deformed without injuring the owner, see the article by Beatrice Blackwood and P. M. Danby, "Artificial Cranial Deformation in New Britain," *Jour. Roy. Anthrop. Instit.*, Jan.-Mar., 1955, p. 191.

[68] "The Supposed Evolution of the Human Skull," in this volume.

[69] Chambers, Robert, "Vestiges of the Natural History of Creation," Churchill, London, 1844.

[70] Wallis, W. D., "The Structure of Prehistoric Man," in *The Making of Man*, ed. V. F. Calverton, Modern Library, N.Y., 1931, pp. 72-73.

we could not say that we were approaching a common ancestor. The similarity would not be due to the transmission of qualities from a common ancestor of a remote past. If this be true, it is equally true that an increase in similarities as we push back the time period does not imply common ancestry.... It seems clear that mere resemblance does not constitute an argument of phylogenetic descent.

This is not a new concept by any means. It has been admitted freely by many authorities, Portmann, Wallis, Hooten, Howells, Hrdlicka, Ackerknecht, Johnson, Coon, Pycraft, Wood Jones, and Gladwin. The phenomenon can be best described as illustrating what is commonly called Convergence, in which living organisms approach each other in form when they are subjected to the same environmental pressures. Since this must often occur in nature, it is not surprising to find Leo S. Berg stating that "convergence and not divergence is the rule, not the exception. It appears to be all pervasive both among plants and animals, present, recent and extinct."[71]

In summary, therefore, it may be said that quite apart from disease, a normal, healthy, human cranium can be brutalized merely as the result of a series of factors in the total environment which have nothing to do whatever with animal ancestry. And it becomes possible for the possessor of a fine intelligent brain to leave behind a skull which would be interpreted by anthropologists as being far down the scale of evolving man. We tend to assume that the painters of those extraordinary subterranean art galleries in Europe must have had features and head forms of noble and benign appearance. In point of fact, they may have been quite brutal in appearance. This may *not* have been so, but some of the skulls which have been reconstructed in our museums into half-ape half-men creatures *may* in fact have been the housings of highly intelligent and refined minds. It is true that one would expect a high intelligence to enable its possessor to live a more refined existence, an existence which would minimize the harsh effects of food and climate upon the bony structure of the skull. But modern Eskimos, who still follow the traditional ways of living for the greater part of their lives, show at least some of the features which characterize the skull of an ape, a powerful jaw and a mild form of keel in the roof of the skull where the attachment of the muscle has reinforced itself, a slightly depressed forehead and strengthened brow ridges, and a face which from the front is seen to be widest at the level of the zygomatic arches rather than in the temporal region as in those whose upbringing has been gentler. Yet

---

[71] Berg, Leo S., *Nomogenesis: of Evolution Determined by Law,* English trans. Constable and Co., London, 1926, p. 174.

these same people give evidence of having plenty of intelligence and no little artistic skill.

There is also the factor of disease. Neanderthal skulls are sometimes held to be diseased skulls, and some of the stoop attributed to certain fossil specimens is now believed to be a result of bone disease of various kinds. Moreover, it is still well established that certain disorders of the endocrine glands can have the effect of greatly modifying the bone structure, and always in such a direction as to tend towards the brutalization of it in its appearance.[72] In view of the fact that disease is believed to have been in evidence in only a few instances of fossil man, we shall not enlarge upon it, but the reader will find much interesting and relevant information in the works of the following: Brody, Dorsey, Haddon, Keith, Mason and Swyer, Speer, and Soffer.[73]

There is, therefore, little from history to support the evolutionary interpretation of the development of intelligence in man from a low to a high level. One cannot *assume* evolution, and then use the assumption to arrange the evidence in such a way as to provide the proof of it. We have no knowledge of any normal child born in health into even the most primitive tribe of which we have any record, who was any less intelligent or educable in the right conditions than our modern hospital babies. And conversely, we do know that a modern hospital baby can grow up to be more brutal, savage, and inhuman than any primitive people have ever shown themselves to be. Neither tools, art, head form, cranial capacity, nor facial features will support the supposed evolution of man. An arrangement of the evidence can be made which superficially may look as though it is supporting this theory, but the whole artificial structure is undermined by the unexpected discovery (one might almost say, unwelcomed discovery) of a completely modern type who appears to be earlier than his supposed ancestors — like Swanscombe and Fontechevade Man, for example.

---

[72] For example, see Jesse William's textbook of *Anatomy and Physiology,* Saunders, Phila., 5th ed., 1935, fn. p. 49.

[73] Brody, S., "Science and Dietary Wisdom," *Sci. Monthly,* Sept., 1945, p. 216; George Dorsey, *Why We Behave Like Human Beings,* Blue Ribbon Books, N.Y., 1925, pp. 108-109; A. C. Haddon, *History of Anthropology,* Thinker's Library, London, 1949, pp. 34 f.; Sir Arthur Keith, quoted by Sir John A. Thompson, *The Outline of Science,* Vol. IV, N.Y., Putnam, 1922, p. 1097, and "Evolution of the Human Races in the Light of the Hormone Theory," *Johns Hopkins Bulletin,* 1922; A. Stuart Mason and G. I. M. Swyer, *Major Endocrine Disorders,* Fairlawn, N.Y., 1959, pp. 15-17; Robert Speer, *Of One Blood,* N.Y., Friendship House, 1924, p. 11; and Louis J. Soffer, *Diseases of the Endocrine Glands,* Lea and Febiger, Phila., 1956, pp. 103-104.

One problem which has plagued the whole study of the origin of man has been to define what *is* man as opposed to what is animal. Although the definition that I am going to propose in the Epilogue could hardly be considered a satisfactory one from a scientific point of view, because no conceivable experiments could be performed to test it out, from the theological point of view, it has much to commend it — and this definition will therefore be explored as a Christian rather than a scientific concept. This might appear to be quite unsatisfactory in approaching a subject which most people would consider to be essentially a physiological matter. There are two things which may be said about this, however: first, that the Christian faith does not look upon man as a spiritual being rather incidentally provided with a body as a temporary measure, but as a spiritual being indwelling a body which was uniquely designed as a proper house without which the spirit cannot express itself completely. Thus, the nature of man's body is very important in the Christian view. And secondly, anthropologists themselves have been quite unable to come up with a definition of man, as opposed to the animals, which will provide a clear cut guide in the assessment of fossil remains. So there is some justification for seeking a Christian definition of man to distinguish him from the animals. Our need is to be able to identify the hallmark of humanness, and as man now is, I believe this hallmark must be sought in the realm of the soul, not the body. I am persuaded that un-Fallen man was distinct from animals physiologically as well as spiritually, but this is the subject of another Doorway Paper.[74]

---

[74] "If Adam Had Not Died," in Volume V.

Epilogue

TO MANY PEOPLE who have read this essay, there may be a number of confusing issues. It is well, therefore, to state very briefly what we do know with reasonable certainty about Early Man. In the first place, from the Christian view of history, there were strictly speaking "no prehistoric times." Within Adam's lifetime, men multiplied until there was sufficient population to support specialized industries, metallurgy, tentmaking, music, agriculture, and indeed city life — for Adam's son built a city. There is no doubt that the word "city" in this context means merely a small cohesive body of people living in a confined area with some measure of community life and a shared culture. Cities in those days often occupied only a few acres of land. This is one fact.

A second virtual certainty is that the same situation repeated itself after the Flood when the population had once again been reduced to a single family. Only, this time, every member of this family already had a certain cultural heritage which must have been quite advanced in nature.

A third assumption is that as this second start in populating the world was made, individuals, families, or splinter groups would break away from the central nucleus and begin the pioneering of the world. There is no reason to suppose that people were essentially different in this respect than they are today. There are always those who move out, who have the urge to explore, who seek to be free and alone. In spite of the hostile nature of the environment, an Eskimo young man will take his wife and head for open country and establish himself, perhaps hundreds of miles from any other fixed settlement. It is even more certain that men would do the same where the environment was temperate and pleasant, and offered every possibility of survival, just as it was inviting to those pioneers in the New World who felt the call of the wide open spaces. It is said that Daniel Boone, when he observed one morning smoke of a fire on the dim, distant horizon, said to his wife, "We're moving on; it's getting crowded."

And, as I have indicated, there is no reason to suppose that human nature has changed in this respect very much.

Thus, as the population at the center gradually grew, individuals and families would undoubtedly move further and further out, seeking freedom from crowding or interference until both Europe and the Far East, and even the New World, would begin to receive its first-comers. As Kenneth Macgowan has pointed out,[75] a man could easily make the trip from China, across the Bering Sea, and well down into the New World in a period of twenty years.

But pioneers like this would inevitably be forced to surrender many elements of their cultural heritage. The circumstances are such, as we visualize it, that they would not only, in the very nature of the case, tend to lose those elements of culture which they had once shared at the center but which no longer contributed directly towards their survival. But they would retain those elements which *did* contribute to their survival. And the basic character of these retained elements would naturally, at least at the beginning, show many similarities wherever men settled, for initially they sprang from the same pool of resources. This is precisely what is found: namely, that the shape and conception of many basic tools, weapons, and artifacts is remarkably similar in areas of the world as widely separated as Central Europe and South America. This has sometimes been attributed to the fact that the same tasks had to be performed by people of like ways of thinking, using materials which were everywhere the same. However, there are a very large number of parallelisms in structural form and embellishment which are not easily accounted for on this basis.

Now to my mind, for the most part it is with these early pioneering and adventurous individuals that we have to do when we are discussing Paleolithic Man. I realize only too well that this runs very much counter to the whole modern conception of what Paleolithic Man represents in terms of evolution and prehistoric processes generally. But I think it is easier in many respects to view the fossil remains of all individuals who are now generally classed as genuinely human as what might be called waifs and strays, fragments of a completely human population thriving at the center and increasingly thinned out and reduced in cultural stature towards the periphery.[76]

One thing seems to me quite certain, and this is that it is impossible on the basis of the head shape or size, or on the basis of

---

[75] Macgowan, Kenneth, *Early Man in the New World*, Macmillan, 1950, p. 3 and map on p. 4.
[76] "A Study of the Names in Genesis 10," in Volume I.

cultural remains however simple they may be, to say with any assurance that this is evidence of man in the making. It is just as likely to be, indeed more likely to be, man in the breaking. Certainly if we allow the present to speak with respect to the past, this is easy to substantiate, as this essay has shown. History provides us with no solid evidence that a human being or even a small family of human beings as reduced in circumstances as fossil man seems to have been, has ever by a natural process of evolution evolved into a highly cultured society. Yet there is no evidence, either, that people so reduced are potentially any less completely human than ourselves.

The simplest proof of this last observation is the testimony of missionaries over the past century or so, and this testimony serves also to provide us with a useful definition of what constitutes true humanness.

When Darwin visited the tip of South America, he found there groups of people living in an environment and under conditions so inimical, so restricting, and so full of discomfort that he found it difficult to understand why human beings, if they *were* truly human beings, would stay there, or indeed could survive. The Tierra del Fuegians were forced by circumstance to spend the larger part of their lives in open canoes in which the children grew up, the adults slept and cooked and spent their daily lives, and the aged died. These people, as a consequence, grew up deformed and with an extraordinarily limited experience. They seldom congregated in groups beyond the size of a family and their artifacts were simple in the extreme. Darwin himself being, of course, well-bred in the ways of the cultured European, was unable to see in these people the human qualities and the social "attainments" which later revealed themselves to a more perceptive student like Bridges.[77]

And since at that time, descriptions of the weird and wonderful ways of primitives from other parts of the world were much in vogue and were eagerly read by many people who felt vastly superior by the reading of them, there was a tendency to exaggerate a little bit and to present the picture of such people in the worst (or best — depending on how you look at it) possible light. Sir John Lubbock said of the Tierra del Fuegians:[78]

These poor wretches were stunted in their growth, their hideous

---

[77] The Rev. Thomas Bridges, a Scottish missionary, arrived among these people in 1863 and spent the rest of a long vigorous life caring for them. Some of his perceptive writing on these people will be found in C. S. Coon, *A General Reader in Anthropology*, Holt, N.Y., 1948, pp. 84-116.

[78] Lubbock, Sir John, *Prehistoric Times*, New Science Library, Hill and Co., N.Y., 1904, p. 201.

faces bedaubed with white paint, their skins filthy and greasy, their hair entangled, their voices discordant, their gestures violent and without dignity. Viewing such men, one can hardly make oneself believe they are fellow creatures and inhabitants of the same world.

Sir John Lubbock was, of course, expressing a secondhand view which allowed him a certain amount of liberty, but this was not true of Charles Darwin. In his *Journal of Researches* he wrote:[79]

> It was without exception the most curious and interesting spectacle I ever beheld. I could not have believed how wide was the difference between savage and civilized man. Their very attitudes were abject....
>
> The language of these people, according to our notions, scarcely deserves to be called articulate. Captain Cook has compared it to a man clearing his throat!

We know now that such opinions were misrepresentations and resulted from a quite insufficient understanding of the true nature and character of these people and their language. Better acquaintance showed that these people were not at all inarticulate, their language containing probably as many words as Shakespeare was able to command.[80] And, of course, they were in full possession of one art which Coon believes to be the only absolutely open and shut mark of distinction between man and the animals, namely, fire.[81] Nevertheless, while we have today a much higher opinion of the intelligence of these primitive people, though they are very nearly extinct, yet it must be admitted that they remain among the most primitive people in the world.

It was not long before the challenge of such a community presented itself to Christian people, and a Mission was organized. When Darwin heard of it, he must have smiled to himself for he was confident that such a mission was a fool's errand; it could not possibly succeed. The story of what was achieved by the first missionaries is, in some respects, a little difficult to sort out precisely, because the events which followed have been presented to the public in two rather different, and in some respects, contradictory ways. We are told by anthropologists of how the pattern of living which these people had developed and by which they had found the way to survive was so disrupted that the whole moral fabric of the society was undermined. Those who had at first been received with open arms and whose ministry had led to a number of conversions were viciously turned

[79] Darwin, Sir Charles, *Journal of Researches,* Ward, Lock and Co., N.Y., 1845, p. 206.

[80] Bridges (see ref. 77) composed a dictionary of some 30,000 Tierra del Fuegian words.

[81] Coon, C. S., *Story of Man,* Knopf., N.Y., 1962, p. 63.

upon and destroyed. According to some versions they were actually eaten by the natives.

However, if we allow Darwin to speak, it would appear that in the comparatively brief interval between the first coming of the missionaries and the final influx of the White Man's pagan civilization, some remarkable changes for the good were effected among these people. Some years later, Darwin wrote to Admiral Sir James Sulivan who was greatly interested in the Tierra del Fuegian Mission:[82]

> I had never heard a word about the success of the Tierra del Fuego Mission. It is most wonderful and shames me, as I had always prophesied utter failure. It is a grand success. I shall feel proud if your Committee think fit to elect me an honourary member of your Society.
> With all good wishes, and affectionate remembrances from ancient days,
>
> Believe me, my dear Sulivan,
your sincere friend,
Charles Darwin.

The missionary efforts undertaken by Bishop Stirling are enthrallingly set forth in a book by his son, A. M. W. Stirling, entitled *Life's Little Day*. Here is revealed how impossible Darwin felt it would be to humanize these natives but Stirling records the fact, which we have already noted, that subsequently Darwin became an annual subscriber to the orphanage of the South American Society.[83] The true humanness of these lowest and most primitive of people is proved beyond doubt by the fact that they could respond to the claims of Jesus Christ, the only perfect Human Being we have knowledge of.

When Captain Cook visited one particular island, he named it Savage Island because the people were so fierce that it was impossible for him to land among them. Later a John Williams tried to evangelize them but was driven off. But in due time, a converted Samoan made a journey of three hundred miles to try to win them for Christ. Within twelve years, out of the 5,000 inhabitants of the island, only eight remained actively heathen. The people as a whole became transformed into a proverbially kind and hospitable community and, according to accounts, they sent every year the sum of £400 (over $1000.) to the London Missionary Society. When a ship was required for a New Guinea Mission, costing £500, they voluntarily undertook to raise the whole amount. When a Home Missionary Group sent £50 to them to meet some extra expenses, the islanders sent it back with thanks, preferring to complete the work themselves. By that

---

[82] This letter is from the biography of Darwin written by his son, Sir Francis.

[83] C. W. H. Amos, D.D., in a letter to the Editor, *The English Churchman and St. James' Chronicle,* Jan. 16, 1959, p. 9.

time thirty married teachers had gone out from that island to New Guinea.[84] Once again, the transforming power of the gospel was proved among people who must have seemed otherwise lacking in humanness and utterly savage.

Here, then, we have the basis for a definition of man. Man is the one creature on earth who can respond to the love of God in Christ and be redeemed, knowingly, effectively, transformingly, and gloriously. Man is the only creature capable of sainthood, the only creature in whom the perfect Man, Christ Jesus, can appropriately reincarnate Himself in a measure. This is the answer to the question, What is Man? It makes no difference how ugly, how deformed, how ignorant, how progressive, how backward, how anything, a creature is. If he is redeemable, he is man. And man's identity as man and his true potential does not depend upon his I.Q., the nobility of his countenance, the complexity of his culture, or the period of world history in which he was born, but on whether the Lord Jesus Christ, the only Perfect Man, can, with dignity and propriety, take up residence in his heart. All other standards of judgment are hopelessly inadequate. Until we know, which we cannot yet, whether Paleolithic Man was redeemable, we cannot know whether he was truly man. This is the simple truth of the matter and every effort to establish the status of fossil man by any other terms of reference will suffer from uncertainty until the Day of Judgment. But in the meantime, we should be very careful not to misjudge by using standards which it can be shown are quite inadequate.

---

[84] Orr, James, *God's Image in Man*, Eerdmans, Grand Rapids, 1948, p. 164.

Part IV

The Supposed Evolution
of the Human Skull

The Supposed Evolution of the Human Skull

> One and the same piece of evidence will assume totally different aspects according to the angle — palaeontological or historical — from which we view it. We shall see it either as a link in one of the many evolutionary series that the palaeontologist seeks to establish, or as something connected with remote historical action.... Let me state clearly that for my part, I have not the slightest doubt that the remains of early man known to us, should be judged historically.
>
> A. Portmann, *Das Ursprungsproblem,*
> Eranos - Jahrbuch, 1947, p. 19.

PRIOR TO MORE recent developments of techniques for dating by means of radioactive materials, there were fundamentally only two methods of estimating the age of a fossil. The first was the geological level at which the specimen was found. The second, applying more particularly to human fossils, was the general appearance: whether apish and "primitive," or essentially like modern man. These two criteria are still largely applied, since the majority of the more ancient remains of early man are completely fossilized and C–14 methods of dating cannot be used.

But it has long been recognized that if the fossil remains of early man are arranged according to their degree of primitiveness, the order will be found to contradict the series arranged on the basis of antiquity as established by the levels at which they are found. This led Franz Weidenreich to formulate the following rule:[1]

> In determining the character of a given fossil form and its special place in the line of human evolution, only its morphological features should be made the basis of decision: neither the location of the site

---

[1] Weidenreich, Franz, "The Skull of Sinanthropus pekinensis: A Comparative Study on a Primitive Hominid Skull," *Paleontologica Sinica,* N.S.D., No. 10, Whole series 127 (1943) : 1.

where it was recovered, nor the geological nature of the layer in which it was embedded is important.

More recently, Leigh van Valen,[2] of the Committee on Evolutionary Biology at the University of Chicago, in reviewing *Evolutionary Biology* by Theodosius Dobzhansky et. al., notes that "three of the contributors (all paleontologists) conclude that stratigraphic position is totally irrelevant to determination of phylogeny and almost say that no known taxon is derived from any other. . . ." It certainly seems brash, therefore, of the proponents of an African genesis for *Homo sapiens* to keep putting man's beginnings further and further back on the basis of the estimated age of the strata in which the fossils are being found.

Now the view held by Weidenreich had become necessary because, if read in any other way, the record had begun to make evolutionary nonsense. On the one hand we had modern types in levels earlier than those in which their supposed ancestors were to be found; and on the other hand in some of the very latest levels, primitive types which "belonged" at the very beginning of the series. Thus Robert Braidwood had written:[3]

> There are one or two early finds of pre-modern types that we need to catch up on. Like Piltdown, there was another questionable find made long ago in England. This was a skull and skeleton (badly broken), found at Galley Hill in gravels of the second interglacial period. The bones looked almost too modern to be so old, for the time is that between the second and third great glaciations of the Ice Age (about 275,000 years ago). But in 1935 the bones of a similar pre-modern skull appeared in gravels of the same geological age at Swanscombe in England. Also, an equally early skull although rather less modern in appearance, turned up in Steinheim, Germany. So it seems pretty certain that a partially modern type of man was already alive a long time ago. In fact these men were alive even before the *main* Neanderthal group.

For the sake of the reader who has a good general idea of accepted anthropological views regarding fossil man, and to whom such terms as Neanderthal Man are familiar in a way, but yet who has no exact mental picture of the sequence in which these types are usually ordered, it may be helpful to give a very brief summary of the picture as seen until recently by anthropologists as a whole.

During the ice age, the alternating cold and warm periods are believed to have witnessed the appearance and disappearance of various types of fossil man. Some were cold weather types, some warm weather types. This accounts for the waves which came and went.

[2] van Valen, Leigh, book review in *Science,* 180 (1973): 488.
[3] Braidwood, Robert, *Prehistoric Men,* Nat. History Museum, Chicago, 1948, pp. 25, 26.

These "waves" are of course an assumption only. The actual remains known are very small, but it is supposed that such finds as we have represent only a tiny proportion of the population at any one period. Neanderthal Man lived in caves, and in popular imagination came to represent the cave-man type, slouching, apish, low browed, and not very intelligent; yet he was a tool maker, and therefore truly human. It is a moot point whether he became extinct with the coming of modern man (Cromagnon), or whether he was absorbed into this new race that displaced him. But long before the appearance of Neanderthal Man, other more primitive types, such as the Far Eastern specimens represented by Pithecanthropus erectus, and Sinanthropus, etc., had been roaming about only to disappear with the passage of time. So that although Neanderthal Man was primitive enough (especially as reconstructed for museum display purposes) he was quite advanced when compared with those who had preceded him by thousands of years, and his skull was much larger.

This was a nice orderly arrangement. Unfortunately, as stated earlier, fossil remains kept on cropping up, which came from levels antedating those in which Neanderthal Man had been customarily found, but which instead of being more primitive (as required by the scheme), were actually quite modern in appearance— in fact, were virtually indistinguishable from present European types. These were obviously displaced somehow, and because they did not fit, they were laid aside "for further consideration." But this trend persisted, and from time to time further out-of-order specimens kept on turning up. Yet the circumstances were always such that the finder, when challenged, could not completely satisfy the experts that he really had found the specimen in the levels he claimed. In some cases, the find had occurred when the excavator was quite alone and had no other witness.

At last, in the summer of 1947, Mlle. Germaine Henri-Martin from a cave at Fontechevade near the village of Montbrun, in France, brought to light a modern-type fossil from a level well below that at which Neanderthal Man was customarily found.[4] All the circumstances of this find were such as to guarantee its acceptance by anthropologists everywhere. In fact, the bones came from an undisturbed level sealed below a thick layer of stalagmite that in turn underlay the Neanderthal level in this area. There could never be any argument as to the validity of this find. Modern man here preceded his onetime supposed predecessors.

---

[4] Eiseley, Loren, "The Antiquity of Modern Man," *Sci. American,* July, 1948, pp. 16-19.

G. Heberer has given a short and instructive summary of the present state of our knowledge of Homo sapiens.[5] First, we know that modern types were contemporary with Neanderthal Man; secondly, the two types sometimes appear intermingled in a single deposit; and, finally, before the appearance of Neanderthal Man there existed individuals, more like modern man than the Neanderthals were themselves.

What this really boils down to is that instead of a nice orderly series of fossil specimens, passing from very primitive to quite modern types, we in fact find the record supports no such pattern. Some of the lowest levels present us with fossil remains that are to all intents and purposes completely modern in appearance, while some of the latest levels throw up specimens which nicely fit the preconceived picture of what the earliest representatives of man are supposed to have looked like. Naturally there had been some tendency to disregard these misfits by questioning whether the levels at which they were found had been correctly reported—until Fontechevade.

At the Cold Spring Harbor Symposia of Quantitative Biology in 1950, devoted to the subject of *The Origin and Evolution of Man,* T. D. Stewart presented a paper dealing with this problem, in which he quoted Henri Vallois, a European authority on this latest find:[6]

> The interest of the Fontechevade discovery is that it clarifies the problem. In contrast to earlier finds of human remains we have here, in effect, a specimen which is well dated and found in a stratigraphic context which allows of no dispute: this is the first time that man, certainly not Neanderthal, although earlier than the Neanderthals, has been found in Europe under such conditions. Now this type . . . taking all its characters together, aligns itself with the Swanscombe form. . . .
>
> To this extent the problem is clarified: in and before the last interglacial period there existed in Europe and probably elsewhere, men with less "primitive" cranial features than those of the succeeding more advanced cultural period — the Neanderthal man of the Mousterian Age.

Not only do we find this kind of reversal in which the modern precedes the ancient by appearing far too early in the geological strata, but we also find the opposite, in which very primitive specimens are found in the very latest geological strata. Thus Rhodesian Man, whose skull is illustrated in Fig. 6 (d) , and who, as A. L. Kroeber

---

[5] Heberer, G., "Der Fluor-test und-seine Bedeutung fur das Pra-sapiens'-Problem," *Forschungen und Fortschritte,* 26th Annual Report.

[6] Vallois, Henri, quoted by T. D. Stewart, "The Problem of the Earliest Claimed Representatives of Homo sapiens," in *The Origin and Evolution of Man,* being the Cold Spring Harbor Symposia on Quantitative Biology, 15 (1950) : 101.

rightly points out, is more primitive than Neanderthal,[7] nevertheless comes from a cave deposit at Broken Hill, in Northern Rhodesia, which is of unknown date, but which according to Alfred Romer is "not improbably *late* Pleistocene," and therefore belongs to the most recent period.[8] For a similar reason the South African manlike apes found by Dart and Broom, and termed the Australopithecinae, are by some of the best authorities rejected as possible ancestors of man because they too come from geological levels which are far too late in the Pleistocene.[9]

At the risk of being tiresomely repetitive, it must be pointed out once more that dependence upon morphology to establish the correct sequence for a series of fossils had seemed the only reasonable course. The fact is that modern man was continually being found in rocks older than those in which his ancestors appeared. This made man older than his forebears, which is ridiculous. But it is only ridiculous if we insist that the more primitive forms *are* his forebears. Evolutionary theory demands that this is so, and consequently has to arrange the series according to morphology or physical appearance.

On the other hand, dependence on morphological details can be equally misleading. One of the best authorities in England, S. Zuckerman emphasizes the fact that such characters may be the result of factors which have nothing whatever to do with the geological age or the supposed relatedness of the fossil to earlier animal forms. Zuckerman put it this way:[10]

> Some students claim, or rather assume implicitly, that the phyletic relations of a series of specimens can be clearly defined from an assessment of morphological similarities and dissimilarities even when the fossil evidence is both slight and noncontinuous geologically. Others, who in the light of modern genetical knowledge are surely on firmer ground, point out that several genes or several gene patterns may have identical phenotypic effects, and that when we deal with limited or relatively limited fossil material, correspondence in single morphological features, or in groups of characters, does not necessarily imply genetic identity and phyletic relationship.

For the sake of those readers to whom some of these terms will be unfamiliar, Zuckerman is saying in effect that there is no justification for arranging a series of specimens simply because they look as though they might be so related, particularly when the geological levels from which they came are of uncertain age. For, as he points

---

[7] Kroeber, A. L., *Anthropology*, rev. ed. Harcourt, Brace, N.Y., 1948, p. 99.
[8] Romer, Alfred, *Man and the Vertebrates*, Univ. Chicago Press, Chicago, 1948, p. 214.
[9] Ibid., p. 187.
[10] Zuckerman, S., "Morphological Series of Hominid Remains," *Jour. Roy. Anthrop. Instit.*, 81 (1951): 57.

out, modern genetics has shown that quite unrelated species may
now and then give rise to forms quite similar in structure, so that
mere similarity is no guarantee that the specimens have anything in
common genetically. Morphology can be totally misleading. We shall
return to this point later on.

The manner in which this dependence upon physical appearance
can distort the interpretations of an able scholar is well illustrated
in the case of Weidenreich's handling of certain Far Eastern specimens. Speaking of this, William Koppers from Vienna remarked how
Weidenreich established a chronological order of hominid remains
beginning with the cranium of Piltdown Man, which now that the
fake jaw has been disposed of, appears to be a genuine fossil of early
geological age. He then established a morphological series of hominid
remains in which he *ends* with Piltdown Man, because the cranium,
early though it is, is quite modern in appearance. Koppers does not
say how the reconciliation is effected.[11]

In the earlier days of anthropology, such problems never existed.
For as far as the public was aware, the finds did indeed fit into a fine
series. However this appearance had often been neatly secured by the
simple expedient of removing from the record any skulls which did
not suit the arrangement. Koppers may be quoted again in this
connection:[12]

> It should interest the wider public to know that in the same con-
> text, the distinguished anthropologist Broom, frankly acknowledges
> that sapiens-like remains from early times have shown a strange ten-
> dency to disappear. He quotes the discoveries made at Ipswich in 1855
> and at Abbeville in 1863 as special examples, and offers the following
> explanation: "During the latter half of the nineteenth century every
> apparently early human skull that was found, if it was not ape-like,
> was discredited, no matter how good its credentials appeared to be."

Thus with the passage of time, the situation has become more
and more embarrassing as fossils have continued to appear which
can neither be hidden from the public, nor introduced sensibly into
the series. Today each new find seems to create more problems than
it solves. Evidently a basic premise is at fault somewhere. This
premise is that human forms must be derived from animal forms,
and transitional forms must therefore be provided. The time scale
is rearranged accordingly to agree with the assumed scale of evolutionary development. Suppose we allow the levels in which the fossils
are found to speak for themselves in each instance, is there then any

---

[11] Koppers, Wilhelm, *Primitive Man and His World Picture*, Sheed and
Ward, London, 1952, p. 221.
[12] Ibid., p. 238.

other explanation for this peculiar mixing of forms, this morphological contradiction of evolutionary theory?

In view of all that has been said thus far, it becomes evident that of the two systems of establishing which fossils in any series are the earlier ones, the only valid one is to fall back upon the supposed geological age at which each fossil was found. While there may be some disagreement as to the exact age in any given case, the general order is likely to be reasonably well established. But in doing this we have lost the nicely graded series entirely. How are we then to account for those forms which look so primitive and which although found in the wrong order, in many respects approach so closely to the ideal "missing link" type?

For many years it has been observed that food and environment may have a profound influence in modifying bone structure. Recently it has been recognized that the human skull is particularly sensitive in this respect. Many of the more remarkable aspects of the skeletal remains of fossil man may indeed be accounted for by such means, so that any series arranged morphologically, without respect to age levels, is really meaningless. Seen in this light it is often possible to view a particular skull as owing its peculiarities not to any genetic relationship with the lower anthropoid forms, but to a certain community of habit and environment causing convergence and having absolutely nothing whatever to do with derivation. The form may be due to historical processes and have no palaeontological significance whatever. This was Portmann's contention.

C. S. Coon also attributed Neanderthal's form entirely to disease and to cold adaptation, with long trunk, short limbs and arms, deep chest, etc., exactly like the Eskimo.[13] Even man's teeth can be profoundly modified by conditions of life. Singh and Zingg noted that two of the more recent feral children found in India (both of whom are now dead) had developed longer and more pointed canines, presumably as a result of the eating of raw meat without the use of any cutting utensils.[14] Another feral child, Clement of Overdyke, had noticeably projecting teeth due to an uncooked vegetarian diet. The "Wild Boy of Aveyron" had developed canines conical in shape and very sharp, besides their being longer than normal. Finally, Kaspar Hauser, kept captive in a small dungeon for perhaps 12 or 14 years, had, in spite of being given cooked food, developed a markedly depressed frontal region as though "pressed down from above."

---

[13] Coon, C. S., *The Story of Man*, Knopf, N.Y., 1962, pp. 40, 41.
[14] Singh, J. A. L., and Zingg, Robert M., *Wolf-Children and Feral Man*, Archon Books, Shoe String Press, Hamden, Conn., 1966, p. 18.

Of the Australopithecines there are believed to have been two types, A. *africanus,* and A. *robustus. Robustus* is considered to be a later type, but less human. *Africanus* had no saggital crest, or "keel," *robustus* had. J. T. Robinson sees this, and *stresses* it is the result of diet, and *robustus* was a plant eater.[15] The gorilla is also a plant eater, in whom the saggital crest is enormous. Plant fibers can clearly be a tougher diet than meat.

Robert B. Eckhardt, in an article entitled "Population Genetics and Human Origins," observed wisely:[16]

> Indeed, are there any grounds for assuming that morphological evidence alone makes it possible to draw a valid distinction between the majority of these early hominids and some ancestral hominid that may be concealed among them? In view of the morphological variability among living hominoids, I think not.

So neither stratigraphical position nor morphological form is a safe base on which to establish either age or relationship. With no possibility of applying the test of actual breeding for assessment of relatedness, what really is left but pure guesswork?

Although it seems little attention was paid to his remarks at the time, Wilson D. Wallis some years ago pointed out:[17]

> The evidence of prehistoric human remains does not in itself justify the inference of a common ancestry with the apes. We base this conclusion on the fact, if fact it be, that practically all the changes in man's structure traceable through prehistoric remains are the result of changes in food and habit.
>
> The most notable changes are found in the skull. Briefly the story of changes is to: a higher frontal region, increased bregmatic height, smaller supercilliary ridges, increased head width, less facial projection, decreased height of orbits and a shifting of the transverse diameter downward laterally, a more ovoid palate, smaller teeth, diminished relative size of the third molar, shorter, wider and more ovoid mandible, decrease in size of condyles, decrease in distance between condylar and coronoid processes, and in general greater smoothness, less prominent bony protuberances, less of the angularity and "savageness" of appearance which characterizes the apes. This is evolution in type, but the evolution is result rather than cause....
>
> Practically all of these features of the skull are intimately linked together so that scarcely can one change without the change being reflected in the others.... Change is most marked in the region in which chewing muscles function.... The adjacent walls of the skull are flattened and forced inward as well as downward, producing the elongation of the skull. The temporal muscles reach far up on the skull,

[15] Robinson, J. T., "The Origin and Adaptive Radiation of the Australopithecines," in *Evolution and Hominization,* ed. G. Kurth, Fischer, Stuttgart, 1962, pp. 123-127.

[16] Eckhardt, Robert B., "Population Genetics and Human Origins," *Sci. American,* Jan., 1972, p. 96.

[17] Wallis, Wilson D., "The Structure of Prehistoric Man," in *The Making of Man,* Modern Library, N.Y., 1931, pp. 69 ff.

giving rise to a high temporal ridge: they extend forward as well as backward, giving a more prominent occipital region, and a more constricted forward region, resulting on the forehead region of the skull in the elevation of the supercilliary ridges and intervening glabellar region. Projecting brow ridges are associated with stout temporal and masseter muscles and large canines. . . . Constriction of outer margins of orbits produces the high orbits which we find in apes, and to a less marked degree in prehistoric human remains.

Even the nature of the soil can have its effect in modifying bone structure. Coon observed: "In my North Albanian series, I found that the tribes of man living on food raised on granitic soil were significantly smaller than those who walked over limestone."[18] We really have no idea at present, how extensively our conditions of life modify our bone structure, nor the exact mechanisms involved. So we simply do not know precisely why the typical fossil remains of early man were so brutalized. Certainly it need have had absolutely nothing to do with an animal ancestry.

With respect to the Eskimos, there is some question as to whether their diet of frozen meat, cooked or otherwise, is really as tough as might be supposed. Some authorities claim that frozen meat has a consistency little tougher than deeply frozen canned salmon, the freezing process having a kind of tenderizing effect. It is also argued that the Eskimo habit of chewing skins very thoroughly to soften them for clothing is limited to the womenfolk, whose facial modification is less pronounced than in the male population.[19]

Fig. 4, however, shows a characteristic Eskimo male face, with the skull form outlined to indicate that the greatest width is at the jowls and not in the temple region. The head of Gainsborough's *Blue Boy*, in Fig. 5 however, shows how a refined diet tends to produce a head form of another kind with the greatest width in the temporal region. The drawing of the Eskimo is taken from a magnificent photograph reproduced on the front cover of *Ciba Symposia* of July, 1948. This particular issue was devoted to aspects of Eskimo life, and the articles were all contributed by Edwin H. Ackerknecht, who pointed out that:[20]

> The cheekbones and jaws of the Eskimo are very massive, possibly under the influence of the intense chewing he has to practice, which also results in a tremendous development of the chewing muscles. Eskimo teeth are often worn down to the gums, like animal teeth, from excessive use.

[18] Coon, C. S., ref. 13, p. 286.

[19] Hooton, E. A., *Up from the Ape*, Macmillan, N.Y., 1935, p. 405. He nevertheless admits that "there is something to be said for the functional theory" (p. 406).

[20] Ackerknecht, Erwin H., "Eskimo History," *Ciba Symposia* 10, 1 (July, 1948) : 912.

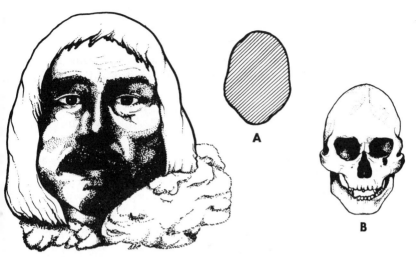

Fig. 4. Contrast the form of this Eskimo head with the head of "Blue Boy" in Fig. 5. This drawing is based on a photo reproduced on the cover of Ciba Symposia, Vol. 10, No. 1, and is quite exact in its proportions: (A) a simplified outline; (B) an ancient Eskimo skull, showing the keel (slightly exaggerated) on the top and the front of the head.

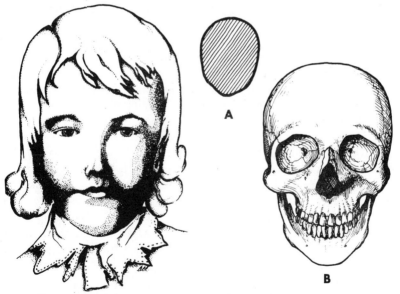

Fig. 5. This head is based on Gainsborough's painting, "Blue Boy," and is drawn to exact scale. It shows clearly the influence of what may be termed a cultured diet. The wide part of the head is at the temples. (A) Cranial outline for comparison with Eskimo head in Fig. 4. (B) Modern European skull.

It has also been pointed out that the Eskimo skull occasionally shows a "keel" along the top, which results directly from the need for a stronger attachment or anchorage for the jaw muscles which are used much more extensively. This will be noted in Fig. 4 (b), and should be compared with the keel indicated in the skulls of three supposedly human fossils in Fig. 6 (c, d, e). It is very clearly marked in the case of the gorilla skull in Fig. 6 (a). William Howells pointed out:[21]

> Gorillas have a heavy and very powerful lower jaw, and the muscles which shut it (which in man make a thin layer on and above the temple, where you can feel them when you chew) are so large that they lie thick on the top of the head, about two inches deep, practically obscuring the heavy brow ridge over the eyes which is so prominent on the skull, and giving rise to a bony crest in the middle merely to separate and afford attachment to the muscles of the two sides.

In the Eskimo skull and in the gorilla skull, there is therefore sometimes a certain parallelism which is in no way any indication of genetic relationship. The explanation of the Eskimo keel is a historical (i.e., cultural) one, and it is in this sense that Portmann refers to historical action as being the explanation of those aspects of fossil remains which have tended hitherto to be interpreted as evidence of biological relationship with the anthropoids. Again, Howells may be quoted:[22]

> The powerful jaw of these animals in chewing, gives rise to a terrific pressure upward against the face, and the brow ridges make a strong upper border which absorbs it.

If man is subjected to uncooked food and forced in the absence of knives to tear it from the bone, the developing muscles will find a way of strengthening their anchorage along these bony ridges. Moreover, if there is not in the diet that which will harden the bone in the earlier years of life when such strains are first encountered, it is inevitable that the skull will be depressed while still in a comparatively plastic state, and the forepart of the brain case will be low and sloping so that it lacks the high vault we tend to associate with cultured man. Thus the massive brow ridges of Sinanthropus, so similar to those of Pithecanthropus, are, as Ales Hrdlicka pointed out some years ago, "a feature to be correlated with a powerful jaw mechanism."[23]

It is obvious now that such a circumstance could tend to reduce

---

[21] Howells, William, *Mankind So Far*, Doubleday Doran, N.Y., 1945, p. 68.
[22] Ibid., p. 131.
[23] Hrdlicka, Ales, "Skeletal Remains of Early Man," *Smithsonian Instit. Misc. Coll.* 83 (1930): 367.

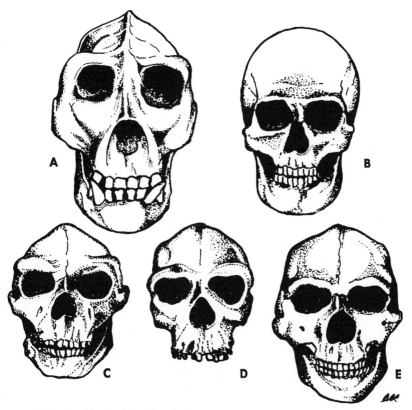

Fig. 6. (A) Gorilla, showing marked keel and wide zygomatic arch. (B) Modern Man with high vault and widest dimension at the temples. (C) Pithecanthropus. (D) Rhodesian Man. (E) Sinan-thropus.

the high vault of the human skull which we usually associate with man's superior mental capacity. One of Weidenreich's last papers was intended to show that there is no real correlation between intelligence and cranial capacity.[24] Anyone who reads this paper will be convinced that he was perfectly right. Yet he still argued that it was man's greatly enlarged cranial capacity which gave to him his superi-

[24] Weidenreich, Franz, "The Human Brain in the Light of its Phylogenetic Development," *Sci. Monthly,* Aug. 1948, pp. 103f.

ority over the other primates. Weidenreich was of the opinion that for some unknown reason, man's brain suddenly began to increase in size. This had the effect of "ballooning" the skull on an arc centered approximately at the junction of the lower jaw and the skull proper, as illustrated in Fig. 7 (c). Not everyone has taken this theory too seriously. Howells referred to it rather contemptuously as "a feeble argument with no proof behind it."[25] He offered no alternative.

But Weidenreich's argument is based essentially on the fact that if we rather arbitrarily draft a series of skulls, in this case the gorilla, Pithecanthropus, and modern man, and in a side view impose upon them as indicated in Fig. 7 a series of arcs centered approximately at the ear, we have a series of forms with increased ballooning from the true animal to the true man. As indicated in Fig. 4 however, Weidenreich's original drawing was hardly fair, since he exaggerated the effect by using a different scale for the various skulls.[26] Moreover, the gorilla and modern man are contemporaries, and the series does not therefore represent anything historically factual *as a series*.

There is another explanation of such a series however, in which we merely assume that the first true man had a high vault, but that the circumstances of his early history were such as to deprive him of some of the essentials of culture thus forcing him to adopt the use of raw meat, which in time greatly developed the jaw muscles and thus "deflated" the high vault with which his ancestors had been endowed. This is exactly the reverse of Weidenreich's theory, but it has this at least in its favor, that there is historical evidence to support it. The evidence of history, as observed in the actual time sequence of many of the fossils which Weidenreich was forced to arrange out of order, is manifestly against his theory. The objection to our alternative, of course, is that we must assume that man was equipped with a high vault and presumably a large brain to go with it, from the very first.

It could also be argued that if at first, man's genetic heritage provided him with the means to grow a high vault, then when this could not develop, the mechanism compensated itself by building a much thicker vault instead. It might happen therefore that the high vault with normal bone thickness is more or less exactly represented by a low vault with a much thicker bone shell. The weight of both forms of skull would presumably be quite similar. Some of the early skulls show this thickening.

---

[25] Howells, William, ref. 21, p. 76.
[26] Weidenreich, Franz, *Apes, Giants and Man,* Univ. Chicago Press, Chicago, 1946, fig. 36.

Weidenreich elaborated his ballooning theory in his book *Apes, Giants and Man*. He assumed that man started with a powerful jaw mechanism. Then he explains what he thinks must have happened:[27]

> The reduction of the jaws went hand in hand with a reduction of the chewing and cervical muscles. The space required for the attachment of these muscles to the skull surface consequently became smaller, and so did the power of the whole chewing apparatus. The superstructures which reinforce a primitive skull in the forms of crests and ridges diminished accordingly....
>
> Exaggeratedly expressed, the evolution of the human brain case proceeds like the inflation of a balloon; and it looks as though the enlargement of its content the brain, was the driving factor.... The transverse axis around which the skull is bent runs approximately through the jaw points.... All the smaller structural alterations of the human skull are correlated with and dependent upon each other and the extent to which they are governed by the trend of the skull transformation as a whole. All fossil human forms, from the more ancient morphological stage to the most advanced ones, show that the state of the minutest structure of the cranial bones corresponds in some way to that of the entire skull form and thereby proves that all forms must once have passed through the same principal phases....

Now reversing the pattern we can view the process quite differently. Let us assume, for the sake of argument, that early man was subsequently forced to eat tough food, after the initial family had multiplied and wandered apart; and that this food lacked that which would harden the skull in its formative period of development: then the strengthening of the chewing and cervical muscles would go hand in hand with the building of a superstructure of bone to provide the necessary anchorage in the form of crests as well as ridges in the front, at the rear, and on the top of the skull, but the skull itself would remain pliable enough that it would undergo considerable distortion.

The "keel" which is so noticeable in the case of the gorilla, naturally tended to appear in early man because the muscles pulled the sides of the skull in, under the increased tension. This is indicated in Fig. 8.

When the jaw was used for cracking bones, etc., the chief point of stress would regularly occur at the chin, since the clamping action between the teeth would normally be one-sided. This again led to a certain degree of compensatory thickening. But unlike the apes, man is a talking creature and makes much more use of his tongue. There is reason to believe that the reinforcement of man's chin takes the form of a bony ridge outwards rather than inwards, on this account, and this gives the prominence which is characteristic of the human jaw. The apes and other anthropoids on the other hand have the

---

[27] Ibid., ref. 26, p. 33.

reinforcement in the form of a ledge which reaches inward instead, and this is known as the simian shelf. In some fossils of early man there is some evidence of a simian shelf, and presumably this is a reinforcement in addition to that which is normal for man's chin, by way of compensation for the added load placed upon the structure at this point. Tugging at flesh in the absence of satisfactory "cutlery," or maybe just bad table manners, contributed quite possibly to the alveolar prognathism which is often found in these early remains. The increasing muscle development which rose up under the zygomatic arch naturally forced the latter outwards and required a stronger form.

It is quite likely therefore that the functioning of the jaw mechanism determines whether the skull will be depressed or not. The fossil human forms then show clearly that the entire series has been affected to a large degree by the same depressive and compressive forces. Thus if early man were to have been utterly deprived of culture it seems quite certain his fossil remains would have revealed an extreme primitiveness which might easily be misinterpreted as evidence of a recent emergence from some anthropoid stock. Yet in point of fact it could happen that individuals might become degenerate at any period in history and leave behind them a cemetery of the most deceptive fossil remains. Humphrey Johnson remarked in this direction:[28]

> It seems likely that in very early times the human form possessed a high degree of plasticity which it has since lost, and that from time to time such exaggerations of certain racial characters, probably brought about by an unfavorable environment, have occurred. In the Pekin-Java branch of the human family, the exaggeration of the apelike traits has occurred to a very high degree: it later took place, so it would seem, though not quite so pronouncedly in Neanderthal Man, and has occurred again though to a far lesser extent in the aborigines of Australia.
>
> Some of the low features of the Australians may, as Prof. Haddon thinks, be due to racial senility and thus the resemblance to Neanderthal man may be regarded as secondary or convergent. By a wider application of this principle we may consider that "convergence" has played a part in bringing about the resemblances of paleoanthropic men to the anthropoid apes.

And quoting Wallis once more:[29]

> If the above interpretations are correct it follows that a return to the conditions of diet and of life which characterized prehistoric man would be followed by a return to his physical type. Yet if there were this transition to a type more simian we could not say that we were

[28] Johnson, Humphrey, *The Bible and the Early History of Mankind*, Burns and Oates, London, 1947, p. 89.
[29] Wallis, Wilson D., ref. 17, pp. 72 ff.

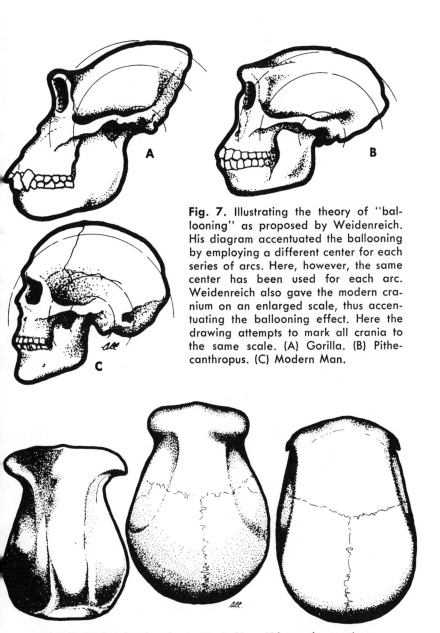

Fig. 7. Illustrating the theory of "ballooning" as proposed by Weidenreich. His diagram accentuated the ballooning by employing a different center for each series of arcs. Here, however, the same center has been used for each arc. Weidenreich also gave the modern cranium on an enlarged scale, thus accentuating the ballooning effect. Here the drawing attempts to mark all crania to the same scale. (A) Gorilla. (B) Pithecanthropus. (C) Modern Man.

Fig. 8. Skulls of a female gorilla (left), a Pithecanthropus (center), and a modern Papuan native (right), viewed from above. The marked formation of the supraorbital ridge and the postorbital narrowness are evident. Such marked differences can almost certainly be attributed to the development of powerful muscles for chewing and biting.

approaching a common ancestor. The similarity would not be due to the transmission of qualities from a common ancestor of a remote past. If this be true it is equally true that an increase in similarities as we push back the time period does not imply common ancestry if the changes are due to changes in function, following changes in diet.... It seems clear that mere resemblance cannot constitute an argument for phylogentic descent.

Wallis then points out with great pertinancy that in any given group of human beings, the male is likely to resemble the anthropoid ape more nearly in bone structure than the female; and yet it is obvious that the male cannot be more closely related than the female. So he concludes that the more muscular male converges towards the ape which is more muscular than man simply because he is more muscular. He attributes the comparative inattention of physical anthropologists to this whole subject to the fact that "an age with its mind made up to evolution of a unilinear type has seen what it looked for."

Moreover, it is not necessary to assume that such functional changes take a very long time to leave their mark. In fact, C. S. Coon pointed out that the case is quite otherwise:[30]

Head form, although it changes with much less speed than stature, for it is not directly concerned with gross size, nevertheless responds to the stimuli which control it and we must not be surprised if long heads have in some instances become round heads during the course of hundreds of generation.

The evidence today is making it very clear that there is less and less justification for the tendency to demand great lengths of time for "evolutionary" change. The truth is that the living body is amazingly plastic and highly responsive to environmental pressures, though precisely what the mechanism is, has so far eluded us.

We have already noted how feral children may develop canine teeth of quite exceptional form. If by chance their skulls were excavated some centuries later, physical anthropologists would be quite wrong were they to make the assumption that this particular tooth structure had taken centuries to form. We know, in fact, that it probably took less than ten years. And the researches of Boas and others into the change of head-form among the successive siblings of immigrant parents to the United States from an area of long-headedness, shows that such changes can occur with remarkable rapidity — again, within a matter of a score of years or less. The earliest born children resemble the parents. Later born children begin to vary in the direction of the new home-country, until the last born children have head-forms quite different from their parents. Thus

[30] Coon, C. S., *The Races of Europe*, Macmillan, N.Y., 1939, pp. 28f.

THE HUMAN SKULL • 211

Boas[31] showed that the influence of environment makes itself felt with increasing intensity according to the time elapsed between the arrival of the parents and the birth of the child. The curious thing is that those *children* who were born in the old homeland still maintain the head-form of the parents, even though they grow up in the new land. Evidently the head shape is determined during prenatal development so that if prenatal development occurs in the old country the influence of the new country is not felt. Boas' work has since been confirmed by H. L. Shapiro.[32]

Coon also mentions that modifications in the skull form resulting from dietary habits, particularly the eating of raw meat and the absence of bone hardening substances in childhood, may occur, under sub-Arctic conditions, with remarkable rapidity. He notes that these changes are functional changes and he concluded:[33]

> Metrical and morphological differences in physical type which appear during the course of the millennia may imply, in some instances, a response to environment rather than a diversity of origin.

We have, then, a mechanism that might account for all the variant forms of fossil man without recourse to hundreds of thousands of years of evolutionary history. Such changes appear to persist so long as the environmental conditions which provoked them persist. And there is evidence that even when the environmental conditions change somewhat, reversion to the original type may be delayed a little. It is generally thought that this kind of inheritance of an acquired character is effected through the cytoplasm, through so-called plasmagenes as opposed to nuclear genes.

The significance of such facts here is that there may be a measure of persistence or carry-over in facial forms which have been developed in response to certain environmental pressures, which thus provides us with racial characteristics which are then traceable not to a diversity of stocks, but to a historical circumstance. It does not require any great feat of imagination to see that as man began to multiply and spread into new areas where new types of food became available and new environments led to modified living habits, changes might take place in his physical form. Wood Jones pointed out,[34] the needs created by any well-defined ecological situation are likely to be met

---

[31] Boas, Franz, *Changes in Bodily Form of Descendants of Immigrants*, Government Printing Office, Washington, 1911; repr. Columbia Univ. Press, N.Y., 1912.
[32] Shapiro, H. L., *Migration and Environment*, Oxford Univ. Press, N.Y., 1939.
[33] Coon, C. S., ref. 30, p. 29.
[34] Jones, Wood, *Trends of Life*, Arnold, London, 1953, p. 76.

by all living things subjected to them by directive responses of a similar kind. The pliability of living forms is great. Ralph Linton put it this way:[35]

> If we are correct in our belief that all existing men belong to a single species, early man must have been a generalized form with potentialities for evolving into all the varieties which we know at present. It further seems probable that this generalized form spread widely and rapidly and that within a few thousand years of its appearance small bands of individuals of this type were scattered over most of the Old World. These bands would find themselves in many different environments, and the physical peculiarities which were advantageous in one of these might be of no importance or actually deleterious in another. Moreover, due to the relative isolation of these bands and their habit of inbreeding, any mutation which was favorable or at least not injurious under the particular circumstances would have the best possible chance of spreading to all the members of the group. It seems quite possible to account for the known variations in our species on this basis without invoking the theory of a small number of originally distinct varieties.

Or we may quote Franz Boas in the same connection:[36]

> If we bring two organically different individuals into the same environment they may, therefore, become alike in their functional responses and we may gain the impression of a functional likeness of distinct anatomical forms that is due to environment, not to heredity.

It is abundantly clear by now, therefore, that we are dealing here with a fact which is very widely recognized. Yet, in spite of this, it is seldom referred to when the search for the missing link seems to be getting warm.

When Broom found a number of items, teeth, parts of the jaw, and parts of the cranium, etc., of the specimen subsequently named Australopithecus *transvaalensis,* the matter was reported in the *Illustrated London News* with pictures of the then most recent additions to the finds, and a reconstruction of the "head." The significant factors in this find, according to Broom, lie in the presence of a clearly apelike form of the head and the obviously humanoid aspect of certain of the teeth. No one would doubt, we are told, seeing the skull, that it was the skull of a variety of chimpanzee or an anthropoid ape. But looking at the teeth apart from the rest of the skull he said:[37]

> If casts of these teeth had been sent to all the anatomists of the world, probably 95% would have certified that they are human. The size, the arrangement and the wearing are all human characters....
> We need not at present discuss the exact position of Australopithecus, but we can without hesitation state that here we have an anthropoid ape with a brain capacity probably between 450 and 650 cc., and

[35] Linton, Ralph, *The Study of Man,* Appleton Century, N.Y., 1936, p. 26.
[36] Boas, Franz, ref. 31, p. 133.
[37] Broom, *Illustrated London News,* May 14, 1938.

thus definitely an ape, but which has teeth which are almost typically human. The incisors, canines, premolars, and first molars are hardly to be distinguished from human teeth. The second and third molar are considerably larger than in man, but very similar to human teeth in structure.

It seems to me that these human characters are much more likely to indicate affinity with man, than that such characters have been twice independently evolved.

But in the same paper there had already been reported by W. P. Pycraft[38] some three years earlier, a remarkable series of finds in South America of three skulls belonging to quite unrelated animals in which a particular bone structure on the lower jaw had assumed substantially the same striking form entirely in response to diet and having nothing to do with common descent. These three skulls belonged to marsupials and at the time were described by Sir Arthur Smith Woodward as perhaps the most remarkable "mimics" (as he called them) hither discovered.

The famous saber-toothed tiger had an extraordinary long upper canine which projected far below the lower jaw when the mouth was closed. This necessitated the hinging of the lower jaw in a special way so that it would clear the upper canines and allow the animal to seize its prey. In Fig. 9 first the jaw of a typical cat is shown, opened to its maximum extent. This may then be compared with the jaw of the saber-toothed tiger which must be dropped much further to clear the saber teeth. The surprising thing about these newly discovered skulls is that in all three the very long saber teeth are protected, when the mouth is closed, by bone flanges on the lower jaw along which the upper canines lie. In Fig. 9 this structure can be clearly seen. The other two skulls show a parallel development, although the photographs of them available to the public do not show quite as clearly the precise form of the protective flange; but there is no doubt about the parallelism in structure. The important thing is, as Pycraft observed, that these flanges illustrate "the molding effects of particular modes of life which more commonly than is generally realized, *start with the choice of food*" (emphasis mine).

Perhaps it is not so remarkable after all to find Australopithecinae with teeth so strikingly like human teeth.

We may quote Wood Jones once more:[39]

All these needs are met by the development of structures directed towards their satisfaction. It seems therefore certain that structures developed for the satisfaction of these common needs may bear a considerable likeness to each other, although the animals manifesting them

[38] Pycraft, W. P., *Illustrated London News,* Feb. 16, 1935.
[39] Jones, Wood, ref. 34, p. 71.

may be utterly unrelated by kinship or descent. Since so many basic needs are common to all animals and these functional needs are satisfied by the development of appropriate structures, it is to be expected that a common ground plan of parts and organs might be detected as underlying the very varied superstructures of large groups of animals.

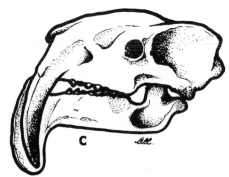

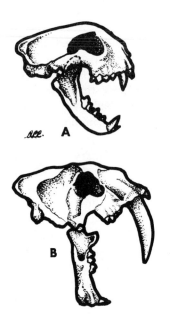

Fig. 9. Skull forms of (A) typical cat with jaw opened to its maximum distance; (B) saber-toothed tiger with jaw opened to its maximum distance, clearing the saber teeth; (C) Thylacosmilus atrox, one of the three entirely unrelated marsupial saber-tooth forms, showing the bone plate protecting the teeth when the lower jaw is in the closed position.

Yet the slightest resemblance between an early human fossil and the skull or other parts of some lower primate is at once taken to mean genetic affinity, and it is seized upon as proof in part of the general theory that man has been derived by some such steps from an animal ancestor. Against such hasty assumptions we must now be much more ready to examine the parallelisms to see whether they may not be explained satisfactorily on other grounds. In this connection it is well to underscore the words of LeGros Clark, who over twenty years ago pointed out:[40]

> In the evaluation of genetic affinities anatomical differences are more important as negative evidence than anatomical differences are as positive evidence. It becomes apparent that if this thesis is carried

to a logical conclusion it will necessarily demand a much greater scope for the phenomenon of parallelism or convergence in evolution, than has usually been conceded by evolutionists. The fact is that the minute and detailed researches which have been carried out by comparative anatomists in recent years have made certain that parallelisms in evolutionary development have been proceeding on a large scale and it is no longer to be regarded as an incidental curiosity which has occurred sporadically in the course of evolution. Indeed, it is hardly possible for those who are not comparative anatomists to realize the fundamental part which this phenomenon has played in the evolutionary process....

The influence of environmental pressures in modifying the structure of an organism is so common in fact, that it would almost seem as though convergence of unlike forms until they are alike is more frequent in nature than the reverse — divergence of like forms until they are unlike. And yet the latter is the fundamental requirement of evolution.

Although too little attention seems to have been paid to his work, Leo S. Berg, in a book devoted to this question, argued:[41]

Convergence and not divergence is the rule, not the exception. This appears to be all pervasive, both among plants and animals, both present, recent, and extinct. We do not find a few simple forms giving rise to a great variety; we find a great variety assuming similarities that have in the past led, or misled all naturalists into thinking that the opposite was taking place....

In studying extinct forms of life, it is most unusual to find a common ancestor for any series of living animals or plants living today. The common ancestor almost invariably turns out to be in some respect or other more complicated than its alleged descendants.

It ought not to surprise us therefore to find anthropoid forms appearing in varying degree among true *Homo sapiens*.

With respect to the influences of temperature on body form and color, a remarkable case is given by A. F. Shull who reported some experiments in which pupae of certain butterflies were subjected to abnormally low temperatures.[42] There emerged from them insects having a pattern and colors resembling a more northerly variety of the same species, and there was reason to believe that the two varieties were genetically similar but in the different environments in which they occurred naturally, they had appeared as different varieties. When transported into a similar environment, the variation was reduced markedly. In a lesser degree there is some evidence that human beings may respond to environmental pressures to become alike in certain respects. Cold climates tend to stimulate a lengthening of the

---

[41] Berg, Leo S., *Nomogenesis; or Evolution Determined by Law*, English trans., Constable, London, 1926, p. 174.
[42] Shull, A. F., *Evolution*, McGraw Hill, N.Y., 1936, p. 249.

nose, perhaps to create a longer passage of warming for the air inhaled, before it reaches the lungs. Limbs may be shortened slightly, for the same reason, to reduce radiation of heat from the body. In very hot climates the air passage to the lungs may be shortened by a corresponding shortening or flattening of the nasal passages.[43] And there are other even more striking bodily modifications in response to heat and high humidity that lead to the Nilotic Negro type and the Pygmy type, in both of which the body has increased its surface area (for radiation purposes) relative to the body mass, in one instance by assuming a very long thin form, and in the other by reducing the total size. Both the Nilotic Negroes and the Pygmies of the Ituri forest in Africa, share a similar environment of high temperature and high humidity.[44]

Thomas Gladwin points out that animals are modified in the same way as human beings in environments of this extreme kind. When F. B. Sumner reared white mice at 20° and 30° C., he found that at the higher temperatures they developed longer bodies, tails, ears, and hind feet.[45] Yet, surely it has nothing to do with genetic relationships.

We must also consider the possibility in some particular instances that some fossils may occasionally represent diseased types. Disease will produce some striking changes in the human form, and often these changes are not merely in the general direction of what must be termed "ugliness," but specifically they tend towards the anthropoid character. Thus Jesse Williams pointed out:[46]

> Degenerate types show characteristic markings that are known as stigmata of degeneration. Common stigmata are — (1) receding forehead, indicating incomplete development of frontal lobes of the brain; (2) prognathism, a prominence of the maxillae; (3) the canine ear; (4) prominent supercilliary ridges; (5) nipples placed too high and supernumerary nipples.

Among the disorders which commonly operate to effect a modification of bone structure, those which are related to glandular disturbances are the most common. In fact a few years ago there was a remarkable

---

[43] On these points see further: "Stature and Geography," *Sci. American,* Apr., 1954, p. 46; Montagu, Ashley, "A Consideration of the Concept of Race," in Cold Spring Harbor Symposia on Quantitative Biology, 15 (1950) : 325 ff.; and "Physical Characteristics of the American Negro," *Sci. Monthly,* July, 1943, pp. 58ff.

[44] Gladwin, Thomas, "Climate and Anthropology," *Amer. Anthropol.* ns. 49 (Oct.-Dec., 1947) : 607 ff.

[45] Klotz, J. W., *Genes, Genesis and Evolution,* Concordia, St. Louis, 1955, p. 28.

[46] Williams, Jesse, *Textbook of Anatomy and Physiology,* 5th ed., Saunders, Philadelphia, 1935, fn. p. 49.

man by the name of Maurice Tillet, a wrestler better known in some circles as "the Angel," who was so Neanderthal in aspect that Henry Field who knew him very well, induced him to pose appropriately dressed as a caveman, with axe and loin cloth, among a group of reconstructed Neanderthal men in the Field Museum of Natural History. It appears that he was so readily lost among the wax figures that surrounded him, that he could not be singled out until at a given signal he plunged forward with an unearthly howl while Pathe Cameras ground away! The sudden coming to life of this apparently prehistoric figure was quite a shock to all who subsequently viewed the film.[47]

Henry Field says of this man, however, that he was highly intelligent, a graduate of the University of Toulouse, and spoke in addition to his mother tongue, Spanish, English, and a little Russian, for his father, a French geologist, had once worked in the Urals. The secret of his extraordinary Neanderthal appearance was in the most unusual enlargement of his pituitary gland. He was examined by a number of experts and it was unanimously agreed that this was a clear case of acromegaly caused by hyperpituitarism for which, fortunately in his case, nature had made some special provision, so that he had survived into adulthood. So enlarged was the gland that he would certainly have died long before but for the fact that a space of unusual development had been left for the growth of this ductless gland. He died in September, 1954. Field considered him a true Neanderthal type.

Speaking of the operation of these glands, A. C. Haddon remarked:[48]

> During recent years it has been recognized that certain glands discharge internal secretions, or hormones, which alter stature, length of limb, size of jaw, shape of nose, growth of hair, texture of skin, and other characters which are in the main those wherein one race of mankind differs from another. Sir Arthur Keith suggests that racial characters are determined largely by the activity of the hormones and that the inherited condition of the glands provides a mechanism for the fixation of racial types. It must not be supposed that the facts adduced by Keith imply that such groups as Mongols or Negroes are in any sense pathological, but merely that for some reason or another certain ductless glands function in some respects more actively, or less so, in these than in other groups. It remains to be shown what conditions of life or nutrition induced the supposed increased or decreased production of the hormones in question, or whether the conditions were "sports" which have been fixed by heredity. It has yet to be

---

[47] Field, Henry, *In the Track of Man,* Doubleday, N.Y., 1953, pp. 230 f.
[48] Haddon, A. C., *History of Anthropology,* Thinker's Library, Watts, London, 1949, pp. 34 f.

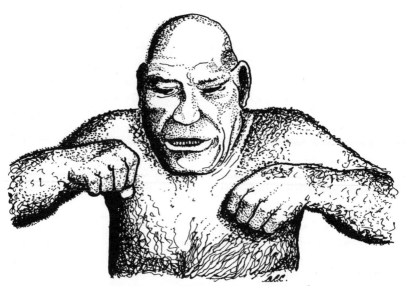

Fig. 10. Maurice Tillet, from a photograph.

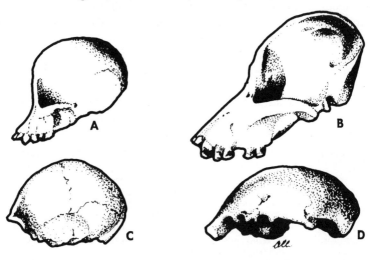

Fig. 11. Two skulls (top) from Borneo illustrate that the vault of the infant is ballooned in appearance, but the adult shows the characteristic flattening presumably due to the development of strong jaw muscles. (A) Infant orangutan. (B) Full-grown orangutan. (C) Infant human skull from Modjokerto. (D) Skull cap of Pithecanthropus from Trinil, Java.

It seems probable that, unlike the orangutan, man's natural headform in the adult stage parallels that of the infant stage in its basic form. Normally both are ballooned. Pithecanthropus is flattened as a result of a tough diet which developed a powerful jaw mechanism. These drawings are based on photos in the "Illustrated London News," 11 December 1937.

proved that these hormones are alone responsible for all racial differentiation, though they may well be contributing factors.

Since Neanderthal Man is usually considered as a "race," the possibility that racial characteristics of this kind could in fact be the result of pituitary or other glandular disturbance, is greatly strengthened by the case of Maurice Tillet. We thus have, in addition to the influences of diet and eating habits, the possible influences of glandular abnormality. It is conceivable that the giantism which has been found to characterize some early fossils of man, could be traced to the same factor. In this case *history* as opposed to *genetics,* in Portmann's sense of the terms, would possibly explain Gigantopithecus and Meganthropus, and so forth, as well as the grossness of some European forms; and any attempt to fit them into a genetical series would be a waste of time.

But it is not only the pituitary gland which can so modify the human form. Sir Arthur Keith, in another work on this subject, pointed out that the characteristics used as physical criteria by ethnologists for distinguishing different racial stocks are affected by several glands in the body. Of these the chief are the pituitary and pineal glands, but the thyroid gland in the throat and the adrenal glands in the kidneys are also of importance. Abnormal growth of the pituitary leads as we have seen to enlargement of the chin, nose, and brow. These features to some extent are common to almost all so-called cavemen. Keith put it this way:[49]

> We are justified in regarding the pituitary as one of the principal pinions in the machinery which regulates the growth of the human body and is directly concerned in determining ... the tendency to strong eyebrow ridges.

Such brow ridges are among the features of fossil man which have tended, in the public mind, to give the most apelike cast to the face. It is curious that such ridges are more marked among Europeans, i.e., the White Man, than among some of the other races. In fact Charles Darwin and Thomas Huxley showed quite marked brow-ridge formation, and it has been suggested by some physiologists that such prominences are evidence of great energy.[50] This could speak well for men of prehistoric times.

Speaking of the thyroid gland, Robert Speer pointed out:[51]

> Many characteristics which have hitherto been regarded as heredi-

[49] Quoted by Sir John A. Thompson, in *The Outline of Science,* Vol. 4, Putnam, N.Y., 1922, p. 1097.

[50] Mottram, V. H., *The Physical Basis of Personality,* Penguin Books, Hammondsworth, Middlesex, England, 1949, p. 79.

[51] Speer, Robert, *Of One Blood,* Friendship House, N.Y., 1924, p. 11.

tary or racial, may be due to environmental causes; it is probable, for example, that stature and longheadedness may be caused by higher or lower activity of the thyroid gland, and that this may in turn be influenced by food, particularly iodine.

Among animals, the changes due to food, temperature, etc., can be quite remarkable. George Dorsey has given an interesting list of some of the changes which can be induced. He wrote,[52]

> For example, tadpoles fed on thymus gland become big dark tadpoles — but never develop into frogs; if fed adrenal gland, they become very light in color. Larvae of bees fed royal jelly become queens; on bee bread unfertile females or workers. Canaries fed on sweet red pepper become red in color. The germ as the "bearer of heredity" is meaningless or monstrous apart from its usual environment. . . .
>
> The hormones actually known are definite and specifically acting indispensible chemical products which modify development and growth of other organs, especially during embryonic life, and the entire metabolism, including that of the nervous system, during adult life. Then, too, there is a collective operation of the endocrines as yet not definitely known, but summarized by Barker as follows:
>
> "More and more we are forced to realize that the general form and the external appearance of the human body depends to a large extent upon their functioning. Our stature, the kinds of faces we have, the length of our arms and legs, the shape of the pelvis, the color and consistency of our integument, the quantity and regional location of our fat, the amount and distribution of hair on our bodies, the tonicity of our muscles, the sound of the voice, and size of the larynx, the emotions to which our 'exterieur' gives expression — all are to a certain extent conditioned by the productivity of our hormonopoietic glands. We are, in a sense, the beneficiaries and the victims of the chemical correlations of our endocrine organs."

Keith pointed out that a poorly developed thyroid leads to stunted growth, to undeveloped nose and hair, and to a flat face. These are characteristic of some of the so-called Mongolian peoples, and it is possible that decrease in thyroid has affected the people of East Asia as a whole. So also the Hottentot and the Bushman differ according to his theory, from the Negro, along lines which might be explained in part by deficiency in thyroid. The adrenal further controls sex characters such as hairiness of the face and body. These are characteristic of European and Australian people, whereas the Negro and Mongolian are perhaps immature in this respect. At any rate, such was Keith's thesis.[53] We may point out what Samuel Brody observed:[54]

---

[52] Dorsey, George, *Why We Behave Like Human Beings,* Blue Ribbon Books, N.Y., 1925, pp. 108, 203.

[53] Keith, Sir Arthur, "Evolution of Human Races in the Light of the Hormone Theory," *Johns Hopkins Bulletin,* 1922.

[54] Brody, Samuel, "Science and Dietary Wisdom," *Sci. Monthly,* Sept., 1945, p. 216.

Congenital blindness, missing kidneys, missing limbs (hardly likely to be inherited), cleft palate, harelip, and other abnormalities were apparently produced in calves, pigs, and rats by withholding vitamin A (and also vitamin B2 in rats) from the pregnant mother's diet. Richardson and Hogan observed about a dozen cases of hydrocephalus — characterized by a great skull with little brain — in newborn rats from mothers fed a "synthetic diet" complete in all the *known* dietary constituents. Deficiency of some unknown essential dietary factor may account for this abnormality.

It might be argued that such observations are not really relevant since it is in the skull form and in the limb proportions that fossil man shows the closest resemblance to anthropoid apes, etc. However, it would not do to overlook the possibility that all these factors may operate in varying degree, each making its impress upon the skeletal remains in its own way and to a different extent when in concert with other influences. Some of the groups of fossils, particularly Neanderthal specimens, seem so much alike as a whole, and so uniformly different from modern man, that it has been customary to assume they represent a true and independent race. The same was thought of the Anthropus series (Pithecanthropus and Sinanthropus, which some authorities now classify simply as Homo sapiens).[55] But we now have instances in which Neanderthal types are found intermixed with, and quite clearly contemporaneous with, men of completely modern type. This is true of the discoveries on Mount Carmel in Palestine, which revealed a mixed population that made any clear distinction between the two types impossible in this instance.[56]

There is a further consideration. As men multiplied on the earth and began to crowd out the original settlements, weaker elements in the population would be driven out. Such people might become waifs and strays, and could well perish in isolation because of the hardships encountered in a new and unfamiliar environment. Possibly it is such people whose remains we find, for as a rule the fossils represent only a very small group, and often only a single individual. That these remains should show varying degrees of primitiveness is not surprising.

The extent to which a whole community may suffer in such a manner was unhappily illustrated some 300 years ago in Ireland. Robert Chambers has given the story:[57]

The style of living is ascertained to have a powerful effect in

---

[55] "The Names of Fossil Man," note in *Science* 102 (July, 1945) : 16.

[56] Howells, William, ref. 21, p. 202. Howells refers to the skull finds in the following terms: "It is an extraordinary variation. There seems to have been a single tribe ranging in type from almost Neanderthal to almost sapiens."

[57] Chambers, Robert, *Vestiges of the Natural History of Creation*, Churchill, London, 1844.

modifying the human figure in the course of generations, and this even in its osseous structure. About 200 years ago, a number of people were driven by a barbarous policy from the counties of Antrim and Down in Ireland, towards the seacoast: there they have ever since been settled, but in unusually miserable circumstances.

And the consequence is that they now exhibit peculiar features of the most repulsive kind, projecting jaws with large open mouths, depressed noses, high cheek bones, and bow legs, together with an extremely diminutive stature. These, with an abnormal slenderness of limbs, are the marks of a low and barbarous condition all over the world. It is peculiarly seen in the Australian aborigines.

This is not an isolated instance. Here is a case in which the "primitive" appearance of a whole group of people is entirely the result of historical factors. Undoubtedly these people, given the proper opportunity, were quite capable of proving themselves in every sense completely human and probably quite as intelligent as any so-called "modern" man. Yet if it ever happened that without any knowledge of the circumstances, their remains were exhumed by some archaeologist, they might well lead the finder to suppose he had run across a mass burial of prehistoric men.

Moreover, small isolated populations whether of animals, insects, or people, tend to vary more widely than large populations. Viktor Lebzelter formulated the principle that where the population is large, the culture will be heterogeneous and the physical type homogeneous, but where the population is small, the physical types will be heterogeneous but the culture homogeneous.[58] The reasons for this are fairly obvious. A small community will be closely knit in its behavior patterns and problem solutions and decorative motifs, etc. But at the same time there will be a measure of inbreeding that will tend to bring mutant genes together in a state of homozygosity so they will then manifest themselves in varieties of new kinds. This is less likely to happen where the population is large.

But it is also found that when a single species is introduced into a new environment there is a tendency for a large number of new varieties to arise almost immediately. This was first noticed by geologists in studying the sudden appearance of many new varieties of a species once they appeared at a certain level in the rocks for the first time. Sir William Dawson referred to it many years ago.[59] Ralph Linton confirmed it for man.[60] Charles Brues illustrated it from entomology.[61] Adolph Schultz, in the Cold Spring Harbor Sympo-

[58] Lebzelter, Viktor, *Rassengeschichte de Menscheit,* Salzburg, 1932, p. 27.
[59] Dawson, Sir William, *The Story of the Earth and Man,* Hodder and Stoughton, London, 1903, p. 360.
[60] Linton, Ralph, ref. 35, pp. 26 f.
[61] Brues, Charles, "Contributions of Entomology to Theoretical Biology," *Sci. Monthly,* Feb., 1947, p. 130.

ia for 1950 referred to it in connection with all primates.[62] Colin
·elby discussed the mechanism in a paper entitled "Modern Views
·f the Origin of Species."[63] The fact is very well known. Yet, once
gain, it is not too often that one hears of its relevance to the present
·ssue. But it is entirely relevant, for one of the most remarkable
·spects of many of the major finds of fossil man is the variability of
·ypes found in a single deposit.

This is true of the fossils from the Upper Cave at Choukoutien,[64]
·f the discoveries at Obercassel,[65] and of the group discovered in the
·abun and Skuhl caves on Mount Carmel in Palestine.[66]

In conclusion we could not do better than to end with a quota-
·ion once more from Wilson Wallis, himself a veteran anthropologist
·nd one who in spite of his views in this matter, would still derive
·nan from some lower form of animal life. His honesty in facing the
·acts and his courage in stating his convictions so forthrightly are
·herefore all the more commendable:[67]

> As regards prehistoric human remains we cannot conclude that the
> increasing resemblance to apes as we go back in time implies simian
> ancestry, seeing that these changes may be due to changes in food and
> posture, representing the acquisition of form growing out of function
> or closely correlated with function. In that case prehistoric man's in-
> creasing resemblance to apes has some other explanation than descent
> from a common ancestor, being, if our interpretation is correct, a case
> of convergence, the response of similar form to similar function....
>
> We cannot afford to close our eyes to facts because we shy away
> from their implications. A good case is not strengthened by adducing
> poor reasons in support of it, and no fear of giving comfort to the
> enemy should lead us to suppose that a partial concealment of truth,
> which arises from a concealment of part of the truth, can compensate
> for the loss of unprejudiced consideration of the facts of life whether
> they seem to fit into our schemes of evolution or fail to fit.
>
> Since the day of Darwin the evolutionary idea has largely domi-
> nated the ambitions and determined the findings of physical anthro-
> pology, sometimes to the detriment of the truth.

[62] Schultz, Adolph, "Man and the Cararrhine Primates," *Cold Spring Har-*
·or Symposia 15 (1950): 50.
[63] Selby, Colin, "Modern Views of the Origin of Species," *Christian Gradu-*
te, Inter-Varsity Fellowship, London, June, 1956, p. 99.
[64] "Homo sapiens at Choukoutien," *Antiquity* (England) 13 (June, 1939):
·43.
[65] Weidenreich, Franz, ref. 26, p. 86.
[66] Romer, Alfred, ref. 8, p. 220.
[67] Wallis, Wilson D., ref. 17, p. 75.

Appendix
Note on S.L. Washburn's Experiment

For those who may happen to be familiar with the experiment carried out by S. L. Washburn, Department of Anatomy, College of Physicians and Surgeons, at Columbia University, and reported in the *Anatomical Record* (Vol. 99, 1947, pp. 239-248), in which he tried to demonstrate experimentally the theory of ballooning as propounded by Weidenreich, the following observations are written.

By severing the chewing muscles of rats, no alteration was found to occur in the skull form. It was evidently not possible by such a means to obtain a higher vault. Washburn's conclusion was therefore that Weidenreich's theory was without foundation. He went even further when he summed up his convictions as follows:

> Constriction of the brain case by the temporal muscles could not be demonstrated in the rat, nor does it seem probable that it occur in man.

However, this is going considerably beyond the evidence. There is no reason to suppose that the rat's gene complement has the capability of supplying the material necessary to provide a higher vault, if did permitted. With man the case is quite otherwise.

Had Washburn *added* to the muscular tension instead of reducing it, he might well have obtained some *reduction* in what vault there is, and this would then have supported the thesis we have been proposing in place of Weidenreich's. (See Fig. 11.)

224

Part V

The Fallacy of
Anthropological Reconstructions

The moment we *want* to stop believing in anything we have hitherto believed in, we not only find that there are many objections to it, but also that these objections have been staring us in the face all the time.

George Bernard Shaw

The Fallacy of
Anthropological Reconstructions

Fig. 12. Mr. and Mrs. Hesperopithecus, reconstructed from the tooth of a wild pig found in Nebraska. These figures are redrawn from the "Illustrated London News" in 1922. This explanatory text accompanied the sketch: "The poise of the head should be noted, large muscles from the occiput to the back and shoulders have to counteract the prognathous head and heavy jaw — a simian character." It is amazing what can be guessed from the tooth of a wild pig. The gullible public can never really know how much imagination and how little science enter into such reconstructions.

IN A UNIVERSITY, although the spirit of competition between disciplines is not overt as it is in the business world, there is nevertheless a certain competitiveness. The amount of money which is budgeted for each department is quite naturally related to the enrollment in the courses it offers, so that there is a certain amount of rivalry when it comes to attracting students. Very large universities, of course, or wealthy universities, do not have to worry too much when classes are mere handfuls. When we were studying cuneiform in the University of Toronto, there were only three of us; yet it was probably at that time the largest class of its kind in the world. . . . The university could afford to sustain it for prestige, if nothing else.

The factor which decides for a large proportion of students what courses they will enroll in is public interest at the time. And by interest I would include also what might be called "market demand," which of course is a reflection of public interest. So there is a tendency in learned circles where the subject matter lacks the advantages of immediate practical importance, to seek to arouse public interest by methods which are not always strictly scholarly. Anthropology has been, I think, one of the chief offenders in this respect, yielding all too frequently to the temptation of attracting attention by advertising in ways which are more entertaining than scholarly.

Some disciplines like psychology always have a wide appeal, and it is not too difficult to obtain student enrollment or a publisher for even very commonplace observations. Astronomy appeals because the very magnitudes involved lend wings to the imagination. The applied sciences make their way with ease, novelty or practical advantage having their own compulsions. But anthropology has somehow or other always been tempted to emphasize, a little bit at least, the grotesque aspects of its subject matter in order to gain a hearing. This was particularly so at the beginning, a hundred years ago. But it is still unfortunately the case. One of the best ways to introduce a subject, either to a class of students or to a reading public, is by the so-called historical method, in which the complexities are led up to by tracing their supposed course of development through simpler stages — as though one might explore the complexity of adult human behavior by tracing back to the stages of childhood development. For some reason, where most other sequences start with the simple and proceed to the complex, anthropology seems to lean towards a policy of starting with the *ugly* in order to lead to the refined, making the assumption that in the historical process of development, "first things" (even faces) must always be ugly. In any sequence of illustrations, man's ancestors will always be assumed to be uglier as they are more ancient. This is entirely presumptive, for the first man need not have been ugly at all. But once this evolutionary assumption is made, it becomes self-validating for the simple reason that fossils are thereafter arranged in sequences to demonstrate it. Reconstructions, by which I mean pictures or models of man's supposed ancestors, could on this

THE FALLACY OF RECONSTRUCTIONS

principle be put in the "right" order by a child who knew absolutely nothing about human history. He would only have to be told that the ugliest were the earliest — and the rest could be left to him. This may seem like an absurd oversimplification or even downright misrepresentation. And it may actually be an exaggeration. Nevertheless, we shall show that anthropologists themselves, ancient and modern, seem to enjoy reinforcing the popular philosophy in this way, not because the facts warrant it but because the public expects it. And this is one of the favorite ways of achieving notoriety — or in more scholarly terms, "recognition." A man's reputation is "made" if he can find some fragment out of which to create a very ancient (and ugly) ancestor.

Anthropology saw its first heyday of popularity with the sudden emergence of volume after volume devoted to the curious ways of savage people. Once it had been agreed that these "savages" represented a necessary stage in human history before man achieved his present civilized condition, it was inevitable that the process should be extended backwards and that those representatives of the human race who stood in the same chronological relationship to primitives that primitives do to us, should be as utterly brutish and bereft of culture relative to native civilizations as native civilizations were felt to be towards the civilized European. Thus no matter how upright and noble our first parents may have been in actual fact, it was absolutely essential to present them as anything but noble and upright. Indeed, if Adam and Eve had actually been dug up with the appearance which we believe they must have had when they came from God's hand, they most certainly would have been rejected as frauds. This is no exaggeration. Quite a number of *modern* skulls have been dug up from strata which demonstrated that they were very early examples of modern-type men, and virtually without exception they have at one time been rejected on one pretext or another and "smitten from the record."

So, reverting to those earlier days of anthropology, we find museums coming into being and taking the form of a kind of Madame Tussaud's where the wonder-weary public were invited to enjoy the questionable stimulus of viewing their supposed ancestors whose chief glory was their bestial appearance. Even animals have some beauty. But these really have none. The slightest excuse served to create a missing link out of some tiny fragment of doubtful identity. And even before Darwin's *Origin of Species* was published, P. T. Barnum

---

[1] Barnum, P. T., see A. O. Lovejoy, *The Great Chain of Being*, Harvard 1942, p. 236.

was inviting the public to see his collection of curiosities including some genuine "primitives," and other miscellaneous fossil items. In 1842 Barnum's Circus Exhibit (by combining it with Scudder's and Peele's Museums) became the basis of the American Museum in New York City, enlivened with freak shows and stage entertainment. It is said that Queen Victoria was once told an "offcolor" joke and that her shattering response was, "We are not amused." But, unlike Queen Victoria, the people of her time were highly "amused" by these anthropological displays, and it has only been in very recent years that museums have begun to tone down some of their more entertaining reconstructions of man's supposed ancestors.

A. E. Hooten, in one of his many informative and entertaining volumes, told the story of a certain prelate who ridiculed the Hall of Man in New York in which so many of these reconstructions had been neatly lined up to give the desired effect. He pointed out how Henry Fairfield Osborn, who was responsible for it, denied the accusation that this was not science; and in an article in a newspaper, closed by saying triumphantly, "The Hall of Man still stands." Next day, apparently, the prelate in his reply closed with the words, "The Hall of Man still *lies!*" Hooten remarked:[2]

> There is just enough truth in that statement to make it cut. Some evolutionary exhibits and reconstructions of extinct men have been carried out with the elaboration of details and assumption of omniscience which are not justified by the scientific data on hand. It is absolutely impossible to infer from the human skull the morphological details of the eyes, the ear, the tip of the nose, the lips, the form and distribution of hair, and the colour of skin, hair, and eyes. So that I think the laugh was on the side of the archbishop because the scientists have overreached themselves and gone beyond their evidence.

Hooten was always known for his keen wit and I think he must have been a very healthful influence in his day, but evidently his words were not heeded, for the making of these reconstructions has proceeded apace. The above had been written in 1937, but ten years before this, Hooten had referred to another astounding piece of nonsense:[3]

> A well known Latin American Paleontologist worked the pampas formations to such an extent that he caused a fossil monkey to evolve into a Homunculus patagonicus, and created from an Indian atlas bone and the femur of a fossil cat, the common ancestor of all existing men!

Perhaps a classic example of this kind of fallacious reconstruction revolves around the appearance and disappearance of Hesperopithe-

---

[2] Hooten, A. E., *Apes, Men, and Morons*, Putnams Sons, N.Y., 1937, p. 60.
[3] Hooten, A. E., "Where Did Man Originate?" *Antiquity*, 1 (June, 1927) : 133.

cus. In 1922 a single molar tooth was found in a Pliocene deposit in Nebraska. A Professor Osborn described it as belonging to an early type of pithecanthropoid, which he named Hesperopithecus. At the same time the eminent Elliott Smith in England induced the *Illustrated London News*[4] to publish a double-spread reconstruction of Mr. and Mrs. Hesperopithecus — all on the strength of this small tooth. Subsequently, it was established that the tooth belonged to a peccary, and Hesperopithecus disappeared from view. However, in the 14th edition of the Encyclopedia Britannica, since the previous edition had listed Hesperopithecus with all honors, it was necessary to make some reference to the fact that this specimen had vanished. But the horrid truth was concealed as far as possible by disclosing no more than that the tooth was eventually found to belong to "a being of another order," which is another way of spelling "wild pig."

It was a great day in the annals of evolutionary anthropology when, in 1857, a fossil skull was found by Fuhlrott near Dusseldorf, at a place ever since universally known as the Neanderthal Cave. This skull was precisely what the doctors had ordered because it lent itself to reconstructions which would satisfy, in terms of ugliness, even the most demanding of viewers. The reconstructions which have been made of this much maligned gentleman are legion and they are a clearer evidence of the stimulating effect of imagination than they are of scientific objectivity. The fact of the matter is that Neanderthal Man was evidently suffering from chronic osteoarthritis,[5] an ailment which forced him to adopt a stooped posture, inviting a comparison with the gait of an ape while in fact having absolutely nothing to do with it.

In 1940, in the University of Knowledge Series, published in collaboration with a number of eminent authorities in various fields, there is a volume entitled *The Story of Primitive Man,* which is the joint work of Mabel Cole and Fay-Cooper Cole of the Department of Anthropology in the University of Chicago. The jacket cover has a reconstruction of Neanderthal Man with his head thrust forward and an almost entire absence of neck (a peculiarly apelike feature). The same gentleman, his apishness slightly more accentuated, if possible, carries his club across the frontpiece on page xii. On page

---

[4] *Illustrated London News,* June 24, 1922, pp. 942-943: "The earliest man traced by a tooth: an astounding discovery of human remains in Pliocene strata."

[5] Coon, C. S., *The Story of Man,* Knopf, N.Y., 1962, p. 40. Also A. J. E. Cave, 15th International Congress of Zoology, London, reported in *Discovery,* Nov., 1958, p. 469.

Fig. 13. This is Neanderthal Man as constructed for the Field Museum of Natural History, Chicago. Until recently, the exhibit portrayed Neanderthal as a stooped man — his wife and son stooped accordingly. At present, however, the display shows him upright rather than stooped, for the reasons stated by the author in this volume. Photos used by permission of the Field Museum of Natural History, Chicago.

40 a closeup gives the reader an even clearer picture of this vacuous-looking idiot, while on the opposite page the book pictures his family, including a child of about eight or ten years of age who looks even more stooped than his elders. Fig. 13 shows a recent reconstruction — the stoop at last removed!

It is common knowledge, now, not only that Neanderthal Man walked erect precisely as healthy modern man does but that he actually had a greater cranial capacity, in excess of 1600 cc., compared with modern man's 1400 cc. Many today believe that Neanderthal Man is still with us and that we would scarcely look at him twice were we to meet him on the street in modern clothes. The impressions which can be created by an artist, starting with the same basic skull, are apt to be quite varied indeed, as will be seen by the three drawings in Fig. 14 which I have copied from the sources indicated.

In 1939, a year earlier, Alberto Carlo Blanc and Sergio Sergi reported in *Science* the finding of a Neanderthal skull in a cave at Monte Circeo in Italy:[6]

> Two other Neanderthal skulls have been found in Italy, one in 1929 and the other in 1935, both in the Sacopastore region near Rome, but neither is as well preserved as the new discovery. However, the occipital opening at the base of one of the skulls was particularly well preserved enabling Professor Sergi to establish for the first time that Neanderthal Man walked erect and not with an ape-like posture with head thrust forward as previously believed. The horizontal plane of the opening in the skull shows that the bones of the neck fitted perpendicularly into the opening, causing the posture to be erect as in present day man.

It is true that this news may have come too late for the printer to agree readily to making any changes in the dustjacket of the book or the illustrations in it, yet it seems likely that if this had been a publication dealing with physics or chemistry in which a basic error of such importance to fundamental theory had been made known to the author one year before his book was published, he would most assuredly have made some attempt — for his own reputation's sake, if not in the interests of truth — to correct the error, either by changing the text or appending a correction notice. But anthropology apparently does not feel any such necessity.

A report from the Associated Press[7] on the finding of Tepexpan Man not far from Mexico City underscores the uncertainty of popular reconstructions. Following the usual custom, the public had at first

---

[6] Monte Circeo: reported in *Science,* 90 (1939) supplement, p. 13.

[7] Newman, M. T., *Globe and Mail,* Toronto, April 4, 1951.

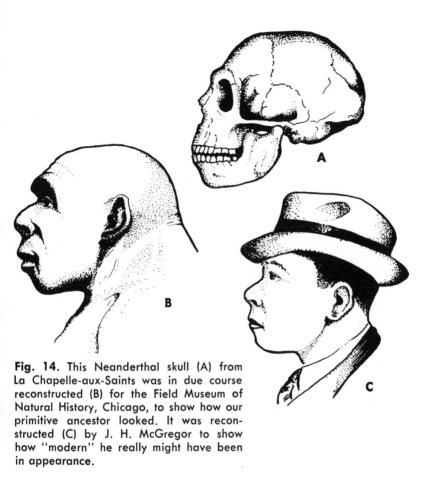

Fig. 14. This Neanderthal skull (A) from La Chapelle-aux-Saints was in due course reconstructed (B) for the Field Museum of Natural History, Chicago, to show how our primitive ancestor looked. It was reconstructed (C) by J. H. McGregor to show how "modern" he really might have been in appearance.

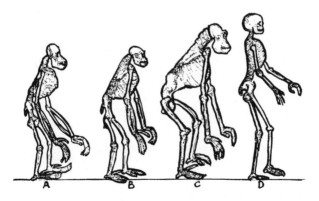

Fig. 15. Huxley's falsified figures of primates and man.

been presented with a portrait of this gentleman, appropriately down-graded in appearance to fit current theories of man's evolution. But in an interview, M. T. Newman said, "Look at some of the reconstructed heads of this individual. . . . They look thick-headed, stupid, and bestial. But now we are trying to be more realistic. . . . Obviously, early man had to be intelligent or he would not have survived." The Smithsonian Institute had taken the same skull, and T. D. Stewart and a Washington artist, Leo Steppat, set to work reconstructing the head. The result was, in the words of Dr. Newman, "Not a bad looking fellow — not too far removed from a typical southwestern Indian." The fact is that there is a strong tendency on the part of anthropologists to take advantage of public gullibility and to supply, upon the slightest pretext, hypothetical missing links, because as Wilson Wallis said,[8] "Since the day of Darwin, the evolutionary idea has largely dominated the ambitions and determined the findings of physical anthropology, sometimes to the detriment of the truth."

Recently, in a notice in the *American Journal of Physical Anthropology,* which I presume was written by the editor (the same T. D. Stewart) , the following warning with respect to such reconstructions was issued:[9]

> From the skull, it is quite impossible to reconstruct the character of the hair, eyes, nose, lips, ears, eyebrows, skin creases, fullness, or expression. In short, it is impossible to reconstruct the appearance of the face.
> Nevertheless, such fancy reconstructions are to be found in almost every book dealing with the evolution of man. It is highly desirable that they should be dropped for they do real harm. Their creators have endowed them with traits and expressions which follow the formula that the earlier the type, the more brutal; the later the type, the nobler of expression. The probabilities are that the expression of early man was no less benign than our own.

How completely true this observation is was beautifully borne out in 1937 when Karl Absolon reported his amazing findings at Vestonice. A summary of his work appeared in the *Illustrated London News*[10] and here we have a series of photographs of the beautiful carved head, done in ivory. In Dr. Absolon's words, it is "the earliest known portrait of a human being." In his article, he remarked:

> There was little hope of obtaining anything clearer anthropologically than current reconstructions. It can therefore be imagined what a surprise it was for anthropology when the sculpture portrait of fossil man was brought to light in Vestonice. Some heretic, some sacrilegeous

[8] Wallis, Wilson, "The Structure of Pre-Historic Man," in *The Making of Modern Man,* Modern Library Series, 1931, p. 75.
[9] Stewart, T. D., in *Amer. Jour. Physical Anthropol.,* 6 (1948) : 321 f.
[10] Absolon, Karl, *Illustrated London News,* London, Oct. 2, 1937.

man had deserted the religion of his fathers, and in defiance of all tradition carved the portrait of a true face. The portrait shows a very noble, fine, animated face — a long nose, arched ridges over the eyes, and a long chin.

Absolon remarked, "The face recalls some classical portrait from some old oriental civilization, or even a modern drawing, such as the head of Christ by the Dutch painter, Jan Toorop, in his *Night in the Cathedral*."

Wood Jones was always speaking out against reconstructions of any kind, which were merely intended to prejudice the viewer's mind in favor of an evolutionary history. He said, with some scorn:[11]

> In the story of the origin of the protohuman stock, and the subsequent emergence of man, there is but little legitimate room for most of the fancy portraits with which pseudoscience has been so ready to arrest uninstructed attention. We have all grown used to the picture of the slouching brute with shaggy hair and elongated arms that is lumbering into a stage of partial uprightness as it toils along the pathway of the origin of man.
>
> One of the most recent and most sumptuous publications upon the comparative cerebral anatomy of the primates has shown this progress in graphic form that renders the ascent the more vivid, since it depicts it as taking place up the laborious slopes of a hillside. Here the slouching hairy beast toils lumbering upwards, seizing sticks and stones as weapons by the way, and passing from stark hirsuit nakedness to the comparative modesty of a skin apron and ultimately to the decent obscurity of a cave.
>
> Were it well attested that man was derived from the stock of the large brachiating anthropoid apes, especially were there any justification for the greatly laboured "gorilloid" heritage in man, these pictures might claim sanction, as do those of the ancestral horses from the findings of comparative anatomy and paleontology; but this sanction is wholly lacking.
>
> There is no justification for the picture of the slouching, semierect Ape Man, though every investigator who … attempts an interpretation of the remains of some ancient human skeleton seeks first to determine evidences of the presence of these characters.

If one were to compare the impression created in the mind by the carved head found by Dr. Absolon and the reconstruction of Neanderthal Man which was displayed in the British Museum, there is no doubt that, of the first, one would certainly say, Here is a thoughtful, intelligent individual — perhaps even a philosopher. And one would say of the other, Here is a brutal man little influenced by culture and probably with essentially animal tastes and little power of reflection. We associate a low intelligence with unrefined features. Sometimes the association is justified, but sometimes it is not. If one compares the reconstructed face of Pithecanthropus erectus shown in

[11] Jones, F. Wood, *Man's Place Among the Mammals*, Arnold, London, 1929, pp. 362-365.

Fig. 16 with the photograph of a Russian delegate to the Cairo Conference which took place in 1958, the fallacy of such association becomes at once apparent. For however much we may disagree with Russian ideology, the fact remains that this delegate must have been a shrewd and highly intelligent man, since the Russians would not make the mistake of sending an idiot to represent them. It may be that this delegate did indeed have a larger brain than Pithecanthropus, with whom we are comparing his head form. But it is not at all certain that cranial capacity is related to intelligence, and therefore Pithecanthropus could have had much more intelligence than we give him credit for, in spite of the fact that his cranial capacity, according to Howells,[12] was between 950 and 1000 cc. in volume. According to Jan Lever,[13] Anatole France had a cranial capacity of only 1100 cc., as did also Gambetta and Justus von Liebig. Franz von Weidenreich questioned seriously whether anything at all could be determined with respect to intelligence on the basis of cranial capacity.[14] Franz Boas expressed the same opinion:[15]

> By analogy we associate lower mental traits with brute-like features. In our naive everyday parlance, brutish features and brutality are closely connected. . . . We are also inclined to draw inferences in regard to mentality from a receding forehead, a heavy jaw, large and heavy teeth, perhaps even from inordinate length of arms, or an unusual development of hairiness. It appears that neither cultural achievement (in this case, associated weapons, etc.) nor outward appearance is a safe basis on which to judge the mental aptitude of races.

It is not surprising, therefore, to find Gaylord Simpson,[16] in a review of LeGros Clark's *History of the Primates: An Introduction to the Study of Fossil Man,* remarking with manifest approval, "The book contains no restorations of prehistoric men or other fossil primates, and is not provided with a graphic phylogenetic tree." Simpson adds, "This is a well written, modest book, for which we should be duly thankful." After all this, it is amazing to find Sir Gavin de Beer publishing an impressive *Atlas of Evolution* in 1964, which is replete with "wholly speculative portraits" of fossil protohominids and men such as Proconsul, Java Man, Pekin Man, Neanderthal Man, etc.[17] As an illustration of how wildly such modern reconstructions of a

---

[12] Howells, William, *Mankind So Far,* Doubleday Doran, N.Y., 1945, p. 138.

[13] Lever, Jan, *Creation and Evolution,* Grand Rapids Internat. Pub., 1958, pp. 158, 159.

[14] Weidenreich, Franz von, "The Human Brain in the Light of Phylogenetic Development," *Sci. Monthly,* Aug., 1948, p. 103.

[15] Boas, Franz, *The Mind of Primitive Man,* 2nd ed., N.Y., 1939, pp. 16, 17.

[16] Simpson, G. G., in *Science,* 110 (1949) : 455.

[17] Cousins, Frank W., *Fossil Man: A Reappraisal of the Evidence,* Evolution Protest Movement, England, 1966, p. 46.

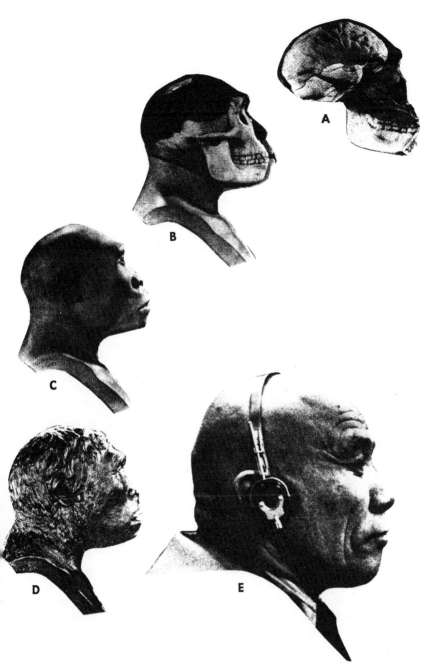

Fig. 16. This series of four photographs (A, B, C, D) shows the stages of reconstruction of Pithecanthropus erectus. (E) The Russian delegate to the 1958 Cairo Conference.

single specimen can differ from each other, Fig. 2 (page 23) shows three alternatives for Zinjanthropus, which many anthropologists, including a number of Christian anthropologists, believe to have been one of man's ancestors. I venture to suggest that *"one* of man's ancestors" is an understatement. If there is any scientific validity whatever in these three reconstructions, Zinjanthropus must have been *three* of man's ancestors! It makes one wonder if anthropologists are even taking themselves seriously, let alone expecting the intelligent public to do so.

There are other kinds of reconstructions which are equally deceiving and more so, because the deception is so subtle. The originators of such illustrations must know that they are less than honest, and yet they do not hesitate to adorn their works thus nor is any protest against such misrepresentations raised by their colleagues.

An excellent example of what I mean will be found in an authorative work by Weidenreich entitled *Apes, Giants, and Man*. In Fig. 17, which is redrawn with precision from the original, two series of three skulls in section are shown, with the brains indicated by stippling. The object of this particular series is to show how the brain may be enlarged progressively in two different "species." I have put the word "species" in quotes for a very good reason. In column 1 we have three animals who genuinely belong to one species, an Irish Wolfhound, an English Bulldog, and a King Charles Spaniel. In column 2, as a parallel series, are shown the skull of a gorilla, of Pithecanthropus, and of a modern European. The object of these two series of skull outlines with the size of the brain indicated, is simply to convince the unwary that just as a wolfhound can become a spaniel (by artificial selection, of course), so the gorilla can become man (by natural selection, of course). What has changed the facial form of the first series is the fact that the brain has been enlarged for some reason by a process of breeding. The assumption is then made that the same thing probably took place with respect to man, his enlarged brain resulting in the kind of facial form which so distinguishes him from the apes. Pictorially, the two series of skulls present a convincing parallelism. But anyone who does a little thinking about the matter will soon see that there are several major fallacies in this scheme. To begin with, it is obvious to any lover of dogs that despite the affectionateness and gentleness of spaniels which makes them such desirable pets, they do not have the intelligence that the wolfhound has, i.e., the intelligence of the Alsatian type of dog, the type used for police dogs and for "seeing eyes" for blind people. And if it came to survival, there is not much doubt whether

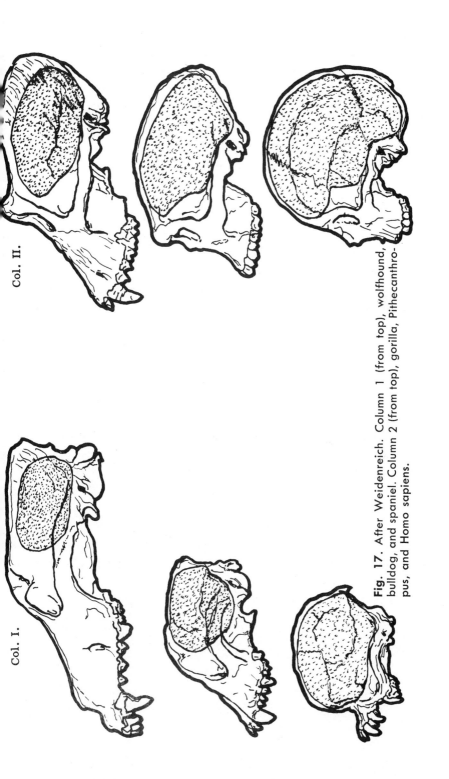

Col. I.

Col. II.

Fig. 17. After Weidenreich. Column 1 (from top), wolfhound, bulldog, and spaniel. Column 2 (from top), gorilla, Pithecanthropus, and Homo sapiens.

the first animal or the last animal in Weidenreich's series would stand the best chance. Altogether, then, even granting that these are indeed one species so that some kind of *natural* selective process might by a strange freak of circumstance bring about the evolution of the spaniel out of the English Bulldog out of the Irish Wolfhound, it would certainly be a freak circumstance and not the normal pattern as visualized by the evolutionists themselves. If the spaniel were turned wild, it is almost certain that after a few generations it would revert to the wolfdog type, so that Weidenreich's canine series really demonsrates precisely the opposite of what he is trying to prove.

Turning, then, to column 2, we have an even more ridiculous situation, really, because we know that gorillas and modern men do *not* belong to the same species — whatever may be said of Pithecanthropus. Thus, in reality, the whole business is not merely unscientific, it is positively deceitful. It only shows how a false concept can so dominate the thinking of an otherwise highly intelligent man that even devotion to truth is weakened. In any struggle between the first specimen and the last specimen in column 1, the first specimen would undoubtedly be the victor. By contrast it is most likely that the reverse would be true in column 2. In what sense, therefore, does this contribute anything either for or against the theory of the evolution of man?

It is interesting to find in the same volume which contains this highly deceiving series of drawings, that the learned author draws attention to the way in which Thomas Huxley committed the unforgiveable sin of presenting the same kind of deceptive diagram. Weidenreich reproduces the famous series of four skeletons (Fig. 15) from Huxley's original work, in which we see an orangutan walking behind a chimpanzee, walking behind a gorilla, walking behind a man. The "message" is clear. However, Weidenreich points out that the first three figures have been "doctored," the apes being depicted in an abnormally erect position. On the other hand, the man has been depicted with a slight stoop. As Weidenreich put it,[18] "In other words, the individual skeletal elements in Huxley's drawing are nearly correct in their form and proportions, but the poses Huxley has given them are artificial and not characteristic." Thus, the stooping gorilla becomes "Pithecus erectus" and the upright man becomes "Anthropus ebentus" in order to fool the public. It is rather like the pot calling the kettle black to find Weidenreich commenting thus on Huxley's diagram.

---

[18] On Huxley's diagram, see F. Weidenreich, *Apes, Giants, and Man,* Univ. Chicago Press, 1948, p. 6.

Huxley was by no means alone in this tendency to doctor drawings to suit. He was apparently accused by his colleagues of "dishonesty" in this regard, and his words of admission are rather revealing:[19]

> I should feel utterly condemned and annihilated by the admission, were it not that hundreds of the best observers and biologists lie under the same charge. The great majority of all morphological, anatomical, histological, and embryological diagrams are not true to nature but are more or less doctored, schematized, and reconstructed.

Thomas Huxley mentions embryological reconstructions. In a paper entitled, "Darwin and Embryology," Sir Gavin de Beer[20] made this statement:

> Seldom has an assertion like that of Haeckel's "theory of recapitulation," facile, tidy, and plausible, widely accepted without critical examination, done so much harm to science.

De Beer then shows how determined an effort was made to demonstrate his theory by a number of workers in the field, especially Hyatt and Wurtenburger who, as he points out, published a beautiful series of fossil ammonites. These were arranged in sequences which seemed to prove the theory of recapitulation. De Beer then remarked:[21]

> So seductive did this picture appear that some years were to go by before A. Pavlov in 1901 showed that, if ammonite shells are arranged in such a sequence, the *stratigraphical order of the geological succession has to be reversed* (his emphasis). In other words, Wurtenburger's and Hyatt's series falsified the evidence and were utterly valueless.

A similar case is reported in much more recent times by Professor G. Gaylord Simpson:[22]

> In fishes, there is a recent seriation from forms with no bone to forms with extensive bone. Comparative anatomists formerly unanimously agreed that this corresponded with a historical sequence in the stated direction, but directly historical studies (by A. S. Romer) now indicate that the real time sequence was *in the other direction* (emphasis mine).

In short, unanimous agreement among the experts is no guarantee whatever of truth. One wonders whether, if a Christian palaeontologist had conducted the historical studies which Romer did, would he even have been able to find a publisher, let alone have convinced Gaylord Simpson of the truth of the matter? Science is far from the

---

[19] Huxley's reply as given in *Dawn*, Sept., 1931, p. 267.
[20] de Beer, Sir Gavin, "Darwin and Embryology," in *A Century of Darwin,* ed. by S. A. Barnett, Heinemann, London, 1958, p. 159.
[21] Ibid., p. 160.
[22] Simpson, G. Gaylord, "Historical Biology Bearing on Human Origins," *Cold Spring Harbor Symposia on Quantitative Biology,* 15 (1950): 56.

objective exercise it would appear to be in the eyes of the general public. Reconstructions leave so much to the imagination that they invite sensationalism and this strongly appeals to the public, helping to promote sales and thus to provide a wider exposure of a man's ideas — always a rewarding experience.

We are still in the company of pots calling kettles black, for this particular form of public entertainment (or deception — Barnum equated them) is still as popular as ever. Speaking at the Cold Spring Harbor Symposia on Quantitative Biology in 1950, G. Gaylord Simpson made this remark:[23]

> In passing, I may say that a prudent paleontologist is sometimes appalled at the extent of restoration indulged in by the anthropologists, some of whom seem quite willing to reconstruct a face from a partial cranium, or a whole skull from a piece of the lower jaw, and so on.
> Of course, this temerity is inducted by the great popular interests of the subject and the fact that fragments do not impress the public.
> Then, too, the worst examples are in popular publications and are not likely to mislead the professionals, but still. . . . !

This quotation terminates precisely as Simpson terminated it. One might suppose from this that he would himself avoid at all costs the presentation of reconstructions of any kind which involved the slightest element of deceit. Yet, unfortunately, he was himself so dominated by evolutionary philosophy that he could not limit himself to the evidence but extrapolated always in such a way as to make the evidence support the view he held. In presenting experimental findings for publication in scientific journals, it is important to avoid adding to the data on the basis of pure assumption. For example, in

---

[23] Ibid., p. 57.

Fig. 18. The suppressive effect of Atropine on sweating in man.

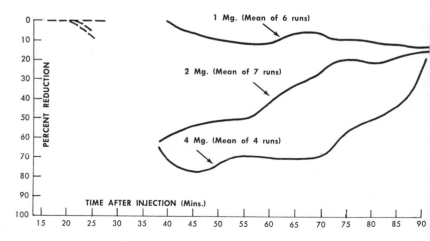

Fig. 18 are shown three curves which reveal the course of the effect of a certain drug on one particular physiological function of man. For reasons which are not important in the present context, we had this information for only that part of the experimental time interval covered by the solid line. Since we knew, obviously, that the drug effect was zero at zero hour of injection, we knew that the solid line would ultimately start from the y axis at zero minutes at the point marked with an asterisk. The temptation, of course, was to join the asterisk to the beginning of the solid line with a smooth curve, thus completing the graph. But this would have been quite improper from a scientific point of view: for there is no *evidence* to show what the course of the effect followed by the drug was during that interval. It would have been pure assumption. Yet Simpson's works are frequently accompanied by geological trees intended to show the relationships between animals in a series, in which the solid lines represent what is known of these relationships with reasonable certainty and then dotted lines are used to assure the viewer that ultimately all the lines stem originally from a single source, thus reinforcing the "truth" of evolution. Remember that the dotted lines are purely presumptive. Although they would possibly be correct if evolution were true, from a purely scientific point of view there is still really no justification for them since actual evidence is entirely lacking. To this extent, the unsuspecting reader is deceived.

Some authors avoid putting in the dotted lines and to this extent are being more strictly scientific — or at least appear to be. They are fulfilling the letter of the law, as it were, but not really the spirit of it. For it is not at all difficult to so curve the lines towards each other without actually joining them, in such a way that the eye itself inevitably completes the process of making a "tree" out of what is otherwise merely a group of loose twigs. The "message" is the same, and it gets across to the reader. As an illustration of what I mean by this, Fig. 19 is reproduced from an excellent study of the subject by Frank Cousins[24] whose diagram was taken from de Beer's work. The absence of actual connecting links tends to be entirely overlooked.

The extent to which this kind of pastime can be carried is rather well shown in Fig. 20 taken from a paper by Kermack and Mussett entitled "The First Mammals."[25] The most casual study of this "suggested family tree of the vertebrate animals" will show that it doesn't remotely resemble a genealogical tree. Not one twig is joined to

---

[24] Cousins, Frank W., ref. 17, p. 21.
[25] Kermack, K. A. and Frances Mussett, "The First Mammals," *Discovery*, April, 1959, p. 145.

Fig. 19. Animal Phylogeny, after Sir Gavin de Beer.

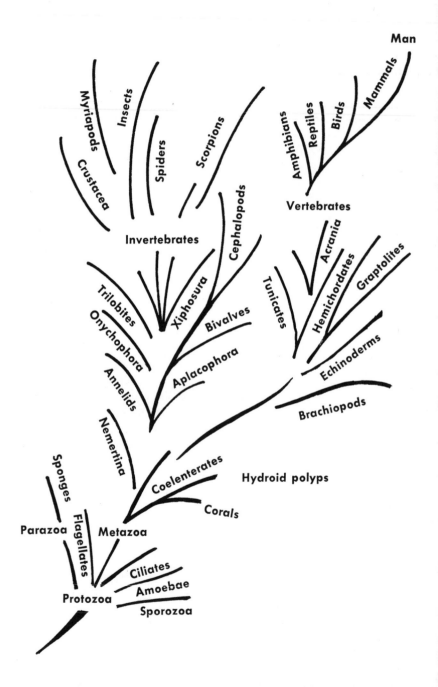

another. There are more disconnections than connections and the dotted lines which provide the only justification for titling the diagram as a *tree* are, of course, competely hypothetical. Yet the public becomes so accustomed to this kind of propaganda that it is no longer recognized for what it really is, but is taken as factual evidence for evolution.[26]

One cannot help but recall the statement made by W. D. Wallis in a paper entitled[27] "Presuppositions in Anthropological Interpretations," in which he pointed out that at least two generalizations are usually implied, though never stated. The first is that more data may be inferred from older remains than would be considered sound to infer from contemporary remains. There is much less danger of being found out if one is wrong. And the second is that in dealing with prehistoric man, inferences may be made on material much less abundant than would be necessary if contemporary man were being discussed. To use his words, "The further we proceed into the gloom of the prehistoric, the clearer our vision. Hence things which could not possibly be inferred if the data were contemporary man, can, thanks to this illumination in the gathering dusk of remote ages, be inferred with confidence."

This paper has been entirely negative and it would be a pity to close it without saying something on the positive side. For there is, no doubt, much to be said in favor of attempting such reconstructions if the object is genuinely to inform rather than indoctrinate or deceive.

It has often been observed, and Wood Jones was one of those who wrote about the matter at some length, that a change took place in the method of research, and in the central theme and prime concern of the life sciences once Darwin's work had established the evolutionary approach to nature. Previously, great interest had been attached to the study of the relationship between form and function.

---

[26] It is most encouraging to note that the Geological Society of London has recently published a symposium entitled, "The Fossil Record" (Burlington House, London, 1967, xii and 828 pp.), which contains papers by 126 authorities, occupying a total of some 800 pages, with innumerable charts and graphs. The encouraging thing is that approximately 90% of these elaborate charts and graphs indicate only the overlap in time of the various animal forms which have characterized the successive geological ages, and do not connect them by hypothetical lines, such as are common to almost all other textbooks. This notable volume demonstrates clearly that such information can be displayed usefully *without* making evolutionary assumptions. This I would consider to be objective reporting of the data at its best.
[27] Wallis, Wilson, "Presupposition in Anthropological Interpretations," *Amer. Anthropol.*, 50, July-Sept. (1948) : 560.

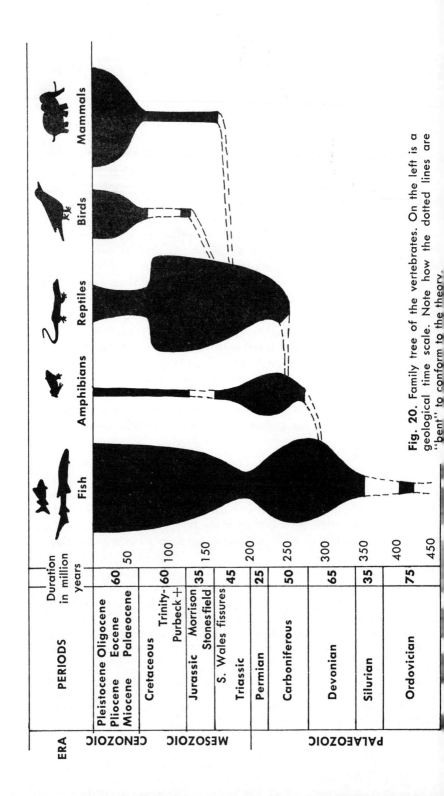

ERA	PERIODS	Duration in million years
CENOZOIC	Pleistocene Oligocene Pliocene Eocene Miocene Palaeocene	60
MESOZOIC	Cretaceous — Trinity- Purbeck +	60
	Jurassic — Morrison Stonesfield	35
	S. Wales fissures	45
	Triassic	25
PALAEOZOIC	Permian	50
	Carboniferous	65
	Devonian	35
	Silurian	75
	Ordovician	

Fig. 20. Family tree of the vertebrates. On the left is a geological time scale. Note how the dotted lines are "bent" to conform to the theory.

After Darwin, this interest declined rapidly and the consuming interest became the question of structure.

The great object was now to establish relationships between different species of animals rather than relationships between form and function within the animal. Since the governing principle here was structural similarity, the assumption being that animals which looked alike were related and that the more nearly they looked alike the more closely related they were, nothing else mattered much except to underscore these homologies. Series of homologous structures were sought with great eagerness and set forth pictorially in just the right way to strengthen the impression that each was merely a modification of the other and that all had a common genetic relationship. The argument that the Great Designer had employed a basic principle of operation, modifying it only as needs required, was forgotten entirely. For the same reason the question of function had been forgotten or overlooked. It was no longer a matter of interest.

Wood Jones pointed out that the older paleontologists scored their great triumphs of reconstruction because they understood so well the relationships which exist between any particular bone and the special purpose which it serves in the whole animal; and they understood also that not infrequently a specialized bone structure serving a specialized purpose usually meant a special kind of animal. Thus they saw living forms as beautifully effective integrated systems, and they were often able on the basis of a single bone to reconstruct the whole animal. Again and again their reconstructions were subsequently validated to an extraordinary degree when further remains were brought to light.

One of the most notable of the older naturalists was Georges Cuvier who enunciated his famous Law of Correlation which stated that if an animal develops one organ in an unmistakable manner, one can infer from it the development of its other organs.[28] Animals with horns and hoofs, for example, invariably possess teeth adapted to vegetarianism. Animals with claws and ankle bones are necessarily equipped with carnivorous teeth. Reptiles with a closed system of teeth are vegetarian, while those with interlocking systems feed on other animals.

According to Cuvier, this correlation applied in the smallest detail and it must even be theoretically possible, he claimed, to reconstruct the entire body of an animal of which only a single organ is known. Wendt said, "Cuvier really was able to reconstruct the

---

[28] Cuvier, Georges: see Herbert Wendt, *I Looked For Adam*, Weidenfeld and Nicolson, London, 1955, p. 152.

complete specimen from a single bone, from the fragment of a jaw (for example)."[29] This ability was demonstrated to his students by Cuvier on a number of occasions when the students were invited to bring him a single bone from some animal of which they had the remainder, and he would then take and reconstruct it, after the Sherlock Holmes manner, into the complete animal.

Towards the end of his book, Wendt records how some of Cuvier's successors showed an extraordinarily "subtle detective sense" which enabled them to interpret apparently barely decipherable fragments. Weinert and Kalatsch appeared to have acquired the ability of looking at fossils through a kind of mental "X-ray apparatus."[30] It was this ability which made it possible for these masters of the art of reconstruction to describe an animal such as Phascolomys, which was living at the time though quite unknown to science, from some sub-fossil bones.[31]

Whereas, today, the majority of reconstructions which mar the work of anthropologists are built up essentially on the basis of an evolutionary philosophy, the older naturalists were not dominated by this philosophy but were guided by a clear understanding of the relationship between form and function. In so far as our museums are now furnished with reconstructions based upon this solid foundation, they are serving the cause of truth. In so far as they are furnished by reconstructions which are inspired primarily by evolutionary philosophy, they become centers of propaganda unworthy of the name of science.

Imagination is a wonderful thing — but man's imagination can, as Scripture says, quickly become "vain." This is particularly so when he deliberately rejects what God has seen fit to reveal about his origin and nature — each of which bears on the other. "Convincing" as such constructs of the imagination may be, one should not put one's trust in them where man's supposed ancestors are concerned. They may be entertaining, but they are seldom scientific, and often they are most misleading.

---

[29] Wendt, Herbert, ref. 28, p. 162.
[30] Ibid., p. 421.
[31] Jones, F. Wood, *Trends of Life*, Arnold, London, 1953, p. 87.

Part VI

Who Taught Adam to Speak?

Speech is the best show man puts on. It is his own "act" on the stage of evolution, in which he comes before the cosmic back-drop and really "does his stuff."

Benjamin Lee Whorf
Language, Thought and Reality

Who Taught Adam to Speak?

MANY YEARS ago Humboldt observed that if there was a transition from animal to man, that transition took place with the acquisition of speech.[1] But he added with rare insight, that in order to speak, man must already have been human. The problem of accounting for the origin of speech appeared to him therefore to be insoluble. Apart from revelation, it still is.

Because of the influence of Darwin's theories, it seemed at one time unnecessary to question the derivation of human speech from animal cries. Essentially the two were the same; it was merely a question of the degree of complexity. Following in the steps of earlier social anthropologists, who were arranging the various primitive cultures in a sequence from the simple to more complex, thereby illustrating man's supposed climb to Parnassus, those who philosophized about language assumed that the strange grunts, clicks, and grimaces of the lowliest "savages" were evidence that speech, like all else, had evolved by barely perceptible steps from simple to complex.[2]

[1] This observation is referred to by Lyell, in his *Antiquity of Man*, 4th ed., 1873, p. 518. A very useful passage from Buffon on the same basic point is quoted by J. C. Greene, *The Death of Adam*, Iowa State Univ. Press, 1959, pp. 202, 203.

[2] A. Goldenweiser has a beautiful illustration of this principle: "What is the theoretical justification for designating as historical, i.e., actual, a series of instances never observed in this successive form in history? The only answer the evolutionist could give here would be that according to the general principles of evolution such were the stages, and that now they were concretely illustrated; therefore the evolutionary hypothesis is correct.... The argument is therefore circular; something that is to be proved, or an inherent part of that something, is assumed in order to make the proof valid. The evolutionist, unable to discover his stages in the historical perspective of one tribal culture, for the simple reason that such a perspective is never available except fragmentarily, proceeds to substitute an instance found in one tribe as a stage succeeding upon an instance drawn from another, and so on until the entire series is completed. The resulting collection of in-

But little by little it appeared that the problem was more difficult. To begin with, more careful studies of the most primitive societies, made by men in the field who spent enough time to learn to *use* the native languages they were studying, began to reveal that far from being simple, they were often exceedingly complex.[3] Indeed so rich in terms did they eventually prove to be in many cases, that such an authority as Levy-Bruhl came to doubt (perhaps unjustifiably) whether they even thought as we do. The difference could no longer be measured in terms of "higher" and "lower" but as a different way of conceiving reality, indeed from one point of view, a more complex way of viewing it.[4] G. G. Simpson rightly remarked:[5]

> At the present time no languages are primitive in the sense of being significantly close to the origins of language. Even the people with least complex culture have highly sophisticated languages, with complex grammar, and large vocabularies capable of naming and discussing anything that occurs in the sphere occupied by their speakers.

Eric Lenneberg has said that primitive languages actually require *more* intelligence to learn than our so-called sophisticated languages do.[6] That language of a highly abstract nature must have been with man in very, *very* early times seems to have been recently confirmed by the finding, reported by Alexander Marshack,[7] of what appear to be clearly mathematical notations on a number of bone fragments dated (expansively) at 15,000 to 13,000 B.C.

In fact, the simpler the culture, the more complex in this sense

---

stances is therefore historically a hodge-podge. What makes the collection an historical or a presumed historical series is once more the assumption of uniformity of development which makes the evolutionist feel at liberty to fill in the gaps in the series of instances wherever found.... Throughout then *we find that what is to be demonstrated, is already assumed to validate the demonstration*" (our emphasis). *Anthropology*, Crofts, N.Y., 1945, p. 508.

[3] A. L. Kroeber remarks in this connection, "Dictionaries compiled by missionaries or philologists of languages previously unwritten, run to surprising figures. Thus the number of words recorded in Klamath, the speech of a culturally rude American Indian Tribe, is 7,000; in Navaho, 11,000; in Zulu, 17,000; in Dakota, 19,000; in Maya, 20,000; in Nahuatl, 27,000. It may safely be estimated that every existing language, no matter how backward its speakers are in their general civilization, possesses a vocabulary of at least 5,000 to 10,000 words." Kroeber then adds this note: "Jesperson, who allows 20,000 words to Shakespeare, and 8,000 to Milton, cites 26,000 as the vocabulary of Swedish peasants." *Anthropology*, Harcourt, Brace, N.Y., 1948, p. 231.

[4] His book, *How Natives Think*, trans. Lilian A. Clare, Allen and Unwin, London, 1926, is full of fascinating material illustrating this point.

[5] Simpson, G. G., "The Biology of Natural Man," *Science* 152 (1966) : 477.

[6] Lenneberg, Eric, *The Biological Foundations of Language,* Wiley, 1967, p. 264.

[7] Marshack, Alexander, "Upper Paleolithic Notation and Symbol," *Science* 178 (1972) : 817 f.

was its language likely to prove. Evidently therefore, the whole concept of arranging these cultures in an evolutionary scale was quite wrong.[8] Abandoning this principle cleared the way for a more careful investigation of the origin of human speech, and attention was turned to the problem from several different directions. To begin with, an answer was sought to the questions, What is the *nature* of human speech, and Do animals "speak" to one another at all? If so, are the two forms of communication related or comparable? If they are not, we cannot easily derive the one from the other. Since, as we shall see, a negative conclusion was reached by a number of investigators, the origin of human speech remained a profound mystery.

Further investigation soon revealed other complications. Speech was always assumed to be instinctive. But the discovery from time to time of "wild" or feral children without speech, showed clearly that it results only where there has been social contact. Moreover such contact must be with speaking individuals, for it was further discovered that someone else has to start the process off for each one of us. Company alone does not create communication by speech. Without the spark from one party already the possessor of the faculty, there is no conversation.

Having arrived at this point, it was felt that human beings should be able to encourage animals to speak, unless the organs of speech were different in the latter. In the course of time it was concluded from investigation of the anatomy of the higher apes that the organs of certain animals are not basically different, and that they therefore ought to be able to speak as we do.[9] And indeed, there are some creatures such as parrots, which, though not in the supposed evolutionary base line from amoeba to man, can be taught to repro-

---

[8] Clyde Kluckhohn in his prize-winning book, *Mirror for Man*, McGraw-Hill, N.Y., 1969, p. 148, remarks: "In contrast to the general course of cultural evolution, languages move from *complex to simple*" (our emphasis).

[9] A. L. Kroeber remarks, "All indications are that no subhuman animal ever has any impulse to utter or convey such information. This seems to hold as essentially for dogs and apes, or for that matter for parrots, as for insects.... Chimpanzees, with larynx, tongue, and lips similar to ours, do not even try to learn to reproduce human words to which they respond in their behavior. There is an old epigram that the reason animals do not speak is that they have nothing to say. Its psychology is somewhat crude, but fundamentally correct." *Anthropology*, Harcourt, Brace, N.Y., 1948, p. 41.

Munro Fox asks, "Can animals ever learn to understand our human language? Most pet-lovers would answer unhesitatingly in the affirmative. But usually a dog learns the tone of voice, not the actual words. If you say to a dog in a cheerful voice, 'I'm going to beat you,' he will wag his tail. If you tell him in a mournful tone, 'I've got a bone for you,' he will put his tail between his legs." *The Personality of Animals*, Pelican Books, London, 1952, p. 28.

duce all the sounds of common speech successfully. Yet apes and monkeys cannot speak. . . . Indeed, as J. B. Lancaster[10] rightly observed:

> The more that is known about (communication systems in monkeys and apes) the less these systems seem to help in the understanding of human language.

And G. G. Simpson, commenting on this, wrote:[11]

> Many other attempts have been made to determine the evolutionary origin of language and all have failed.

Maybe language did not evolve at all!

On the other hand, history soon provided instances of human beings who lacked all the normal faculties of speech, i.e., sight, hearing, and voice, and yet who learned to speak (with their fingers of course) and to communicate ideas at a very high level of abstraction. This once more seemed to indicate that the real secret lay in the structure of the brain, or in some other quality of human nature, and not in the organs of the voice.

It was therefore concluded that some genetic strain must suddenly have appeared to alter the structure of the human brain in some way at present unknown, thus paving the way for the appearance of this peculiarly human faculty.[12] Yet this does not answer the main problem, even if such a mutation could be shown to have occurred. For we have on record the case of two feral children, brought up entirely in the wilds, without any human companionship except that they were themselves companions in isolation, who never between them spoke a single word of any form whatever. Thus we find that even the presence of another human being, and the possession of a truly human brain (for subsequently they were taught to speak, though always with limitations) do not in themselves constitute the necessary framework within which speech must inevitably appear.

We are still left therefore, with the problem as to who started the process, for the process must be started by someone. While it is true that a few authorities believe that the human race may be an amalgam of several distinct and independently originated stocks, springing from lower forms of life, there are many others equally committed to an evolutionary origin for man, who hold that he must be derived from a single stock.[13] In this single stock we must have a

---

[10] Lancaster, J. B., *The Origin of Man*, ed. P. L. DeVose, Wenner-Grenn Foundation, N.Y., 1965.

[11] Simpson, G. G., ref. 5, p. 477.

[12] Cassirer, Ernst, *An Essay on Man*, Yale, 1948, p. 31: it should be noted that he has to fall back simply on the concept of some unusual mutation, never again repeated.

[13] The official statement of UNESCO is to the effect that the human race

first man and a first woman. It matters little what we call them, whether Adam (which simply means "man") and Eve (which really means "child bearer," i.e., mother) , or some more technical name, we are still dealing with the same two individuals. What is to account for the fact that they began to talk to one another and this has continued wherever their descendants are found, and without exception, for no people on earth are known without a fully developed language. People are known in one part of the world or another without almost every faculty which we hold to be essentially human, even without mother-love, but not one people has ever been found without the faculty of speech.

It may be stated simply then, that scientifically the question is beyond our reach. About all that scientific investigations can do is to demonstrate what *cannot* be the origin. In Genesis, however, the story of the first conversation on earth is revealed. And since it is the only story that shows insight into the nature of man's first steps at conversation, it is of peculiar interest no matter whether we view it as fancy or as fact, for all about us every day are children learning to speak for the first time and showing us consistently a certain pattern of learning which by its very persistence leads us to suppose that it is the only pattern by which man ever learned to speak. Not merely the subject of conversation of the first pair, but the consequences of it, and the circumstances in which it came to pass, are of real significance for all those who today are concerned with the problem of human nature and conduct. For it is man's power of speech which has enabled him to do what he has done and to be what he is, whether for good or for ill. The power of speech involves the power of abstraction and of self-consciousness, and of delayed reaction and decision. It has in short made man in part a free-willed agent. But it has also enabled him to learn in a unique way and to pass on the substance of his learning so that culture has become cumulative.

But let us revert once more, and consider the points raised in the foregoing in greater detail. It is strange how frequently what is obviously true turns out to be quite false. For centuries it was obvious to everyone that the sun moved around the earth; and until acceptance of this obvious fact was entirely undermined, no further progress in astronomy was possible.

That animals talked to one another was equally obvious. In times of danger a shrill warning was uttered, and the answering pre-

---

is to be derived from a single stock. *Man,* Roy. Anthrop. Instit., London, June, 1952, p. 90, section 125. In Europe there are some dissenting voices, although in the New World almost all authorities agree with this.

cautions of flight were undertaken by those who heard the signal, obviously indicating that they clearly understood what was being "said." Curiously enough some of the most profound observations regarding the real nature of so-called animal speech have finally come not from a man who was a naturalist, but a man who was basically a philosopher interested in the nature of human nature. George Herbert Mead[14] showed in a way which virtually compels assent that animals are not self-conscious and therefore can only *utter* signals, which are not expressions of thought or of emotion. Such sounds are uttered involuntarily, like the "Oh" and "Ah" of a man too deeply moved for speech. The excited whining of a dog in anticipation of food is not the dog's mind expressing anticipation, but a reflex expressing itself. The dog does not express emotion consciously, but the emotion expresses itself. Raymond Pearl has pointed out that herd leaders are not leaders in the sense that human beings may be, for no thought or reasoning is involved.[15] They serve rather as a special sense organ for the whole herd, and their position as leader is in a way an accident of biological processes. Thus Mead distinguishes between a sound which is a sign, and a sound which is a symbol. The first is shared by all creatures able to express emotion, including fear and anger, hate and love, and of course in man, laughter. But a sign of such a nature is involuntary as a rule; always involuntary in the case of animals, but not always so in the case of man who is such a prodigious actor. The "Oh" of a man suddenly injured is not "thought" out. It expresses itself. Naturally we understand it all; the scream of fright, the roar of laughter; both are read, but neither are truly language. Mean points out that it is not until a child discovers what the meaning of his *own* sound to *others* is, and then deliberately makes the sound with this meaning attached to it, that the child speaks. In this sense speech might be held to start when a child discovers that it can cry (without compulsion) merely to gain attention to its self. Such an attitude arises out of self-consciousness, and the consciousness of others as being similar to oneself.

A child thus discovering the trick of gaining attention becomes an actor. Darwin was interested in the question of "acting" because he felt it threw light on the origin of language.[16] He felt that the

---

[14] Mead, George Herbert, *Mind, Self, and Society,* Univ. Chicago Press, 7th ed., 1948.

[15] Pearl, R., *Man the Animal,* Bloomington, Ind., 1946, p. 115.

[16] In his book, *The Expression of the Emotions in Man and Animals,* Darwin has shown that expressive sounds or acts are dictated by certain biological needs and used according to definite biological rules. Thus a sneer was held to be the remnant of "baring the teeth," and so on. However it is

actor in "pulling a face" to indicate anger was only doing what a dog might do when it bared its teeth to frighten its enemy. But this assumed that the dog is conscious of the face he is pulling and realizes that by doing it he can frighten his opponent. In actual fact it seems quite certain now that for the dog "the face is pulling itself," and no self-consciousness is involved. To the other dog it is a sign which he responds to in a characteristic manner. But because the originator is moved by emotion and not by abstract or self-conscious thought, no speech is involved. It is a sign and not a symbol, for symbols have a nature arbitrarily (and therefore consciously) assigned by user and reader alike. The actor pulls a face consciously, knowing that it will be interpreted in a given way, and his thought so expressed in a symbolic form, read and understood by the audience, is communicated deliberately by what must be termed symbolic language. In common speech we may speak of a sign language, but it seems desirable to distinguish between what is in reality a symbol language and the unconscious sign of anger which an animal may express in the presence of an enemy.

That animal cries are emotional only, and not conceptual, is now the considered opinion of those who have made a study of the matter. Cassirer pointed this out:[17]

> Everyone who examines the different psychological theses and theories with an unbiased and critical mind must come at last to the conclusion that the problem cannot be cleared up by simply referring to forms of animal communication and to certain animal accomplishments which are gained by drill and training. All such accomplishments admit of the most contradictory interpretations. Hence it is necessary, first of all, to find a correct logical starting point, one which can lead us to natural and sound interpretation of the empirical facts. This starting point is the definition of speech.... The first and most fundamental stratum is evidently the language of the emotions. A great portion of all human utterance still belongs to this stratum. But there is a form of speech that shows us quite a different type. Here the world is by no means a mere interjection; it is not an involuntary expression of feeling, but a part of a sentence which has a definite syntactical and logical structure.... As regards chimpanzees, Wolfgang Koehler states that they achieve a considerable degree of expression by means of gesture. Rage, terror, despair, grief, pleading, desire, playfulness, and pleasure are readily expressed in this manner.
>
> Nevertheless one element, which is characteristic of and indispensable to all human language is missing; we find no signs which have an objective reference or meaning. "It may be taken as positively proved," says Koehler,[18] "that their gamut of phonetics is entirely sub-

recognized today that Darwin had oversimplified the problem of speech by equating it with the ability to make noises and express emotions. His book was published in 1872.

[17] Cassirer, Ernst, ref. 12, pp. 28, 29.

[18] Koehler, W., *The Mentality of Apes*, Harcourt, Brace, N.Y., 1925, p. 317.

jective and can only express emotions, never designate or describe objects. But they have so many phonetic elements which are also common to human languages that their lack of articulate speech cannot be ascribed to secondary (glosso-labial) limitations. Their gestures too, of face and body, like their expressions in sound, never designate or describe objects."

Cassirer added,[19]

Here we touch upon the crucial point in our whole problem. The difference between *propositional* language and emotional language is the real landmark between the human and the animal world. All the theories and observations concerning animal language are wide of the mark if they fail to recognize this fundamental difference. In all the literature of the subject, there does not seem to be a single conclusive proof of the fact that any animal ever made the decisive step from subjective to objective, from affective to propositional language. Koehler insists emphatically that speech is definitely beyond the powers of anthropoid apes. He maintains that the lack of this invaluable technical aid and the great limitation of those very components of thought, the so-called images, constitute the causes which prevent animals from ever achieving even the least beginning of cultural development.

The English neurologist Jackson introduced the term "propositional" language in order to account for some very interesting pathological phenomena. He found that many patients suffering from aphasia had by no means lost the use of speech, but they could not employ their words in an objective, propositional sense. Something had therefore reduced their speech to the level of animal noise which, like the cry of the parrot, was no longer human language at all.

---

[19] Cassirer, E., ref. 12, p. 30. Similarly Munro Fox, ref. 9, pp. 22, 23: "We ourselves, of course, have to learn how to talk, but babies do not learn to make cries of various sorts corresponding to their feelings. Such cries of infants are not learned but are made by instinct. This leads to a most important question. Does an ape, too, know how to make its various characteristic sounds and grimaces by inborn instinct, without any learning, or does it learn its 'language' from its mother? This question has been answered by keeping an ape quite alone from its birth until it was five years old. For the first five years of its life this ape did not hear or see any other apes. The investigator found that the animal was able to express itself in ape language just as well as any other ape of that species. All its cries and expressions were made by instinct; they had not been learned. It is clear that the language of these animals has nothing in common with our speech; it resembles cries we may make such as 'Oh' and 'Ah', or shouting for joy, or weeping."

Subsequently, on p. 29, he writes: "The chief difference between the sound-language of animals and human language is that while animal's sounds or movements express its feelings, and may communicate feelings and intentions to its fellows, we do more than this. We have words for things, and words for thoughts, and we make these words into sentences. With animals this is, of course, not so. If I take a banana away from a chimpanzee, he can show that he is angry; if he wants a banana, he can show that he is hungry; if he gets a banana, he can show that he is glad. His movements and expressions indicate that he is angry, hungry, or glad, even if they are made unwittingly. *But the chimpanzee cannot say anything about a banana.* Animals have no conversation."

Meanwhile the clicks and grunts which in popular imagination were taken to be a major part of some primitive languages actually take a very minor place in the structure of such languages. It can be said that the languages of the most primitive people, as for example the Australian aborigines, are exceedingly full of terms and are definitive and specific in the extreme. Indeed they are so rich in terms and names for things that abstract thought becomes well-nigh impossible, for there are no such simple things as "classes"; everything is individual and specific.[20] We may quote Cassirer again,[21]

> Hammer-Purgstall has written a paper in which he enumerates the various names for the camel in Arabic. There are no less than five or six thousand terms used in describing the camel; yet none of these gives us a general biological concept. All express concrete details concerning the shape, the size, the colour, the age and the gait of the animal. . . . In many American tribes we find an astounding variety of terms for a particular action, for instance for walking or striking. Such terms bear to each other rather a relation of juxtaposition than of subordination. A blow with the fist cannot be described with the same term as a blow with the palm, and a blow with a weapon requires another name than one with a whip or a rod. In his description of the Bakairi language — an idiom spoken by an Indian tribe in Central Brazil— Karl von den Steinen relates that each species of parrot and palm tree has its individual name, whereas there exists no name to express the genus "parrot" or "palm." "The Bakairi," he asserts, "attach themselves so much to the numerous particular notions that they take no interest in the common characteristics. They are choked in the abundance of the material and cannot manage it economically. They have only small coin, but in that they must be said to be excessively rich rather than poor."

The languages of primitive people all over the world show this same amazing wealth. Here objectivity is a characteristic in excess. What is specifically lacking therefore in animal forms of communication, is here exemplified to the nth degree . . . and yet it was formerly thought that such societies would provide us with the very links between civilized man and the primates below him.

Levy-Bruhl has gone into this question very extensively. It is true that his views of primitive mentality are questioned today in many quarters, but the question mark is placed against his use of the con-

---

[20] Levy-Bruhl can be quoted to good effect in connection with this: "The (Australian) languages bear witness to this, for there is an almost total absence of generic terms to correspond with general ideas, and at the same time an extraordinary abundance of specific terms, those denoting persons and things of whom or which a clear and precise image occurs to the mind as soon as they are mentioned. Eyre had already remarked upon this and noted that such terms as tree, bird, etc., were lacking, although specific terms were applied to every variety of tree, fish or bird." Lucien Levy-Bruhl, *How Natives Think*, trans. Lilian A. Clare, Knopf, N.Y., 1925, p. 170.
[21] Cassirer, Ernst, ref. 12, p. 135.

cept of "prelogical" thinking. He argued that native people did not use the kind of logical constructions in their thinking that we do. But it is quite evident today that they are as capable of logical thinking as we are, though their premises are different. Allowing for this misconception, if misconception it be, Levy-Bruhl nevertheless has done great service in showing the amazing degree of language development which characterizes the most primitive people known to us. Certainly such people do not provide a missing link from animal grunts and cries to cultured speech. Thus Levy-Bruhl wrote:[22]

> This concept, that in the evolution of thought the simplest is the earliest, is a concept which undoubtedly proceeds from Spencer's philosophy, but that does not make it any more certain. I do not think it can be proved in the material world, and in what we know of the world of "thought" the facts would seem to contradict it. Sir James Frazer (who was committed to the evolutionary principle) seems to be confusing the simple with the undifferentiated here. Yet we find that the languages spoken by peoples who are the least developed of any we know — the Australian aborigines, Abipones, Andaman Islanders, Fuegains, etc. — exhibit a good deal of complexity. They are far less simple than English, though much more primitive.

Similarly he quoted the experience of Livingstone in South Africa:[23]

> It is not the want, but the superabundance of names that misleads travellers, and the terms used are so multifarious that good scholars will at times scarcely know more than the subject of the general conversation. We have heard about a score of words to indicate different varieties of gait — one walks leaning forward, or backward; swaying from side to side; loungingly or smartly; swaggeringly; swinging the arms; or only one arm; head down, or up, or otherwise, and each of these modes of walking was expressed by a particular verb.

Levy-Bruhl stressed the specificity of native languages from various parts of the world, drawing on the reports of many travelers of the last century:[24]

> Eyre remarks upon this with the Australian Aborigines. He states that generic terms such as tree, fish, bird, etc., were lacking although specific terms were applied to every variety of tree, fish or bird. . . . In western Australia, the natives have names for all the conspicuous stars, for every natural feature of the ground, every hill, swamp, bend of a river, etc., but not for the river itself. Lastly, not to prolong this list unduly, in the Zambesi district, every knoll, hill, mountain, and every peak on a range has its name, and so has every watercourse, dell, and plain. In fact, every feature, or portion of the country, is so distinguished by appropriate names that it would take a lifetime to decipher their meaning.

We could go on indefinitely. The Aymara Indians of Chuciutu

---

[22] Levy-Bruhl, Lucien, ref. 20, p. 21.
[23] Livingstone, David, *The Zambesi and Its Tributaries*, 1865, p. 537.
[24] Levy-Bruhl, Lucien, ref. 20, pp. 170-174.

in Peru have 209 distinct words for potatoes, and such northern people as the Eskimo of Canada and the Chukchee of Siberia have an almost unlimited number of names for snow and ice, in every conceivable form, yet not a single word for "snow." Suffice it to say, therefore, that primitive languages may be primitive only in so far as they do not permit the refinement of abstract ideas, such a refinement as is essential for the construction of a pure science. But this lack by no means implies that they have a deficient language. Their terms for dealing with objects exceed our own many times; their dictionary would be correspondingly many times the length of ours.

We have pointed out that no people are without a language. From this observation and because all subjects investigated up till a few years ago had possessed the power of speech no matter how primitive their culture, it was assumed that speech was instinctive.[25] But in time it became apparent that this was not so. We may repeat that throughout the centuries of historical record, so-called "wild" or feral children have been reported. It was not till comparatively recently that such children were found and studied by men whose judgment and scholarship were sufficient to guard them against sensational conclusions intended to stimulate public imagination. Such children have always been found to be without speech.

Recently a very complete treatment of all known cases of feral children up to 1966 was republished by J. A. L. Singh and Robert M. Zingg, under the title *Wolf-Children and Feral Man*.[26] In all, 36 cases believed to be reasonably well documented are dealt with in some detail. Many are well attested, others rather less so, but the cumulative effect is to show that such children have indeed been brought up, due to early total isolation, by animals which include wolves, bears, pigs, a jackal, and even a leopard. Without exception, they did not learn to speak a word while in the wild and almost nothing even when later attempts were made to reeducate them.

Susanne Langer remarked in this connection:[27]

---

[25] Edward Sapir, an incomparable scholar of linguistics, wrote: "The gift of speech and a well-ordered language are characteristic of every known group of human beings. No tribe has ever been found which is without language, and all statements to the contrary may be dismissed as mere folklore.... The truth of the matter is that language is an essentially perfect means of expression and communication among every known people." Article on "Language," *Encycl. of the Social Sciences,* Macmillan, N.Y., 1933.

[26] Singh, J. A. L. and Robert M. Zingg, *Wolf-Children and Feral Man,* Archon Books, 1966, xli and 379 pp., ills., with forewords by R. Rugglesgate, Arnold Gesell, F. N. Maxfield, and K. Davis.

[27] Langer, Susanne, *Philosophy in a New Key,* Mentor Books, New American Library, N.Y., 1952, p. 87.

The only well-attested cases are Peter the wild boy, found in the fields of Hanover in 1723; Victor, known as the "Savage of Aveyron" captured in that district of Southern France in 1799; and two little girls, Amala and Kamala taken in the vicinity of Midnapur, India, in 1920. Even of these, only Victor has been scientifically studied and described.

One think however we know definitely about all of them: *none of these children could speak in any tongue, remembered or invented* (her emphasis). A child without human companions would of course find no response to his chattering; but if speech were a genuine instinct, this should make little difference. Civilized children talk to the cat without knowing that they are soliloquizing, and a dog that answers with a bark is a good audience; moreover Amala and Kamala had each other. Yet they did not talk. Where, then, is the language making instinct of very young children?

It is as though Providence had secured for us by historical "accident" the materials we particularly need for testing all such hypotheses. Had we on record merely the instance of lone waifs and strays such as Peter and Victor, we might still have argued that they did not speak because they did not have company. Quite apart from the observation which Langer makes — that children talk to animals without sensing any incongruity (as adults do too!) — we have also the record in very recent times of the finding of two children who shared their strange childhood upbringing in the wild and still never spoke one word to each other. Moreover, every subsequent effort to teach the boy Victor the use of language failed conspicuously, and when the question is asked, Why did *he* fail, when others succeeded in part (though very inadequately), the answer seems to be in Langer's own words, "Because he was already about twelve years old. . . ." In other words, when Victor was found, he had evidently passed the stage of development where he *could* learn a language, whereas the other children in varying degree, were still young enough to be taught at least a few words and expressions, though none of them developed into normal human beings.

We may draw a further conclusion from all this, therefore, that the capacity is latent in every child for the learning of a language, even in those who are reared in the wild, but this capacity does not guarantee that language will automatically arise of its own accord. On the contrary in each of the four children known to us, no language whatever did appear of its own accord. It was only after they were spoken to, that they spoke in turn, and even then only provided that the capacity for acquiring the faculty of thinking in words had not been outgrown and lost through lack of use.[28]

Having arrived at this point, the question immediately arose as

[28] See J. W. Tomb, "On the Intuitive Capacity of Children to Understand Spoken Language," *Brit. Jour. Psychiatry*, 16 (1925): 553-55.

to whether it might be possible to teach animals to speak as men speak. We have already mentioned that the absence of speech among animals cannot be attributed to the absence of the secondary glosso-labial anatomical structures, for they have many phonetic elements which are also common to human languages. Granted that some of the sounds we make might be beyond the capacity of some animals, at least they ought to be able to reproduce a kind of dialect of their own. But they never do. It is felt that this must therefore be due to some lack in the brain. Formerly it was customary to assume that the essential difference in animal and human thinking processes was one merely of degree. But it seems now that it is one of kind rather. Briffault pointed out some years ago:[29]

> Between the mental constitution of the rudest savages and that of any animal, including the anthropoids, there is a wide gap, and that gap consists of more than a difference of degree; it amounts to a difference in kind. Primarily that difference depends upon the conceptual character of human mentality.

This conceptual character in man permits speech.

Again from the pen of Henri Bergson:[30]

> The same impression arises when we compare the brain of man and that of the animals. The difference at first appears to be only a difference in size and complexity. But judging by function, there must be something else besides. . . . Between man and the animals the difference is no longer one of degree, but of kind.

Efforts have been made for years, and continue to be made, to open up lines of communication with animals. The prodigious and patient labors of the Kelloggs (1933),[31] Hayeses (1951),[32] Gardners (1967)[33] and Premack (1969)[34] have revealed some surprising facts. It is certain that animals do communicate with each other successfully, and man ought therefore to be able to establish contact by this means, as indeed he may with his horse or his dog. But apparently in those animals which seem therefore capable of understanding speech, they do not themselves have the capacity to speak. Such creatures as Premack's chimpanzees did "talk" by signs, but vocalization has proved

[29] Briffault, Robert, "Evolution of Human Species," in *The Making of Man,* Modern Library, Random House, N.Y., 1931, p. 762.

[30] Bergson, Henri, *Creative Evolution,* Mod. Library, Random House, N.Y., 1944, pp. 200, 201.

[31] Kellogg, W. N. and L. A., *The Ape and the Child: A Study in Environmental Influence on Early Behaviour,* McGraw Hill, N.Y., 1933.

[32] Hayes, K. J. and C., *The Ape in our House,* Harper, N.Y., 1951.

[33] Gardner, R. A. and B. T., reported in an article, "Teaching Sign Language to a Chimpanzee," *Science,* 165 (1969) : 664-672.

[34] Premack, David, "Language in Chimpanzee?" *Science,* 172 (1971): 808-822.

quite beyond their physiological capacity thus far. By contrast, birds which can vocalize meaningfully to the hearer, seem nevertheless without the mind necessary to make their own vocalization meaningful to themselves. Birds have vocal organs adequate to the task but no mental equipment to make the capability useful to them. Other animals may have the mental equipment but no vocal organs adequate to communicate their thoughts usefully to men.[35] At the present time it does not seem that any animal communication system could possibly account for the human one. This is as Eric Lenneberg concluded:

> The rather widespread belief that many animals have a language of a very primitive and limited kind (or that the animal pupils of English instruction can enter the first stage of language acquisition) is easily refuted by a comparison with man's beginnings in language.

Animals do not speak, nor have they thus far been taught to speak, not because they lack the mechanical means, the muscles in the tongue and throat, etc., but evidently because they do not have the brain structure necessary to permit conceptual thought.

On the other hand, and this is of profound importance, a human being can be lacking in all the normal requirements for speech and yet, because of the structure of the brain, the mechanical and secondary handicaps can be overcome, and conversation be carried on at a very high level of abstraction. It would almost seem as though Providence were again at work in history, for we have two examples of individuals who were blind, deaf, and dumb, and yet who developed a high degree of understanding and education, one becoming an internationally famous spokesman for her fellow sufferers. Both the fact that such handicapped people could learn to communicate ideas and the circumstances surrounding the first steps by which they learned to speak at all, are of very great significance for our purposes. Moreover when it is found that both individuals passed from speechlessness to speech by the very same kind of process, it is a matter of considerable interest here.

The names of these two blind deaf-mutes are Helen Keller and Laura Bridgeman. Their story, in so far as it immediately concerns us, is best told in the words of their teachers and their own. It is desirable to comment that in the experience of both individuals, they had learned to tap out with their hands certain signs communicating needs as they arose. In the experience of both individuals a day came when the real meaning of these signs was discovered by each in turn.

Miss Sullivan, the teacher of Helen Keller, has recorded the exact

---

[35] See the Doorway Paper, "Is Man an Animal?" in Volume IV.

date on which the child began to understand the meaning and function of human language:[36]

> I must write you a line this morning, because something very important has happened. Helen has taken the second great step in her education. She has learned that everything has a name and that the manual alphabet is the key to everything she wants to know.
> This morning, while she was washing, she wanted to know the name for "water." When she wants to know the name of anything, she points to it, and pats my hand. I spelled w-a-t-e-r and thought no more about it until after breakfast.... (Later on) we went out to the pump house, and I made Helen hold her mug under the spout while I pumped. As the cold water gushed forth, filling the mug, I spelled w-a-t-e-r in Helen's free hand. The word coming so close upon the sensation of cold water rushing over her hand seemed to startle her. She dropped the mug and stood as one transfixed. A new light came into her face. She spelled "water" several times. Then she dropped on the ground and asked for its name, and pointed to the pump and trellis and suddenly turning round she asked for my name. I spelled "teacher." All the way back to the house she was highly excited and learned the name of every object she touched, so that in a few hours she had added thirty new words to her vocabulary. The next morning she got up like a radiant fairy. She has flitted from object to object asking the name of everything and kissing me for very gladness. Everything must have a name now. Wherever we go she asks eagerly for the names of things she has not learned at home. She is anxious for her friends to spell, and eager to teach the letters to everyone she meets. She drops the signs and pantomine she used before, as soon as she has words to supply their place, and the acquirement of a new word affords her the liveliest pleasure. And we notice that her face grows more expressive each day.

What a simple account this is, and yet how dramatic. It is almost like being present at the birth of a soul! And how significant do the names of things become. What this is to be called, and what that, is now of supreme importance, for the name of the thing is the thing itself. To possess the name is to possess the very object.

But we also have Helen's own account of this experience:[37]

> We walked down the path to the well-house, attracted by all the fragrance of the honeysuckle with which it was covered. Someone was drawing water, and my teacher placed my hand under the spout. As the cool stream gushed over my hand she spelled into the other the word "water," first slowly, then rapidly. I stood still, my whole attention fixed upon the motion of her fingers. Suddenly I felt a misty consciousness as of something forgotten, a thrill of returning thought; and somehow the mystery of language was revealed to me. I knew then that w-a-t-e-r meant the wonderful cool something that was flowing over my hand. That living word awakened my soul, gave it light, hope, joy, set it free. There were barriers still, it is true, but barriers that in time could be swept away.

---

[36] Sullivan, Anne M., in the Supplement to *The Story of My Life,* by Helen Keller, Grosset & Dunlap, N.Y., 1905, p. 315.

[37] Keller, Helen, *The Story of My Life,* ref. 36, pp. 23, 24.

I left the well-house eager to learn. Everything had a name, and each name gave birth to a new thought. As we returned to the house every object which I touched seemed to quiver with life. That was because I saw everything with the strange new sight that had come to me.

It seems presumptuous to attempt to interpret Helen's experience, as it would be foolish for a blind man to describe the color of a sunset. But it appears that Helen realized for the first time that w-a-t-e-r was not a sequence of taps indicating her need, but a substance which stood apart from her need, though it could also supply it. It stood apart from her need, objectively — it was the substance in its own objective existence. W-a-t-e-r was not her supply, but *water*, whether from the pump or in a cup, or in the rain, or in a stream. Naturalists often remark that one of the chief delights of a walk in the country is that they can identify the plants and animals of which they know the name. When we know the name, in some peculiar way we understand the nature of a thing. It is this kind of conviction which prompted Moses to ask God His name. To most primitive people a name is most secret, for when one has obtained the name of a person, one has obtained a peculiar power over him. Indeed if a child in its first few months, turns out to be constantly unwell, the Chukchee of Siberia believe it has been given the wrong name, and they will change it. The Eskimo do not believe the child has a soul until it has a name, and thus no murder is involved in infanticide so long as the child is still unnamed. Recently there is on record the case of a child in a psychiatric ward who having reached a certain point in her recovery, decided to change her name; and no one could persuade her to retain the name she formerly had.[38] It is strange how often names suit people, and yet it is obvious that the name is given before the personality is developed to match it. Edward Sapir remarked on this:[39]

> Language is heuristic...in that its forms predetermine for us certain modes of observation and interpretation.... There is a widespread feeling, particularly among primitive people, of that virtual identity or close correspondence of words and things which leads to the magic of spells.... Many lovers of nature, for instance, do not feel that they are truly in touch with it until they have mastered the names of a great many flowers and trees, as though the primary world of reality were a verbal one and as though one could not get close to nature unless one first mastered the terminology which somehow magically expresses it.

Cassirer gives us the record of Laura Bridgeman's experience:[40]

---

[38] Bettelheim, Bruno, "Schizophrenic Art: A Case Study," *Sci. American*, 1952, pp. 31 ff.

[39] Article on "Language," in *Encyclopedia of Social Sciences*, Macmillan, N.Y., 1933, p. 157.

[40] Cassirer, Ernst, ref. 12, p. 37. He quotes Miss Drew, her teacher (p. 35):

Long before Laura Bridgeman had learned to speak, she had developed a very curious mode of expression, a language of her own. This language did not consist of articulated sounds but only of various noises which are described as "emotional noises." She was in the habit of uttering these sounds in the presence of certain persons. Thus they became entirely individualized. Every person in her environment was greeted by a special noise. "Whenever she met an acquaintance unexpectedly," writes Dr. Lieber, "I found that she repeatedly uttered the word for that person before she began to speak. It was the utterance of pleasurable recognition." But when by means of the finger alphabet the child had grasped the meaning of human language the case was altered. Now the sound really became a name; and this name was not bound to an individual person but could be changed if the circumstances seemed to require it. One day, for instance, Laura Bridgeman had a letter from her former teacher, Miss Drew, who, in the meantime by her marriage had become Mrs. Morton. In this letter she was invited to visit her teacher. This gave her great pleasure, but she found fault with Miss Drew because she had signed the letter with her old name instead of using the name of her husband. She even said that now she must find another noise for her teacher, as the one for Miss Drew must not be the same as that for Mrs. Morton. It is clear that the former "noises" have here undergone an important and very interesting change in meaning. They are no longer special utterances, inseparable from a particular concrete situation. They have become abstract names. For the new name invented by the child did not designate a new individual, but the same individual in a new relationship.

Laura Bridgeman subsequently studied arithmetic and geography, and actually became a successful teacher of others who were both blind and deaf, and like Helen Keller she manifestly lived an amazingly full, interesting, and genuinely enjoyable life.

From both these instances there is much to learn. In the first place, there seems to be some form of inborn capacity to make emotional noises, and this is shared by animals. That this is not dependent upon mimic is evident from the fact that animals brought up in entire isolation make all the ordinary cries and calls of their species, although trained animals and domesticated animals, develop certain additional sounds or variant cries. It is generally held, for example, that dogs only bark when domesticated, howling only when entirely wild. The second thing that we may note is that both girls developed an entirely different, and it may be said specifically *human* personality, once they had acquired genuine speech. Moreover, in the initial stages of this acquisition, it was a hunger for the names of

---

"I shall never forget," writes Miss Drew, "the first meal taken after she appreciated the use of the finger-alphabet. Every article she touched must have a name; and I was obliged to call one to help me wait upon the other children, while she kept me busy in spelling new words" (See Mary Swift Lamson, *Life and Education of Laura Bridgeman, the Deaf, Dumb and Blind Girl*, Houghton Mifflin Co., Boston, 1881, pp. 7 ff.).

things which most rapidly built up the power of speech, and not the desire to understand the things they could name.

This is characteristic of all children. Dr. David Major wrote in this connection:[41]

> By the beginning of the twenty-third month, our child had developed a mania for going about naming things, as if to tell others their names or to call our attention to the things examined. He would look at, point towards, or put his hand on an article, speak its name, then look at his companions.

Commenting on this, Cassirer remarked:

> The hunger for names which at a certain age appears in every normal child and which has been described by all students of child psychology proves ... that he learns to form the concepts of those objects, to come to terms with the objective world.
>
> Henceforth the child stands on firmer ground. His vague uncertain fluctuating perceptions and his dim feelings begin to assume a new shape. They may be said to crystallize around the name as a fixed center, a focus of thought. Without the help of the name, every new advance made in the progress of objectification would always run the risk of being lost again the next moment.

As Eric Lenneberg points out,[42] in Greece in the period of Classical philosophy, the relationship of the name of a thing to the thing named was the focal point of discussions on language. The question was, Did the object predetermine the name in some way? But the object can hardly do this since different languages appoint to it their own identifying tags appropriate to their world-view as a language. In his dialogue *Cratyles,* Plato (427-347 B.C.) sought a solution to this relationship of name and thing, but his answers do not really clarify the problem today and certainly we are no nearer solving the problem of origins for ourselves.

The question still remains for us, as we consider this extraordinary and long overlooked or minimized trait of human nature, Where and how did it all begin? We have the case of two Indian children, Amala and Kamala, neither of whom had spoken one word between them, although they shared each other's company. Reverting back to the very first pair, whom we may most reasonably refer to as Adam and Eve for purposes of identification, who or what first induced them to talk to one another?

Names stand for processes, and knowing the name seems to deceive us into thinking we understand the process. Those committed to the evolutionary origin of man must fall back upon the use of a magic word for the appearance of the special kind of brain man has

---

[41] Major, David, *First Steps in Mental Growth,* Macmillan, N.Y., 1906, p. 321.

[42] Lenneberg, Eric, ref. 6, p. 445.

which makes speech possible for him. They tell us it was a "mutation" of some sort! And there we have the whole "explanation." But even if a name were an explanation, they still have not told us who spoke first to start the process off, nor are we told what kind of a conversation would be most probable — though we might have guessed by now that the one who began the process must be one who was other than Adam and Eve, and prior to them and must already have been a speaking person. And we might have guessed too that the first words would have to be a list of the names of things.

In the first chapter of Genesis we are constantly told that "God said...," and not merely that God did.[43] Moreover in the creation of man a peculiar change takes place in the narrative, for having noted the recurrent phrase "Let the sea bring forth" or "Let the earth bring forth," as though directions were given to that which is inanimate to obey the word thus spoken, when the creation of man is in view, we are immediately presented with a conversation in heaven.[44] That God was not speaking to the heavenly host of angels when He said, "Let us make man ..." is clear from the fact that *man* was to be made in *His* image, and after His likeness. This surely means that man was made in the likeness of God, and not in the likeness of the angels. When God therefore said, "Let us make man in our image..., He was not addressing Himself to the angels at all. This conversation was therefore originated and carried on within the Godhead. He who first spoke *to* Adam was God, who had already been *conversing* about him.

What follows in the story is of real importance. Any thoughtful reader must surely be struck by the frequency with which the idea of "naming" things occurs in this early record. In some books one finds the glossary of terms at the end. Although they are needed at the beginning, it is discouraging to find oneself faced with such a list before some interest has been aroused in the subject matter. But in this instance, and for reasons which are obvious in the light of what we now know of the faculty of speech which man was given, the meaning of the first words and the names of the ordinary phenomena about which God wished to inform Adam, were given to him in some detail. Thus a name is given to the heavens, and to the earth, making more specific the general reference to them in Genesis 1:1. It is as though God had said, "Now I wish to tell you about these phenomena; and henceforth therefore we will refer to the sky as heaven, and to the soil upon which you stand as earth, to the

---

[43] Genesis 1:3, 5, 6, 8, 9, 10, 14, 20, 22 and 24.
[44] Genesis 1:26.

light as day and the darkness as night, to the waters as sea, the atmosphere as the firmament, and we will name the rivers, and the sun and the moon, and even the stars." Then two trees are singled out and given compound names, the tree of life and the tree of the knowledge of good and evil.

Then Adam received his own name. But there is a break in the narrative at this point. Having established a frame of reference, Adam was now invited to speak for himself.[45] Most of us like to name our own pets. Part of the commission given to Adam was that he should govern the animals, and it was natural therefore that he should be invited to name them for himself. None of them *had* any name up till then, and thus with artless simplicity the record says that whatever Adam called any creature, that was thenceforth its name.

Now we are not told how he named them. We do not know whether he was guided by their color, size, shape, or the cries they made. But what followed this naming ceremony seems to imply that there was a more significant reason for giving him the task. There are some who believe that Adam was merely one of many such representatives of manlike creatures, perhaps a special Homo sapiens singled out by the Creator who had then given him the benefit of a unique spirit. But the record seems in a remarkable manner to go out of its way to make it clear that Adam was the only man alive at that time. In Genesis 2:5, we are told that "there was not a man to till the ground." In Genesis 2:18, we are told that God had remarked, "It was not good that man should be alone." In Genesis 2:20, we are told that "there was not found a companion for him." And finally in Genesis 3:20, it is stated that Eve became the mother of *all* living. It seems clear from the wording of Genesis 2:18-23, that God wanted Adam to discover for himself that he could never find among the lower forms of life a suitable companion in his loneliness. It seems manifest too, that if Adam had been a slouching half-ape creature, God might well have brought to him other creatures little different from himself of the primate stock, which might have sufficed for his half-intelligent mind as an appropriate mate. However, with proper insight, Adam gave to each animal brought to him a name by which he signified in some way his reaction and his evaluation of its relative position with respect to himself.

That this is so seems clear when one reads what followed this naming process, for, removed into a state of unconsciousness, perhaps tired by the exercise of judgment in such a critical matter, he is "divided" and from himself is taken a true help-meet. Awakening

---

[45] Genesis 2:19.

from this sleep, and quite probably still supposing that the process of naming must continue, he is presented with this creature in whom he instantly recognizes a true help-meet, and a very part of himself.

The whole story is so simply written and so profound in its insight into the nature of speech and the forms which it first takes in childhood, and the true significance of the use of names for things, that it is almost as though God had cast the record in such a form deliberately that it might shed its own light on one of the profoundest of all mysteries. At any rate it is the only light we have. There is no other from any other source.

Susanne Langer made a significant admission therefore when she wrote:[46]

> Language though normally learned in infancy without compulsion or formal training, is none the less a product of sheer learning, an art handed down from generation to generation, and where there is no teacher there is no learning. . . .
> This throws us back upon an old and mystifying problem. If we find no prototype of speech in the highest animals, and man will not say even the first word by instinct, then how did all his tribes acquire their various languages? Who began the art which now we have to learn? And why is it not restricted to the cultured races, but possessed by every primitive family from darkest Africa to the loneliness of the polar ice? Even the simplest of practical arts, such as clothing, cooking, or pottery, is found wanting in one human group or another, or at least found to be very rudimentary. Language is neither absent nor archaic in any of them.
> The problem is so baffling that it is no longer considered respectable.

At the risk of over-loading a paper already more than a little weighted down with quotations, valuable as they are, I cannot refrain from one last one by Roger Brown in his *Words and Things* who sums the situation up very effectively by writing:[47]

> Neither feral nor isolated man creates his own language these days, but must not such a man have done so once in some prehistoric time and so got language started? Actually the circumstances in which language must have begun represent a combination for which we can provide no instances.
> We have animals among animals, animals in linguistic communities, and humans among animals; but in none of these cases does language develop. We have humans raised in linguistic communities and in these circumstances language *does* develop. What about a human born into a human society that has no language? We don't know of any such societies, and so we don't know of any such individuals. But these must have been the circumstances of language origination.

Revelation is all that remains to us, and that revelation has been

---

[46] Langer, Susanne, ref. 27, pp. 87, 88.

[47] Brown, Roger, *Words and Things,* Free Press, Collier-Macmillan, London, 1968, p. 192.

set forth in clear simple terms. God spoke to Adam first. And in due time Adam learned to speak with God. This is the unique relationship which man has with God, the capacity for conscious fellowship and communication, and all that these imply.

For this fellowship he was created, and without it he is like a feral child, an orphan and terribly alone. To communicate with others is necessary for the generation of a soul in the personal sense of the term. To communicate with God it is necessary for that soul to be truly alive, and this kind of communication involves a fellowship based upon a true reconciliation between God and man.

Part VII

Light From Other Forms
of Cultural Behavior on Some
Incidents in Scripture

Introduction

A T LEAST ONE book and quite a few papers have been written
exploring the light which the customs of other cultures throw
upon many passages of Scripture, especially in the Old Testament.
But almost all of these have concerned themselves primarily with
peoples from the Middle East area, both ancient and modern.

For example, H. B. Tristram in 1894 published a volume entitled, *Eastern Customs in Bible Lands*.[1] It can still be obtained in
secondhand bookstores and is a thoroughly worthwhile book to read,
shedding a great deal of light on both the Old and New Testaments,
and on the beliefs of the Jewish people particularly in the time of
our Lord. In 1896, a very well-known Oriental scholar of that day,
Hormuzd Rassam, presented a paper before the Victoria Institute in
London.[2] This, too, is full of interesting observations. Much more
recently, Ernest Gordon in 1945 contributed an article in *The Sunday
School Times* entitled,[3] "Light on the Old Testament from Primitive Society."

All of these have this in common, that they deal with people
who in one way or another have shared in the historical stream of
events which form the immediate background of the biblical record.
To my knowledge there has been no serious attempt to show how
primitive and advanced cultures which have not shared this common
background have nevertheless developed patterns of cultural behavior
which shed unexpected light on many parts of Scripture. Now and
then one will run across casual comments in a work such as Living-

---

[1] Tristram, H. B., *Eastern Customs in Bible Lands,* Hodder and Stoughton,
London, 1894.

[2] Rassam, Hormuzd, "On Biblical Lands, Their Topography, Races, Reli-
gions, Languages, and Customs, Ancient and Modern," *Trans. Vict. Instit.,*
London, 30 (1896-97) : 29-85.

[3] Gordon, Ernest, "Light on the Old Testament from Primitive Society,"
The Sunday School Times, Nov. 3, 1945, p. 851.

stone's *Travels in Africa*[4] or Lubbock's *Origin of Civilization*,[5] but nobody has thought to pull together this kind of incidental commentary on the Scriptures into a single essay.

The only exception to this is a volume such as Barton's *Archaeology and the Bible*,[6] which gives numerous references to cultural parallelisms in the Middle Eastern literary texts such as legal codes, collections of stories, poems, and prayers, and religious documents of various kinds, both in Cuneiform and hieroglyphics. For this reason we have not included any illustrations from such contiguous sources. The material of this Doorway Paper has been derived almost entirely from records of cultural behavior which owe little or nothing directly to Middle East tradition.

This is not a paper which one would ordinarily read straight through as a continuing text, but rather a source of reference. A few of the comments do not deal strictly with cultural parallels but were felt to be intriguing enough to justify their inclusion — and it is not too likely that the average reader would discover them otherwise.

This collection of comments has simply grown by accretion from a fairly wide range of studies which have taken me into the highways and byways of biblically and non-biblically oriented literature over the past 35 years or so. Hence the reader should understand that this material did not result, strictly speaking, from a study of Scripture itself, though by investigating some particular passage listed in the Index, he will often find a great deal of information on Scripture. This kind of material was rather extracted from studies of primitive people made in depth by anthropologists who lived with them for a time. In many instances the writer was not aware of the fact that he was shedding interesting light on Scripture. In a few cases the parallelisms are not precise but reflect the underlying philosophy of the biblical pattern and to this extent help one to understand better. Some things that people did in the Old Testament seem, if not unforgiveable, at least somewhat cruel, and yet when the underlying philosophy is illuminated by reference to some other culture, the situation often appears in a much less unfavorable light.

---

[4] Livingstone, David, *Missionary Travels and Researches in South Africa*, Harper, N.Y., 1858, xxiv and 732 pp.

[5] Lubbock, Sir John, *The Origin of Civilization*, Appleton, N.Y., 1882.

[6] Barton, George A., *Archaeology and the Bible*, The American Sunday School Union, Phila., 1916.

Chapter 1
The Rationale of Cultural Patterns

IN GENESIS 2:24 it is written, "Wherefore a man shall forsake his father and mother and shall cleave unto his wife." It is amazing how many repercussions in the cultural behavior of people can hinge upon some apparently inconsequential fragment of the total behavior pattern. That a man should leave his home and take up residence with his wife's people rather than that a woman should leave hers and take up residence with his people seems on the face of it of not very profound consequence. And yet there stems from this single procedure a whole chain of consequences which can be traced in virtually every kind of culture in the world, both high and low, and which sheds a wonderful light on a surprising number of events in Scripture.

That it should be the first distinct reference to cultural behavior in Scripture suggests that the writer recognized its prime importance. And, incidentally, it raises the interesting question as to how the passage got in at this place in Genesis, since it is reasonably certain that Adam himself did not insert it — unless under divine inspiration he was instructed to set down as a guide to marital conduct in the future something about which he could not possibly have had personal experience at the time.

For many years biblical scholars have held that the book of Genesis was originally composed of 11 brief histories which had accumulated from Adam to Moses and which Moses took and combined into a single narrative. This view holds that the first narrative was written by God Himself and terminated with the words (in Gen. 2:4), "This is the history (generations) of the heavens and the earth, etc." That God should write such a record is by no means impossible. He wrote the Ten Commandments on tablets for Moses;

276

and He wrote on the wall of Belshazzar's palace. This first record was presumably put into Adam's keeping who subsequently added a historical record of his own, a record which terminates with the words, "This is the book of the history (generations) of Adam,..." (Gen. 5:1). There are 11 of these in all, and when Moses put together the book of Genesis they formed the basis of his account. To these he added a few explanatory "editorial" notes, which, for example, recorded the identity of places which had since changed in name. To this History he then added the other four books, so that with complete justice the whole Pentateuch is credited to Moses, but with the significant restraint that no quotation in the New Testament from Genesis itself is ever actually attributed to Moses. It is therefore possible, but by no means certain, that Genesis 2:24 was added by the hand of Moses by divine instruction.

Why should the man leave his home rather than the woman leave hers? Primitive societies are primitive chiefly in the sense that their dominion over their physical environment rests on a slender margin. The term "primitive" has nothing to do with intelligence or wisdom in dealing with social problems. There are many anthropologists and sociologists who have expressed the belief that the most primitive people are often the most socially sophisticated. They do not always reason out why they have adopted some customs which contribute to the general well-being of their society, but perhaps they learned more quickly by trial and error than we tend to do. In the present context they saw very clearly that when the wife's mother receives into her household the new husband, she has *gained* a son. By contrast if the wife moves into the husband's home, his mother has *"lost"* her son. Since from time immemorial the feelings of the matriarch have carried more emotional weight in the home than that of the male, who is very likely to spend far less time at home in any case, it is a sound principle for the well-being of the community to take steps to lessen as far as possible the emotional conflicts which are almost certain to arise when a woman with rights enters the household of another woman with rights. The introduction of the man into the wife's household rather than the reverse is a custom that is very widespread. It is worth noting certain things which follow from it as a principle.

Were each man to bring his wife into his own family circle, several brothers or a number of males within a village might well end up bringing together a number of women who were virtually strangers to one another and belonged to different tribes with somewhat different patterns of culture, who would then be called upon to live together in harmony when their husbands might, for one reason or another, be all absent from the village for long periods of time. In most societies of the world until *very* recent times, the males were likely to be away at war, hunting, or engaged in some form of work away from home. The woman is inevitably in such cases left to care for the children, the hearth, and the animals and the garden. When the husband has settled in his wife's home, it comes about that the women in the community who must live together and work together rather closely will by this very arrangement already belong to the same basic family, sharing the same cultural idiosyncrasies of the tribe.

The consequences of this practice of residence had other interesting repercussions with respect to the children. Since the children grew up in their mother's home territory, they naturally learned to behave as members of the mother's tribe, and they were in fact accredited to her tribe and her family and not to his. As a consequence, when the husband happened to have inherited "property," and by property is meant rights, titles, movable wealth, and so forth, he might be reluctant to see it pass out of his hands into the hands of his wife's tribe. Now he could get around this difficulty, if he so desired, by adopting an orphan, or a slave, or a youth captured in war, as his own son, and then passing over to him, rather than to any of his own children, all his wealth. As we shall see, adoption of those who were not sons into full sonship occurs in Scripture. Indeed, when the husband is away for extended periods of time either trading, fighting, or hunting, there is always some question of whether all the children born to his wife are really his children. As a result, there has been a very widespread practice of having the father officially "adopt" his own children. And until this adoption has been publicly declared in some simple ceremonial way, even his own legitimate children cannot claim him as their father.

In our culture, we are very much concerned with physical paternity, that is, with the man's role in conception. In many other cultures physical paternity is either not even recognized as a fact or is considered of little consequence. In almost all societies other than our own, children are so welcomed that the question of who is the legitimate father is very secondary. Indeed, an unwed mother who has a child, particularly a man-child, is likely to be sought eagerly in marriage because she has demonstrated that she is capable of bearing children. The Chukchee even had a particularly happy name for such an unwed woman: they called her a "fawn mother."

A further point of logical consequence is that since the woman has not left her home, her brothers are present always while her children are growing up and they, so long as they remain bachelors, are likely to take a larger part in the education of these children than the father himself does. As a consequence, the children grow up with a rather special attachment to "uncles" as a class. Every daughter in a household looks forward to receiving a bride price from her intended husband, and in the natural order of things it has worked out generally that one particular brother becomes especially attached to one particular sister and that sister will probably turn over to him much of the bride price which she receives, so that he in turn will be in a position to find a wife for himself. This special brother-sister relationship persists throughout life, and since his sister will in all probability be married before he can be, she is apt to have children before he does, and as a result, he will take particular interest in her children as opposed to the children of other sisters in his family. He will be the one who will discipline or reward them. His sister's husband will not be allowed to punish his own children, and indeed he will generally be very happy not to be required to do so. This uncle relationship is reflected interestingly in the Old Testament in certain important ways.

Another consequence of the matrilocal principle is that in many cultures which are polygynous — that is, in which the man may have a number of wives— his second wife, and indeed as far as possible all his wives, will be sisters. The reasons for polygyny will be considered briefly below, but the point I am trying to make here is that if a man married two women who were not sisters and if he was by custom to live with his wife's parents, then he would logically have to live in two places at once. The fact is that many societies expect the man who has married one daughter to take in succession each of the other daughters, so that in the end the whole family stays together. The first wife will have the priority due to her, which is nothing less than the priority she had in her own family as the eldest daughter in any case. To marry one of the younger daughters first would, in the eyes of such a culture, give rise to an impossible situation in which a daughter who had been junior in the family would "lord it over" her seniors. The reader may see the relevance of this to one well-known biblical event. But as we shall show, every one of the points which we have considered thus far sheds light on events in Scripture — and this not only in the Old Testament but also in the New.

Because in a polygynous society a man's wives are likely to be close relatives, the children as a whole will be apt to call any adult female "mother." Indeed, since the father is common to them all, they not unnaturally look upon every female as a potential mother, and this is reinforced by the fact that in many such societies any one of the women will without hesitation suckle any hungry child. As a result, children will reserve the use of a given name only for their true mother in order to identify her. The child will, therefore, call every woman "mother" except the individual who happens to *be* his or her mother, and this individual will be addressed by her first name. By the same token, the women will refer to the child by the true mother's name as a means of particular identification. It would not serve the purpose to identify the child by its father. Thus while Indo-Europeans habitually attach the determinative -son (i.e., John, Johnson, etc.), other societies in which physical paternity was not so critical used such a form as Mary, Maryson, etc.

But this is only one of many names which a child is likely to receive, names which identify the tribe, and which even summarize the individual's personal history.

We cannot leave this subject without touching upon one particular concept of marriage which I believe must virtually be absent in every culture except that of so-called Western Man. This is the concept of romantic love as the basis for engagement. People in primitive cultures as well as high non-Western cultures do not marry for love except on rare occasions, and do not marry to legitimize sex. For the most part marriage serves two purposes which are clearly recognized: the first is that, by it, the individual achieves adult status, and the second is that the children may be legitimized. And by "legitimized" is meant here that the children will have a recognized relationship to everyone else in the community. They belong in an orderly way.

It should be emphasized that genuine love often develops between man and wife even when it has had little or no part in the original marriage. When I said that romantic love is not the basis of engagement, I meant only that it is not as a rule the reason for becoming married in the first place. But there are many accounts in the anthropological literature of strong attachment between two married people which has developed as the result of living together. It has been said that any two people of the opposite sex who are thrown together closely for a sufficient length of time and whose background makes them congenial to one another will have a tendency to become increasingly attached in the course of time. There is still much to be said for the once common practice, even in European society, of arranging marriages on the basis of overall appropriateness rather than prerequisite affection. Unfortunately, all too frequently, romantic love is based upon too shallow a foundation to survive the stresses and strains of individual growth of the two parties.

In many cultures, it is very firmly believed that in procreation the man provides the spirit of the child whereas the woman provides only the body. Since such societies are less materialistic than we are, it is honestly believed that at the time of birth the man makes a greater sacrifice than the woman does and is in greater danger. One interesting consequence of this concept of the relative roles played by the man and the woman in procreation is that the marriage of brothers and sisters is very often considered incestuous, and therefore abhorrent, *only* when the two children are the offspring of the same mother. Having the same mother, they are believed to have the same kind of body — which forms a dangerous union. On the other hand, having the same father is not nearly as serious. Two children of one father, then, whom we would therefore consider as brother and sister may marry legitimately, provided that they are the children of two different wives. A very interesting story in the Old Testament involving two of David's children might have ended differently if the young man had realized the implication of his exact relationship to the girl he violated.

As we have already noted, earlier cultures tried to make provision for the achievement of familial harmony by insisting upon the union in marriage of people who were related in a special way. They wished to see joined together people who were closely enough related by blood that the involvement of the equally closely related relatives would stabilize the marriage as far as possible with the least emotional disturbance for all concerned, especially when the husband was likely to be absent from home a large part of the time. But they also wished to avoid bringing into the world defective children, an eventuality which people had very early observed was more frequent if the blood relationships were *too* close. Since each brother in the family tended to be paired off in a special relationship with a particular sister, his sister's children became of special concern to him. When these children grew up, it was often taken for granted that the ideal marriage partner for them would be one of his own children. Thus a man's son would ideally marry his mother's brother's daughter, i.e., a cross cousin. This can be set forth diagrammatically as follows:

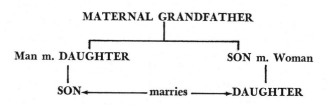

However, among Semitic people another kind of cousin relationship seems to have been preferred. In this case the ideal marriage partner was not the mother's brother's daughter but the father's brother's daughter, a relationship known as parallel cousin marriage. This is set forth diagrammatically as follows:

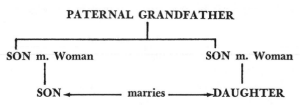

Frequently, tied in with this parallel-cousin relationship, was a further principle which is as follows. If my brother marries a woman and dies at a time when his wife may still bear children, then I will assume the position of husband towards his wife. When this happens, his children would then become my children. However, since I am not related by blood to his wife, her children would not be considered related bodily to my children because they have received their bodies primarily from their mother. It thus comes about that although her children have now become my children and are thus *counted* as brothers and sisters to my children, since I am the appointed father of them all, yet it is perfectly legitimate in societies so structured in this way for such children to be joined in marriage. Indeed, a son may marry a "sister" so that his spouse is both wife *and* sister, a circumstance which illuminates one particularly well-known story in the Old Testament. He truthfully marries his sister; and yet because she is the daughter of his father (by a process of "adoption") she is not the daughter of his own mother. It is this last fact which earlier cultures saw as being crucial. It depends entirely on the concept that incest is dangerous because of the close relationship of two bodies derived from the same mother, and not the close relationship of two spirits derived from a common father. This is why a man may not marry his own mother or his own sister by *his* mother.

It is abhorrent to us that a man should have several wives at once, and yet for thousands of years polygyny has been practiced very widely. One reason for this is that there was a tendency for the succession of wives to be sufficiently closely related that they were already well conditioned to living together. The notion of romantic love introduced a most disruptive of all forces in human relationships, namely, jealousy. And there is no jealousy as divisive as that which stems from wounded love. The jealousy which stems from wounded pride is bad enough, but there are often ways in which it can be compensated for on a social plane. The simple fact is that the practice of a number of women sharing a single husband does not automatically lead to family chaos. The rights of each wife and her children have almost always been protected by custom. And, curiously enough, it is not infrequently the women themselves who insist upon other women being added to the "community." This is partly a question of social prestige, for as each wife is added all the previous wives move up in rank by one order. Moreover, a man who can support successfully a number of wives is generally considered to be a superior individual to the man who has only one or two wives. In addition to this is the plain fact that, in many such societies the women far outnumber the men. Not only do they tend to mature sooner and live longer, but the very occupation of men keeps the male population down. The hazards of war, hunting, traveling in general, cause a steady attrition of the male population. In some societies this is so serious in fact that the balance is preserved by destroying a large number of female infants at birth. Only in Western culture are people comparatively indifferent to the plight of the widow. In non-Western cultures a widow would not be left to grow old by herself, she would be married to a man able to provide her with the associations of "family." This factor also contributes to polygyny. In short, polygyny, unlike the harem, is a social arrangement not really prompted by sex at all.

There is a further extension of the connected lines of thought regarding marriage which is logical enough, granted the other premises. Since the element of romantic love does not usually enter into the contract of marriage, the marriage bond is in no way weakened seriously in the eyes of the community merely because the husband and wife are constantly at loggerheads. But there is one element in the union which is quite critical, namely, that the wife must bear children. In the event that she proves barren, the man may take one of several alternative courses of action. He may divorce his wife and reclaim in full the bride price, since the "contract" has been broken. As a second alternative, he may demand from the bride's family the next oldest sister, not as a substitute for his first wife but as an addition to his household to bear his children. It is just such a possibility as this that in many societies leads to the feeling that the bride's sisters are potential wives of the oldest sister's husband. And this probably led in some cases to the potentiality becoming a reality, with the end result that the man by custom married all the sisters whether his first wife was barren or not. There is a third alternative, and this is that the wife who finds herself unable to bear children has the privilege of providing her husband with another woman to raise children for him, the children as they are born being laid at once upon her knees so that they accept her as true mother from the very first. The important point here is that the husband himself is not allowed, *in this arrangement,* to choose the second wife. And it must be supposed that the first wife will take care to ensure that the second wife will be one who will not forseeably compete with her own privileges as the first wife. The husband has no choice in this matter, it is entirely for the wife to decide and it is she who "gives" the substitute to her husband and not the husband who makes the choice himself.

The opposite of barrenness which is considered a breach of contract is the birth of more than one child at a time, which is frequently felt to be undesirable. The birth of twins has been interpreted in a number of ways by primitive people, some believing it is a good omen and others not a good omen. It is considered a good omen by those who desire only to have a large number of children in their household and who are not *unduly* superstitious, although in some circumstances even those who love children find it necessary to destroy one of them by exposure since the mother cannot support both because of the harshness of their environment. Those cultures in which the forces of evil are more manifest, and some societies like the Dobuans which are absolutely impregnated with black magic, the birth of twins is looked upon with distaste, suspicion, fear, or horror. Those who look upon the event with distaste are people who usually believe that it is most improper for a human being to parallel the behavior of animals by bearing more than one child at a time. It is an animal, not a human, practice and is felt to be degrading. Those who look upon the event with suspicion believe that it is evidence of infidelity on the part of the woman. In order to bear two children at once she must have "known" two men, one of whom would, of course, not be her husband. In this case action is likely to be taken by the mother in order to avoid suspicion, and one of the two children may either be destroyed by "exposure" or farmed out to some other family. Those cultures which look upon the phenomenon with fear believe that no good can possibly come of such an event if the sex of the two children is different, since it implies in their mind that a brother and sister have been far too closely associated together in the womb. It is a kind of prenatal incest, which is taboo. Finally, and in the context of this paper perhaps more significantly, those who view the event with horror do so because they believe that one of the two children is born of an evil spirit. They therefore destroy both children, being unable to tell which child is the evil one. It is possible that this particular belief arose in the course of time as a consequence of certain events in the early history of mankind which, as we shall see, may also be implied in certain passages of Scripture.

Although the father is not believed to be important in the *physical* birth of the child, he is believed to be nearly, if not wholly, responsible for the child's spiritual soul. As a consequence, physical malformation is blamed on the mother as a rule. On the other hand, where it happens that the child grows up to look like the father, it is either totally improper to draw attention to it or it is attributed to the fact that the father has played so much with him and been familiar with the child as he grew.

So close is this "spiritual bond" that when a child turns out to be notably good, it is credited entirely to the father; and when the child turns out to be particularly bad, it is blamed upon the father. This is not unreasonable, and it is reflected in Scripture in some very interesting ways.

One final aspect of family life relates to the fact that in simpler societies, or in the higher cultures which have a very stable diet, all the members who "belong" have a tendency to develop the same characteristic body odor. A foreigner has a body odor which is different and for that reason apt to be "unpleasant." Food has a tremendous effect in this respect when it is not varied from meal to meal and when washing of the body is not an important part of daily life. One of the first things that a man will do when he returns after a period of absence is to bury his nose in the necks of his children in order to delight in the familiar odor which is apt to be most readily detected here where the clothes are vented. Our noses are challenged with so many conflicting odors that we become comparatively indifferent. In biblical times it was not so.

In our culture a man's will is not usually read until after his death, though he may reveal some of its content to those concerned while he is still alive. To many cultures this would appear to be a strange procedure, for it makes it impossible sometimes for those who are to benefit to make any long-range plans. And with us it is a rare thing for a benefactor to pass on his wealth to any of his children while he is yet alive, thereby anticipating the terms of his will. This again seems foolish to many peoples because the aged are robbed of the pleasure of *seeing* their wealth do some good and indeed of benefitting reciprocally themselves.

Other cultures have often tended to adopt the principle of allowing children upon demand to be given their inheritance. Since the assumption is generally made in such societies that only sons will share the inherited wealth, if it happens there is only one other son, that other son automatically becomes possessor of all that his father has, a circumstance which is vividly reflected in a well-known New Testament parable.

We shall now consider these matters in somewhat greater detail, using illustrations drawn from cultures in many different parts of the world.

Chapter 2
Illustrations From Other Cultures

1. Primitive Sociology

As an illustration of the sociological sophistication of a primitive people we may quote the conclusions of Claude Levi-Strauss writing in one of the UNESCO publications:[7]

> In all matters touching on the organization of the family and the achievement of harmonious relations between the family groups and the social group, the Australian aborigines, though backward in the economic sphere, are so far ahead of the rest of mankind that, to understand the careful and deliberate system of rules they have elaborated, we have to use all the refinements of modern mathematics. It was they in fact who discovered that the ties of marriage represent the very warp and woof of society, while other social institutions are simply embroideries on the background. . . .
>
> The Australians, with an admirable grasp of the facts, have converted this machinery into terms of theory, and listed the main methods by which it may be produced, with the advantages and drawbacks attaching to each. They have gone further than empirical observations to discover the mathematical laws governing the systems, so that it is no exaggeration to say that they are not merely the founders of general sociology as a whole, but are the real innovators of measurement in the social sciences.

2. Groom to Leave Home

Among the Iroquois there existed eight separate tribes, and no member of any one tribe could marry within his or her own tribe. The husband joined the tribe of his wife and the children were all named after her, not after him. As a result all the women of any one tribe remained together and all the children were relatives in a special way, and would receive an inheritance in the same tribal territory. By this means, by requiring that the husband be from another tribe but take up residence with his wife and not the reverse, tribal territories and

---

[7] Levi-Strauss, Claude, *Race and History*, UNESCO publication, 1952, p. 28.

wealth were preserved intact but the tribal stock itself was constantly regenerated by the introduction of new genes.[8]

It will be remembered that Laban insisted that Jacob ought to remain with him in his territory after marrying his two daughters.

Since there is apt to be a closer emotional attachment between a mother and her son, it naturally leads to more acute jealousy if the son brings a woman into the mother's house. Hence patrilocal marriage, i.e., marriage in which the woman forsakes her own home and goes to live with her husband's household, is more rare, particularly where romance enters marriage — which it does in a few cases, though this, too, is rare. As an illustration, we may note that the Reddi, a tribe living in India in the Bison Hills, according to Haimendorf, have adopted the practice of requiring the bride to live in the bridegroom's house until they can set up house for themselves. Haimendorf comments,[9] "there is usually pretty hard feeling between the mother-in-law and the bride."

It is not always true that the man leaves his father and mother while the woman stays at home, for very often *both* leave home and set up house together. The principle is rather that if the couple due to circumstances (lack of house or money) have to live with one of the parents, it is usually with the wife's family, and where it is not, there are apt to be emotional conflicts. In a few cases the husband goes to live with the wife's family only until she has borne her first child, after which he takes her away and they set up house independently. According to Driberg,[10] the Lango (Africa) do not require the man to provide a house for his wife until a child is actually born. This is to validate "the contract" which requires that the woman shall give children to her husband. A few cultures, the Hopi of Arizona,[11] for example, turn the tables on the husband somewhat by requiring him to stay with the wife's family until he has proved himself a good provider by fulfilling certain household tasks to their satisfaction, so fulfilling *his* part of the contract. All of which reflects the wisdom of obeying the injunction of Genesis 2:24 where independent residence for the newly married couple is not immediately possible.

---

[8] Dawson, J. W., *Fossil Men and Their Modern Representatives,* Hodder & Stoughton, London, 1880, p. 317.

[9] Haimendorf, Christoph von Furer, *The Reddi of the Bison Hills,* Macmillan, N.Y., 1945.

[10] Driberg, J. H., *The Lango, A Nilotic Tribe of Uganda,* London, 1923.

[11] Murdock, George Peter, *Our Primitive Contemporaries,* Macmillan, N.Y., 1951, p. 344.

3. ADOPTION

The principle of adoption is very widely illustrated throughout the world. For example, Sir John Lubbock said:[12]

> The mere tie of blood relationship was of no account among the Romans. The most general expression and comprehensive term indicating relationship in Roman Law was *cognatio* (meaning, "I recognize"), that is to say, the tie between persons who are united by the same blood *or* those reputed by law as such. But cognition alone, whether it proceeds from legal marriage or by any other union, does not place the individual within the family nor does it give any right of family. Even at the present day, in some parts of Africa, a man's property goes not to his children as such but to his slaves.

In speaking of kinship, Robert Lowie had this to say:[13]

> In pre-Christian German law, a newborn child did not automatically enter the family of its unquestioned begetter; the latter was obliged formally to recognize the child as his, if such were his wish, and was also at liberty to disown it.

By African custom a man who could not possibly be the true father of a child is rated as its parent provided he fulfills certain legal conditions of fatherhood. In Jewish custom these conditions involved naming the child officially and teaching him a trade.

With us the question of physical paternity is decisive if it can be demonstrated according to law, but in a society where the husband may be away from home for great long periods of time as Roman soldiers often were, it was not easy for him to generate his own offspring and yet children were greatly desired. Since marriage was not based on any concept of romantic love (except upon occasion) the returning husband was quite happy to find that his family had increased provided that his wife was the mother. He would therefore by a very simple gesture adopt them and they became *his* sons in the eyes of the law.

Among the Eskimo adoption, even if he is not a true son, may entitle a man to be heir to all the family possessions if he happens to be older than the other sons.[14] In Central Africa the practice of adopting children is very prevalent indeed, especially among the Feletabs and, though they have sons and daughters of their own, the adopted child generally becomes the favorite and heir to the whole property.[15] Perhaps our own adopted children might be encouraged if they knew some of these things.

In Africa among the Banyoro it is customary for a male child of

---

[12] Lubbock, Sir John, ref. 5, p. 100.
[13] Lowie, Robert, *Social Organization*, Rinehart, N.Y., 1948, p. 57.
[14] Lubbock, Sir John, ref. 5, p. 96.
[15] Ibid.

five or six years, to be adopted by someone traced in the male line as a relative.[16] The adopted child's true family in the meantime adopts another child from another family which bears an inverse relationship to themselves. Thus the families are not really blood units at all, but there are many bonds of association that tend toward cohesion.

The Lango, another African tribe, treat their captives very handsomely.[17] They are adopted into the village as equals and welcomed as additional hands. The men adopt younger girls who are captured as their own daughters, the older ones being immediately married into the village. In Arabia the Muti Ali capture slaves and promptly adopt them into their own household with all the rights of the children of the house.[18] Some slaves have climbed up to the position of chieftain. In the Northwest, although the Iroquois were almost continually at war from around 1650-1785, they actually had a larger population when they finished than when they started, due entirely to their practice of adopting the majority of their prisoners into the tribe. It is generally held that by about 1700 they had more foreigners in their tribes than actual natives. Even aged people were adopted if some particular family was lacking a grandparent, for example, in order to make the household complete again. Robert Briffault pointed out that among primitive people mother love is not based so much on the fact of actual birth but on a deliberate process of adoption.[19] As he put it, "It is the adoption of the offspring, and not the relationship, intellectually viewed, which constitutes maternity."

4. PHYSICAL PATERNITY

It is not surprising, perhaps, that in days gone by, or in cultures where a knowledge of what takes place at conception was very hazy, people should naturally attribute the development of a child's body to the mother but be somewhat less certain about the part played by the father. In some societies it was questioned whether the father had any physical part to play at all. For example, the Trobrianders held that supernatural beings conceived the child, though only after the passage had been opened for them by the male.[20] The Australian aborigines held that the male sperm merely feeds the supernaturally

[16] McIlwraith, I., "Lectures in Social Life of Pre-Literates," at University of Toronto, 1953.

[17] Driberg, J. H., ref. 10.

[18] Tayyeb, Ali, himself a native of Arabia, in a seminar on Cultural Anthropology presented to the Anthropology Dept., Univ. of Toronto, 1953.

[19] Briffault, Robert, "Group-Marriage and Sexual Communism," in *The Making of Man*, ed. V. F. Calverton, Modern Library, N.Y., 1931, p. 497.

[20] Herskovits, Melville, *Man and His Works*, Knopf, N.Y., 1950, p. 292.

conceived embryo in its initial stages.[21] If it is pointed out to either of these people that the child sometimes bears a remarkable physical likeness to the father, they account for it by pointing out that the father fondles and plays with his children so much that it affects their appearance. The Australian aborigines believe that the supernatural being is a kind of spiritual animal of some particular recognized species. If the animal happens, in a particular tribe to be a kangeroo for example, then the spirit of the child *is* kangeroo, though the body of course is human. The child grows up to believe he is kin to the kangeroo family and he may not eat kangeroo meat except on one very solemn occasion which is a kind of annual memorial communion service.

Among the Ainu of Northern Japan,[22] it is believed that both the spirit and the intellect of the child are derived from the father and not from the mother; consequently, as in many other tribes, the father feels he is losing spiritual strength of a very vital kind when the child is born. The woman is merely losing part of her body which is much less demanding. So he is the one who endures the suffering of childbirth and gets all the sympathy from his neighbors who look after his pigs and cultivate his yam patch while he enjoys complete rest. When the child is born, the wife is expected to return to work at once and generally does so without any ill effects.

And this brings up another important point. It is only because of our materialistic view of life that such a "spiritual" view of things seems unrealistic — indeed, absurd. The father who by an act of will adopts an unrelated individual as his own son looks upon such an individual as genuinely related in a way that his own children are not. Thus it comes about that in a polygynous society children of different mothers are not looked upon as brothers and sisters in our sense of the terms, even if they share the same father. A man who has two wives, one of whom bears a daughter and the other a son, would not deny the right of those two children to marry since in his view they are in reality unrelated in any *physical* sense. Granted his premise, that he is not physically their father in the sense that the mother is physically the mother, his conclusion is reasonable enough. The principle sheds an interesting light on one of the tragic stories of the Old Testament.

Reverting once more to the Trobrianders,[23] and they are merely one of many peoples who might be used as an example, it may be

---

[21] Murdock, G. P., ref. 11, p. 34.
[22] Ibid., p. 179.
[23] Goldenweiser, Alexander, *Anthropology*, Crofts, N.Y., 1945, p. 419, n. 8.

noted that since the legitimate father is not considered as related in the way that the mother is, he is to some extent treated as a stranger, yet not entirely a stranger but rather a "special friend." Resemblances are never denied but they are never made the basis for speculation as to the possible role of the father in procreation.

It is difficult to see how the fact of physical paternity would not force itself upon their thinking, these people being intelligent as they actually are. But the facts of life are such that if a man has constant intercourse with his wife the period of gestation might never come to be recognized, especially where children are born to a wife acceptable to the husband even when he has been away for more than nine months at a time. Moreover, ignorance on this whole matter is surprisingly widespread even in our own society. Recently a case was reported in a New York hospital where a woman had eleven children before she and her husband discovered "where they came from," as she put it.[24]

Herskovits underscores the happy relations which almost always are apparent between the father and the children of his wife. Speaking of the Trobrianders, he said:[25]

> He fulfills the role within the family of nurse and playmate. The relations between him and his children are described as wholly delightful. He fondles them, amuses them, spoils them, but never corrects them and never punishes them.

5. MOTHER'S BROTHER

No matter how idyllic the total environment of a culture may be, children still have to be *taught*. And teaching, if it is to be effective, must involve sanctions of some kind. Since the father has such a delightful relationship with his children, it seems clear that the necessary discipline as a child grows up must be applied by someone else. All corrections and punishments are administered by the mother's brother, the uncle on the mother's side. This principle is also very widely observed in cultures all over the world, even — though somewhat vaguely — in our own. With us, as boys, uncles were invariably looked upon as sources of tips and surprise gifts in a way that the father was not. In English society many parents send their children to private school, partly because of their reluctance to risk the loss of warm associations by having to take disciplinary action. It is easier to have a governess discipline the children when they are very young and the school authorities as they grow up.

---

[24] Jackson, Dugauld, C., "Engineering's Part in the Development of Civilization," *Science,* 89 (1939) : 234.

[25] Herskovits, Melville, ref. 20, p. 292.

Speaking once again of the Trobianders, Malinowski[26] says that a child soon comes to look upon his mother's brother, one particular brother actually, as a very special person whom he calls his *kada*. This individual lives probably in the same locality, but he may live at some distance in another village. It makes no difference. Malinowski says, "The child (also) learns that the place where his *kada* resides is also his, the child's own village; that there, he has property and his other rights of citizenship; and that there his future career awaits him." The reason why the maternal uncle is so important will become apparent in the next section.

5. BROTHER-SISTER AND BRIDE PRICE

In the previous section we qualified the word "uncle" as being a maternal uncle; that is, a mother's brother rather than a father's brother. But we also qualified the statement by saying that it is one particular brother who acts in this special relationship.

In almost all societies in which the groom must *acquire* the guardianship, or proprietary right to the "service" of his wife, a special relationship arises between one brother in the family and the sister who is nearest to him in age and is given public recognition as a result of the fact that the brother, in order to get married must himself be able to raise the bride price required by custom in order to obtain *his* wife. The man who seeks this particular sister's hand in marriage will bring to her a comparable "bride price" which will make it possible for him in turn to achieve his status as a married man. He thus has a special interest in this particular sister and in the kind of husband she gets, and in the course of time this concern and interest is extended to her children. And thus it comes about not only that he becomes their disciplinarian, but he also looks upon his own children after he is married as the most suitable marriage partners for them. So has arisen a practice which is very widespread indeed, namely, the marriage of a man to his mother's brother's daughter or of a woman to her father's sister's son.

It has always appeared superficially to the European that the concept of "bride price," or as it is referred to widely in Africa, the *lobolo,* reduces the wife to a purchased article, a kind of chattel. Generally speaking, this interpretation is quite erroneous. With a certain amount of social logic, the father of a girl who is to be married will point out to the enquiring White Man that he has kept the girl and brought her up and in return has received her service in

[26] Malinowski, Bronislaw, "The Relations Between the Sexes in Tribal Life," in *The Making of Man,* ref. 19, p. 569.

terms of household duties performed. When she is taken away from the house, her husband will benefit by her past training, whereas the father will be sacrificing a pair of useful hands. Why, then, should he not be "compensated"? The Chukchee argue that the daughter who has served her father, when she is married, will end up by serving her father-in-law and that therefore the father-in-law should be required to contribute towards the bride price which will go to the girl's father.[27] But this is only one part of the logic.

There is another side to the coin. Unlike our way of arranging these things, other cultures have usually made it a costly business to get married, but comparatively easy to obtain a divorce. We adopt precisely the opposite policy, by making it easier to get married than to get a driver's license, and a very expensive process to obtain a divorce. We invite two young people to join themselves together with the greatest of ease into a union which is supposedly for life, which, if it does not turn out, we leave them to struggle through years of psychological torture either because they have inadequate resources to obtain the necessary release without an extended process of further anguish, or, which is perhaps even worse, because their moral standards are too high to allow them to take the simplest course for the obtaining of a decree of divorce on the grounds of adultery. In short, one can walk in without the slightest hesitation, but one can only get out through an experience which leaves scars for life.

In other cultures than our own, the situation is such that it often takes almost every near relative to help a man to accumulate the necessary *lobolo* before he can obtain a wife. It is not a question of making a snap decision and going through a five minute ceremony. Everyone in the neighborhood has some stake in the undertaking. If a man finds he has made a mistake and that his marriage cannot continue, he cannot lightly consider divorcing his wife since he must marry again to maintain his adult status and this would involve going around to all his former sponsors and asking them once again to invest a considerable amount of wealth in a second try. Needless to say, the certainty that he is going to have to make a second round of entreaty is a quite adequate deterrent against casually deciding to get married in the first place, or casually deciding to terminate a marriage that has once been contracted. So, in point of fact, such societies tend to hold that a man is only going to seek divorce if the situation is so bad that the consequences of having to raise a second bride price are to be preferred. It does make a certain amount of sense.

[27] McIlwraith, I., ref. 16, quoting from W. Bogoras, *The Chukchee,* Vol. II, Amer. Mus. Nat. Hist. Memoirs, 1904.

Among the T'honga,[28] a people living on the border between Natal and Portuguese East Africa, the collection of the bride price begins several years before the ceremony. Much haranguing and argument accompanies the discussions as to the proper amount between the in-laws. The man may only be a lad when the process begins, when he obtains a promise from his father of three cows, from his father's brother of two cows and two goats. He may go to his father's brother's son and get the promise of another six cows and an additional seven sheep from his father's brother's son's son. In the meantime, he has to accept gracefully long speeches of instruction, of advice and precaution from the subscribing parties. Everyone seeks to ensure that the lad will not come back to them again; the longer the period of preparation, the greater the opportunity each side has to expound the virtues of their respective offspring. If the wife proves a bad one, he may divorce her and demand a refund. She, then, has to go around and collect back from everyone who shared in her bride price the goods which had been passed on to them — no mean process of recovery. It must, indeed, be a very stabilizing factor.

If the woman proves barren, the husband may ask for the return of the bride price. If there is little chance of success in this, he may decide to ask his wife instead to provide him with another wife as a kind of compensation. In most cases, probably in nearly all, the wife will have her next oldest sister join the household as a second wife.

The bride price is also to some extent an indication and a recognition of the value which the groom and his family attach to the girl and her family. Among the Anglo-Saxons the supposed "sale" of a daughter by the parents or guardian to the husband was not the sale of a woman as a chattel but the transfer of the "right of protectorship" over the woman.[29] Whatever may be said about our interpretation of this exchange of wealth, Diamond notes that where contact with the White Man has led to the abandonment of this practice,[30] marriage has proved to be much less secure and more easily broken up.

Where a man, for one reason or another, cannot call upon an extended family to help him "raise the necessary funds," he may work for his bride by accepting temporary enslavement. This happens where the suitor is far away from home or is without resources. It may happen in a nomadic society where a woman is necessary to a man's survival and if the man happens to lose his wife while away

[28] McIlwraith, I., ref. 16, quoting H. A. Junod, *Life of a South African Tribe*, 2 vols., Neuchatel, 1912.
[29] Cairns, Huntington, "Law and Anthropology," in *The Making of Man*, ref. 19, p. 355.
[30] Diamond, A. S., *Primitive Law*, 1935, p. 230.

from home. Bogoras mentions this of the Chukchee.[31] And it happened to Jacob. According to P. Dobell, the custom is prevalent among the Karaikees (northeastern Asiatics).[32] If a young man should fall in love with a girl and he is not rich enough to obtain her by any other means, he enslaves himself to her father as a servant for three, four, five, or ten years, according to agreement, before he is permitted to marry her. When the term agreed upon expires, he is allowed to marry her and live with the father-in-law as if he were his own son. The same custom prevails among the Kamtchadales where the suitor of a particular maiden asks her parents permission to serve them for a time with a view to obtaining her as a wife.

7. MARRYING SISTERS

The practice of validating a marriage contract only after children have been born with the proviso that if the woman proves barren, the man must be fully compensated by the girl's family very naturally led to the principle that he might claim as a second wife one of her sisters to bear him children. According to Schapera,[33] at the present time the Tswana in South Africa require the family of a barren bride to substitute or provide in addition the next older sister. There was always the possibility, of course, and it must have happened upon occasion that even the second sister failed to provide him with a child. It was very seldom that the man himself was suspected of being to blame, though in one or two societies this possibility was recognized. On the whole, it was customary to allow for this contingency and to "hold" the other sisters for the husband of the eldest one. Even if children were born to the first wife, it was often felt quite proper for all the other sisters to join his household, since in the event of her death prematurely he could still claim one of the sisters. According to Briffault,[34] in some Indian tribes a widower could demand as a "replacement" wife her next oldest sister even if she was already married to someone else! According to the same authority, in the Central Celebes Islands, a man cannot marry a younger sister unless he has first married the elder. In the Philippines generally, a man usually took as wives all the sisters of the family. In the Marshall Islands when a man marries a woman, he is automatically regarded as married to all her sisters. In fact, if the husband

---

[31] Bogoras, W., ref. 27, p. 579.
[32] Dobell, P., quoted by A. G. Morice, "Northwestern Denes and Northeastern Asiatics," *Trans. Roy. Can. Instit.*, Univer. of Toronto Press, 1(1915) : 177.
[33] Schapera, I., *A Handbook of Tswana Law and Custom*, London, 1938.
[34] Briffault, Robert, ref. 19, pp. 207-210.

does not find it convenient to take charge of all the sisters, there is no alternative for the latter than to contract casual alliances; they become in fact what we would call prostitutes. In the Marquesas a man had marital rights over all his wife's sisters, whether these subsequently married other men or not. The substitution of a sister for a wife who has died prematurely is extremely widespread, being found among the Tartars, the Kalmuks, and many other Siberian peoples. Among the Wabemba of the Congo, if a man's wife dies and all her sisters are married, the husband of one of them must allow his wife to cohabit on specified occasions with the widower. If the sister happens to be an infant she is nevertheless handed over to the widower but a slave girl is sent with her to act as a substitute until she comes of age. Among the Kaikari of Central India, a man may marry his deceased wife's younger sister but may not marry her older sister. The principle, far from being distasteful, is therefore found all over the world.

That the sisters should be betrothed in the right order according to age is also a principle universally accepted as far as I know. The Hindus always avoid giving a younger daughter in marriage before an older one.[35] The Kurnia of Gippsland in Australia insist that a man's first wife must always be older than his second wife, hence where sisters follow in marriage they do not allow the taking of a younger sister first.[36]

8. NAMING AFTER THE MOTHER

In cultures other than our own, names are apt to have somewhat wider significance. There are at least three different kinds of names. First, there is the name which is inherited in the sense that it identifies the lineage of the child in terms of blood relationships. It has chiefly social significance and because the identity of the father is not always as clear as the identity of the mother, this kind of name reflects the mother's rather than the father's line. The second kind of name is psychological, one might say person-al. This kind of name is usually given by the family, who after consultation decide that they wish some ancestor to return to be with them in the household, taking up residence in the child so named. The third kind of name has more a magical connotation. Anyone who can "get hold of it" has, by doing so, a powerful insight into the character of the person to whom it is given. It gives one power over an individual to know

---

[35] Gordon, C. A., "Notes on Philosophy and Medical Knowledge in Ancient India," *Trans. Vict. Instit.*, Lon., Vol. 25 (1891-92) : 236.
[36] Coon, C. S., *A Reader in General Anthropology*, Holt, N.Y., 1948, p. 247.

what this name is, and consequently it is kept very secret. The Indians of North America were either allotted this name privately by an individual specially appointed as "Keeper of Names," or they went out and sought it in a kind of private religious ordeal which might involve some self-mutilation and entering into an ecstatic trance. It was only shared thereafter with certain very personal friends. According to McIlwraith,[37] the Bella Coola added names to individuals occasioned by some personal experience, so that men or women might often have ten or even twenty names. And knowing these was like knowing their personal history. In England two or three generations ago, one did not address an individual by his given name until he had established a certain intimacy — except where class distinction so set a gulf between two individuals that they either would not or could not take advantage of it. Looking back on my own public school days, I'm quite sure that I never learned the given name of any one of the many boys with whom I lived and played and studied for eight years or so. It was not considered proper to address a fellow by his Christian name.

The giving of a name may also signify an invitation to the spirit of one departed to return, via the present bearer, to the family circle. If the child becomes seriously ill, it is customary to change the child's name, as is done by the Chukchee for example. Curiously enough, very sick children, mentally ill, may upon recovery — even in our own society — decide to adopt a new name as though they had become a different person.

In all primitive societies and in some higher ones, the name is identified with the character of the holder, whether animal or human. A logical extension of this identification is that to reveal a person's name is to reveal his character, a procedure which must be avoided at all costs if one is a friend or a relative, because it allows others to make use of this information. Murdock says that the Ainu wife never mentions her husband's name, for to do so would rob him of part of himself.[38] Very often the soul has no existence in the individual until he has received his name, and among American Indian tribes a certain woman would be appointed as "Keeper of Names," to whom application had to be made before a child could receive full personhood.[39] However, once the name was given and the soul was lodged, the name could be safely forgotten. It was like a key to open the way to personality, which once used could be thrown away. But without a

[37] McIlwraith, I., ref. 16.
[38] Murdock, G. P., ref. 11, p. 197.
[39] Goldenweiser, Alexander, ref. 23, p. 337.

name, nothing had any real existence. Thus the great Sumerian Creation Epic speaks of past eternity as a time when "Heaven was not named, Below to the earth no name was given."[40]

In some cases although the person's name is known to everyone, he is not *directly* addressed by it but is spoken to as the son of whatever his mother's name was. If a wife and a husband have names like Dorothy and John, for example, the husband will be addressed as Dorothy's husband and the wife as John's wife, so that neither is actually addressed by name.[41]

Ernst Cassirer says much about the significance of naming things in a child's growing ability to come to terms with the world.[42] Once he has hold of the name, he has hold of the object itself. This "learning of names" process is far more than merely increasing one's vocabulary. It is more than the mastery of labels, it is mastery of the things labelled. To know a person's name is to "know" the person for what he is. This is not so true in our philosophy, but it is almost universally so in other cultures.

9. ROMANTIC LOVE

It is difficult for us to realize that our accumulated social wisdom does not mark the high point in history but may reflect rather a retrograde view. We find it almost impossible to see how a society could operate without "discovering" the excitement of falling in love. Nevertheless, many societies know nothing of this particular form of cultural behavior. It is certainly not, apparently, one of the so-called "universals." Some societies recognize it as a possibility and reject it outright as being stupid. Twenty-five years ago, and perhaps even today, in China, a man who falls in love is considered insane.[43] And I learned recently that even today American films with a romantic theme are tremendously popular with Mongolian audiences because they treat them as comedies. The Samoans laugh incredulously at tales involving jealousy due to love.[44] According to Haimendorf,[45] among the Reddi of the Bison Hills the individuals concerned in a proposed marriage not only have no choice in the matter, the selection being entirely a parental affair, but the couple are virtually not even interested. One might suppose that such an indifferent union between the newlyweds might seem likely to poison their feelings

---

[40] Barton, George A., ref. 6, p. 287.
[41] Coon, C. S., ref. 36, p. 190.
[42] Cassirer, Ernst, *An Essay on Man,* Yale Univ. Press, 1944, p. 132.
[43] McIlwraith, I., ref. 16.
[44] Murdock, G. P., ref. 11, p. 72.
[45] Haimendorf, C., ref. 9.

toward their children and thus make them feel unwanted. Contrary to psychological doctrine, this does not appear to be the case at all. The children in such cultures appear to live remarkably happy lives. Frank Speck,[46] speaking of the Naskapi Indians in Canada says that although marriage is based entirely on convenience, "the children are quiet and well behaved, and are well loved. There is no corporal punishment but a spirit of real comradeship." This is a constant refrain in the literature of anthropology which deals with patterns of culture. It suggests that some of our conclusions that the waywardness of children is due to lack of discipline or the absence of love between the parents may require some revision. Certainly photographs of Naskapi children reflect their sunny dispositions. A notable exception is found among a people whom we have referred to more than once previously, the Trobrianders. Malinowski, who made these people his special interest, says that permanent attachments between boys and girls spring out of passion, genuine affection, and intellectual companionship. As soon as this occurs, the girl is "seen" with the boy during the day and is then considered married. In a sense we reverse this process.

10. INCEST

It may truthfully be said that there is an almost universal "horror" of incest, that is to say, the marriage of a brother and sister who are children of the same mother, or of a mother and son. These two are singled out in particular by virtually all societies. But, there are many cultures which do not consider the marriage of a man to his daughter as incest since it is not felt that the daughter received her body from him. Similarly, it is not felt to be incest when a brother and sister who are children of one father but not of one mother, are married — for the same reason. One only has to remember that it is believed that the mother supplies the body and it is the uniting of two *bodies* from the same source which is viewed with such distaste.

For reasons which geneticists feel they can explain satisfactorily, the marriage of all very close relatives is apt to have undesirable results; and records show that in highly inbred isolated societies, even in Scotland for example, the incidence of deaf-mutism and other congenital deformations is considerably higher than normal. It is quite likely that primitive people who are very keen observers took note of this fact.

It will be perhaps of more interest to refer very briefly to the

---

[46] Speck, Frank G., *Naskapi Indians,* 1935.

fact that in many primitive or older high cultures, whenever a brother-sister marriage which was by definition incestuous could be "got away with" without ill effect on the offspring, the family was generally considered to be superior stock just on this account... as indeed they may very well have been. Such families gained this advantage over others, namely, that all wealth, privileges, rights, and titles remained undivided within the family. The two circumstances combined, the reputation for being superior stock and the accumulation of wealth, afforded the family aristocratic rank. The Inca chiefs married their sisters, and the Ptolemies of Egypt married their sisters.[47] It will be remembered that Cleopatra was the seventh generation of brother-sister marriages, and there was certainly nothing inferior about her, though her younger brother appears to have been less notable, indeed perhaps even slightly imbecile. It may be that the superior stock was already beginning to lose its genetic excellence.

11. CROSS COUSINS AND PARALLEL COUSINS

It should be underscored that while the concept of a cross cousin as the "ideal" marriage partner is exceedingly common all over the world, it is not the only acceptable cousin marriage relationship. By contrast with the cross cousin relationship, there is what is known as a parallel-cousin, by which is meant the mother's sister's daughter or the father's brother's daughter as opposed to the mother's *brother's* daughter or the father's *sister's* daughter. To marry one's mother's sister's daughter would be to all intents and purposes by definition incest in some cultures. In fact, it is incest but one generation removed since the couple are then children of two sisters who in turn derived their bodies from the same mother. This incest principle is not, however, applied to the marriage of a father's brother's daughter. It applies only to bodily or blood relationships, not to such spiritual relationships as are felt to exist in fatherhood. Female incestual relationships of this kind have never been favored in any society. What is found among the Hebrew and the Muti-Ali (an Arab people), and not altogether unexpectedly, is the marriage of parallel cousins who are the children of *brothers*, since this is not considered to involve incest by their definition.[48] In short, I, as a son, would marry my father's brother's daughter. This is much more allowable because our two bodies will almost certainly be derived from two different mothers.

---

[47] Murdock, G. P., ref. 11, p. 417. See also, J. G. Frazer, *Adonis, Attis, and Osiris,* London, 1906, p. 323; and Gordon Brown, *Melanesians and Polynesians,* London, 1910.

[48] Tayyeb, Ali, ref. 18.

C. S. Coon[49] notes that as the Israelites became more settled and well-to-do after the conquest of Canaan, they tended to favor a cross-cousin relationship, whereas previously they had favored the parallel-cousin relationship adopted chiefly by the Arabs. Among the representative people who marry cross-cousins are the Reddi of the Bison Hills in India, the Hopi of Southwestern United States, the Nunivak Eskimo, the Chukchee of Siberia.

12. LEVIRATE MARRIAGE

The principle that marriage is a contract which is broken if the wife dies while the man might still hope for children, in which case the dead wife's sister substitutes for her, is in some societies paralleled by a reverse agreement. In other words, if it is the husband who dies at a time when the wife is still young enough to have children, then it is her turn to be compensated, and this compensation is not guaranteed by her being given her dead husband's brother as a "private" husband, but she is allowed to claim her dead husband's brother as a father not only to the children she already has but as a "substitute" husband to provide her with more children. By this means she can raise a family without her children being illegitimate. This practice, which is not only found in the Bible but found among primitive people occasionally (the Nunivak Eskimo, for instance), is an example of the somewhat rare acknowledgment in other cultures of the equality of the wife with the husband in terms of the marriage contract. Although it is a mistake to suppose that the term bride price signifies that the wife was little more than a chattel, a purchased possession as it were, for quite other reasons women have tended to be treated as such by their husbands in many cultures. The levirate, wherever it is found, is a recognition of the right of the woman to enjoy the raising of a family for her own protection and provision, just as the provision of a substitute sister recognized the right of the man to raise a family of his own. It provides for the birth of legitimate children to a partner of a contract whose rights are not otherwise protected.

There is a phenomenon which is very widespread in primitive societies and which is referred to as a "joking relationship." This permits a relationship of excessive familiarity between a man and a woman under certain conditions. The man may raise her dress, exposing her in public; and she may retaliate in kind. This is a rather surprising circumstance. Among the Crow Indians it prevails between

---

[49] Coon, C. S., "Race Concept and Human Races," *Cold Spring Harbor Symposia on Quantitative Biology,* 15 (1950): 251.

a man and his sister-in-law,[50] i.e, between a man and his brother's wife. Among the Nahma Hottentots, the relationship exists between cross cousins.[51] To my knowledge wherever a joking relationship is recognized in a society, it exists always between two people who may become man and wife. In the case of the cross cousins, it exists primarily between cross cousins who are most likely to end up as man and wife. Not all cross cousins will do so, of course. In the case of the man and his brother's wife, the same potential exists; namely, in the event of the brother's death. It is a kind of privileged relationship of familiarity, which may perhaps be not altogether unlike the familiarity which used to exist in England between a boy and a girl in their childhood, who in the normal course of events might be expected to marry when they grew up.

The privilege of "exposure" by uncovering nakedness was strictly limited to those who might be expected to marry, hence it was a severely punishable offense where such an expectation could never be realized.

13. POLYGYNY

I suppose that polygyny is most commonly associated in the mind of the White Man with Africa, and perhaps it is here that the phenomenon is most frequently observed. As a matter of fact, when large parts of Africa were under British Colonial administration, every administrator when he visited a village would immediately look for the central house or hut which had the largest number of huts adjoined to it. For this was a sure sign of a man with many wives, who could be pretty safely judged to be, as a consequence, an able administrator like himself. It takes a good man, as one of my professors used to say, to run a women's college successfully!

I am not suggesting that such a custom is desirable once a society has reached the point that its male members are likely to live out their lives to a reasonable age, and once a society has found ways and means of caring for its older womenfolk. But in the absence of these two requisites, I do not think that polygyny in itself *need* involve all the evils which we tend to associate with it. This is particularly so when two other factors are borne in mind: first, that the womenfolk are likely to be of the same family or quite closely related; and secondly, that the emotional tensions which are involved in a marriage

---

50 Murdock, G. P., ref. 11, p. 273.
51 Ibid., p. 490.

that is predicated primarily on romantic love are absent, the marriage being essentially a contract agreeable to all parties.

14. BARRENNESS

With respect to barrenness, enough has already been said to indicate that since marriage is not for the gratification of sex, but is rather a contract wherein the man undertakes to care for the woman and the woman undertakes to provide the man with children to continue his line and his name, it follows that virtually without exception a childless wife is considered a contract breaker with respect to her husband, a disturber of normal behavior with respect to her society, and a source of great potential embarrassment to her family. The last stems from the fact that having broken her contract, the husband can claim back her bride price, a circumstance which can be disastrous to a family since the gifts may already have been widely distributed — even slaughtered and eaten in fact. And in terms of the social organization of the community, the groom's gifts to the bride's parents may already have been used by her special brother for the "procurement" of *his* wife. In short, reverberations are likely to occur throughout the whole community. It is therefore no wonder that the grief of a barren wife is a recurrent theme all over the world, and not least in the Old Testament.

To my knowledge only one society other than our own has ever thought to acknowledge the fact that the husband himself and not the wife might be to blame. Unfortunately, it would be difficult to prove except by some form of adulterous action in which the man demonstrates his virility with some other woman than his wife.

15. BIRTH OF TWINS

On the whole, pastoral people, who have many flocks of sheep, can employ their children usefully at an earlier age than those societies which are either hunters or farmers. Hunters clearly would be handicapped by very small children (while engaged in hunting), and farmers who must do hard physical work cannot employ very young children either. But those who herd animals can and do use children at a very young age indeed. Such societies tend to welcome children born under any circumstance whatever.

On the other hand, people whose environment is harsh, such as the Eskimo for example,[52] do not have the means of accommodating too many entirely dependent children at any one time, nor do they

---

[52] Garbar, Clark, "Eskimo Infanticide," *Sci. Monthly,* 1947, p. 100.

have foods, apart from the mother's milk, which are suitable for exceedingly small infants. An Eskimo mother will nurse her child anywhere from four to six years. She cannot nurse two children and infanticide is therefore practiced (or used to be practiced) not only when twins were born but if children appeared in too short an interval. It is important to realize that the Eskimo, like the Chukchee and many other primitive people, do not believe that the infant has a soul until it has received a name. To them a nameless baby is almost, though not quite, a *thing*. The mother *may* show no grief when she puts the unnamed baby out in the snow to die. Mother love is *not* found in all societies.

Almost universally twins have been considered an ill omen in many societies. Sometimes it is explained by a native spokesman that only animals have multiple births and that it is not proper for a human beings to behave like animals.[53] The attitude of other native people is based on a much more profound distrust, namely, that one at least of the children is the offspring of an evil spirit.[54] Since such a child should be destroyed immediately, the problem is to know which one to destroy. And since this cannot be known with certainty, either both babies are killed at once, or the whole family may be ejected from the village. The Peruvians in *some* cases agreed that it was a bad omen,[55] in *others* they rejoiced in it as evidence of exceptional fertility.

Livingstone notes that among South African tribes one of the twins is killed.[56] Among the Arunta of Australia,[57] twins are usually killed immediately as being "unnatural," but there is no ill treatment of the mother. The Arunta chiefs apparently do not know how the custom arose. In Melanesia where brother-sister relationships are so strongly avoided, if a girl and boy are born together, one will be put to death immediately in order to avoid having to raise them in proximity.[58]

16. HONORING PARENTS

The principle of crediting to the father the goodness of his son or blaming him for his wickedness is found very widely in non-Western cultures. It is a principle of great importance where it is observed, and the westerner does well to heed it when in their com-

[53] Lubbock, Sir John, ref. 5, p. 34.
[54] Ibid., p. 35.
[55] Ibid.
[56] Livingstone, David, ref. 4, p. 577.
[57] Coon, C. S., ref. 36, p. 230.
[58] Goldenweiser, Alexander, ref. 23, p. 302.

pany. Peacekeeping forces in the Middle East have on more than one occasion run into unexpected problems by personally rewarding some young Arab who performed them a kindness. This was taken as an insult to the father who believed that *he* should have received the reward directly, and it was distasteful to the village because it undermined their system of cultural values by improperly paying attention to one of the younger members of the society. The result has been to alienate the whole village by an act which was supposed to do precisely the opposite. If the father had been rewarded instead, as would have been proper, everyone would have been happy: the father because he would have been richer, the son because he would have maintained a reputation as dutiful, and the village as a whole because the outsider's behavior would have been a tacit recognition of the reasonableness of their culture pattern which they themselves took for granted.

The Japanese, at least the older generation, even today take this principle very seriously. Not very long ago a young man who brought disgrace upon his family by some dishonorable act would be quite likely to commit suicide in order to redeem his father's honor. Some primitive cultures, such as the Samoans, punish a whole family — father, mother, brothers and sisters — if any one member of the family does some particularly disgraceful thing.[59] The individual has never assumed the kind of personal importance in any other culture that we allow to the individual in ours.

17. Body Odor

Almost all societies except our own have a tendency to adopt a comparatively simple and comparatively stable diet. Some live on maize (American Indians), some live on rice (Chinese), some live on potatoes (Aymara of Peru), others live on the meat of a single species (reindeer: Chukchee), and so forth, and in most cases very little change or embellishment of the diet is either desired or possible. The consequence of this food stabilization is that a characteristic body odor is developed in association with each particular diet. This body odor becomes pleasant by familiarity and is preferred or considered "natural" by all those who happen to share it. All foreigners or strangers who do not share it, or who may happen to have no detectable body odor at all, are considered distasteful in this respect.[60] One of the first things which the Eskimo hunter does when he returns to his native village is to bury his face in the neck opening of his

[59] Murdock, G. P., ref. 11, p. 61.
[60] Coon, C. S., ref. 36, p. 91.

children's clothing in order to breathe deeply the familiar body odor of home. It is just possible that the European habit of touching cheeks as a form of greeting is not a form of the kiss of welcome but a less demonstrative remnant of the habit of "falling upon the neck."

18. DIVISION OF THE INHERITANCE

The culture of Western man has attached great importance to the accumulation of wealth by "usury," the gathering of interest with time without any further expenditure of energy by the possessor. The longer this kind of wealth is kept in the position where it can accumulate interest, the more valuable it becomes when it is finally transferred to a new owner. Since a father not unnaturally desired that his children shall have the maximum benefit of his wealth and at the same time he is likely to be convinced that he is the best judge of how to invest it, he is apt to retain control of it as long as he possibly can. With this kind of system, an inheritance normally is only passed on to the children when the benefactor can have no further interest in it.

Throughout most of the world's history, the possibility of accumulating interest in this way has been somewhat limited. Where wealth was property, rights, or in the form of otherwise unexchangeable things, the present owner often had no particular reason for maintaining sole ownership until he died. As a consequence, those who were to inherit his wealth often had the right to claim their inheritance at any time.

In his *Ancient Law*,[61] Maine pointed out that in his time among the Hindus the instant a son is born, he acquires a vested right in his father's property which could not be sold without recognition of his joint ownership. When he attained full age he could, if he so desired, compel a partition of the estate, even against the consent of the parent. And if the parent acquiesced, one son could always demand a partition even when the other sons were not in favor of it. Maine pointed out that German tribes in ancient law allowed the same proceeding. If it happened that there were only two sons and the first had demanded and taken his interitance already, all that the father possessed automatically belonged to the other son. Nor was it necessary that the first son to demand his inheritance need be the eldest.

---

[61] Maine: quoted by Sir John Lubbock, ref. 5, p. 464.

Chapter 3
Illustrations in Scripture

ALL THAT WE have presented so far is in one way or another related to family life, and was sparked by a consideration of Genesis 2:24, which lays down the general principle that if a man and his wife when they are first married do not have the means to establish a home of their own, the man should go to live with his wife's family rather than the wife leaving home to live with his family. As a matter of convenience, we broke up our consideration of the rather wide ramifications of this injunction into sections. But, after due consideration, it did not seem the most suitable arrangement to explore the Bible itself under these particular headings in the same order, so we decided instead to follow on from Genesis 2:24 through the Old Testament, pointing out, where appropriate, how the story as it unfolds reflects many of these patterns of cultural behavior. In doing so, it will be seen that these other cultures do indeed shed light upon many events in Scripture which to our western view seem otherwise improper, or at least somewhat irrational.

GENESIS 2:24: Therefore shall a man leave his father and his mother and cleave unto his wife.

Since this passage was largely responsible for initiating the thread of the argument in the first part of this paper, we merely refer the reader to Part I and Part II-2 without further comment here.

GENESIS 4:1-2: And Adam knew Eve his wife; and she conceived,

and bare Cain, and said, I have gotten a man from the Lord. And
she again bare his brother Abel.

The Hebrew original is rather exceptional. Two boys are born
who are generally assumed to have been twins, but the original text
suggests rather that Abel was the true child resulting from Adam
"knowing" Eve — as the text puts it — but that Cain was satanically
originated (רַתֹּסֶף לָלֶדֶת) and unnaturally given prior birth. Even
in the natural order of things sons have been born some hours apart
who are nevertheless not twins in the true sense.[62]
In Genesis 3:15 the promise is given to Eve that One who should
be her seed would finally undo the works of Satan. In the circumstances, it was very natural for Eve to suppose that this Promised
Seed would appear at once; and there is some evidence that she supposed this to have happened when her first child was born. This
event is recorded in Genesis 4:1 and 2, and the Hebrew of the original
is in some respects a little odd. Our text reads: "And Adam knew
Eve his wife; and she conceived, and bare Cain, and said, I have
gotten a man from the Lord. And she again bare his brother Abel."
In the original, Eve's statement "I have gotten a man from the Lord,"
may be translated in several different ways. She may have said, "I
have gotten a man with the Lord," i.e., with the help of the Lord
perhaps. But she may also have said, "I have gotten a man, even the
Lord." In any case, the word "Lord" is "Jehovah" in the Hebrew, a
circumstance to which we shall return in a moment. The phrase
"And she again bare his brother Abel" is also a little strange. It could
possibly be rendered, "And she bare also (at the same time) his
brother Abel." This would be a birth of twins. The only justification
for this translation lies in the fact that the adverb "again" is a verb
in the original which means essentially "to do at the same time," or
"to repeat."
In the New Testament Cain is said to have been born of "that
Wicked One" (1 John 3:12), a phrase which is exactly paralleled to
that in Matthew 1:20 where Jesus is said to have been conceived of
the Holy Spirit. The Greek ἐκ *(ek)* is used in both cases, implying
derivation in a special way, in the one case "out of" the Holy Spirit
and in the other case "out of" the Evil One. Is it possible that Satan
was also mistaken, believing that the first child that Eve bore would
somehow or other be the Redeemer and that in some supernatural
way he tried to see to it that an Antichrist appeared before Christ?

---

[62] *Toronto Globe*, Aug. 5, 1949, reported such a case under the title, "Born
26 Hours Apart: But Two Sons, Not Twins."

If this admittedly speculative idea has any justification, then it seems not unlikely that with Cain exiled by God Himself from the company of his fellows, Satan might soon tempt other men to claim themselves to be the Promised Seed. Although there are other interpretations of Genesis 4:26, it is not impossible that the statement that at this time "men began to call upon the name of the Lord" should more properly be rendered "men began to call themselves by the name Jehovah." The Hebrew allows this, and it may be that notable individuals were tempted to make this claim for themselves openly for the first time.

In Exodus 6:2 and 3 there is a passage the meaning of which has always been a subject of debate. In this passage the Lord says to Moses, "I am the Lord: and I appeared unto Abraham, unto Isaac, and unto Jacob, by the name God Almighty, but by my name Jehovah was I not known to them." It has always seemed strange that the Lord who was about to redeem Israel should say that He had not been known by name to the patriarchs, who met Him and talked with Him face to face. I should like to suggest this possibility. When Mary was told that she would bare a Son who was to be the Redeemer, she was also told what His name was to be, namely, Jehovah the Savior, shortened into the form, Jesus. It seems to me not unlikely that God might have told Eve that when the Promised Seed came His name would be Jehovah. But — and this is the point of importance here — she was not told that Jehovah was God's name. Accordingly, as the knowledge was passed from generation to generation, the tradition was well known that the name of the Promised Seed when He appeared would be Jehovah. But still no one knew that this was God's name. As I see it, God was here saying to Moses, "You know as others have known that when the Redeemer comes his name will be Jehovah; but now I am revealing to you that I, God Almighty, am that Jehovah." Or in very simple words, "I am *that* I am," the second "I am" being a translation in a sense of the word "Jehovah." Moses now knew that the Promised Seed was not a great mortal one but was to be God Himself. This fact was clearly understood by Isaiah (35:4).

There is a further observation that might be made regarding Cain, though I must confess that I am not certain that the text warrants what I am reading into it. Of the descendants of Cain, we are never told of their death. This might be simply the result of the fact that we are not given their age. But there were many subsequent historical figures in the Old Testament who were either enemies of the Lord's children or, though actually Israelites, were without faith, yet these people have their deaths recorded, even though we are not told how old they were when they died.

Some believe that Cain was supernaturally born of Eve through the agency of Satan who thereby hoped to present the Antichrist, supposing that Abel was actually the Promised Seed. The Hebrew of Genesis 4:1-2 has always presented problems to the translator and it almost seems as though Adam knew his wife only once in spite of the birth of two children who are not presented to us in the usual terms reserved for the birth of twins. There is an ancient belief, and one still preserved by many primitive people, that when twins are born one of them is actually a child of the devil. Having no means of identifying which child is the evil one, such societies customarily insisted that all twins must be destroyed at birth.

Now, however fanciful such an idea may be, we are not altogether without some encouragement in holding it in the light of other passages of Scripture which bear upon the subject. If we attach any importance to ancient traditions, we may observe that the legendary giants of antiquity were believed to have had supernatural birth and to have enjoyed a kind of super-natural life. They lived and continued to grow in size as long as they lived, and because they lived for such lengths of time they became giants in size and vastly superior in knowledge. If these beings were descendants of one supernaturally born, they may have formed a race of giants and given rise to the tradition which seems to be reflected in Genesis 6:4. These men were not merely giants in size, they were men of renown. And certainly one gets this feeling of those who are listed as Cain's descendants. While they did not die naturally, they were certainly capable of being slain, as Goliath was. And in Matthew 24:39 speaking of the Flood destroying the old world, we are told not that they died in the Flood but merely that they were "taken away." The abhorrence of twins in some cases reflects a knowledge of details regarding the birth of Cain and Abel which has not been preserved for us in Genesis.

GENESIS 4:19, 22, 23: *And Lamech took unto him two wives: the name of one was Adah, and the name of the other Zillah.... And Zillah, she also bare Tubal-Cain, an instructor of every artificer in brass and iron.... And Lamech said unto his wives ... Hear my voice ... for I have slain a man to my wounding, and a young man to my hurt.*

In Genesis 4:22 the son of Zillah is given as Tubal-Cain, and although the name does not appear in this form of antiquity, R. J. Forbes, one of the outstanding authorities on metallurgy in antiquity, points out that Cain means "smith." And according to the same author, one of the tribes long associated in the ancient world with metalworking was the Tibareni, whom many scholars identify with Tubal, the *l* and *r* being interchangeable.

We may go one step further in this when we discover that the name of the individual who came to be constituted as the god of the Tiber (a clearly related word) was Vulcan. To my mind, there is not much doubt that Tubal-Cain is the earliest form of the name Vulcan, which in its later stages was merely shortened by the omission of the *Tu-*. In his commentary on Genesis, Marcus Dodds points out that everything is so faithfully perpetuated in the East that the blacksmith of the village of Gubbatea-ez-zetum referred to the iron "splinters" struck off while working at his forge as "tubal."

Now the traditions regarding Vulcan are rather interesting. He is, of course, associated with fire and the working of metals, later appearing as the divine smith of the Roman *tubil*ustrum. He is said to have been a cripple, having been thrown out of heaven by Jupiter as a punishment for having taken the part of his mother in a quarrel which had occurred between them.

In Genesis 4:23 there is the rather extraordinary story of how Lamech took vengeance on a young man for wounding him. Lamech's son was Tubal Cain, perhaps none other than Vulcan, subsequently deified. In the brief account in Genesis, it is stated that Lamech had two wives, one of whom was named Zillah. Let us suppose, for a moment, that it was with Zillah that Lamech quarrelled and that Tubal-Cain, the son of Zillah, took his mother's part and got into a fight with his father Lamech. Whatever happened to Lamech is not clear, although he appears to have been wounded, but Tubal-Cain himself was injured sufficiently to become thereafter a lame man. Moreover, it is customary in a society where polygamy is allowed, to name the child not after the father but after the mother, since this obviously assures better identification. In early cuneiform one of the curious words which has puzzled Sumerologists is "parzillu," a word for "iron." Now, surely, this word is none other than a masculinized form of two Semitic words, "Bar Zillah," i.e., "Son of Zillah." In the course of time because the ending *-ah* tended to be reserved for words of feminine gender, the word became "Parzillu," or "Barzillu," with a correct masculine termination.

Putting all these things together, one has a remarkable series of fragments of tradition in which there is a continuity of name-forms, all related in meaning or association and wrapped up in a trade of very ancient origin, attached to a deity who had the strange experience of being ejected from his home and rendered lame for taking his mother's part and who thereafter lent his title, "Son of Zillah," to the Sumerian people as their word for "iron."

Such, then, is the light which this very early story in Genesis seems to shed upon much that is otherwise strange — and even absurd — in ancient tradition. That there is a basis of fact throughout is clearly confirmed by the very continuity of the blacksmith's art. Yet only in some form of Semitic language does one find any meaning to the venerable name, Tubal-Cain, or any light upon the origin of the hitherto mysterious word "Barzillu" or "Parzillu," meaning "iron," a word evidently bearing witness to the very early practice of naming children after their mother wherever polygyny was in effect.

GENESIS 9:20-25: And Noah ... planted a vineyard: And he drank of the wine, and was drunken; and he was uncovered within his tent. And Ham, the father of Canaan, saw the nakedness of his father.... And Noah awoke from his wine, and he knew what his younger son had done unto him. And he said, Cursed be Canaan....

It has often been wondered why Canaan was cursed rather than Ham, who was the true offender against his father's honor. It has been suggested that the curse originally was "cursed be Ham, the father of Canaan," and there is apparently one ancient manuscript to support this view.

But I think perhaps there is a better explanation. As we have seen in Chapter 2, 16, it has in other cultures been customary to attach the credit or blame to the father (in some cases to the whole family) for some good or evil deed performed by a son. By a quite logical process of reasoning, if Noah had cursed Ham he would in point of fact have been discrediting himself, since he was Ham's father. This was avoided by cursing Ham's son and in this way discrediting Ham who was his father.

The principle is very interestingly illustrated in 1 Samuel 17: 50-58. There, David has just performed a deed of great national importance by destroying Goliath. Now David himself was no stranger to Saul, for he had on many occasions played his harp to quiet the king's distracted spirit. Yet here in verse 55 we find that when Saul saw David go forth against Goliath, even though he had actually offered David his armor, he said to Abner, the captain of his armies, "Abner, whose son is this youth?" And although Abner must certainly have known David by name, he replied, "As my soul liveth, O king, I cannot tell."

This has always seemed a strange remark both for the king and for his commanding officer to have made. But I think the explanation lies in a proper understanding of the social significance of verse 58: "And Saul said unto him, Whose son art thou, young man? And David answered, I am the son of thy servant Jesse, the Bethlehemite." This was apparently simply an occasion upon which, following a widespread social custom, Saul was planning to give credit where he saw credit was really due, namely, to the father. Because David was Jesse's son, it was to Jesse that recognition must be given.

In the New Testament we find a further instance in a slightly different form. It is quite obvious that while a man can publicly seek to give credit to the father of a worthy son, it was less discreet for a woman to make reference to a father in complimentary terms for fear of being misunderstood. She therefore refers instead to the son's mother who rightly shares in the worthiness of her children. This fact is reflected clearly in Luke 11:27, where we read of a woman who suddenly perceiving the true greatness of the Lord Jesus Christ, cried out in spontaneous admiration, "Blessed is the womb that bare Thee and the breasts which Thou hast sucked."

GENESIS 11:25-31: *And Nahor lived after he begat Terah an hundred and nineteen years, and begat sons and daughters. And Terah lived seventy years, and begat Abram, Nahor, and Haran ... and Haran begat Lot. And Haran died before his father Terah in the land of his nativity, in Ur of the Chaldees. And Abram and Nahor took them wives: and the name of Abram's wife was Sarai; and the name of Nahor's wife, Milcah, the daughter of Haran, the father of Milcah, and the father of Iscah.... And Terah took Abram his son, and Lot the son of Haran his son's son, and Sarai his daughter in law, his son Abram's wife; and they went forth with them from Ur of the Chaldees....*

GENESIS 12:1, 5, 9-13: *Now the Lord had said unto Abram, Get thee out of thy country, and from thy kindred.... And Abram took Sarai his wife, and Lot his brother's son ... and they went forth to go into the land of Canaan.... And Abram journeyed, going on still toward the south. And there was a famine in the land: and Abram went down into Egypt to sojourn there.... And it came to pass, when he was come near to enter into Egypt, that he said unto Sarai his wife, Be-*

hold, now, I know that thou art a fair woman to look upon: Therefore it shall come to pass, when the Egyptians shall see thee, that they shall say, This is his wife: and they will kill me, but they will save thee alive. Say, I pray thee, thou art my sister. . . .

GENESIS 20:1-12: And Abraham journeyed from thence toward the south country, and dwelled between Kadesh and Shur, and sojourned in Gerar. And Abraham said of Sarah his wife, She is my sister: and Abimelech king of Gerar sent, and took Sarah. But God came to Abimelech in a dream by night and said to him, Behold, thou art but a dead man, for the woman thou hast taken; for she is a man's wife. But Abimelech had not come near her: and he said, Lord, wilt thou slay also a righteous nation? Said he not unto me, She is my sister? and she, even she herself said, He is my brother: in the integrity of my heart and innocency of my hands have I done this. And God said unto him in a dream, Yea, I know that thou didst this in the integrity of thy heart; for I also withheld thee from sinning against me. . . . Now therefore restore the man his wife. . . . Then Abimelech called Abraham, and said unto him, What hast thou done unto us? . . . And Abraham said, Because I thought, Surely the fear of God is not in this place; and they will slay me for my wife's sake. And yet indeed she is my sister; she is the daughter of my father, but not the daughter of my mother; and she became my wife.

The circumstances surrounding these events are wonderfully illuminated by many observations as set forth in the former part of this paper. It is the cryptic statement of Abraham, "Indeed, she is my sister; she is the daughter of my father, but not the daughter of my mother," which really receives the most light in this respect.

Genesis 11:25-27 can be set forth schematically as follows:

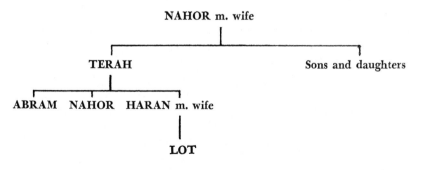

Up to this point, the sons and daughters of Nahor who were Terah's brothers and sisters are not named, but information given in the following verses provides very good grounds for believing that one of these was named Haran. We shall examine this shortly, but for clarity we now modify the above genealogy as follows:

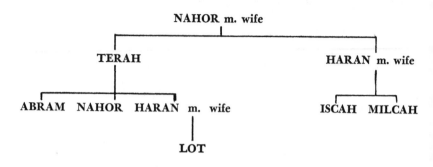

It will be noted that Terah's brother, Haran, had two daughters, Iscah and Milcah. The former of these, Iscah, was Sarah by another name. This identification is very widely agreed upon, was accepted in Jewish commentaries, and is assumed by Josephus in his *Antiquities* (Bk. 1, vi, 5).

It may appear to the reader that large liberties are being taken with the text, but this is not really the case. Like many others, the Jewish people commonly accepted the principle that if a man's brother married a woman and subsequently died before the children married, he took his brother's place and became in effect both her husband and the father of her children. This is the basis of the Pharisees' hypothetical question in Luke 20:27-38. If therefore Terah's brother Haran had died, the duty of becoming in effect the father of Iscah and Milcah would automatically devolve upon Terah. Terah's "new" children would then become sisters to his own sons and when Abraham and Nahor subsequently married Iscah and Milcah, they would, socially, be marrying their own sisters. Genetically they were not, the two girls being cousins. However, they were a special kind of cousin, namely, "parallel cousins." The term has been invented by anthropologists to signify the following relationship. My *father's* brother's children are parallel cousins. By contrast, my *mother's* brother's children are cross cousins. In a Semitic society the ideal wife for a man was one of his parallel cousins. Furthermore, where several sons existed and there were several female parallel cousins, it was assumed that the oldest son would marry the oldest girl and so on down the line. The expected wife for Abraham would therefore be his uncle Haran's daughter of comparable age (Cf. Chap. 2, 11).

Now this seems a little complex, but it is particularly striking in this instance because even today among many Arab tribes in all their love stories the man looks upon his paternal uncle's daughter as his "princess." This is the term by which he refers to her in his poetic moments. In Hebrew the word for prince is *Sar,* the feminine form of which is *Sara,* meaning "Princess." The terminal possessive pronoun "my" is a long *i* so that *Sara* becomes *Sarai* meaning "my princess." This is how Abraham referred to his beautiful wife. Her name was Iscah but he called her "My Princess" or *Sarai.*

Thus Terah's brother Haran, who predeceased him, is identified in verse 29 as the father of Milcah and Iscah, whereas Terah's *son* Haran, who also predeceased him, is referred to as the father of Lot (v. 31). Because his son Haran (no doubt named after his uncle) died prematurely, Lot became in a special sense the charge of Terah and subsequently of Abraham (Cf. Chap. 2, 12). So when Terah's brother died, Terah took his brother's wife and became the father of his brother's children. Because he was also the father of Abraham, this allowed Abraham to say with perfect truth (though with ulterior motives) that Sarai, his princess, was indeed his sister, being the daughter of his own father, but *not* the daughter of his own mother.

There is, therefore, not the slightest element of invention here in so far as the record of Genesis goes. Genesis 11 gives us sufficient information, if carefully read, to see that there is nothing fanciful about the circumstance which so compounded Abraham's relationship with his own wife.

Only one further observation seems appropriate here. And that is that every brother in a society of this nature is given a particular responsibility for the sister who is next to him in age. He bears a special protective relationship towards her and must approve her husband. He will, moreover, be called upon to chastise her children if necessary, while her husband will not be allowed to do so. It was thus important to curry the favor of any brother who was manifestly the protector of the sister whose hand might be sought in marriage, in which position Abraham must have appeared in the eyes of Pharaoh. This is why Abraham felt sure of his own safety, and indeed, of being favored by Pharaoh or anyone else who might be in a position to desire Sarai (Cf. Chap. 2, 6).

GENESIS 15:2-4: And Abram said, Lord God, what wilt Thou give me, seeing I go childless, and the steward of my house in this Eliezer of Damascus? And Abram said, Behold, to me thou has given no seed: and, lo, one born in my house is mine heir. And, behold, the word of the Lord came unto him saying, This shall not be thine heir; but he that shall come forth out of thine own bowels shall be thine heir.

This appears to reflect a custom which, as we have seen, was evidently quite common, namely, the adoption of some member of the household who is nevertheless not a blood relative, who becomes the potential heir of the adoptive father. It would appear from the story, however, that the head of the house in this case at any rate made his adoptive son his heir so long as he had no sons of his own. It seems as though this could not but engender hard feelings if a son should be born unexpectedly. But perhaps if the adopted individual was quite aware of the tentative position he held as heir, his subsequent downgrading in this sense, might not be quite such a blow. On the basis of Genesis 24:2 it seems to me not unlikely that it was the same faithful member of his household who, as it says, was his eldest servant and ruled over all that he had, was sent on the delicate mission of finding a wife for the heir who displaced him. In which case, it is surely an evidence of the humility of his spirit and perhaps more understandable that the Lord was able to meet him so graciously while he was on his mission. At any rate, the adoption of a servant to become an heir of his master is a not uncommon custom among many cultures.

GENESIS 16:1-3; 21:2, 8-14: Now Sarai Abram's wife bare him no children: and she had an handmaid, an Egyptian, whose name was Hagar. And Sarai said unto Abram, Behold now, the Lord hath restrained me from bearing: I pray thee go in unto my maid; it may be that I may obtain children by her. And Abram hearkened to the voice of Sarai. And Sarai Abram's wife took Hagar her maid the Egyptian, after Abram had dwelt ten years in the land of Canaan, and gave her to her husband Abram to be his wife.... For Sarah conceived, and bare Abraham a son in his old age.... And the child grew, and was weaned: and Abraham made a great feast the same day that Isaac was weaned. And Sarah saw the son of Hagar ... mocking. Wherefore she said unto Abraham, Cast out this bondwoman and her son; for the son of this bondwoman shall not be heir with my son, even with Isaac. And the thing was very grievous in Abraham's sight because of his son. And God said unto Abraham,

Let it not be grievous in thy sight because of the lad ... in all that Sarah hath said unto thee, hearken unto her voice; for in Isaac shall thy seed be called. ...

And Abraham rose up early in the morning, and took bread, and a bottle of water and gave it unto Hagar ... and the child, and sent her away.

This is an illustration of the fact that the wife who fails to provide an heir to her husband is aware of having broken part of her marriage contract. Sarai had the alternatives of either finding a sister who could become Abram's second wife, or providing him with some other woman entirely of her own choice. Abram was not permitted, and probably did not seek to choose, a second wife for himself on the specific grounds of a broken contract, but he did accept Sarai's choice. Hagar became his wife and in due course bore him a son, Ishmael. But thirteen years later, Sarah herself became pregnant and bore him a son, Isaac. During this interval Hagar seems to have caused considerable irritation to Sarah but not sufficient that she could demand of Abraham that he dismiss her from the household. When, however, Sarah's child was weaned, it appears that Ishmael was quite unwilling to accept gracefully the reduction of his status as the heir of Abraham, and his behavior became so unpleasant that Sarah demanded the expulsion of Hagar and her son from her household. According to law, a law which is reflected in the Code of Hammurabi, Abraham was called upon to take action on his wife's behalf and he "cast out the bondwoman and her son," albeit with some reluctance (Gen. 21:14). In justice to Hagar, it does seem from Genesis 16:6-9 that Hagar was somewhat less to blame for the situation than her son Ishmael was. In Galatians 4:29 it is Ishmael who is accused.

In Genesis 30:1 and 5 it will be noted that the same custom is applied in the relations between Jacob and Rachel. She gives her maid Bilhah to Jacob who bears a son. Rachel said, "God hath ... given a son" (v. 6). Clearly Rachel really did consider this was her child and the reality of her faith is borne out (vv. 7, 8) when she again gives her maid to Jacob and claims the second child as double vindication.

GENESIS 24:2ff.: And Abraham said unto his eldest servant of his house ... thou shalt go unto my country, and to my kindred, and take a wife unto my son Isaac. ... And he arose, and went ... unto the city of Nahor. ... And (the servant) said, O Lord God of my master

Abraham, I pray thee, send me good speed this day....And it came to pass, before he had done speaking, that, behold Rebekah came out, who was born to Bethuel, son of Milcah, the wife of Nahor, Abraham's brother....And Rebekah had a brother and his name was Laban: and Laban ran out unto the man....And it came to pass, when he saw the earring and bracelets...said, Come in, thou blessed of the Lord....Behold, Rebekah is before thee, take her and go, and let her be thy master's son's wife....

Therefore, Isaac married his father's brother's daughter. It will be remembered once again that this is the marriage of parallel cousins, rather than cross cousins, which is somewhat rarer a practice. Nevertheless, such a marriage is quite acceptable, provided that the man is marrying his father's brother's daughter. It would not be at all acceptable for a man to marry his mother's sister's daughter. The difference in these two alternatives is that in the latter case there is a measure of incest involved because the bride has received her body (according to social belief at the time) from a woman who is too closely related by blood. On this crucial point, see Chapter 2, 10.

Now the circumstances surrounding the search which Abraham initiated for a wife for his son Isaac are particularly beautiful, and the literary form in which the story is cast in Scripture is surely the equal of any such love story in the English language. The old and faithful, though nameless, servant was sent by his master Abraham to find a wife for Isaac from the land from which he himself had come to this present place. So he set forth with camels and gifts and he came to the city of Nahor, that Nahor whose relationship to Abraham has already been established in Genesis 11. In due time, he comes to a well outside the city and there he decides to wait, asking the Lord that He will send out to him the maid of His choice and will reassure him by this sign, namely, that she would offer not merely to all him something to drink but to draw water also for his camels.

It would be a pity to tell the story in any other words than those of the original but we may note that before the faithful old servant had finished praying (v. 51), a girl came to the well, very fair to look at, and her name was Rebekah, "born of Bethuel, son of Milcah, the wife of Nahor, Abraham's brother."

The genealogy which we have already repeated twice is now repeated a third time in order to bring out a striking fact about the relationship in time between Isaac and Rebekah. For the fact is that Isaac was born so late in the lifetime of Abraham and Sarah that he could not appropriately have found a wife in what would strictly have been his own generation, namely, the generation in which Bethuel was born. Had he married a sister, let us say, of Bethuel's, he would have been marrying a woman perhaps twenty or twenty-five years older than himself.

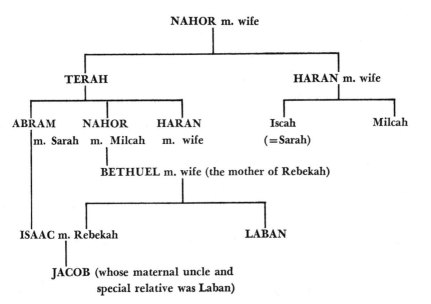

Now the interesting thing about Bethuel is that although he was the father of the girl whose hand was sought in marriage, it is very evident from the record, as Blunt was perhaps the first to underscore, that he is virtually ignored in all the transactions which surrounded the betrothal of Rebekah. It is Rebekah's mother and Rebekah's brother, Laban, who are the chief actors in the story. When the servant first speaks with Rebekah, he asks her, "Whose daughter art thou? Tell me, I pray thee, is there room in thy father's house to lodge in?" She answers that she is the daughter of Bethuel and that there is room. But when he thereupon declared who he was and whence he had come, we are told that "the damsel ran and told them of her *mother's* house these things also." This is not the normal thing for her to have done as is evident by Rachel's behavior when, later, Jacob introduced himself (Gen. 29:12) under somewhat similar circumstances.

This might all be accidental except for the fact that we are then told that Rebekah had a brother whose name was Laban and that "Laban ran out unto the man and invited him in."

This strange circumstance in which Laban acted as host rather than the father of the household has led some people to propose that perhaps Bethuel was dead. But this is clearly ruled out by the subsequent statement (Gen. 24:50) to the effect that Laban and Bethuel together answered the servant's enquiries once he was in the house. So everything is agreed upon and Rebekah is to go with the servant who then makes the presentation of gifts. But these gifts are now presented not to the father but to the brother Laban and to her mother (Gen. 24:53). At the same time, it is suggested she should stay a few days before leaving; and once more the suggestion comes not from Bethuel but from her brother and her mother.

Some encyclopedias, when dealing with Bethuel, propose that he may have been sickly or even imbecile, able to assent to what is proposed but not to make decisions nor to be a sensible recipient of valuable gifts. Personally, I think there is another possible reason for his taking such an insignificant part in all these proceedings which in no way casts doubt upon his character but results from the fact, already noted before, that in Oriental society, as among many native people today, there normally exists a special relationship between each brother in a family and the sister nearest him in age (Cf. Chap. 2, 6).

We have already noted the widespread custom which required that the groom bring a substantial bride price when seeking a wife. We have also noted that the special brother is often largely dependent upon the gift brought to his sister to enable him, in turn, to fulfill the proprieties when *he* takes a wife. It is not at all surprising, therefore, that Laban, who seems to have been Rebekah's "special brother," should have been so interested in the gifts which were brought by the faithful old servant and at the same time should have played such a prominent part in the whole transaction.

But the genealogy as set forth above reveals another fact which might otherwise be missed. Isaac was born under circumstances which in effect made him one whole generation late, being the child of Abraham's and Sarah's old age. Had he been born routinely, Bethuel himself would have been "of his generation." As things transpired, Bethuel's children, not he himself, were of Isaac's generation. In our modern terms, this is perhaps the first generation gap of which we have record. At any rate, it is quite certain that Bethuel himself could hardly have had a sister of appropriate age to be Isaac's wife, for Isaac was young enough, due to circumstances, to be his son. He therefore did not receive the gifts. Because the two families were closely related. it is virtually certain that Bethuel would know very well that Isaac was a special child of his parent's old age. Even if he didn't know this already, the faithful old servant would certainly explain it all while he was in the house; and since he was not looking for one of Bethuel's sisters and did not wish to cause embarrassment to them, he would almost certainly have avoided Bethuel's household. Thus, the two people chiefly interested in the proposal which was being made would be Rebekah's mother, who would be very anxious to see her daughter so well married, and Laban, who would be very happy to see the valuable gifts exchange hands.

GENESIS 28:1-2: And Isaac called Jacob, and blessed him, and charged him, and said unto him, Thou shalt not take a wife of the daughters of Canaan. Arise, go to Padan-Aram to the house of Bethuel thy mother's father; and take thee a wife from thence of the daughters of Laban, thy mother's brother.

GENESIS 29:1, 4-6, 9-28: Then Jacob went on his journey, and came into the land of the people of the east. . . . And Jacob said unto them, My brethren, whence be ye? And they said, Of Haran are we. And he said unto them, Know ye Laban the son of Nahor? And they said, We know him. And he said unto them, Is he well? And they said, He is well: and, behold, Rachel his daughter cometh with the sheep. And while he yet spake with them, Rachel came with her father's sheep: for she kept them. And it came to pass, when Jacob saw Rachel the daughter of Laban his mother's brother, and the sheep of Laban his mother's brother, that Jacob went near, and rolled the stone from the well's mouth, and watered the flock of Laban his mother's brother. And Jacob kissed Rachel, and lifted up his voice and wept. And Jacob told Rachel that he was her father's brother, and that he was Rebekah's son: and she ran and told her father.

And it came to pass, when Laban heard the tidings of Jacob his sister's son, that he ran to meet him and embraced him, and kissed him, and brought him to his house. And he told Laban all these things. And Laban said to him, Surely thou art my bone and my flesh. And he abode with him the space of a month.

And Laban said unto Jacob, Because thou art my brother, shouldest thou therefore serve me for nought? tell me, what shall thy wages be? And Laban had two daughters: the name of the elder was Leah, and the name of the younger was Rachel. Leah was tender eyed;

but Rachel was beautiful and well favoured. And Jacob loved Rachel; and said, I will serve thee seven years for Rachel thy younger daughter. And Laban said, It is better that I give her to thee, than that I should give her to another man: abide with me. And Jacob served seven years for Rachel; and they seemed unto him but a few days, for the love he had for her.

And Jacob said unto Laban, Give me my wife, for my days are fulfilled, that I may go in unto her. And Laban gathered together all the men of the place, and made a feast. And it came to pass in the evening that he took Leah, his daughter, and brought her to him; and he went in unto her. And Laban gave unto his daughter Leah Zilpah his maid for an handmaid. And it came to pass, that in the morning, behold, it was Leah: and he said to Laban, What is this thou hast done unto me? did not I serve thee for Rachel? wherefore then hast thou beguiled me? And Laban said, It must not be so done in our country, to give the younger before the firstborn. Fulfil her week, and we will give thee also this for the service which thou shalt serve with me yet seven other years. And Jacob did so, and fulfilled her week: and he gave him Rachel his daughter to wife also.

In Genesis 28 above we have a beautiful illustration of a potential cross-cousin marriage. The Hebrew people accepted either a parallel or cross-cousin marriage, in the latter instance the man being permitted to marry either his father's sister's daughter or his mother's brother's daughter. In neither case is there taint of physical incest. As we have already noted, Laban was evidently Jacob's mother's "special brother." So Jacob went to find Laban.

Evidently Rachel was a remarkably beautiful girl. In verse 17 the Authorized Version tells us that "Leah was tender-eyed; but Rachel was beautiful and well favored." The Hebrew in this passage is interesting, for there is a suggestion that in fact Leah was "weepy-eyed," more literally, "watery-eyed." For Rachel the original implies not only beauty but a certain fire. Rachel sparkled! Perhaps it is no wonder that Jacob loved her at first sight.

We have noted that whenever a suitor sought the hand of a man's daughter but came without the requisite bride price to demonstrate the seriousness of intent, or wherever there was little portable wealth in terms of jewelry and precious metals (such as had been given to Laban), which would have enabled the bride to depart immediately with her new husband, the husband-to-be could agree to work for a certain length of time to compensate the father-in-law for losing a pair of working hands (Cf. Chap. 2, 6).

Evidently Jacob did not enquire carefully enough as to the rules of the society. Had he been a student of social anthropology he might have realized that marrying a younger daughter before an older one could create real problems. Perhaps if Laban, in his turn, had been completely honest with Jacob, he might have told him to begin with: but then he ran the risk of not having an extra pair of hands for 14 years. It always strikes me as being a particularly beautiful touch that the writer tells us how the time flew for Jacob on account of "the love he had for Rachel," though it must be noted (in v. 20) that it was the *first* seven years which thus passed so quickly. One wonders about the second period of servitude.

GENESIS 38:2-30: Judah saw there a daughter of a certain Canaanite, whose name was Shuah; and he took her, and went in unto her. And she conceived, and bare a son; and he called his name Er. And she conceived again, and bare a son; and she called his name Onan. And she yet again conceived, and bare a son; and called his name Shelah....

And Judah took a wife for Er his firstborn, whose name was Tamar. And Er, Judah's firstborn, was wicked in the sight of the LORD; and the LORD slew him.

And Judah said unto Onan, Go in unto thy brother's wife, and marry her, and raise up seed to thy brother. And Onan knew that the seed should not be his; and it came to pass when he went in unto his brother's wife, that he spilled it on the ground, lest that he should give seed to his brother. And the thing which he did displeased the LORD: wherefore He slew him also.

Then said Judah to Tamar his daughter in law, Remain a widow at thy father's house, till Shelah my son be grown: for he said, Lest peradventure he die also, as his brethren did. And Tamar went and dwelt in her father's house.

And in process of time the daughter of Shuah, Judah's wife died; and Judah was comforted, and went up ... to Timnath.... And it was told Tamar, saying, Behold, thy father in law goeth up to Timnah to shear his sheep. And she put her widow's garments off from her, and covered her with a veil, and wrapped herself, and sat in an open place, which is by the way to Timnath; for she saw that Shelah was grown, and she was not given unto him to wife.

And when Judah saw her, he thought her to be an harlot.... And he turned unto her by the way, and said, Go to, I pray thee, let me come in unto thee; (for he knew not that she was his daughter-in-

law.) And she said, What will thou give me, that thou mayest come in unto me? And he said, I will send thee a kid from the flock. And she said, Wilt thou give me a pledge, till thou send it? And he said, What pledge shall I give thee? And she said, Thy signet, and thy bracelets, and thy staff which is in thine hand. And he gave it her, and came in unto her, and she conceived by him. And she arose, and went away, and laid by her veil from her, and put on the garments of her widowhood.

And Judah sent the kid by the hand of his friend the Adullamite, to receive his pledge from the woman's hand: but he found her not. Then he asked the men of that place, saying, Where is the harlot, that was openly by the way side? And they said, There was no harlot in this place. And he returned to Judah, and said, I cannot find her; and also the men of the place said, that there was no harlot in this place. And Judah said, Let her take it to her, lest we be shamed: behold I sent this kid, and thou hast not found her.

And it came to pass about three months after, that it was told Judah, saying, Tamar thy daughter in law hath played the harlot; and also, behold, she is with child by whoredom. And Judah said, Bring her forth, and let her be burnt. When she was brought forth, she sent to her father in law, saying, By the man whose these are, am I with child: and she said, Discern, I pray thee, whose are these, the signet, and bracelets, and staff. And Judah acknowledged them, and said, She hath been more righteous than I; because that I gave her not to Shelah my son. And he knew her again no more.

And it came to pass in the time of her travail, that, behold, twins were in her womb . . . therefore his name was called Pharez. And afterward came out his brother . . . and his name was called Zerah.

This story provides a beautiful illustration of how the Levirate practice was applied and how God judged a man for being indifferent to it when it suited his purposes. The text supplies us with the following genealogical data:

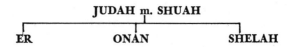

JUDAH m. SHUAH

ER   **ONAN**   **SHELAH**

Er married a girl named Tamar but the Lord destroyed him for his wickedness, and Tamar was left a widow. According to custom she was then given to Onan, Er's next oldest brother, but Onan refused to play his part (v. 9) and his life was also taken by the Lord. Judah then promised that the next son, Shelah, who was yet a child, should be given to her as a husband when he grew up. But then Judah betrayed his promise, for when Shelah was grown he was given another wife instead of Tamar who in the meantime continued to live with her father (v. 11). Tamar then took things into her own hands when she found that her father-in-law had denied her a lawful husband, and by pretending to be a harlot she compromised him. When Judah discovered what he had done (v. 26), he immediately admitted his guilt but in the meantime twins were born to Tamar, namely, Pharez and Zerah. In due course the great grandson of Zerah was he who greatly troubled Israel and caused many to lose their lives (Josh. 7:1).

According to Numbers 26:20 Judah's younger son, Shelah, did marry but not Tamar, and he and his children were therefore disqualified from the royal line. Tamar, on the other hand, was strictly the wife of Er, the firstborn, and on this account her children were considered strictly as children of Er, the son of Judah. The circumstance illustrates the fact that the mother, whose identity is always known for certain, is more important than the actual father, in terms of the children born. According to *law,* the question is, Who is the legal husband? — not, Who is the actual father? This matter is of prime importance in the case of Joseph, who was the husband of Mary and therefore the legal father of Jesus. Meanwhile, the royal line is traced through Pharez, the son of Tamar, and therefore by law the son of Er, the son of Judah.

In the beautiful story of Ruth and Naomi, there is an illustration of this custom. Ruth insists on staying with Naomi, but she tries to discourage her on the grounds that "if I should have a husband this very night and should bear sons" (Ruth 1:12), it would still be a long time before one was old enough to be given to Ruth as a husband to compensate her for her loss. Hence Naomi asks her, "Would ye tarry for them till they were grown?" (Ruth 1:13).

LEVITICUS 18:17: Thou shalt not uncover the nakedness of a woman and her daughter.

The terminology used here has seemed to many commentators rather odd. The injunction itself is clear enough, the object being to state clearly those relationships in which marriage is not permissible. But I think the use of the phrase "uncover the nakedness of . . ." may be a reflection of the implications involved in the "joking relationship" to which reference is made in Chapter 2, 12.

2 SAMUEL 13:1: And it came to pass after this, that Absalom the son of David had a fair sister whose name was Tamar; and Amnon the son of David loved her....

When this verse is analyzed, it is obvious that Absalom and Amnon were brothers, both being sons of David and that Tamar was a sister to both of them. But what we know now from the cultural habits of other people indicates that the situation was not quite so simple. David had more than one wife, and Tamar was the daughter of one of these wives, whereas Amnon was the son of another of these wives. Absalom was evidently a true brother to Tamar and bore that special relationship which we have noted that one particular brother will bear to a particular sister. Tamar was Absalom's special sister (Cf. Chap. 2, 6).

According to the views of many cultures with respect to the definition of incest, Tamar was not related to Amnon in any incestuous way, for, although David was the father of both, they did not share the same mother and their bodies were not therefore derived from the same source (Cf. Chap. 2, 10).

According to verse 2, what really vexed Amnon in his relationship with Tamar was that for some reason he could not conveniently have his will with her. It was then that a certain "friend" of his offered to arrange things for him. In verse 4, Amnon told his friend that he loved Tamar, "my brother Absalom's sister." I think this is clear recognition on the part of Amnon that Tamar was not his *own* sister. And it is a little difficult to understand, therefore, why he did not go to David and ask him frankly for Tamar's hand in marriage. It may be that he did not want to *marry Tamar*, that his intentions were not honorable. Tamar herself pointed out to Amnon that he was wronging her unnecessarily for she said (v. 13): "Now, therefore, I pray thee, speak unto the king; for he will not withhold me from thee."

One can only assume, therefore, that Amnon's heart was evil and that he had no good intentions towards Tamar except to satisfy his own lust. The story in its sorry detail is not so much a record of the evil effects of incest, for such a marriage would not have been counted incestuous. But it is a record rather of the ultimate evil of lack of self-control in human behavior.

Absalom's vengeance undoubtedly stemmed from his genuine feelings towards Tamar, but it may have been reinforced in his own mind by the realization that Tamar could no longer supply him with the help he might have expected from her dowry towards the obtaining of his own wife (Cf. Chap. 2, 6).

It is important to realize that God in His graciousness meets the needs of people within the framework of their own culture. In the present instance the Word of God sets forth Tamar's words to the effect that her father, David, would not deny her as a wife to Amnon in such a way that Tamar is not judged for making this observation — though to us it would seem quite an improper proposal . . . an important point which missionaries have to face up to.

MATTHEW 1:25: And (he) knew her not till she had brought forth her firstborn son: and he called his name JESUS.

Joseph fulfilled the conditions which were required by law to constitute him as the father of Jesus and therefore to make Jesus officially his heir, not only by giving him his name but by teaching him the trade of carpentry (See also Chap. 2, 3).

LUKE 15:11, 12, 31: And he [Jesus] said, A certain man had two sons: And the younger of them said to his father, Father, give me the portion of goods that falleth to me. And he divided unto them his living. . . . And he said unto him [his elder son], Son, thou art ever with me, and all that I have is thine.

Once again, little comment is necessary in view of what has already been said in Chapter 2, 18. But it is worth noting a significant departure from the expected wording of the father's response. We are told that "he divided to *both* his living." In other words, having only two sons and having already been requested to give the younger son his inheritance, the older son at the same time received his, since now it was a foregone conclusion. As was customary, the older son did not wait until his father died to come into possession of his due inheritance. Since there were only these two boys, the elder son naturally received and at once possessed "all that his father had," exactly as it is stated in verse 31.

I suppose part of the elder brother's concern was that his younger brother would now be in a position to rob him of some of *his* possessions after having squandered his own. After all, the fatted calf which was slaughtered potentially belonged not to the father but to the elder

330 • LIGHT FROM CULTURAL BEHAVIOR

son, *"all* that I have is thine." Yet apparently he had not been asked if he would surrender this choice animal. There is a sense in which he had a legitimate grievance, and yet the father was right. The conflict of interests, the conflict between what is "good" and what is "right," is common.

A final comment is perhaps in order. According to Old Testament injunctions, the oldest member of the family, i.e., the firstborn, was always given a double portion of the inheritance in order that he might have sufficient wealth to redeem a brother who got hopelessly into debt. In this instance, therefore, the inheritance had not been divided in a 1-to-1 ratio but in a 2-to-1 ratio, so that the older brother would actually have been provided with the requisite means to redeem the prodigal in any case. In this sense the old father was justified in using his son's property. . . . But perhaps he should have advised him or asked his permission before doing so. Evidently he had not done this (vv. 25-28).

LUKE 15:20: And he arose, and came to his father. But when he was yet a great way off, his father saw him, and had compassion, and ran, and fell on his neck, and kissed him.

Very little comment is necessary here in view of what has already been said in Chapter 2, 17. Although the young man's diet had probably been changed sufficiently that his body odor was no longer familiar, the old man fell easily and at once into the old way of showing his affection by burying his face where body odor had once been sensed as a proof of belonging.

The custom is reflected in the behavior of Jacob when he met his defrauded brother Esau after a separation of many years (Gen. 33:4); as also when Joseph was united with his brethren (Gen. 45:14). It might appear that when Isaac blessed Jacob, he too was being guided by body odor (Gen. 27:21f.), but I rather think here that it must have been the clothing itself which provided the identifying odor for presumably Jacob and Esau shared the same table.

GALATIANS 4:1, 4, 5: Now I say, That the heir, as long as he is a child, differeth nothing from a servant, though he be lord of all. . . . But when the fulness of time was come, God sent forth His son . . . to redeem them . . . that we might receive the adoption of sons.

It seems strange to us that a man, though he is born in the

family, should not automatically be recognized as the heir. But as we have seen (in Chap. 2, 3), even true sons have to be officially adopted by the father in many societies in which the father is likely to be away from home for long periods of time. Moreover, where there are no children, servants or even captives may be adopted as legal heirs with the full rights of true sonship. In writing to the Galatians, Paul probably had in mind the need to emphasize to the Jewish people that they were not children of God automatically, merely because their father Abraham was God's special child; nor are the children of Christian parents automatically children of God. There must be a clearly defined process of adoption in which the relationship of true sonship is established by an act of the Father.